THE PURSUIT OF EQUALITY IN THE WEST

THE
PURSUIT
OF
EQUALITY
IN THE WEST

ALDO SCHIAVONE

Translated by

JEREMY CARDEN

HARVARD UNIVERSITY PRESS
Cambridge, Massachusetts
London, England
2022

Originally published in Italian as *Eguaglianza: Una nuova visione sul filo della storia,* Giulio Einaudi Editore
Copyright © 2019 by Aldo Schiavone

Library of Congress Cataloging-in-Publication Data
Names: Schiavone, Aldo, author. | Carden, Jeremy, translator.
Title: The pursuit of equality in the West / Aldo Schiavone ; translated by Jeremy Carden.
Other titles: Eguaglianza English
Description: Cambridge, Massachusetts : Harvard University Press, 2022. | Originally published in Italian as Eguaglianza: una nuova visione sul filo della storia, Giulio Einaudi Editore, 2019. | Includes bibliographical references and index.
Identifiers: LCCN 2021048398 | ISBN 9780674975750 (cloth)
Subjects: LCSH: Equality—History. | Equality before the law—History.
Classification: LCC JC575 .S3513 2022 | DDC 320.01/1—dc23/eng/20211122
LC record available at https://lccn.loc.gov/2021048398

CONTENTS

PREFACE

This is not a political book, nor is it an ideological manifesto.

It is a work of historical interpretation and conceptual proposition that, while holding together different perspectives, seeks to contribute to defining the terms of a crucial issue of the present age.

I believe it is important to say straightaway that readers will not find here a history of equality in the West—a project far removed from my goals—but just a path within it. An itinerary aimed at identifying some key loci, from which an alternative and as-yet-unexplored paradigm can be constructed.

The idea of equality is a constitutive feature of our tradition. But for some time now, since before the new century even started, the value and perhaps the very meaning of this presence have been lost. Events of great consequence, sometimes very distant from each other, have led to its eclipse. We therefore run the risk of mislaying something essential, which, it seems to me, we need more than ever before.

To elude this danger, new thinking is required, capable of grasping the challenge that is being laid down for us. Historic research is always in some way preparation for the future. The story presented here aims to be so in an even more visible way than is normally the case. The past, if we know how to speak to it, is a living laboratory, not a storeroom of discarded objects.

The theme has preoccupied me for many years, at least since the concluding chapter of *Ius: L'invenzione del diritto in Occidente* (2005; 2nd ed., 2017), published in English as *The Invention of Law in the West* (2012). I devoted a series of lectures to it at the Collège de France in 2008, and the Jerome Lectures in 2014, at the University of Michigan in Ann Arbor, and at the American Academy of Rome. The idea for the book arose from these initial approaches to the topic, and was discussed and appraised with Sharmila Sen, whom I wish to thank most warmly for having wanted from the outset to make it a book for Harvard.

Fara Nasti read the whole Italian manuscript and made many very helpful suggestions. The work would have been unimaginable without her contribution.

Finally, a warm thank you to Jeremy Carden, who translated my complex Italian with care and sensitivity, and my gratitude to everyone at HUP—a constant and irreplaceable presence in my studies over the years.

THE PURSUIT OF EQUALITY IN THE WEST

PROLOGUE

The Most Beautiful of Lives

On the final page of the third and last book of his *Essays,* Montaigne writes:

> It is an accomplishment, absolute and as it were God-like, to know how to enjoy our being as we ought. We seek other attributes because we do not understand the use of our own; and, having no knowledge of what is within, we sally forth outside ourselves. A fine thing to get up on stilts: for even on stilts we must ever walk with our legs! And upon the highest throne in the world, we are seated, still, upon our arses.
>
> The most beautiful of lives to my liking are those which conform to the common and human model, with order but without miracles and without extravagance.[1]

These words were not dashed off by their author. The examples of the stilts and the throne, and the reference, in the final section, to the human and to order, were added after the first print version, as we learn from the manuscript notes in the margin to the copy of the *Essays* on which Montaigne worked until the end of his days.[2]

Indeed, they touch on a point that troubled him perhaps more than any other: "I am expounding a lowly, lacklustre existence. You can attach the whole of moral philosophy to a commonplace private life just as well as to one of richer stuff. Every man bears the whole Form of the human condition," we read at the beginning of the second essay of Book 3.[3] It was necessary to describe and to emphasize that part of us which, though not identifying with the particular experiences of each person, includes them all, and constitutes the common ground we have long called (as Montaigne already did) the "human condition."[4]

We are in the years between 1588 and 1592, one of the darkest periods in the history of France and of Europe. The country had been racked for decades by an almost uninterrupted succession of religious wars: implacable hatreds between faiths brandished like arms, and a reciprocal desire to annihilate the other. But though his eyes were filled with the havoc of such lacerations—or perhaps precisely because he saw nothing around him except that unspeakable horror—Montaigne was able to reverse the perspective, and to place in the center not the rupture but the rediscovery of the bond; not the emptiness of divisive destruction but the fullness of identification and contact.

"The whole form of the human condition," in the second essay; "the common and human model," in the final one. The later addition of the words "and human" to the "common model" present in the text of 1588 condenses all of Montaigne's concern: the fear, which evidently still troubled him, of not having been sufficiently clear on a vital theme.[5] What is really "common," what makes all lives comparable—from the most obscure to the brightest—is exactly what makes them unmistakably "human."

The "human," then, was nothing other than the "common," the shared. But the only way to fully grasp this unifying thread, to render evident the substance and force of the connection, was, according to Montaigne, to take the apparently opposite path of an endless journey within the irreducible singularity of one's existence, in search of the most secret and hidden attitudes as they revealed themselves—day after day, event after event, thought after thought, reading after reading—to his dissecting gaze. The maximum determinateness, as a way of achieving the maximum inclusion, the cancellation of every particularism, of every closure:

to enable the discovery of the universal human—"the whole form"—as it unfolded in all its fresh and objective nudity.

We will search in vain in Montaigne's beloved classics—Seneca, Plutarch, Horace, Lucretius, the Skeptics, and the ancient Stoics—for something more than a preliminary intuition of this itinerary that began from the singularity of his own inner landscape, but whose sole objective was to go beyond, in order to reach, in the remotest layer of the self, a universally shared imprint. This was no longer the ancient world, even though Roman humanist motifs (perhaps not all of which were familiar to Montaigne) can still clearly be discerned, from Terence to the intellectuals of Hadrian's court—Gellius, Favorinus, the great jurists of the imperial council—bent however to describe another matter, integrated into another substance.[6]

Montaigne was not announcing the dawn of the bourgeois world either. What we have here is the outline of a less well-known modernity, another way out from antiquity, completely different from the one that would soon delineate the extraordinary path of modern individualism in its successful blend of economics and philosophy, law, politics, and literature. Montaigne is not Defoe, or Locke, or Descartes: there is no continuity or progression between them. And the figure that speaks in the first person in the *Essays* has very little in common with the one who says "I" in the *Adventures of Robinson Crusoe* (less than seventy years later in the—slightly backdated—fiction of the novel).[7] Here too we are witnessing the lighting up of a feature through unexplored paths, and we can detect the presence of traits that had never previously appeared on the stage of history. This time, though, the protagonist recognized himself only in doing; he was defined entirely and exclusively by the actions he performed. In short, he was nothing other than his labor—incessantly transforming, producing, and accumulating—and he entered into a reflective relationship with his mind only through the trace left on the things surrounding him.

We tend to forget it, but the early phases of modernity were not marked by the linear course of just one renewed construction of the self, the intellectually compact formation of a single new form of subjectivity. In that crucial age, we glimpse instead the outline of separate roads, just one of which would become dominant—and it was not the one indicated in the *Essays.* The horizon they offer a view of appears all the more precious, then, because it has the flavor of an alternative, and of an occasion that has not, thus far at least, been developed.

❋ ❋ ❋

Montaigne was entirely caught up by his discovery: by having found that the ultimate substance of our "being"—we are accustomed to say, of our individuality—carries, inscribed within it, a feature describable through what he called a "common model," which is reproduced identically in each of us.[8] On it the circumstances of the existence of single persons, the infinite variety of accidents and opportunities, construct sometimes enormous differences, without predefined limits: stilts and thrones as opposed to "lowly, lacklustre" lives.[9] But, he thought, it was necessary to look beyond the false absoluteness of singularities, to trace the element to which all lives must relate in order to be truly understood. Montaigne resorted to a striking image to express the power of this return, which was not a reduction but a revealing. It evoked the ineludible physicality of the bodies to which we are bound, the hardness of their anatomical structure, which is the same for everyone: "our legs," "our arse" (the word is not coarse, but arresting; there was this too in sixteenth-century Europe, before the consolidation of the Counter-Reformation or of "good manners" in the salons of Paris, London, and Vienna: think of Rabelais, or, in Italy, of Aretino and of certain letters by Machiavelli).[10]

"The most beautiful of lives . . . are those which conform to the common and human model," said Montaigne. The aesthetic judgment ("the most beautiful of lives") masked the moral evaluation. The idea of "conforming" introduced the unexpected one of the rule, the norm: of a parameter that is reproduced, intact, in each person. Subjectivities are not extinguished by complying with this yardstick but perfected through recognition of it: "with order but without miracles and without extravagance." It is in this way that it is possible for each person to perceive "the whole form of the human condition": the "human norm"—as E. M. Forster, perhaps the most important English writer of the twentieth century and certainly the last to have an idea of what the British

Empire had been like, would write centuries later in a page of *A Passage to India* that appears to be a late counterpoint to Montaigne—as the only path toward "harmony" and "beauty."[11]

As in the *Essays,* so too in Forster the aesthetic judgment hid the moral appraisal. French humanism tempered by the ravages of civil war, and an already post-Victorian and postimperial English classicism came together on the cusp of the same idea, which Forster also called "Mediterranean": the universality of measure as the discovery of equality in the human.[12]

※ ※ ※

Montaigne was writing on the threshold of a great change.[13] Just a few decades earlier the New World had begun to invade the imagination, intellects, and even the everyday life of Europe with the previously unknown produce of its lands; with its riches, its spaces, its marvels; and ships bristling with sails and cannons had not long since begun to regularly ply the Atlantic, suddenly no longer a boundary but a channel.

His relationship with antiquity was still deeply felt, even if it was a past seen as an inexorably fading universe, already immersed in the deceptive, albeit golden, light of the Italian Renaissance.

In his eyes, though, modernity had not yet acquired the features that would soon become familiar and indelible: it was, as it were, merely announced more than truly realized (unlike what would be seen by Defoe—we have just mentioned his *Robinson Crusoe*—who was writing when the die of capitalist development was almost cast), and Europe had not definitively embarked on the path of bourgeois transformation that we all know. The profile of the modern world was barely sketched and open to various solutions. In many ways, Montaigne behaved like a frontiersman, suspended between two ages. And it is for this too that his thought is so compelling—because it does not flow within schemes that would only later become the acquired forms of a whole epoch.

But in his own time there was already a new and different atmosphere in French, English, and Dutch—but also German, Portuguese, Spanish, and Danish—cities. A sudden and disconcerting expansion of the borders within which it had until then been permitted to live, and a new abundance of goods, capital, labor, and ideas was thrusting Europe into a totally unknown dimension. At the same time there was a spreading perception of a changed—and previously inconceivable—relationship between land and sea, rootedness and mobility, geography and history, that rendered even the unthinkable realistic.

The breaking of old barriers was already all there in Montaigne. His point of view could not have formed if he had not interiorized the definitive breach of a historic boundary, of a cage of restrictions—material and cultural—that until not long before had given a shape and a countenance to the course of the Old World: a basis of facts and interpretations on which the image, first elaborated by Italian humanists, of ancient antiquity as completeness and as the satisfaction of the finished had just been constructed. Perfection, but in closed forms.

This network of limits had already begun to dissolve centuries earlier—commencing with the thought and social practices of Italian cities at the end of the thirteenth century, Dante and Florence above all—but it was not long since that it had really disintegrated. Montaigne enjoyed the freedom of a gaze that could venture for the first time beyond the barriers of the past; but which, at the same time, did not yet know the outcome of what was starting to come into being, nor where and how the new equilibria of the epoch that was being ushered in would be reached. He was thus able to move with a fluidity and lack of prejudice that he seized as an unexpected gift.

From such a privileged position—the last point of contact between the old and the new, the ancient and the modern—Montaigne said he was unable to conceive the "human"—the "condition" and the "model" of a human that historically was already completely outside antiquity and its echoes, but not yet completely molded by the new age—without at the same time conceiving equalness, and without going beyond, in order to do so, the excluding shell of the "I."

※ ※ ※

We will find it very hard to fully position Montaigne in Western thinking about equality, which he only touched from a tangential position—a reflection at the boundaries between ethics, history, and philosophical anthropology.

His point of view did, however, reflect an exceptional historic time—the dawning of the modern: a state of suspension in which everything was still possible. Past and future—what had definitively ceased to be lasting but had not yet completely slipped away, and what had already begun, but was not yet fixed in a stable grid of characteristics, either social, economic, or cultural—blurred together in the same oscillating indeterminacy: a fluidity enabling the achievement of vertiginous depths.

The order of thoughts entrusted to the *Essays* did not have—nor did it wish to have—strictly philosophical, and far less political, implications. Instead it stuck to the representation of a morphology of the interiority of the human—of all the human—that projected it onto a backdrop with as-yet-unknown and nebulous traits, in which one feature, albeit only barely outlined, was emerging: the force of the entanglement between the idea of the universal, the consciousness of self, and the intuition of equality—of a particular and barely glimpsed equality: the impersonalized and common measure of each life—as the true destiny of a civilization. It is for this reason that we have begun our story with him.

At the time when Montaigne was writing, the modern developments of that idea were not even imaginable, though a long history had already accrued around some of its elements. It is these paths that we must now tread, following the traces of lost threads that we shall use in an attempt to extend our gaze and look forward.

CHAPTER ONE

THE GREEK ALTERNATIVE

Nature or Politics?

Anatomies

The beginning of our journey takes us far back in time. The setting is the eastern shores of the Mediterranean, in the decades between the sixth and fifth century BC, when the outline began to form of what would later be called, in a way as suggestive as it was overstated, the "Greek miracle": an age of great innovations, when features took shape that would leave their mark on the whole of the ancient West.

As far as is known, reflection on equality first began to crystallize in relation to one of the most significant events of this period: the birth of the *polis;* that is, of the city as a politically organized body that we would call sovereign—though the ancients themselves had no such concept.

In the new communities, whose independent existence often stemmed from the crumbling of vaster territorial entities, in Greece and along the coasts of Ionia colonized by the Greeks, the experience of complete political autonomy led the inhabitants to form very close ties among themselves. Reciprocal and equal, these bonds were not just between the old aristocracies, but also included people of humbler stock—peasants, artisans, shopkeepers, traders, seafarers—and prompted a distribution of government tasks that involved the whole community, rather than just being concentrated in tight-knit oligarchies or in the hands of a monarch.

The *poleis* regenerated from this new sociality quickly became the context for a peculiar management of power, which was soon called "democracy"—a word that Aeschylus, in *The Suppliants*, written in Athens probably around 460 BC, already showed that he knew, working deftly around the terms forming it: *demos* and *kratos*—people and power, combined in a previously unimaginable short circuit.[1]

In the newly refashioned cities there was plenty of discussion (and writing too): more complex modes of social organization and of the division of labor freed up, albeit for just a few, time and resources to devote to activities that we would describe as intellectual. People began to publicly ask questions about themselves, the value of their choices, the characteristics of the societies that were developing, the mysterious regularity of nature, and the hidden meaning of life and of the world. They debated the exact significance of the peculiar symmetry between citizens induced by democratic politics, and what the limits were of this condition.

Parity within the bounds of one's own circle had already long been common among various aristocratic groups at the time—as is clearly shown, for example, in Homer's poetry. But something different was emerging now: the democracy taking root in centers along the coasts of the Aegean was at once the presupposition and the result of a leveling not limited to a narrow circle of important families but extending to the whole social fabric of the city. It is in this framework that we come across an announcement that has reached us mutilated and decontextualized but which, due to the essentiality of its content, has been part of European and Western history ever since: in a certain sense, the point of origin of the path we are trying to reconstruct.

Expressed in it, probably in highly assertive and polemical terms—whether for the first time exactly we do not know, but undoubtedly in an already very definite and complete way—was a radical idea, that of equality as a "natural" feature of the human; and some decisive implications of this discovery were clearly set forth:

We know them and we respect them [perhaps: "our customs, our laws": the integrations to render this incipit are conjectural and controversial]; but those of people who live far away we neither know nor do we respect them. Thus in this regard we have become barbarians towards each other, since, in nature at least, we are all fitted similarly by nature in all regards to be both barbarians and Greeks. It is possible to observe what is necessary by nature for all human beings and what they possess in relation to their needs in conformity with <the same> needs, and in all this none of us can be defined as either b<arbaria>n or Greek. For we all breathe into the air through our mouth and nose; <we laugh when we are happy in our mind> or we weep when we are grieved; we take in sounds by our hearing, and we see by means of light with our eyes; we do work with our hands and we walk with our feet.[2]

It is possible, as has been suggested, that these words were paradoxical or even provocative, and that their author was not exactly a friend of democracy, whose limitations and incompleteness he wished to denounce.[3] But no attempt to piece together a background can extinguish the objective force of this thought, presented with the impact of a drastic pronouncement open to all "human beings."[4] The boundaries of citizenship in the new *poleis* were breached in a single blow; the declaration went further even than the whole sum of their inhabitants, to include nothing less than the entire human species.

❀ ❀ ❀

Writing in this fashion, around 430 BC, in a work consisting of various books and probably entitled *On Truth*, was a man devoted to "philosophizing," as Pericles, the great Athenian politician, put it in those same years. His name was Antiphon, and his words have survived in a fragment known to us through two of the Oxyrhynchus Papyri.

Antiphon lived in Athens—at the height of the democratic experience—and his master had probably been Anaxagoras, who came from Clazomenae on the coast of Asia Minor: a man of learning versed in the doctrines of the Ionic physics that had accompanied the establishment of popular governments on the Asian side of the Mediterranean.

An Ionic inspiration—the intellectual environment between Miletus and Abdera—shines through in Antiphon's text: the naturalism supported by the empirical observation of reality typical of early Greek science, which had yielded the conceptions of Thales, Anaximander, and Leucippus, and would run through to Democritus. A universe that is now almost lost to us (something can be intuited through Lucretius), due to the drastic selection made in late antiquity when saving classical texts—a choice dominated by the Christian canon, which, by no longer transcribing works deemed incompatible with the new religion, effectively consigned them to oblivion—like those of the early Ionic scholars, too imbued with materialism. Their analytic force can be almost only detected in an indirect way, through the screen of Platonic and Aristotelean writings that would intercept and readapt their memory. But unfortunately, here too we are conditioned by a thick filter erected by the two philosophers, who forced the richness and originality of that tradition into the categories of the metaphysical and spiritualistic turn that distinguished Greek thought from Plato onward (we shall see an example shortly).

To push his reasoning to its most extreme consequences, Antiphon evoked an alterity well known to fifth-century Athenian culture, constitutive of the Greek certitude of their own superiority: we, the Greeks, on the one hand, and the barbarians on the other. A contrast based on a primary negation, a path of self-recognition determined above all by exclusion, in opposition to the other: not slaves, not women, not peoples unable to speak a Greek dialect.

Instead, Antiphon stripped those differences of meaning, erasing them completely, and in so doing reached the horizon of an absolute inclusion: the space of the universally equal (the philosopher did not mention women, but he probably included slaves in his formulation, though whether here or in another text we cannot say, as we shall see more clearly further on—they must also have fallen within the scope of the equality he imagined). Every identification obtained solely through opposition was superseded at a stroke, to the point of including within the same field also what appeared at first sight to be completely extraneous to it: the barbarian, or the slave, recognized as being perfectly equal.

Any distinction constructed on the basis of social conventions, however deep rooted, was cancelled out by the evidence of a more important uniformity, founded on objective recognition of fundamental characteristics shared by all human beings, distinguished by the same anatomy and the same functioning of the body. Such uniformity had to come first, because—and this was the real heart of Antiphon's reasoning, implicit but crystal clear—everything belonging to the world that we would call social-historical should be related—and to a certain extent subordinated—to the natural-biological datum. The corporeality of bare existence was elevated in this way to the measure of every human relation. Not just the common functions of survival (breathing), but also those enabling sociality and community life (seeing, moving, working, laughing, crying), performed by means of the same anatomical base (the mouth, nostrils, feet, eyes, hands), make humans entirely similar; and from this Antiphon derived consequences that could connect nature and society, observation of reality and the correct formation of the rules that should guide all dealings between human beings.

The affirmation, as formulated, had the effect of bringing life—grasped in its barest essentiality—directly into politics (the declaration inevitably had political implications), projecting the materiality and functionality of bodies not only onto the social profile of the *polis,* but even onto relations between different peoples commonly perceived as opposites. And life was brought in not as an inert object over which to exercise an omnipotent command—the unquestionable authority of the law, of *nomos*—but rather as the unbreakable foundation of collective action: an intent that, with time, would become the genetic feature of all democratic radicalism.

✳ ✳ ✳

In Antiphon's interpretation, the experience of politics—whatever the philosopher's actual position within it—was evoked and, as it were, placed between parentheses, while it was the discovery of the natural character of equality that was placed in the foreground. As if, to truly comprehend its import, it was necessary to give that idea a completely external grounding with respect to the constitution of the *polis.* To conceive it as evidence of a nature pushed beyond itself and interpreted as norm and as destiny—an attitude also known to Greek thought irrespective of this particular vision. And it was the conquest of a prepolitical horizon that made it possible to arrive at that otherwise precluded universality which, once achieved, had a socially and culturally explosive significance.

The boundaries of nature, in fact, did not coincide with those of the *polis*. The discovery of equality held true also and indeed above all outside the city; it could go beyond the specifically political sphere to include the whole species, precisely because the affirmation was not the outcome of an achievement within a particular community, but reflected a natural input, a kind of primary self-recognition of the human as such.

What weight and value Antiphon really gave to the proclamation of this boundless unity is not known. It is likely that he himself thought it wise not to exaggerate its significance, sterilizing its practical and political meaning, reduced to a declaration of principle, perhaps even with paradoxical overtones, and without any immediate consequences for the established order of an entire civilization.

The fact remains, however, that it is impossible to erase the effect of destabilizing relativity that the affirmation—whatever its intention—ended up radiating. A whole system of persuasions was called into question and oscillated dangerously, observed with the estranged gaze of someone judging it in the light of another truth.

Cities of Equals

In the Greece of the second half of the fifth century BC, Antiphon's pronouncement was an isolated, though, as we shall see, not forgotten case. From what can be reconstructed, it would appear that no one developed his strand of thinking directly, though someone must have picked up on it.

Equality was discussed, though above all in relation to a different and less radical version—narrower, but more widely shared. A paradigm directly linked this time to politics and to the democratic turn being experienced by the Greek world. It too was destined to have a very long history.

A trace of it can be found in a well-known passage from Herodotus, written in the second half of the fifth century and drawing probably on a source that should once again be linked to Ionic thought. The historian expounded, in the shape of a dialogue, a kind of elementary theory of forms of government, setting them against each other in the search for the best one. His classification would prove very influential and long-lived, from Plato to Aristotle to Polybius and all the way through to the founders of modern political science—Machiavelli, Hobbes, and others.[5]

In the tale the comparison was developed enigmatically by three Persian men of learning.[6] Each one defended a different type (Herodotus was perfectly aware of the strangeness of attributing to Easterners what must have seemed to his readers to be authentic Greek thinking, and though the reason for his choice is not revealed, the anomaly was evident to him):[7] one of the three, Darius, speaks up for the monarchic form; another, Megabyzus, for the oligarchic one; while Otanes, who speaks first, prefers the institutional setup based on the power of the people: "The rule of the many . . . has, in the first place, the most beautiful of names, to wit, isonomy"—literally, "equality of law."[8]

Herodotus did not use the word "democracy," already fairly widespread in his time, but referred instead to a notion connected to an essential aspect of the democratic constitution: that of the equality of the law with respect to all citizens: *isonomia.* Antiphon's *omoios,* which perhaps had more of a morphological and naturalistic semantic field, was replaced by Herodotus with *isonomos,* more loaded with political and, we would say, specifically constitutional allusions. For him, equality with respect to the law was the soul of democracy, because this is what made it possible to place the power to govern the *polis* in the hands of the people.

There was, however, something further hidden in Herodotus's tripartite division (monarchy, oligarchy, isonomy), which made the role of *isonomia* even more central. In the sequence, democracy only figured as one of the possible forms of politics in the city: alongside it, and on the same level, were the other two, oligarchy and monarchy. But that was not how things actually stood. This position, whereby democracy (and the equality that made it possible) was just a part within a broader whole (the three forms of politics together), was nothing more than a retrospective fiction, formulated to create an effective systematic construction.

From a historic point of view, the experience of politics—and, let's say, its birth as a specific way of organizing and managing power in the *polis*—had not preceded democracy (*isonomia*), but had accompanied and, if anything, followed it as its consequence. Politics, in its entirety, coincided genetically with democracy and was not simply an antecedent.

* * *

To better understand the identity of what we are talking about, and its implications for our theme, we must move on to Aristotle, who, around a century later, in the third book of the *Politics,* drew on Herodotus's classification (already used and modified by Plato), and in turn listed the three forms of government indicated in the *Histories,* though with some changes to the nomenclature: government of one, of a few, of many.[9] For the government of many—what Herodotus had defined as *isonomia*— Aristotle used the word *politeia,* the same one he employed to denote, generically and neutrally, the political setup of every city, what we would call its constitution.[10] The same term thus came to designate, in his writings, both the political constitution in general and a particular form of it—the democratic one; and the philosopher himself did not fail to emphasize the surprising superimposition (without offering an explanation), for which there were no alternatives. Evidently, the "government of many" was not just one of the types of *politeia,* whose name it stole. Its existence was the indispensable condition for being able to think of the *polis* as a "political" order (that is, for being able to use, to describe it, the word *politeia*).

The lexical overlap revealed the historic connection that had produced it: the government of the people, and that alone, had opened, in the West, the age of politics—of any politics, of *politeia* itself as constitutional order—and had enabled the *polis* to become what we know.

But in turn—and this is the aspect of greatest interest here—politics brought equality onto the scene: Aristotle defined the *polis*—any *polis,* not just the democratic kind (another revelatory clue)—as a "community of equals" (*koinonia ton omoion*), once again using the word we found in Antiphon.[11] For Aristotle, there was no *polis*—no genuine city—if there was no equality among citizens. And on the same occasion, shortly before the text mentioned at the beginning, Aristotle referred to the political order in general—to any order that could be called "political"—as a system based on the equality of citizens.[12]

In his eyes, then, politics, democracy, and equality were woven together in an inseparable web, which appeared to be the result of a specific historic process, mirrored by philosophical reflection. Without equality there could be no democracy, and without democracy no politics—that is, the possibility of a constitutional order of any kind. There could only exist an unspeakable and immense power, like in the despotisms which, in the view of the Greeks, had always characterized the Eastern empires.

Subsequent history, far beyond antiquity, would contribute to dissipating the force of this original connection, obscuring its significance and value: and the loss would have important consequences. It would be forgotten that the generative core of politics in the West only succeeded in taking shape through the inclusion of citizens in the government of the community, and their active adherence to a framework of rules and shared institutions. It had been this participation that formed, in each person, a new self-consciousness that included a precise, albeit limited, idea of equality. It is entirely correct, then, to see, as the Italian historian Santo Mazzarino has, the birth of politics as being bound up with the discovery of its indissoluble connection with the development of moral life.[13]

* * *

One further word should be said about Aristotle. We have seen that the philosopher, in his definition of *polis*, returned to the term *omoios* previously used by Antiphon—and it is possible that this is the oldest word in the Greek lexicon of equality. But in the fifth book of the *Politics*, it is *isos* that dominates, in its meaning of quantitative, measurable, and divisible equalization.

Isos and its compounds had in fact marked, already from the middle of the fifth century—and so roughly around the time of Herodotus—the season of the democratic wave that was sweeping across the whole of the central and eastern Mediterranean, from Ionia to Sicily, pushing all the way to the banks of the Tiber, where republican Rome was taking its first difficult steps. And *isonomia* above all had occupied a privileged place in this spread: equality with respect to *nomos,* to the law as a now exclusively political and secular command within the *polis.*[14] In the composition of the word, the presence of *isos* was not the only novel element. In the middle of the fifth century, *nomos* also appeared with a transformed meaning.[15] Any religious allusion (that it might originally have had) had been lost, and it had begun to unambiguously denote the written law dictated by the new politics on which democratic equality was founded.

It is possible that, at first, *isonomia* also denoted, still in a limited manner, merely aristocratic forms of parity. But when Herodotus described it as "the most beautiful of names," more than fifty years after the Athenian reforms of Cleisthenes, it already related unequivocally to the new democratic regimes. For Herodotus the "beauty" of the word evidently lay in its connection with the flourishing and development of a world of political ideas and behaviors that expressed—or at least had the potential to do so—a form of community that had not previously seen the light of day.

The opening up of unexpected areas of opportunity—from increasingly intense trade to the colonization of extensive territories beyond the sea, and to the exploration of the inner self ("I have investigated myself," we read in a fragment of Heraclitus), all of which were well known to Herodotus—was breaking down the former hierarchies and old structures of power, from Greece to Asia Minor.[16] The new equilibria were judged not only to be wiser, but also more "beautiful": the two terms—wisdom and beauty—coexisted in the democratic culture of the late fifth century, and the beauty of the object was projected into the beauty of the name that denoted it.[17]

Antiphon
Herodotus
Aristotle

Democracy

Herodotus expressed opinions that were fairly widespread in Greece in the second half of the fifth century. Other thinkers, not many years apart, were reflecting even more fully on the relationship between equality (a particular type of equality) and democratic regime. Pericles's oration for those who had fallen in the first year of the Peloponnesian War, reported by Thucydides, can be regarded as the first manifesto of democratic thought on democracy in the history of the West: and equality—but not Antiphon's version—occupied a prominent position.

Pericles was speaking in the winter of 431–430 BC, when events still seemed to be going Athens's way. Thucydides, who was relating it, was writing around twenty years later.

> We use a constitution which does not seek to emulate the laws of our neighbours, we being more of a model [*paradeigma*] for others than their imitators. And its name is democracy [*demokratia*], because on the one hand it rests not on the few [*es oligous*], but on the many [*es pleionas*]; and on the other, while before the law [*kata . . . tous nomous*] all men are equal [*pasi to ison*] for the settlement of their private disputes, if however, according to the evaluation received, each man has a good reputation in something, he is not chosen to hold public office on the basis of his wealth more than for his merits; nor, due to poverty, if someone can do something good for the city, is he prevented from doing so by obscurity of rank.[18]

The combined use of "democracy" and "isonomy"—though obscured by a not entirely limpid style that has caused great difficulties of interpretation—outlined what we would call a kind of sovereignty, of popular sovereignty, which for Pericles (as we know him through Thucydides) acquired exemplary value for the whole of Greece. In it, the idea of equality was determined by the actuality of politics and achieved efficacy solely in the ambit of the latter, and of its boundaries, commencing with the distinction between the private sphere ("private disputes") and public life (access to "public office").

Antiphon's naturalistic and universalistic perspective was entirely absent. His path seemed to have led nowhere. Now equality figured as a direct consequence of the political constitution; the government of the people was the sole condition for its maintenance and development. It was an equality *in politicis,* as has rightly been observed: effective in this field alone.[19] And not just in the sense that it was limited to what we would call "political rights" (the right to free speech, to vote, and to hold public office). But also in the more substantive meaning that concerned only those recognized as having the status of citizens, that is, as having access to politics—the model used a century later by Aristotle as the basis for his thinking.

It was, in short, a construction subordinated to the existence of a civic body—the *demos,* the people—who could administer—*oikein*—power in the community through the authority of the law—of the *nomos;* with this latter term including a reference to the notion of dividing up (which sat well with the quantitative idea of *isos,* of equal). An authority understood in the sense of "sovereign law"—of *nomos basileus*—according to the image elaborated by a line of thought stretching from Pindar to Herodotus, and on through to Plato, Aristotle, and Chrysippus.[20]

This type of equality was thus rooted entirely within the grid of exclusions and negations that defined, as we have seen, the space of citizenship in the *poleis* of classical Greece—the opposite of what Antiphon had tried to suggest by turning to Ionic knowledge and its capacity for description and analysis.[21]

Moreover, in general it did not even concern the poorest in society, as ownership of land, however little, almost always featured as a prerequisite for being fully considered a citizen. It was a privilege for free adult males able to bear arms and with a minimum of standing. In a word, the prerogative of a minority (we should not forget that there were large masses of slaves in the Greek cities of the fifth century BC, especially in Athens and in the other urban centers of its empire), even if a minority not just made up of aristocrats. Hardwired into the notion of equality was the idea of the boundary, of something blocked and fenced off, regarded as insuperable and constitutive of its essence.

As on other occasions, and precisely where it seemed to reach the height of maturity, ancient civilization showed itself to be an imprisoned society, surrounded everywhere by barriers. A world that accepted limitation and was gratified by it. Almost as if closure was the price to pay for constructing the formal perfection and harmony that would one day be called "the classical."[22]

Antiphon's position—intrinsically open, projected toward universality, and with no excluding determinations—is all the more striking, then, standing in utter solitude but at the same time extraordinarily pre-cursory and destined not to fade away in silence, even in the ancient tradition itself. A dazzling beam of light, the product of an avant-garde Ionian knowledge that would never be hegemonic but illuminated an environment to which that light never truly pertained, and which re-mained standing thanks only to an insuperable network of exclusions.

These exclusions enabled the strict hierarchy of roles and the divi-sion of labor that had made possible, in the economic and technological conditions of the time, the development of a superior culture. The uni-versality intuited by Antiphon could never have been realized without destroying the very foundations of the civilization that had managed to conceive it, albeit on the margins of its thought. The equality he glimpsed was not of that world. For things to change there would need to be a true rupture in history. A catastrophe, and a new beginning—exactly what we call the end of the ancient world.[23]

❋ ❋ ❋

An entirely different issue is what we might describe as the extension of the range of that equality only *in politicis,* with respect to the living con-ditions of each citizen. If, that is, it should only concern political rights, or take in other aspects of the social organization of the community as well, involving, for example, a rebalancing (if not exactly parity) in the distribution of wealth. In other words, given that, in a *polis,* there could be no democracy without equality, how much was needed for the model to function properly?

In *Areopagiticus,* written around 380 BC, Isocrates appears to touch on the problem when he talks about "two recognized types of equality—that which makes the same award to all alike and that which gives to each man his due," in other words, "that which rewards and punishes every man according to his deserts."[24] But he was only referring to—and criticizing—the possibility of gaining public offices by lot rather than election, without any allusion to measures that might impact economic and social inequalities. And in Greek thought there was never effectively any answer to the question, even though it did hover, as if suspended, over its reflections, before becoming one of modernity's great problems. It must be added, though, that, in antiquity genuine redistributive mechanisms—for example, in land ownership, or through the periodic and general cancellation of debts—were never fully theorized or constituted real models.

Power

The Greeks had a tragic conception of power, which left its mark on the whole history of the West. They were hypnotized by its intrinsic asymmetry. The fullness of its presence as opposed to the emptiness of its lack. So, for them, the exercising of power was inseparable from the arrogance of those who held it and the envy of those subjected to it—unfailing companions, and infallible bearers of ruin. What's more (they thought), power loves to hide in the darkness, concealing its ways from the eyes of others: a sinking into the depths that also attracted tragedy.

Politics, democracy, and equality in the *polis*—the original political order as the first democratic order of equal citizens—was also born out of an attempt to curb such perils. If power is asymmetrical, it must be reduced, at least in the public sphere, to the opposing symmetry of parity: the community must be established as a community of equals, to rid its government of the shadow of catastrophe.

But equality in the democratic *poleis* was, in actual fact, surrounded by the unequal, the asymmetrical, which multiplied on every side, as the inevitable price of a social and economic mechanism that could not do without it. Aristotle expressed this impossibility—the existence, inevitable for his world, of great structures of inequality—with incomparable force. With him, the two paradigms of equality that Greek thinking had elaborated—the naturalistic and universal one proposed by Antiphon, and the political and more limited one expounded by Pericles—reached their point of maximum tension.

And it is to his analysis that we must now return.

❋ ❋ ❋

In the first book of the *Politics*, composed after 342 BC, the great philosopher constructed with amazing clarity (employing Platonic ideas as well) a full-blown ontology of human dissymmetry almost without parallel in the history of Western thought. Perhaps only in Nietzsche can we find something similarly powerful and significant, but that would be another story.

Once again, and unexpectedly, nature returned forcefully to the scene. For Aristotle as well, the foundation of his thought consisted of an interpretation of *physis*—of nature—that, as in Antiphon, was considered the norm and destiny of the human.

The theme from which Aristotle started to expound his theory was slavery: its justification and foundation. The inequality at the root of this institution was constructed as a figure of being, projected in the framework of a metaphysics—or, as it is preferable to say, a metapolitics—of subordination, which spilled into a definitive anthropological condemnation for a whole part of humankind.[25] In silent opposition, it was flanked by an idea of equality that was just as precise and marked; and the two forms, the equal and the unequal, were both, for Aristotle, constitutive elements of the community, delineating a polarity that encapsulated the entire life of the *polis*.

Aristotle's doctrine was not the only concept of slavery developed in classical antiquity. The Romans would devise a different one, less metaphysical and more closely linked to historicity, that took shape during their imperial experience, from Cicero to the jurists of the Severan age (we will return to this in the following chapter). And yet that thinking would carry great weight over time and would lie at the heart of many modern justifications of slavery, through to Confederate political writings in the years of the American Civil War.[26]

The framework within which Aristotle's analysis operated was the image of the *polis* as community—"we see that every city is a community [*koinonia*]"—but of a particular kind: it is in fact a "political community [*koinonia . . . politike*]: that same one which, in the seventh book (probably written between 347 and 344), Aristotle called, as we have seen, a "community of equals."[27]

This equality was not called into question by the philosopher, far less denied. Yet appearing immediately alongside it is a description that opened a completely different horizon: that of the powers inevitably accompanying the existence of every human aggregation: royal or political power (*basilikon, politikon*) wielded over the community as a whole;

domestic power (*oikonomikon*) in the home; and finally, that of the master (*despotikon*) over slaves. And it should be noted straightaway that, to describe the general function of government, Aristotle indicated two different types of command, exercised respectively through royalty or politics; with royalty lying outside politics in the narrow sense of the term, further proof that, for him, the latter was, strictly speaking, just the one based on a rotation in government functions, that is, democratic politics.

Yet, the philosopher continued, the difference between these types of power is not merely quantitative, as it might seem at first sight: depending, that is, on whether rule is exercised over a few, more, or many. Between them is a diversity of form, of kind (*eidos*)—qualitative, of essence. To demonstrate this, according to Aristotle, it was necessary to employ the method of breaking down the whole into its component parts. In our case, the political community—the *polis*—divided into its simplest elements. This could be done in two ways: either through observation "from the beginning" (*ex arches*), or in the shape of systematic analysis.[28]

The first perspective yields the historic sequence that had led, in Aristotle's view, to the formation of the *polis*: from the family to the village to the city. In the other one, by contrast, the order is inverted: only the already constructed city (the whole) gives complete form to its parts (families, villages) and enables them to exist.[29]

In reality, for Aristotle the two paths—the historic and the systematic—were not on the same plane. From an epistemological point of view, primacy lay with the system: with morphology, not history, even though he often turned to historic investigation (as in this case) to verify his doctrines. The city as a community of equals was thus the point of departure.

Within the *polis*, though, continues the *Politics,* as observation "from the beginning" also shows, the single human being is unable to be self-sufficient: here Aristotle writes "each of us" (*ekastos emon*).[30] His language did not have a word to indicate what modernity would call the "individual": the lack of the name revealed the absence of the thing. And as only "beasts or gods are self-sufficient," but not citizens, cooperation was necessary.[31] It could not, however, be symmetrical, at least in its key functions, namely, the reproduction of the species and the organization of material labor. A hierarchy was required, evident right from the elementary cells of the community.

Onto the stage came power, then, with all its harsh consequences. The human being became the locus of a profound and lacerating scission that would never knit together again, at least in the ancient world. The phrases in the *Politics* delineate an ontology of the human condition founded on inequality. Males and masters on one hand, women and slaves on the other; although, Aristotle specified, the kind of power exercised over women was not the same as that exercised over slaves. Words that cannot be read without a shudder: the classical world is also the abyss that distances us from it, though it is a distance achieved very recently, and still incompletely; not just the thread which, fractured and intermittent, continues to bring it among us.

Such crushing subordination had a very powerful justification for Aristotle. From the start it was presented as an unmodifiable objectivity: disparity existed "by nature" (*physei*)—here it is again, after Antiphon! And it is "nature" that "has distinguished between female and slave."[32] In fact, "the male with respect to the female is such that by nature one is superior, the other inferior, one commands and the other is commanded."[33] The same applied to the slave: anyone "that by nature belongs not to himself but to another is by nature a slave."[34]

The "community of equals" thus rested on a rigid asymmetry in the power that enveloped it from every side, enabling its existence: command, and be commanded—*archein* and *archesthai*: a polarity with no way out. But the imbalance was not always identical every time it appeared. As regards politics, the asymmetry was provisional, corrected by the rotation of posts: at least in the democratic regime, which alone could be defined as truly "political"—"commanding and being commanded in turns."[35] On the other hand, the imbalance in the relationship of marriage between man and woman, and that between master and slave, was definitive, because it was formed "by nature": and this was the demonstration of the difference of kind—in other words, qualitative—between the powers exercised in the *polis*.

The continual reference to nature, hammered home on almost every line, is the real underlying thread of the whole analysis.[36] The point of view expressed by Antiphon—adherence to a rigorously naturalistic perspective—seemed paradoxically to be maintained, only then to be spectacularly turned into its opposite in terms of results. It was not equality that figured as a natural (and universal) datum, but, on the contrary, difference and submission, the latter pushed to the point of the complete estrangement of the subjected, to their total alienation, we might say. The slave—Aristotle affirmed—is in fact a man that does not belong to himself: almost evoking the ghost of Hegel's writing in the *Phenomenology*, to say nothing of the Marx of the *Manuscripts* (we shall return to both in Chapter 3).[37]

The equality of citizens was an artificial construct, an outcome of history and civilization, a consequence of the "political" constitution of the city—of its *politeia*—and of the rotation of public offices within it. The only natural thing, on the contrary, was the necessity of total subordination, the vast chasm of the unequal. And it was nature—its order and its characteristics—that explained and justified this complete subalternity of one man to another, and of woman to man, through to the very destruction of their humanity (partial for women; complete for slaves).

The morphology of the forms of power in which the life of the city was articulated coincided, for Aristotle, with a plane of qualitative differences, of essence, removed from human will but rooted in an unmodifiable ontological geometry of social life. In this way, the established order—the social order of the *polis* in its effective historicity, and the politics within it—acquired the armor of metaphysics and assumed the mask of the eternal. Everything else was secondary.

Slavery, as we have said, was a particular focus of attention for Aristotle. The relationship between master and slave—he added—is similar to the one between soul and body ("the rule of soul over body is like a master's rule").[38] The simile projected servile dependence onto the background of what had to appear as the most important discovery of philosophy: the interiority of the self, the infinite superiority of its untouchable lightness over the inert heaviness of the bodies containing it.

It was in this regard that the philosopher recalled how slavery was viewed by some as an institution contrary to nature: "to others it seems that being a master is contrary to nature: for them, in fact, one is slave, the other is free only according to the law; while by nature there is no difference."[39] And shortly after he insisted: "We need to question . . . whether all slavery is contrary to nature."[40]

It is not stated in the *Politics* who the supporters of this thesis were. But Aristotle's whole analysis was an explicit and outright contestation of their view. And it can readily be supposed that behind the doctrine he rejected was the one expounded by Antiphon and his followers (few in number but probably not nonexistent); and that, as we mentioned, in the original version of Antiphon's text as well, or at least in other passages of his work, there was a direct reference to slavery.[41] Such thought, about a century after it was originally affirmed, must still have been important enough to Aristotle for it to deserve such a long, specific, and destructive response.

Greek thinking about equality thus became locked within an implacable contrast: in the frontal clash between two irreconcilable paradigms; in the explicit and specular comparison of two opposite references to nature ("by nature," "contrary to nature"). Within it there was believed to be a dual and incompatible truth: the proof of a radical parity embracing the whole species—pure visionariness, in that world—or the measure— harshly realistic with respect to the times—of a principle of subordination pushed, for those subjected to it, to the point of the annihilation of the human that was in them, of their reduction to a mere thing (a thing "that speaks").[42] Only in the framework of this dramatic asymmetry was it possible, according to Aristotle, to conceive of a community of equals.

"By Nature"

How an outcome like this was reached is not hard to understand. We are faced—on Antiphon's side, and on Aristotle's—by two completely different ideas of nature, from which there derived, with the same coherence, two images of sociality—and of equality—that were entirely incompatible. An unbridgeable gap lay between them, marked by what we described earlier as the antimaterialistic and metaphysical turn of Greek philosophy.

One aspect did however continue to link the two visions: a continuity that eluded the rupture of change. For both, nature—whatever was understood by this term—contained an intrinsically normative value: it fixed, as we have said, the destiny of the human. It was a conviction expressing an original feature of all Greek thought, transmitted in many variants—including the Christian one—to the whole of the West, right into the heart of modernity.

The difference emerged, instead, around the quality of what was called nature.

For Antiphon it was what could be empirically observed by those looking at it in its immediate physicality; it was the anatomy and physiology impressed in the structures and functions of organs and bodies; it was the physiognomy of the living, as it appeared to the eye of those able to investigate it over and above any subjective difference. This inquiry revealed a uniformity of the human species that went beyond any possibility of discrimination, and indicated a path to follow, far beyond the one undertaken by democratic politics. In it, equality appeared to be rooted in the human form itself, visibly displayed by the same observable structure of bodies—and this alone counted.

There was Anaximander above all in this thought, probably filtered through the lens of sophistic reflection; together with the anamnestic bent of early Greek medicine: a deep-rooted belief in the irrepressible materiality of the real.[43] There was the passion and patience for scrutiny of the early Greek astronomers (the same ones derided by Aristophanes) and the first surveyors; and the wisdom of navigators and peasant farmers, who recorded signs in the sky, sea, and land to guide their behavior in advance.[44] Expressed in it was something remote in the history of our knowledge, but also surprisingly topical: science is not just about revolution and impermanence. Contemporary genetics adduces different, and more sophisticated and elegant, motivations capable of bringing to light much more profound and subtle regularities than those suggested by Antiphon, but the epistemological approach and the conclusions are substantially the same.

❋ ❋ ❋

On Aristotle's side, instead, another picture formed. For him nature was something completely different, which had severed any overly binding relationship with empirical observation. The materiality of the real did of course continue to exist; but it was necessary to pierce and go beyond it to see the profile of essences. The philosopher states this with absolute clarity, precisely in the pages we are considering: "nature is end" (*e de physis telos estin*): the formulation of an authentic ontological dogma, which reduced the observation of sensible reality to the search for its metaphysical causes alone.[45] The "end," in fact, could not be anything other than a projection of the investigator's mind, a product of their thought; it was not a property directly distinguishable in things, in bodies, in quantities. The representation of nature thus moved to a different level: from the field of physics to that of ideas; from bodies to relations between essences, as Francis Bacon would perceptively intuit in his own time.[46] Ionic materialism was erased in a single stroke. Nature lost physiology, anatomy, and the experiment, to gain metaphysics and ontology. It took almost a millennium to regain them.

For Aristotle, what appeared to be "by nature" was not so because it reflected the research of physics, the anatomical survey, or the investigation of the material causes of phenomena, but rather because it corresponded to an idea of "Ought," to a system of ends, reconstructed in the mind of the interpreter who drew it from the ethical and social experience of his age, accepted en bloc and uncritically, then to be transfigured into archetypes outside of time. It was a way of proceeding that culminated in an extraordinarily effective metaphysical legitimation of the existent—and of its social and power relations. In the *Politics,* in other terms, with an intellectual path opposite to that of Antiphon, it was the metaphysical (or metapolitical) character of the philosophical perspective that justified the flat realism of the social vision, and not the realism of physical inquiry that permitted the utopia of the ethical and civil conception.

In the shift between the two doctrines, the dark side of the idealistic and metaphysical turn of Greek thought from Plato onward was fully revealed: the same that would produce the greatest epistemological disaster of Western thought, blocking for a very long period of time any capacity for the scientific investigation of nature, and the technological development that went with it.[47]

The materiality of the real vanished from major speculation for centuries and would not be rediscovered until the advent of Renaissance and modern science; in the ancient world, it would become the realm merely of base practitioners, of those engaged in minor trades: a matter for artisans, not for scholars. In its place, under the guise of ultimate and hidden "ends," it was impossible to perceive anything other than a metaphysical masking of the social form of the present and of its prejudices—in a word, of the common sense of the age, substituting empirical observation with the claim to thus see more deeply.

From this perspective, it was quite possible to regard slavery—an institution on which the entire society of the time was based, and which appeared, with some reason in the given technological and economic conditions, without any alternative—as adhering fully to an imaginary and strict cosmic order of the world. If the end of the human species was cooperation, and its most elementary form presupposed, in the existing situation, a rigid division of tasks based on the fixity of roles and on the practice of coercion, only the total subalternity of women and of a proportion of men could guarantee it. And as the *polis* was an institution "by nature" (Aristotle firmly believed this, placing it at the height of human civilization), the inequalities that permitted its existence, however extreme, could not be other than "by nature" and according to an end as well, and therefore corresponding to the very nature of the thing. Equality was of course the high point of politics, but its achievement meant that it had to be surrounded, as paradoxical protection, by a network of negations; by the whole boundless multiplicity of the unequal.

The metamorphosis was complete. An institution with a purely social and cultural foundation was exchanged for an obligatory outcome with no alternative, which mirrored a law of nature. Excluding and repressive mechanisms that were solely the result of a particular historic development—slavery and female subalternity—ended up being legitimated as perennial figures of the human, and as such justified by natural principles. The idea expressed by Antiphon went in a completely different direction; but the representation was doomed from the start, in an environment unable to sustain it—from a social more than a strictly cultural point of view.

In the contrast between Aristotle and his opponents a whole universe was overturned, even if just for a moment, and in that movement was a glimpse, contracted but very clear, like in a hologram, of the entire path of the West.[48]

Ancient Humanists?

The idea that equality might encompass the whole human species, far beyond the borders of the *polis,* survived Aristotelean criticism, and even the end of the Greek democratic wave. It was picked up by the founders of Stoicism, and projected within new cultural contexts: before all else, the reflection on the human being pursued in Hellenistic and Alexandrine circles between the third and second centuries BC.

But that assumption—far removed from the direct practice of democracy and from the debate that had given rise to it—would end up losing all its potential ideological and political incandescence. It transmuted into a generic and inconsequential affirmation, with a vaguely humanistic flavor—the weak ancient humanism from Menander to Terence; to the intellectual circles close to the "enlightened" emperors of the second century AD, that of the "I am man, and I find nothing extraneous to me that concerns men" (first put like this by the Latin poet Terence).[49] All that emerged distinctly in the background was a cosmopolitanism imbued with tolerance and relativism and lying somewhere between ethics and ethnography, but totally sterilized in social and political terms, which would constitute a great part of the new Hellenistic culture. Attitudes and motifs in which it was never possible to give form to that molecular and Promethean idea of the human—of a human unfettered by any kinship or community tie—which would belong to modernity and, as we shall see, would have a decisive influence on the birth of a new civilization. And it is in this sense that we once again encounter the idea of equality at various points of a tradition stretching from Chrysippus ("no man is slave by nature" in an evident anti-Aristotelean polemic) to Eratosthenes—the great scientist and geographer who measured the Earth's circumference—and through to Panaetius and to

Antiochus of Ascalon, and from them to Cicero (whom we will discuss later).[50]

The shift of that thought from social and institutional elaboration—or even one of criticism of the dominant opinion, at any rate in relation to democracy and its tensions—to the plane of merely scholastic pronouncement—a shift, ultimately, from politics to minor ethics—was an irreversible and decisive passage in ancient culture.

Equality would never again be thematized in that world as a political problem with a cultural dimension, a precise vision of the world, behind it. Certainly, Rome at the beginning of the republican age undoubtedly saw some very bitter clashes, with an indubitably egalitarian content: we will return to this shortly. But it was a brief parenthesis, and in any case without any genuine intellectual development behind it—a fleeting appearance relating to the golden age of democracy in the eastern Mediterranean, soon to fade away.

In the city on the banks of the Tiber, instead, thinking about equality would move in a quite different direction. It was still far removed from politics, reencountered only at the end of the path, but it would mark the future of the West and seal its destiny.

CHAPTER TWO

THE ROMAN IMPRINT

Legal Machine and Theological Constructions

Pontifices and Laws

In a passage of his speech for the fallen at the start of the Peloponnesian War, Pericles affirms that one of the features of democracy is that "all men are equal for the settlement of their private disputes," in other words, parity of treatment is guaranteed for every citizen in disputes outside the sphere of politics.[1] Surprisingly, the formula of ensuring equality for everyone in private affairs perfectly summed up—describing it in advance—the function that would be performed by Roman law in the most significant part of its history: from the heart of the republican age through to the final years of the Severan dynasty, in the middle of the third century AD, by which time it had become the point of reference of a world empire. The task had already been quite clear to Cicero since the final decades of the republic, in the period when Roman legal thought was at its most creative: "Let the goal then of the civil law be defined as the preservation, in the concerns and disputes of citizens, of an impartiality founded on statute and custom," we read in a passage from de oratore that almost seems like a literal translation of the one from Thucydides, albeit with the addition of the decisive—and specifically Roman—reference to *ius civile* (civil law).[2]

In contrast, it was precisely in Greek culture, where it had actually first been articulated so clearly, that there was no adequate elaboration of the pointedness of Pericles's declaration.[3] It would in fact be hard to sustain that the principle stressed in it had—then or later—any particular prominence in the experience of Athenian democracy and the culture that informed it. The private equality of citizens was not a goal that ever attracted much attention or led to the adoption of distinct strategies or techniques; it was in the sphere of political equality (or of equality as a general human norm) that a significant part of philosophical reflection was concentrated—in this too philosophy showed itself to be the authentic *logos* of the democratic *polis*.

That objective seemed rather to be the lesser result of an institutional arrangement built around another priority: the primacy of the public and community aspect of city life, and, through it, of democratic politics. A design which consecrated as fundamental the preeminently constitutional role of the *nomoi,* statutes emanated according to the will of the people as expressed in assemblies: the *isonomia* discussed earlier related above all to the field of politics and its rules.

This did not mean statutes could not address issues concerning the private dimension of citizens' lives as well. But it was, so to speak, a marginal part of their remit; and, in such cases, their interpretation was entrusted to the rhetorical culture of the orators in trials, and to the discernment of the popular juries making decisions about disputes. At the same time, no knowledge that we would describe as strictly juridical, no specific expertise or group of specialists would ever be put in place to achieve the aim indicated by Pericles, viewed in any case as of secondary importance compared to the political management of the *polis*.

When Aristotle stressed that the human being is essentially a "political animal" it was this primacy of the "public" that he wished to emphasize; the rest, the "private" sphere of citizens, slipped into the shadows, into a gray area unworthy of much consideration.[4] Anyone who chose to lead their life entirely within this dimension would be reducing themselves, by common consensus, to a diminished and irremediably degraded existence. *Idiotes* in Greek means private, as in separate,

isolated, incomplete; but it is also someone who is rough and un-
couth, lacking something considered essential for being an authentic
human being: politics.

❊ ❊ ❊

But from around twenty years before Pericles gave his speech, and less
than fifty before Thucydides's account, there was, on the fringes of the
Mediterranean area frequented by the Greeks, a city that had established
an isonomic legislation—in all likelihood inspired by the Hellenic example, though much more structured than its probable models—devoted
in large part precisely to regulating the "private" weft of life evoked by
the Athenian politician.

This was the Rome of the Twelve Tables, in the middle of the fifth
century BC.[5]

It is impossible to ascertain the existence of a direct genealogy between the two experiences—Athenian democracy and the Roman republic
in the age of the Decemvirs—though there certainly were contacts. Rather,
we need to think about the effects of the genuine democratic wave that
swept across the eastern-central Mediterranean in the fifth century BC,
reaching Rome as well, where it took the form of Greek-inspired
plebeian struggles against the patrician aristocracy of Tyrrhenian and
Etruscan origin.

Despite having a far less developed cultural environment behind it
than Greece, the Roman legislation of the Twelve Tables was particularly analytical and detailed. This was because it brought together an already centuries-old legacy, totally absent in Greece, which had been
built up by a council of patrician priests—the pontifices—intent, from
the very start, on fixing in an almost oracular way the rules of a difficult coexistence within a highly composite civic fabric that was just beginning to consolidate.

Under the popular pressure that had imposed them, the Twelve Tables
appeared to be the result of an integration of opposing drives: patrician
(priestly) knowledge, transcribed in plebeian (legislative) form. In fact,
they projected into a frame of general and certain equality—with respect
to a civic body of patricians and plebeians that in this respect were
undifferentiated—a more ancient tradition, the expression of an original

feature of the archaic Roman mentality. The tendency, that is, toward a powerful and invasive ritualistic prescriptiveness, infused with magic, suspended between the human and the divine, and not found in other parts of the Mediterranean—with the possible exception of Palestine in the epoch of the *Pentateuch*, though the outcomes would be completely different.

The Twelve Tables had thus established also in Rome a very close link between isonomy in "private" relations and democratic politics: the same one delineated by Pericles. In the middle of the fifth century BC, plebeian democracy and isonomic legislation seemed an irresistible pairing in that distant periphery on the edges of Hellenic colonization in Italy.

But the rapid failure of the design cultivated by plebeian extremism—to transform Rome into a Greek-style democracy, founded on written laws and people's assemblies—plunged into crisis by the reaction of the aristocracy and the compromise soon reached between the ancient patriciate and new plebeian elites—severed that tie precociously. The Twelve Tables would remain as a monument of the republic, but Rome became an oligarchic regime in the hands of a limited number of great patrician-plebeian families—the new *nobilitas*—that was not only very far removed from any notion of radical democracy but did not even correspond to the Periclean model of a moderate government of the majority, with public posts partially determined by lot.

Yet that "private" equality, detached now from any democratic design—though the republic of the nobility never shunned a specific popular base, indeed adopting this feature as its own ideological banner—did not just remain intact but actually became stronger, forming the nucleus of a genuine legal machine of equality that was destined to stretch far beyond antiquity and to traverse the whole of Western history.

Private and Equal

The social and cultural history of Rome developed, then, in a completely different direction to that of Greece. And the specifically legal talent that it had displayed from very early on would take root exactly in the deepest and most acute point of the difference—the marked importance, in concrete facts and in ideas, of the "private" sphere of citizens in the organization of the *polis*.

Rome had also experienced the model of statutory law from very early times, probably even before the Twelve Tables. The *lex,* as it was already called in archaic Latin, very soon became, in the self-representation of republican political culture, the expression by antonomasia of the deliberations of the people gathering together in assemblies. And, as in Greece, even though the statutes did touch on issues regarding the private life of citizens as well, they dealt principally with the city's political arrangements, what we would call its constitution.

But unlike the Greek experience, the other, private aspect had occupied a central position—constitutive of the city and of its culture no less than the collective, communitarian side—from the very beginning of Rome's history, and it was due precisely to this importance that it had been drawn into the specific field of priestly prescriptions we spoke of earlier: not opposed to *lex* but certainly alternative. It was the world of *ius*—which came into being as something intrinsically associated with the social life of citizens, outside of politics.

That word—*ius*—which we render with "law," was untranslatable in every other ancient language. It denoted a wholly Roman body of rules and of disciplining that was completely different from the model of the *nomos* and from that of the *lex* which largely copied it, in a dualism that would again be reabsorbed. It was a set of precepts, initially intertwined with religious experience but then increasingly and more markedly detached from it, drawn up to perform the function suggestively and specifically evoked by Pericles, but otherwise left in the shadows by Greek thought, irresistibly attracted only by the public and political side of community life.

The task of *ius,* as Cicero later wrote, would be exactly to guarantee equality—*aequabilitas*—in the (private) relations of citizens, in that part of their existence unrelated to politics and the community—extraneous, in other words, to what the Romans called *publicum,* that which is of the people.[6]

Privus / privatus (the Latin equivalent of *idios / idiotes*) also designated the single human being (as Aulus Gellius, the famous Roman antiquarian and scholar who lived in the second century AD, still remembered), depicted in isolation, detached and, as it were, incomplete.[7] But this time the word carried no semantic overtones suggestive of a negative value or diminishment, as it did in Greek: the public and the private remained, in social experience and in Roman cultural representations, two separate but balanced spheres. Above all, they had equal dignity, and their harmonic equilibrium (*publicum privatumque*) defined, with no precise hierarchy but with a clear reference to an irreducible difference, the ordered whole of the city.

This diversity of conception—perfectly visible in classical Greece and republican Rome—though apparently unremarkable, as if hidden between the folds of societies with many features in common (early Rome was in many ways "a Greek city," albeit not exclusively so), would have incalculable consequences.[8] If it had not existed, the West would probably not have seen the birth and development of what we call law. The explanation for it remains in part an enigma, as often happens when faced with the genesis of archaic features that appeared from the outset as facts seemingly referring to nothing beyond them. But due to the role that this peculiarity would later acquire, it is worth devoting some attention to it.

* * *

We must go back to remote origins: to specificities linked to the initial formation and consolidation of Rome as a politically recognizable entity.

In that environment—the area that is now Lazio, between the eighth and seventh century—marked by the expansive capacity of wealthy and aggressive aristocracies (Latin, Sabine, Etruscan), the economic and military weight of rigidly patrilinear and patriarchal kinship structures that generated very solid family and clan units—*familiae* and *gentes*, as they were called in Latin—was highly significant. And it remained so even after the aggregation that led, in a geographically favorable location, to the establishment of early Rome. It fixed a cultural and organizational model centered on the solitary figure of the *paterfamilias*, or "father of the family," around whom there revolved a whole system of subordinations and exchanges—economic and matrimonial.

Within this framework, the city took shape on the basis of a kind of compromise, and of integration, between two distinct types of power; and this original duality had a decisive influence on its history.

The first, which acted more as an antecedent or presupposition—certainly systemic and perhaps historic as well—was expressed by the preeminence, closely linked to the functioning of kinship relations, of the single heads of family or clan chiefs, who, though jealous of their prerogatives, had become part of the new and more or less heterogeneous civic bloc. This amounted to a kind of early kin lordship of the *patres* (one might say, improperly but perhaps effectively, "sovereignty"): a position that translated into an irremissible autonomy of command, conserved in the amalgamation of the new city. Many centuries later, the unlimited nature of this original power, which sometimes even extended to putting one's own children to death, would appear to Hadrian, the great humanist *princeps* of the second century—in a reflection lying somewhere between history and ethnography—as a peculiarity that set the Romans apart from other peoples: "there are almost no other men who keep their sons subjected to a power such as our own," reports Gaius (a jurist contemporary to him), citing the thought of his emperor.[9]

The other power, more recent and already in some way "political," arose instead from the initial crystallization of the city's institutions around certain forms of assembly (the first senate, the *comitia curiata*; later, the meetings of the standing army) and the figures of capable and bold warrior kings.

A sort of original polarity was thus established, mirroring the one between *ius* and *lex* (quite clear to later Roman thought)—very strong, and crucial for later developments.

On the one hand was a space structured by strong kinship relations, essential both for the dealings that determined the coexistence, from the point of view of the economy and of matrimonial exchanges, between the *patres*—now citizens as well—at the head of their respective family networks; and for managing the powers of each head of the family within their own group.

On the other was an area marked by the predominance of strictly political relations, relatively fragile at first, and then increasingly more substantial. This concerned the city as a whole, or, to use a word that soon became common, its "people," and not the existence of single families. An area that was in turn the expression of a balance between different components: the aristocratic selection; the pressure of the lower social orders, unified in the plebeian masses, which very quickly became discernible; the charisma of the warrior kings.

The first of these two areas—the non-"political" and therefore non-"public" one, according to the later Roman lexicon, but indispensable for the orderly preservation of the new city—would later, undoubtedly still in the republican age, be defined as "private": because it pertained to the autonomy of power (we have also ventured to call it sovereignty) of "single" head-of-family citizens, in so far as they were *privi, privati,* considered, that is, outside the political tie but within their kinship relations. In this sense, we can say that family and clan structures formed the private sphere in Rome: creating a separation from the "public" space of the community as people—as political subject—which would already appear to historic and legal thought between the second and first century BC to be constitutive, genetically and morphologically, of the very essence of the Roman *res publica*.[10]

It was to protect and regulate this ambit—this nucleus of private sovereignty not dissolved by the prevalence of political relations, but respected as a world apart, in a certain sense foundational with respect to the "public" life of the city—that the disciplining force of *ius* developed from a very remote age: a function integrated at first within sacrality and a heavy magic-religious symbology. When all this became rarefied to the point of vanishing, the adjective *civile* began, probably from the end of the second century BC, to be added to *ius,* forming the expression *ius civile,* that is to say, civil law, understood as *ius civitatis:* the private (not political) order of citizenship.

It did not stem from external interventions, but from inside the space of autonomy to which, through self-regulation, it gave further form and substance. It was a kind of shell, steeped in rituality and symbolism, protective of the power and of the hierarchies expressed by kinship relations; its first lexicon was a nomenclature of that peculiar patriarchal lordship, which Roman thought would always regard as specific to the history of its community. An order realized through pronouncements—made originally by priests, and then by wise men from the leading families of the patrician-plebeian nobility—and rigorously case-based in nature, which was also preserved in later ages.

This framework was never again called into question after the episode of the Twelve Tables. If the plebeian design had definitively taken root, the whole history of Rome would have changed, and its development might perhaps have featured rhetoric and orators in the place of law and jurists. But the project remained unfulfilled. The compromise between the patriciate and the plebeian elites, which from the beginning of the third century BC gave a definitive structure to the republic, fixed its aristocratic form for good, albeit in part corrected by a limited popular presence (ideologically emphasized by the nobility itself).

That agreement also definitively sealed the substantive primacy of (aristocratic) *ius* and not of (democratic) *lex* in regulating the private lives of citizens, entrusting it to a narrow circle of experts, jealous custodians of a particular and increasingly complex and sophisticated technique. It stabilized, that is, the form of *ius* as what we would call that of a jurisprudential case-based law, shaped by experts through their opinions (and later through their written works) and by the magistrates that administered justice with their edicts. A "case law" guided by jurists, rather than a law created by political command ("law at Rome is not so much an ordinance of the State as a creation of the lawyers," as Ronald Syme would tersely and effectively write).[11]

For the whole republican age, juridical isonomy continued to be accompanied by a political citizenship that also managed to maintain an egalitarian bedrock, despite the evident oligarchic weighting. And the paradigm of the people's government (*res publica* as *res populi*) continued to describe the self-representation that Roman thought had built up of its own political constitution—an elaboration unquestionably interpreted with greatest clarity by Cicero. But the equilibrium was not destined to last.

A Natural Law

Even if it was the product of the knowledge of an elite—the jurists were all from families belonging to the senatorial nobility, both of patrician and plebeian descent—the intrinsic egalitarian core, however circumscribed in scope, expressed by *ius* would never be disavowed. The Twelve Tables had consolidated this aspect, inserting it into a solid legislative framework, rather than creating it from nothing. In short, it embodied a remote Roman idea of equality.

It had been like that from the beginning: the most ancient pronouncements—fruit of the secret knowledge of the pontifices—guaranteed peace within the newly formed community; and this could only be maintained by respecting the parity between the *patres* that were part of it. The prescriptions of *ius*—almost oracular responses to questions formulated by citizens—concerned essential areas of social dealings: patrimonial relations (debts, purchases, sales), matrimonial exchanges, land boundary issues, power over children and wives within the family, hereditary mechanisms.

In a young community forged from an unstable fusion, open to and inclusive of different local ethnic groups—secession was an abiding political nightmare for the city—it was important that such decisions should place on a completely level plane the heads of families (both patrician and plebeian, even though the latter perhaps did not have gentilitial forebears), between whom there might arise (or had arisen) some dispute over patrimonial affairs or (strictly exogamic) matrimonial exchanges. In other words, that the response of the priest was totally equidistant with regard to the interests at play, projections of irreducible microsovereignties. Any departure from this line would have led to ruinous intestine conflicts—the ultimate calamity for a city surrounded by enemies, against which the whole of archaic religiosity was deployed, with its rituals, symbols, and sacrifices, to reassure citizens and to exorcize the ever-looming risk of division and chaos.

Parity and symmetricalness lay at the heart of *ius;* a direct consequence, as it were, of its historic and anthropological base, expressed through the strength of kinship relations; a feature inscribed within its genetic nucleus: a glue no less essential than political institutions for holding together the *civitas.*

Later, in imperial Rome, this guaranteeism (with respect to the established social order) and this egalitarianism still appeared to be the most recognizable feature, and the most important function, of *ius.*

It is Cicero, again, who writes in *pro Caecina:*

> He who thinks that civil law should be given no consideration at
> all breaks every community bond, not just concerning judicial pro-
> cedures, but with regard to life itself and the common good. And
> he who admonishes the interpreters of law, declaring them inca-
> pable of understanding it, diminishes humanity and not just civil
> law. And if he then holds that it is not necessary to obey the ju-
> rists, he does not just injure them but shakes the very foundations
> of the laws and of law. Because you must always bear this in mind:
> that in a city community there is nothing that should be guarded
> so jealously as the civil law. And in fact, if it is set to one side, no
> means remain to ascertain what belongs to him and what to others;
> there is no measure of equality that can hold good for all [*nihil est
> quod aequabile inter omnis atque unum omnibus esse possit*].[12]

The distributive balance between citizens enabled the community to
survive without disruptive conflicts. It was not achieved by searching
for a quantitative parity between the patrimonies of the family heads,
but by establishing rules that were the same for everyone. "What belongs
to him and what to others": *ius* seemed the discipline best suited to preserving the bedrock of property ownership underpinning coexistence
between the *patres,* in turn a direct consequence of the mutually excluding nature of kinship structures, which imposed an at least partial
subdivision of land and other assets.[13] If that bulwark had crumbled,
the dark path of anomie would have opened up: there was nothing
worse than the absence of norms, in any field of life, for the Roman aristocratic tradition, grounded in a magic-religious (and then juridical)
prescriptiveness that was to appear almost obsessive to late republican
scholars themselves.

The function of *ius* seemed, then, not just to be distinct from politics
but, in certain circumstances, could even be directed against it. In the
same text, Cicero writes: "What in fact is the civil law? It is something
that influence cannot bend, nor power break, nor wealth corrupt."[14]

Gratia, potentia, pecunia: social relations, corruption through wealth,
power. Without a doubt, what was being evoked here was the degenerate

side of politics, dramatically familiar to any member of the Roman governing orders during the troubled decades of the "sunset" of the republic (Cicero was writing not long before 60 BC)—but it was still politics.[15] Yet *ius* (Cicero believed) was quite different, and immune to the risks to which the latter was always exposed: the declaration did not (just) express the rhetorically heightened sentiment of the moment; it revealed the influence of a long history of separation and alterity that was unthinkable in the Greek world. The certainties of law—the symmetry and parity radiating from its core—had nothing to do with the unstable and tempestuous world of political behavior. What we have here is the "degree zero," as it were, of the millenary ideology of the neutrality of law.

✳ ✳ ✳

Cicero's speech also leads us to another far-from-unimportant difference (we have already touched on it) between the "private equality" of the Greeks, barely outlined and founded on the *nomoi*, and the Roman one, much more fully articulated through *ius*.

While the former was an outcome of democracy, of the *isonomia* imposed by politics, and had no autonomous space—either conceptual or institutional—outside of it, the other one—private equality through *ius*—had been being built in a way that was entirely independent of political action, and would survive intact the end of the limited democratic experience of republican Rome. Indeed, it enjoyed its greatest period of development during the increasingly marked absolutism that distinguished the Principate from Augustus onward: a regime that turned into a full-blown military autocracy, in which even the final traces of the long and highly problematic relationship between legal equality and political freedom (between legal equality in the field of private law and equality of political rights) rapidly dissolved.

The detachment between "public" and "private," or, if we want, between *ius* and democracy, between *ius* and political sovereignty, would appear to Hegel, almost 2,000 years later, as unequivocal proof of the incapacity of Roman law (and of the Roman world) to resolve its incurable contradictions. Those subjects considered and weighed up with great care by *ius* were reduced, outside its domain, to the sole dimension of a subjugated people, exposed to the pressure of an arbitrary and crushing political power, though some significant privileges were reserved for the network of aristocratic circles—from the senatorial nobility in the capital to the small oligarchies of the peripheral cities—that constituted the backbone of the empire.

But the apparently contradictory separation was also the sign of the enduring tendency of that system of rules to distinguish itself from any other competing power, and to protect its own isolation through an ever more demanding and specialized technique—which soon became the most highly structured in the ancient world. To transform its own self-referentiality directly into a force able to interact effectively with the other centers of social and political authority in play at any given time. Cicero had precociously realized this too: "In a question of law, gentlemen, there is nothing like that—no forged document, no dishonest witness; in short, all that undue influence, which is all-powerful in public life, is here, and only here, inoperative; for it has no chance of getting to work, no opportunity to reach the judges, no means even of raising a finger," we read, again in *pro Caecina*.[16]

From then on, the history of the West could not have done without this kind of dialectic—on one hand law, on the other the *nimia potentia* evoked in the oration: powers without measure or order that had emerged from inevitably tumultuous societies. A contrast where the winning position would depend, in the different circumstances, only on the historic conditions of the moment.

Formalism and Ontology

Cicero had grasped the essential point. It could rightly be said that not just the birth but the whole history of *ius* revolved around a single problem: how to guarantee equality in the private relations of a society that had originally been organized in a very basic way but was now, in the imperial age, relatively complex, and how to conserve it outside of politics.

It was in response to this need that, in the course of the first century BC (largely before Cicero's eyes), the cognitive features of Roman legal thinking underwent a great transformation—a genuine intellectual revolution—whose effects can still be seen today. What might be described as "the splitting of forms" was invented in the realm of *ius*, and a framework built for an entirely formal law (in the sense of Hegel, Weber, and Kelsen)—the first in world history.[17]

Drawing on archaic religiosity, *ius* had, from the very beginning—as we have said—expressed a powerfully symbolic and ritualistic tendency. Many of its precepts consisted of nothing other than the imposition of a ritual, of procedures articulated and measured right down to the tiniest detail of wording or gesture, entrusted to the knowledge of priests: anyone who departed from them lost the dispute and had no way of making their case. The original substance of relations and things—and the conflictual charge encapsulated therein—disappeared, yielding to a symbolic transfiguration with a very strong disciplining value that defused all violence.

But later, in a mature, secularized society with imperial growth in full swing, that remote aptitude—suspended between magic practice and empirical astuteness—for distinguishing the world of facts from the field of *ius*, and for entrusting the latter to a universe of symbols, was morphing into something previously unseen.

Contributing to the change was both the memory of archaic customs and the pressure of an only recently acquired and previously inconceivable imperial power that required order and certitudes for an economy and a society that was now of Mediterranean proportions, the most advanced in the ancient world and with levels of production and trade that would not be seen again until Europe was on the threshold of modernity.

A new form of wisdom and a new interpretation of reality came into being, then, within the circle of jurists. Their sole purpose was to achieve social discipline through a technique capable of producing rules presented with the objectivity of incontrovertible enactments—not the result of arbitrary acts of will (still less on the part of political power) but the outcome of pure acts of knowledge.

The secret lay in a hard-won ability that might be described as the splitting of the functional forms and relations considered by *ius* from the social material that constituted them concretely and gave life to them in reality. Commercial transactions, debts, credits, ownership (of land, property, a slave), marriages, subjects (who bought, sold, lent sums of money), and also claims, defaults, inheritances, and legal actions lost the effective determinateness, or singularity, linking them to interests, to settings, to events, to particular cases (a specific bundle of goods, lot of land, head of family, will). Instead, they became abstract figures, formal schemes of acts and behaviors shorn of concrete content, which did not exist other than in the universe of *ius*, but which found in it a decisive justification. They enabled the rule elaborated by the jurist to be connected no longer to the specific event requiring regulation—now an almost boundless myriad—but to the recognized abstract model within it, that is, to the functional form concealed beneath the empirical contingency of every single fact. As a consequence, the legal discipline that was pursued could be linked in a direct and synthetic way to the general figure thus devised, and to the functional equilibria that it expressed, instead of depending only on the evaluation of a multiplicity of cases that the growing complexity of society rendered inevitably elusive and slippery.

Every form constructed according to this procedure would have its own (legal) name: to ascribe one to it was to acknowledge its separate existence in the space of *ius*. And the names, in the thinking of those who assigned them, reflected the (legal) substance of things and were an immediate consequence of their truth.

Almost 2,000 years of usage has made us familiar today with a terminology that we take for granted, a nomenclature that runs through and puts into (legal) form our daily existence: sale, tenancy, mortgage, deposit, will, obligation, mandate; but also good faith, malice, error, fault, possession. And we have forgotten that the weft and the underlying mechanisms of such a universe were created by Roman jurists alone, and over a relatively brief arc of time, certainly no more than five or six generations.

Yet this powerful impetus toward abstraction—toward an entirely formal law—would never distract the ancient jurists from their eminently practical and operative function. It would never transform them into philosophers, although their conceptual elaborations were indebted to a great deal of Greek thought, reworked with total liberty but the same consummate skill. Rather, it would make them protagonists of a previously untested technique and render them capable of performing their task with extraordinary effectiveness. The self-isolation of the guardians of *ius* within a universe of forms alone, of defined and hidden proportions and compatibilities, and the regulating of social reality on the basis of those abstractions, unleashed in fact an immense ordering force, an incomparable grip on life events, temporarily set to one side in juridical reasoning only in order to be better mastered and directed.

❋ ❋ ❋

The concepts built through the formalizing gaze of the Roman jurists would not be considered, by the jurists themselves, just as categories of thought. They were seen, in an ever more defined way, as figures of being as well—as *res incorporales,* "incorporeal things"; some of which were those *quae iure consistunt,* "that consist of law," as Gaius would write in his *Institutiones* in the middle of the second century.[18] They were treated, that is, as real beings endowed with their own life and with an unescapable objectivity, which legal knowledge limited itself to mirroring, in a kind of adjustment of the intellect to the very reason of the observed thing.

Savigny—the greatest German jurist and historian of law in the nineteenth century—grasped this aspect with great subtlety, and in a well-known text written in 1814 described its essential features very effectively:

> It has been shown . . . that, in our science, every thing depends upon the possession of the leading principles, and it is this very possession which constitutes the greatness of the Roman jurists. The notions and axioms of their science do not appear to have been arbitrarily produced; these are actual beings, whose existence and genealogy have become known to them by long and intimate acquaintance. For this reason their whole mode of proceeding has a certainty which is found no where else, except in mathematics; and it may be said, without exaggeration, that they calculate with their concepts.[19]

Whether in this vision of the Roman jurists there were influences of a directly Platonic (ideas as essences) or Aristotelian nature (dualism between form and content and the metaphysical priority of form) we cannot ascertain. But the epistemological revolution of legal thinking was certainly infused with the whole of Greek classical philosophy, which filtered through to contribute to the great change.

The figures of law thus acquired a value that made *ius* a genuine metaphysics, albeit a highly particular one, directed exclusively toward transforming abstract patterns of historically determined social relations into forms of (legal) being, where the concrete experience of life was reduced to within a finite number of archetypal models: a full-blown ontology, posited as the driving force for every development in law. It was a very similar way of proceeding to what we saw in Aristotle with regard to the ontological transfiguration of inequality and slavery. A limited set of concepts (of forms) would from then on become the protagonist of an invisible scene, somehow spectral but able to impact the material reality of life, which came to appear entirely lacking in (legal) sense outside of that contact.

The great invention of Roman legal thought is revealed in its capacity to link in a single circuit the search for a rigorous prescriptive order with the construction of a metaphysics that justified it from a point of view that was not ethical (the justice so beloved to the Greeks) but coldly ontological. From then on—and through to today—legal discourse would appear to be the fruit of a cognitive operation whose every phase could be rationally controlled, standing aloof from the disputability of moral values but also from the possible abuse and will of political command.

This happened precisely when the Roman aristocracy—from which all the most important jurists still came—had succeeded in concentrating enormous power in its hands, with an unprecedented world reach, the result of an extraordinary desire for empire that required a legitimation proportionate to its immense breadth, order and consensus, to fully justify itself. And the demand for a shared order—on a scale that had never been seen before—pushed toward the regulatory force of abstraction: mastery in thought, as an indispensable condition for exercising control and political hegemony. Quintus Mucius Scaevola—a jurist of the final century of the republic and the first protagonist of the turning point, had also been an exceptional governor of the province of Asia.[20] Venerated by those he administered, who lived in a territory of cities, trade, and culture, he had learned first-hand what it meant, for a Roman and for a jurist, to govern the world.

The response was a kind of law capable of acquiring an entirely formal dimension, of venturing somehow beyond its own historicity—in the sense that from its point of view nothing could be perceived other than the abstract form of the real relations considered by it. No naked force, no self-enclosed power, no contingent events, no burgeoning subjectivity; just intellect and essences: a normative order to which the development of a specific instrumental rationality was linked—calculative, quantitative, destined to mark legal argumentation forever and to become identified with the very reason of law.

* * *

Formalism was not just an extraordinary invention from the point of view of juridical technique. It also brought with it a very important consequence: the machinery of law whose realization it permitted would necessarily function from then on as an egalitarian model—the most effective one constructed by the West to date, which took up, emphasizing and strengthening it, the egalitarian tendency present from the origins of *ius*.

It could in fact only perform its task by pressing all the single human beings involved into just one mold, identical for each of them. Every personal particularity disappeared—and so did every difference, as long as one remained within the sphere of law. In their place there was just an abstraction—the abstract form of singularity, we might say: an empty schema, a perfectly neutral profile, indifferent to any concrete content, defined only by the functional position held in the relationship or act under consideration: the buyer, the seller, the creditor, the debtor, the lessor, the owner, and so on, for every figure falling with the scope of the history of *ius*.

Clearly, the inequalities induced by social and economic mechanisms continued to exist, and to produce their effects; not all buyers were equivalent; neither were all sellers, nor all owners of land or slaves. But the differences, however macroscopic, remained outside the legal appraisal. They were (temporarily) set aside when entering the domain of law. For the machine of *ius* to be able to function, each subject had to be interchangeable in their abstraction, defined only by the role they had in the transaction under consideration. It was the invention of the formal equality of law: the most formidable construct of social thought in the West. Without it, we would not be here to talk about it.

In antiquity—unlike what would happen in modern societies—the gap between private formal equality and substantive (economic, social) and also political inequality did not result in particular tensions. It would fade away without leaving significant traces, overwhelmed by the force of other contradictions and conflicts; also because the range of legal formalism was in any case drastically reduced in that context, as that of political equality had been, and its invention remained compressed, without any opportunity to become a truly general rule. Like politics, that equalness did not include slaves—and hence a large part of the world of production and labor—nor, very often, women either; and not even the lowest social orders, especially in the countryside, both in Italy and in the rest of the empire: masses destined to live outside or on the edges of law, as access to *ius* always effectively remained a possibility for the privileged. And it did not concern—or only tangentially touched upon— what we call "public law," even when a first, troubled, and nebulous notion of it began to take shape with the thinking of Ulpian and other jurists in the Severan age, in their attempt to extend the control brought by *ius* to the nascent statehood of their time: tax system, bureaucracy, army, provincial administration. Formalism in the ancient world would always remain largely confined within the limits of private law.

It was not until another history came onto the scene, and the model was transplanted into a different force field, that all the potential contained in its full deployment became apparent.

Person

In Roman legal thinking it was always clear that the function of *ius* could only have meaning if it was intrinsically associated with the concrete life of human beings, each one considered (outside of politics, of the "public") in the network of their private relations. That the world of law was, in other words a creation "for the benefit of single beings," as Ulpian would declare in one of the texts of his *Institutiones* in which he made use of an ancient tradition culminating in the teaching of the great jurists of Hadrian's time, who made the assumption a guiding principle of their work.[21] A long time earlier, after all, Cicero had already been able to write that *ius* was inconceivable if not between men and for men.[22]

Yet Roman law was never a law based on the "human person." Still less was it an order founded on recognition of "human rights."[23] It was rather a kind of analytics (transcendental, one might say) of the relationship between order, subject, and power, founded on an ontology of the juridical being. A framework suspended between Aristotle and Kant. The equalizing capacity that it expressed—its equality machine—rested exclusively on the objectifying and formalizing force of its vision, on the power of the ontological projection with which it was endowed. Where others saw nothing but contingent things, facts, and behaviors—the social dust of bare lives—jurists discovered immutable entities, rigid preestablished proportions, metaphysical balances that were not to be violated. In short, life instituted within forms, without, however, reaching the point of translating it into an individualizing vision of the human—a threshold that was never crossed, just as had been the case for Greek equality. Its foundation was the calculation of private positions and powers, not the construction of the subjectivities or the law of persons— as for the Greeks, politics was about being part of the community, not exalting singularities.

Nor was *ius* ever a constructed order from the point of view of subjective rights—a category entirely unknown to ancient thought, not even in relation to the head of the family's powers. It was not law that, as such, pertained to the subject (even though, in certain circumstances, a quantum of *ius* did belong to each subject); if anything, it was the subject that belonged to law.[24] In the case of the powers of the *pater,* for instance, what was highlighted was the objective web of kinship relations—the overwhelming weight of patrilinear descent in family organization— rather than the individual guarantee for the figure occupying a particular role in that hierarchy. The "benefit of single beings" that Ulpian talked about was never a function creating legal subjectivities in the modern sense of the term. It referred indistinctly to the private network of family nuclei, of properties and exchanges, to singularities formalized only from the perspective of their objective importance: first in the Roman community of the *patres* itself, then in the organization of the empire's citizen elites. At most, what came into relief were statuses: the condition of single entities with respect to the family, to citizenship, to freedom (as opposed to slavery); never the abstract possession of their rights.

The point was that the Roman "single being" did not coincide with the modern "individual": not even when Ulpian, in one isolated text, speaks of *singularis . . . persona.*[25] Something decisive was lacking: social (prior even to legal) control—generalized and on a mass scale—of one's capacity for labor; the historic definition of one's own atomized subjectivity as a producer and (therefore) a consumer. And a philosophy to conceptually elaborate this condition—and hence in terms of (self-) consciousness—was missing too. In a word: the economic and intellectual context of modernity.

Only the nineteenth-century rereading of Roman law—culminating in an interpretation strongly conditioned by Savigny, Mommsen, and Sumner Maine—would mystify the features of this picture, overlaying it with wholly extraneous elements. Characteristics taken from European societies between the eighteenth and nineteenth centuries and from their legal thinking, through to the construction of the full-blown bourgeois-Roman law centering on the figure of the individual property holder, on the "man of having" (as Hegel would say): a real mess in historic terms, but with an extraordinary normative result that would dominate Western legal culture for a long time.[26] We shall return to this in due course.

In Roman thought, by contrast, there never existed what we might call the subjective gaze on *ius,* or, reversing the perspective, *ius* considered from the point of view of the constitution of the subjectivities that would have had to articulate it. And it was also by a similarly negative attitude that the formalism of its equality was nourished. By a continually estranging and a-personalized view, as if from above and outside any subjectivity, which, even when (as often happened) it set out to search for equitability, for the most appropriate solution to the specific case under examination, over and above the application of narrow law, did so by aiming for the criterion of an objective measure, a predefinable calculability. The jurists' vocation was to search for an infinitely divisible measurability, for the quantum of law exactly attributable to the parties involved in each situation: quantity, as it were, without subjects. And this was the sense of the *suum cuique tribuere* ("to each his own") from Cicero to Ulpian: the dispelling of subjectivities in the face of the rigorous and impersonal calculation of quantities.

❊ ❊ ❊

Roman thought was the first to give a social and legal meaning (or at least attributable to *ius*) to the word *persona*, in the sense of a human being to whom legal functions could be related (in any case an unusual use in Latin for this term, drawn from the lexicon of the theater, and which, like the corresponding Greek word *prosopon*, customarily indicated the stage mask, or the character played by an actor): a choice of terminology that, as we shall see, would have very important consequences.

Just after the introductory comments of his *Institutiones*, while presenting a classification that would provide an ordering structure for the whole course of his argument, Gaius writes: "All the law in use amongst us relates either to persons, things, or [trial] actions"—a three-part division destined to enjoy a long-lived if not immediate success (as far as is known, no other Roman jurist would repropose it in the same terms, at least until the fourth century and, later, Justinian).[27]

It is not possible to say whether the original idea for this scheme came from Gaius. Certainly, a contraposition between persons and things (*personae/res*) can already be found in Cicero, in a passage from *de oratore*, albeit in a completely different context.[28] And it was again Cicero, followed moreover by Seneca, who employed the word *persona* to describe conditions and figures of human subjectivity (it is harder to trace the use of the term back to Quintus Mucius Scaevola).[29] It is quite possible, then, that Gaius was reworking an earlier and perhaps rhetorical model that is unknown to us.

But even the use of this category for systematic purposes did not pave the way for any construction of legality from a subjective point of view (a difficulty perfectly apparent to Kelsen, when he says: "The physical or juristic person who 'has' obligations and rights as their holder, *is* these obligations and rights—a complex of legal obligations and rights whose totality is expressed figuratively in the concept of 'person'").[30] Indeed, for Gaius, with respect to *ius,* persons and things ended up being placed absolutely on the same plane (together with actions). No primacy of the subject was even minimally envisaged. Admittedly, the "person" did appear, but was immediately placed alongside things, and it served only to designate a sphere of *ius*—the one concerning it—in a symmetrical separation with respect to the other two fields (things and trial actions). The exclusive view remained that of the legal order as a whole. It was in any case a return to the machine of equality, in its cold, formal objectivity.

And there is much more yet. Immediately after the classification mentioned above, Gaius moved on to deal with the first of the indicated fields—persons—pointing to a new distinction: "The primary division [*summa divisio*] of the law of persons is this—that all men are either free or slaves."[31] Slaves thus seemed to fall fully within the category of persons—those, among them, who are under the mastery of another person [*qui in aliena potestate sunt*]. Indeed, "slaves . . . are in the *potestas* of their owner [*in potestate itaque sunt servi dominorum*]," the jurist later says when he comes to deal with slavery.[32] Aristotle seemed to have been forgotten: slaves were not taken into account at all by law, but they were nonetheless considered persons: the law of slavery—in its powerful Roman specificity (more about this in a moment) was still the law of persons.[33]

Then everything changed. In the second book, when he moved on to discuss things (the second part of the initial classification), Gaius's perspective shifted abruptly.[34] Distinguishing between "corporeal" and "incorporeal" things (we have already touched on the latter), he lists slaves among the examples of the former ("land, a slave, a garment"—*fundus, homo, vestis*), thereby once again reducing the living human being in a state of slavery simply to a thing—in a line that, unexpectedly, reestablished a strong continuity with the Aristotelean tradition. Not a further word was said about the "person"—it literally disappeared.

The change was of no little importance.[35] The center of Gaius's entire system concealed a shift as disorienting as it was irremediable between persons and things: a kind of dual regime of the human, given the impossibility of tracing a clear boundary between subjects and objects. A continually compromised demarcation—between subjects unable to be completely defined as such, and objects which, in turn, were not entirely so—that was thrown resoundingly into crisis precisely by the presence of slavery, especially the Roman version.

Nor was it merely a systematic incongruence, a cold problem of exposition. Emerging into the spotlight in that contradiction was one of the crucial points of rupture that separated antiquity from the modern world: the possibility of a unitary juridical (but not only) consideration of the human. It was a theme to which Roman thinking would once again return.

The Rule of the Empire

The relationship between formalism and equality of law did not mark the end of the ancient jurists' reflections on equality.

In the last great season of their history—between the end of the second century and the first decades of the third, during the age of the Severans—the egalitarian device they had elaborated, which by then had become, at least in principle, the "private" rule of the entire empire and a constituent element of the whole civilization of that world, opened out to encompass another perspective. At first sight completely different, it was actually nothing other than its completion: a strong revival of the doctrine of natural law and its universalistic foundation inspired by the Stoic tradition.[36]

When we speak of natural law what immediately springs to mind is the movement of ideas that ran through the political and legal laboratory of modernity between the seventeenth and eighteenth century. It must immediately be said that nothing even remotely comparable existed in the Roman (or Greek) world. The main reason for this will be explained in due course. In the meantime, another by no means small difference can be noted.

Roman legal culture, with the exception of two narrow windows of time, respectively in the ages of Cicero and Seneca, was never accompanied, as a point of support and reference, by any philosophical or political elaboration worthy of the name. A condition far removed from the entanglement between philosophy and legal science that would distinguish early modernity, and which must be regarded as the real breeding ground of modern thinking on the doctrine of natural law.

Due to this lack, the ethical paradigms first deployed in the history of Roman legal thinking by the Severan masters were very meager in terms of genuine prescriptive content, which remained limited to the generic indications extrapolated by Cicero from a strand of Greek philosophy that was in turn already centuries old: yellowed features of a statically patrimonial and property-based representation of community bonds, closely compatible, moreover, with the original features of the social relations and the economy associated with the Roman kinship system.

Nor, in the age of the Principate between the first and third century, had reflection advanced much in this field. Nothing like a public ethics or a genuine debate had ever come into being, despite the exceptions of Seneca and Marcus Aurelius. It is as if the extraordinary creativity of strictly legal knowledge—always rigorously self-centered, and which excluded any moral evaluation from its formalism—had dried up all the available reserves of public thought and political philosophy in that world. The constitutional framework of the Principate and of the empire itself—totally original, moreover—was, at least until the Severan age, progressively grounded in government and administrative praxis instead of being elaborated or sustained by any conceptual development, either philosophical or legal.[37]

But at the beginning of the third century, when the crisis that would overwhelm the whole of ancient society, and with it the empire, was taking shape, it was becoming increasingly clear that the formal isolation of *ius*, its reduction to a purely reflexive relationship between an ontology locked into immobility by its presumed completeness and an equally abstract Ought—a duty of obedience—constructed as a kind of obligation a priori, was no longer enough.

Jurists were no longer faced by the private disciplining of a social context already firmly unified by an unopposed political hegemony that was still confident of itself and its underlying consensus; but rather the increasingly difficult task of finding a rule and a measure with which a world on the brink of irremediable collapse could identify. And this at a time when the government of the empire, which was beginning to acquire the form of a genuine state such as antiquity had never previously known, was growing increasingly chaotic and unwieldy.

The great masters of the Severan age, Ulpian in particular, therefore posed the problem of transforming legal science—the most advanced and prestigious knowledge of the time (the only "true philosophy," according to a polemical declaration, again by Ulpian)—into the overall ideology of the Romanized world.[38] And to extend it, as far as possible, to the administration of the empire as well, keeping it away only from political bureaucratic praxis and from the invasiveness of the army and of the military high command. They had picked up and developed the legacy of their predecessors from Hadrian's time—of Salvius Julianus, Juventius Celsus, Sextus Caecilius Africanus—that was already moving in the same direction and thought of law as the most mature expression of a civil community stretching over three continents. As the outcome of a long path to integration, albeit in the shadow of an ever-harsher despotism, which they would seek in vain to mitigate (and Ulpian himself paid with his life for this failure).[39]

The explicit adoption of such a perspective imposed on the jurists of this age a new relationship with ethics (however threadbare it had by now become), renewing the connection pursued in his own time by Cicero to justify Rome's dominion over the Mediterranean, and then invariably ignored by subsequent thinking.

It was this change of perspective that oriented the transition from a *ius* indifferent to questions of ethics and justice, to a law committed to the search for a "just" order, suspended between innatism and metaphysics.[40] The choice gave new and unexpected space to the old and forgotten (by the jurists) doctrine of natural law, reproposing a version with completely different ends, which permitted an appraisal of the distance separating the legal thought of Hadrian's age from that of the authors who lived between Septimius and Alexander Severus. Just a few decades had elapsed, but they had been sufficient for a definitive change of epoch.

* * *

Cicero's *de legibus* can be regarded as the founding text of the early Roman doctrine of natural law. With a view to completely legitimizing the now-established imperial power, its objective was to achieve a representation in terms of natural law (that is, of a universally accepted rationality) of the whole juridical experience of the city that now dominated the Mediterranean—a kind of transubstantiation of Roman positive law, elevated to a universal principle of justice.

But when Ulpian was writing, around two and a half centuries later, those were problems of a distant past. The revival of the doctrine of natural law had an entirely different purpose then. The jurist imagined that the outcome of the imperial unification of the world and a reliable brake on the collapse of the values inherited from the Roman aristocratic tradition could come about with the recognition of the primacy of an incomparable science. Of an intellectual practice that had invented, with formalism, the very idea of legality as compliance with the dictates of a hard and strong body of knowledge, and which was now trying to impress its mark on the new state structure emerging in a dramatic age of crisis.

From this perspective, legal thought seemed to be not just the custodian of a highly specialized technique, but also a form of knowledge able to encapsulate the whole meaning of civilization ("Jurisprudence is knowledge of all things divine and human, the science of the just and the unjust," wrote Ulpian in another well-known text).[41] A culture capable of offering a doctrine of justice (a word ignored by jurists until then, but used sensationally at the beginning of his *Institutiones*), in which legal technique, having become an ethical commitment and a life choice, could be transformed into a universal canon of conduct, into the very ideology of human civilization in the shadow of the empire.[42]

It was within the framework of the link between law, justice, and civilization that the doctrine of natural law made its return. No longer to legitimate the empire (there was no need) but to suggest the "natural" existence—a naturalness that was also prescriptive, according to the old Greek tradition—of a just order, the bearer of the "equity" (*aequitas naturalis*) that was now tending to become the ultimate pursuit of *ius*.[43]

❋ ❋ ❋

The new context paved the way for the reworked paradigm to be used in two possible ways. The first, though cloaked in Nicodemism, appeared in the text from the *Institutiones* mentioned above: when Ulpian, in establishing a hierarchy between justice and law (an absolute novelty for jurists), alluded, prudently but unequivocally, to the possible existence of a law that was legally constituted (indubitably of imperial provenance) but not based on justice—a brave declaration, which was not, however, picked up in the Roman age.

The second, on the other hand, leads directly to the theme of equality, conceived—and this too was a novelty for jurists—from an abstractly universalistic point of view. It had nothing to do with the formalizing mechanism of legal science but was the same as had been envisaged by Antiphon, and then by Stoic cosmopolitanism, echoed also by Cicero. Ulpian writes:

> Manumissions also belong to the law of peoples [*ius gentium*].
> "Manumission" derives in fact from the sending out of one's hand,
> that is, granting of freedom. . . . This thing originated from the law
> of peoples, since by the law of nature all men were born free; and
> manumission was not heard of, as slavery was unknown. But after
> slavery came in by the law of peoples, there followed the boon of
> manumission. And while by natural law men are all called by a
> single name [*Et cum uno naturali nomine homines appellaremur*],
> in the law of peoples there came to be three genera: free men, and
> set against those slaves and the third category, freedmen, those who
> had stopped being slaves.[44]

Moreover:

> As far as concerns the civil law [*ius civile*] slaves are regarded as
> not existing [*pro nullis habentur*], not, however, in the natural law
> [*iure naturali*], because as far as concerns the natural law all men
> are equal [*omnes homines aequales sunt*].[45]

We will return in a moment to the meaning of the declaration that
concludes Ulpian's argument in the second of the passages above, and
which is still emotional to read today, given the context of the culture
to which he belonged. Let's start for now by saying that—in relation to
slavery—it was not an isolated position. It reflected the detachment of
slavery from the plane of naturalness, shifting its foundation onto that
of a simple social convention, albeit unanimously accepted by all peoples
and, consequently, reaffirmed the identification between natural condition and freedom of men. In years not far removed from when Ulpian
was writing, at least two other Severan authors shared it: Florentinus
("Slavery is an institution of the law of peoples whereby a man is—
contrary to nature—subjected to the ownership of another"): *contra
naturam* were the precise words he used, and they seem almost like a
literal quotation from Antiphon; and Tryphoninus ("freedom is the
condition of natural law and subjection the invention of the law of
peoples").[46] They were all evidently referring to what was by then a very
widespread doctrine, in which there returned, in a reworked form, a
clear echo of the Stoic views that had come down through the "humanism" of the age of the Antonines, which had revived memories of
them and of their impact.

The novelty was that jurists were now speaking about it, and not (only)
philosophers or writers.

Masters of Slaves

The rejection of the naturalistic paradigm for justifying slavery—the
one, as we saw, embraced in full by Aristotle—was not recent in the
Roman world. Cicero had already abandoned it, in *de republica,* in favor

of a doctrine in which the dominant feature of slaveholding was no longer the placid mirroring of an unmodifiable qualitative difference inscribed in the nature of the human ("rule" and "be ruled" in Aristotle: obedient bodies in the presence of omnipotent minds).[47] Rather, it was the coercive and repressive inclination toward a totally artificial disciplining, harsh and strict, open also to violence, but induced by history alone. From slavery as a projection of being to one as the historic right and duty of masters: an idea that would persist through to American anti-abolitionist literature in the years of the Civil War, not without some support from the Christian Churches.

What was emerging, in Cicero's vision, was the harsh vocabulary of surveillance, punishment, and training: "tame," "castigate," "press." In the change, from nature to history, and hence to artificiality and force, what came prior even to any philosophical genealogy was the concrete experience of Roman slavery, and the problems it had posed at the peak of its spread across the Mediterranean (a sea of slaves, no less than the Atlantic Ocean in the seventeenth and eighteenth century).

In the face of proliferating organizational forms and new and versatile modes of exploiting the labor and skills of slaves, it is entirely understandable that the cold interpretation proposed by Aristotle might seem, from the Roman viewpoint, pale and fuzzy, if not wholly unrealistic. More elastic and dynamic parameters were needed to account for an incandescent social matter, with a pressing requirement for a solid but flexible network of prescriptions and operative roles unknown to the Greek classical world and which, due to a lack of legal specialism, it would not in any case have been able to develop. It was not only "barbarians" who arrived in Rome as slaves, but often men and women from culturally more advanced societies than those of their masters, whose talents had to be fully exploited and with regard to whom it would have been difficult to speak of a "natural" inferiority.

The Severan jurists fully reiterated this approach, confirmed by the most recent legislation of the emperors, which combined repression and integration, inserting it into the background of a conscious and generically humanistic design (albeit the weak and fuzzy "humanism" we spoke of earlier), which had made Stoic teaching one of its foundations, and law the rationality of the empire. They were certainly not hostile to the slavery system, and their pronouncements were not intended to shock or subvert that world in any way. They sought merely to link the formal framework of their knowledge to a universalistic and cosmopolitan principle of legality suited to the conceptual tools available to them; and at the same time to bring doctrinaire order to the functional and cultural peculiarities of the Roman form of chattel slavery. Nor is it unsignificant that both Ulpian (in the first quoted text) and Tryphoninus expounded their thinking in relation to the figure of manumission: an institution that, in its most complex developments, was absolutely typical of the experience of the golden age of imperial slavery between the late republic and the first century.[48]

The separation of the law of peoples from natural law was the fruit of this endeavor and served to give greater depth of field to the jurists' gaze, within what we might call the "general doctrines" regarding personal statuses (in this case, *status libertatis*). It was no longer necessary for the universalization of the Roman legal order to rest directly just on a naturalistic base—as it had been for Cicero, and as still seemed to be repeated by Gaius, probably rather late with respect to his time. The long administration of a vast empire rendered actual what had initially been an inconceivable cosmopolitan and historic-comparative perspective. Now the planes could be distinguished, that of historic events and social conventions from the one of ethics and natural reason, and the latter could be used not to establish normative foundations in the narrow sense (for this it was necessary to stop at the level of *ius gentium*, beyond which it could not go), but rather a prescriptiveness at once weaker and more inclusive, which could be posited as the ideal measure toward which, within the limits of the possible, the actions and designs of governors should aim: something similar to the "natural equity" found in Ulpian.

The confining of slavery within *ius gentium* and *ius civile*, well away from natural law, was therefore like the synthesis of two previously separate needs. First and foremost, the full attainment of a historicized and sociologized notion of slavery, shorn of any dogmatic residue, based on a long-established custom of repression but also of integration (by manumissions, which transformed, through the unappealable decision of any private master, a prisoner who did not even have the guarantee of life into a citizen of the community that was master of the world). And secondly, the attempt, admittedly fragile and insufficient but looking to the future, to identify a notion of the juridical that encompassed the whole of the human—but, as it were, a prehistoric or ahistoric human (a kind of Rousseauian prefiguration)—that in some way dealt with the point left unresolved by Gaius.

* * *

The construction of the paradigm of *ius naturale* away from the field of historicity is what enabled the jurists of the Severan age to make their own the formulation of the principle whereby all men are equal.

The novel feature did not lie in the content of the proposition. As we have seen, that was Greek thought, which appeared first in relation to the most ancient elaboration of democracy, and then returned—without any narrowly political meaning—in Stoic reflection, especially in Hellenistic culture. And it had also been reprised by Cicero, who, once again in *de legibus*, probably transcribing from Antiochus of Ascalon, had sustained, in truth rather scholastically, the "natural" resemblance of everyone who belonged to the human species.[49]

What was totally unusual was to now find that dictate in a legal context: not as a concept taken from philosophers, but as a principle of the world of law, as something relating to *ius*. Without a doubt, it was a fleeting relationship: the "institutionalization" of nature carried out by the Severan jurists (to use Yan Thomas's expression) had, as a counterweight, the evanescence of the rules that were inscribed within it, if not taken also from *ius gentium* or *ius civile*.[50] But it was still *ius;* and the normative value of nature had (as we saw) a long tradition, which now accompanied the device that, in considering human beings as abstract figures, identified only by the formal structure in which they were immersed, meant that they could be treated, in every legal procedure, as perfectly equal subjects.

Roman formalism, the Stoic legacy, and imperial universalism, which until then had developed two different and far-removed models of equality, thus seemed to converge toward the same result. If all men are equal by nature (and free), and the equality of single subjects was after all a condition elaborated by centuries of legal specialism, it could easily have followed that everyone should "by nature" have the same legal treatment in the shadow of the empire.

Instead, an abyss lay on the path to this conclusion: a void that the ancient doctrine of natural law would never fill, fading away without an echo in the silence of the Byzantine libraries, and, even before that, in the indifference of a social reality that was not capable of accepting and championing it. And its equality would remain, despite everything, a rule without any tie with its own time, an aborted pronouncement without consequences. The recognition of an "institutionalized" but inert naturalness, once again sterilized politically and socially, that was unable to go beyond the writing of a book or a scholastic classification to become life, consciousness, contradiction.

The same principle would be formulated by slave masters in the modern world too: Benjamin Franklin or Thomas Jefferson probably owned no fewer than Ulpian did. The key difference was not this, in fact, but rather that in the conditions of modernity those words would acquire the force of an explosive proclamation, capable of unleashing energies, resources, ideas—a dialectic of emancipation—that the ancient world could not experience.

The evanescence of the Roman doctrine of natural law did not just depend on the inability to fully extend the sphere of *ius* beyond the field of private law, and hence on the impossibility of moving from more habitual ground to that of the relations between subjects and sovereign—a fracture that one strand of Severan legal thinking would try in vain to overcome by attempting to stabilize a law of administration, of territorial autonomies, and of imperial government. It was above all a consequence of the lack of a historic force capable of taking on its indications, of making it the ideology of its economic, civic, and intellectual growth; of transforming it into the philosophical, political, and legal culture of an ascending world, rather than reducing it to the reverberation of a dying empire and civilization. Moreover, neither of the equalities we are speaking of—the functional and formal one originally developed by legal thought, and the ethical, naturalistic one that the jurists drew on from the philosophical tradition—ever referred to real "individuals" in the fullest sense of the word. They related only to figures linked to societies that had always elaborated nonindividualistic conceptions of the human, the reflection of an indelible core—economy, kinship ties, community bonds—of a typically ancient depersonalization of life, which had not yet come to terms with the explosive power of the subjectivity of the moderns.

These absences explain the solitude—genuinely tragic in some respects—of the great Roman jurists in the final stages of their history, and the catastrophe faced by their elite in the middle of the third century; to say nothing of the violent deaths—genuine political assassinations— of Papinian and Ulpian.[51] Their knowledge was deployed at the outer edges of a world that no longer had a future and was about to be over-whelmed by one of the most devastating crises ever known in history.

But precisely for this reason, coming from the great Severan authors, that short sentence—"all men are equal"—is charged with resonances that must not be lost. It was the extreme—and very advanced—view of legal culture in the world that had invented it. The point of encounter, albeit shifted as far away as possible, between (ethical) universalism and (juridical) formalism. A contact relating to a dimension of *ius* that, though helpless in the prison of a naturalistic paradigm unable to impact the reality of life, did, however, sum up not just an ancient philosoph-ical doctrine with many echoes, but also the lesson of that dissolution of power and force into the geometric order of forms without which the new West would never have been built.

The Theology of Equality

In a singular overlap, the last season of Roman legal thought coincided nearly perfectly with the early consolidation of Christian theological thought, after Paul and after the Gospels. Almost as if law and theology, later so close in many medieval paths, ceded to each other place and hegemony—together with many conceptual instruments—in the history of the final phase of antiquity.

Unfortunately, it is not possible to dwell here on the cultural impli-cations of this entanglement—the intellectual culmination of a whole epoch—which still awaits an in-depth investigation.

The fact remains that what the jurists had not succeeded in doing (or only to some small degree: Ulpian's dream, and perhaps, before him, that of Papinian) the new religion did, in a theological-legal-political tangle the full implications of which have yet to be explored. To become, that is, the reference and the ideology of the new bureaucratic circles and the ruling orders of the waning empire (also incorporating whole blocks of old legal knowledge, often reworked in the decayed form of an invasive and inconclusive legalism), to the extent that the whole society of late antiquity was shot through with its doctrines and compromises.

❋ ❋ ❋

The shadows that still surround certain aspects of the biography of Tertullian, the inventor of Christian Latin, and perhaps a prominent jurist himself—we cannot rule out linking the mysterious author present with this name in Justinian's *Digesta* with the Doctor of the Church who was such a protagonist of religious thought in the third century—is probably one of the strongest indications of the enigmatic nature of this complex juridical-theological transition.[52]

At the center of the Christianity of the Gospels was an explosive idea of equality—of equality in love—that submerged and redesigned the original framework of the Bible. This superimposition was the heart of the new message of salvation and hope, destined to achieve unprecedented success in a fearful world rocked by a crisis from which there was no discernible way out. If God is love toward everyone ("I give you a new commandment, that you love one another. Just as I have loved you, you also should love one another," says the Jesus of John's Gospel); and if every human being, the object of this love, is God's creature, made "in our image, according to our likeness," as declared in Genesis, that entailed a principle of the absolute leveling of human beings before their creator, which ended up coinciding with recognition of the divine present in each of them: "There is no longer Jew or Greek, there is no longer slave or free, there is no longer male and female; for all of you are one in Christ Jesus," as Paul put it in his dazzling prose.[53]

The connection between love and the proximity of the divine paved the way for the most important innovation in this conception: that God's love does not (only) concern the human universality that dwells in everyone; equality does not involve us (only) as bearers of common traits. If it was a question of this, we might even believe we were in the presence of a kind of spiritualistic overturning of the equality intuited by Greek materialism, and then revived—in terms already less associated with the physicality of bodies—by Stoic thought. But no. Love and equalization in God concern—and this is the literally revolutionary content of the Christian message—the particularity of every single life, of every single human experience, in their ever-different conformations. A previously unconceived dialectic destined to have an enduring and troubled future was established between equality and singularity—with the latter not annihilated, as in Roman legal formalism, but instead emphasized by the former, even if this was due to divine mediation (equal because everyone comes from the Lord). And Tertullian invented the word to denote this irreducible human uniqueness, charged with value as the specific object of God's attention and love: *persona*.

Where did the idea for such a choice come from?

It would be intriguing to be able to link this use to the world of law, and to find a connection—however faint, after having clarified the significance of the word in Gaius—between the legal vocabulary of the second century and that of the Doctor of the Church; and to interpret on this point his theological thinking as having some continuity with that of law—almost a development of it in transcendence. Unfortunately, a precise derivation cannot be firmly established, though it is known that Tertullian had a good grounding in law (irrespective of whether he was the master found in the *Digesta*); and even though it can be stated with reasonable confidence that the *Institutiones* of Gaius must have circulated fairly widely and been quite well known at the beginning of the third century, when the theologian was writing.

In truth, the first use of *persona* was not employed by Tertullian, in his *contro Prassea*, with regard to the human person; instead, he used it to resolve the delicate doctrinal issue of the trinitarian articulation (the Father, the Son, the Holy Spirit) of a God who nonetheless had to remain rigorously unitary: the *Domine Deus une, Deus Trinitas* ("Lord one God, Trinity God"), as Augustine would later say.[54] One substance in three connected persons, explained Tertullian, who, with *substantia* and *persona,* tried to render in Latin the Greek difference between *ousia* and *ypostasis.*[55] It was the same problem that presented itself, in a specular, reversed fashion, in relation to the simultaneously human and divine nature of Christ: where, instead, according to Tertullian, there were two substances in one person.[56] In both cases, the word must have meant for him the minimum unit, distinguishable by difference, with respect to subjectivity—subjectivity in its molecular state, we might say. In relation to the human, it indicated the clot of identity and diversity that makes each life at once identifiable as human but distinguishable from every other one—a person.

A powerful theological mechanism came into being, then, that was completely new with respect to Judaic monotheism. Each minimal segment of the human recognizable as such—every single life, irrespective of its fortunes—precisely due to its distinguishability was endowed with an absolute value, in that its uniqueness was also the sign of the direct relationship with its creator, reaffirmed in the strongest of ways by the human presence of Christ. And in this exclusive relationship with God, it found itself equal to all the others: an equality in difference that seemed able to overcome every previous difficulty in holding together the equal and the diverse, and to stand as a point of arrival and a now definitive redemption.

※ ※ ※

The Gospel Jesus had sustained with lucid conviction—right to the end, in the culminating scene of his teaching, before Pilate—that his kingdom was not of "this world," and that it was necessary to "render to the emperor what is of the emperor, and to God what is of God."[57] Such affirmations marked a drastic break with the theocratic tradition of Jewish culture and paved the way for the modernity of the separation between religion and politics, church and state.[58]

But they also had another no less important consequence. They shifted to the kingdom of heaven, and to that alone, the actuality of that equality between human beings established with the force of an explosive principle. For now, it was only a restrained, curbed equality, as if postponed. This explains perfectly why the rapid spread of Christianity from one end of the empire to the other between the third and fourth century, from Syria to Africa to the provinces of Gaul, was not accompanied by any significant movement of social demands.

On the contrary, the political reception of the new religion as the official cult of the empire, from Constantine onward, would develop entirely in the context of the stabilization of late-antiquity's social hierarchies, without doubt among the most unbalanced in Western history—which, Christianity taught, were due respect and submission, deferring the moment of redemption to heaven. And the Christian bishops in the fourth- and fifth-century cities, from Carthage to Alexandria, to Milan, to Constantinople, were quite ready to preach the Gospel and to be slave owners, seeing no contradiction for the practice of their faith. Nothing more was needed to calm them than a certain humanity, without pointless and unjustified violence.[59]

In this case too, we are in the presence of a new episode—unquestionably the most sensational from the point of view of its historic importance—of what we might call the political sterilization of equality, repeated with different forms throughout antiquity, from Antiphon to Boethius passing by way of the Roman jurists. Its establishment—though radical—was unfailingly accompanied by the weakening of its immediate and concrete significance, reduced in any case to a declaration without consequences, even when made by jurists with responsibilities of imperial government, or—as in the case of the Christian message—to a principle referring to the reality of a world awaiting the end of time.

* * *

The theological construction of the concept of the person, which began with Tertullian, would then be completed by Augustine in *de Trinitate*, a milestone of the new theological thought.

The frame still consisted of the elaboration of the trinitarian formula: how to reconcile the irremissible monotheistic assumption with the three-part articulation of God's presence. Tertullian's solution did not seem entirely adequate to Augustine, though he himself moved in the direction already outlined in the *adversus Praxean*. And the most critical point seemed to him to be precisely the use of the term *persona* to denote each of the three figures of the Trinity.

While for Augustine the forms of the Trinity have a purely relational value—the Father is such solely with respect to the Son, and vice versa; and the Spirit with respect to both—the word *persona* would appear to indicate a minimum unit, absolute and indivisible, complete in itself in its particularity.

> For if to be is said of God in respect to Himself, but person rela-tively [*persona vero relative*]; in this way we should say three per-sons, the Father, Son, and Holy Spirit, just as we speak of three friends, or three relations, or three neighbors, in that they are so mutually [*invicem*], not that each one of them is so in respect to himself. Wherefore any one of these is the friend of the other two, or the relation, or the neighbor, because these names have a rela-tive signification. What then? Are we to call the Father the person of the Son and of the Holy Spirit, or the Holy Spirit the person of the Father and of the Son? But neither is the word person com-monly so used in any case [*neque persona ita dici alicubi solet*]; nor in this Trinity, when we speak of the person of the Father, do we mean anything else than the substance of the Father. Where-fore, as the substance of the Father is the Father Himself, not as He is the Father, but as He is, so also the person of the Father is not anything else than the Father Himself; for he is called a person in respect to Himself, not in respect to the Son, or the Holy Spirit: just as He is called in respect to Himself . . . God . . . and just as to Him to be is to be God, . . . so it is the same thing to Him to be, as to be a person.[60]

Within the theological wrapping—rich in neo-Platonic overtones— the concept of person is roughly hewn (it would then be conclusively shaped by Boethius), and has an unequivocal and solid reference to the human. Pushing through is an idea of the singularity of existences as a value in its own right, and not as a simple fact to realistically take account of—an inerasable richness that feeds on nothing but its own specificity—which ancient culture, either political-philosophical or juridical, had never managed to express. Behind the person of God was the bare life of the human person finally coming into full light. The face of God had the face of man: theology, in short, acted here only as the guise for the philosophical-anthropological intuition and social-historic analysis.

And it is again the theological discourse (in this case the relationship with God) that directly links the theme of the person and that of equality. Once again in *de Trinitate* we read:

> Wherefore, every single man [*singulus homo*] who is called image of God [*imago Dei*] not according to everything that belongs to his nature but according to the mind alone is only one person [*una persona est*] and is, in the mind, the image of the Trinity. Instead, the Trinity, of which man is image, in its totality is nothing other than God, and in its totality is nothing other than Trinity.[61]

If every human being, as a person, is an image of the Trinity, their singularity—their molecularity, we might say—does not impede recognition of equalness, which binds them to all other human beings through the shared relationship with God.

In the construction of the vocabulary of subjectivity as well, Augustine marked a turning point.[62] He set alongside *persona* a new word destined to have a long and not yet exhausted history (to which much of the current account will be devoted): individual—*individuum,* the nominalized form of the adjective *individuus,* indivisible, inseparable, which in classical Latin (for example, in Cicero) was used to denote the atom—the indivisible—in the doctrine of Democritus.[63]

It had probably been Gaius Marius Victorinus, in his Latin translation of Porphyry's *Isagoge,* who first used this term in reference to the human subject (in the original the philosopher employed—and this too was novel—the Greek *atomos*).[64] Augustine detached the function of the new word from that of a simple calque of the Greek term, and made it into a full-blown, philosophically grounded category: "For when I define what man is, which is a specific name [*nomen speciale*], all single men that are individuals [*singuli quicque homines quae sunt individua*] are contained in the same definition, and to it belongs nothing that does not regard man," he writes in *de Trinitate.*[65] And just before: "But if they say that the name of substance or person [*substantiae vel personae*] *nomine*] does not signify species, but something singular and individual [*singular atque individuum*]."[66]

The description of the human is rooted in the conceptual determination of the isolation of single specks in the dust of lives that comprise and shape it. Individual and person, the existential atom and its absolute value, become the poles of a representation that cannot do without equality—the metaphysical relation of persons in their bond with God—as a balance for the fracture between particularity and universality, and as tension toward unity, albeit an equality once again projected beyond the measure of time.

❄ ❄ ❄

With Augustine we are already, in many respects, outside the ancient world. It had in fact been the crumbling of the anthropological background and of the social ties that had characterized imperial society, under the effect of a general system crisis, that permitted the establishment of a different idea of the human, both more shattered—literally, atomized—and at the same time more infused with hope and value. Augustine is the strong and inspired exegete of this new perspective: his thought looks ahead, toward a history in the process of opening, in comparison to which antiquity was now just a large repository of memories and doctrines; an important pillar, but now over.

And yet even the Christian conception—centered for the first time on a "personal" representation of the human—did not escape the limitation upon which every previous ancient doctrine that had tried to make equality a universal principle had foundered: its inevitable sterilization; the deferment of its actuality beyond the bounds of history, onto the plane of an impotent naturality, or of a kingdom of heaven realized only at the end of time.

For ancient equality to yield results it needed to be circumscribed: the privilege of a few, not the right of everyone. And, above all, it had to be, as it were, depersonalized, as in the invention of formalism by the Roman jurists.

It would not be until a new history unfolded that both of these barriers were called into question.

CHAPTER THREE

THE EQUALITY OF
THE MODERNS

Labor, Individuals, and Classes
in the Age of Capital

Labor as Commodity

Now that it is ending, it can be said without rhetoric: the last two centuries have truly been the glorious age of labor in the West.[1] Of labor as total human fact, the spread of which has invaded every aspect of our civilization.

We need to begin from this reality when commencing a discussion about the equality of the moderns. In the era that has just finished, labor and equality developed an increasingly close social and cultural connection that lasted through to a sudden and dramatic point of collapse, with outcomes that still cannot be predicted.

What now lies behind us was not, however, the age of labor in general, but of a particular historic form of it: that of labor as commodity—of labor power sold in exchange for a wage—that in different ways has transformed the world. Above all, in the shape of mass labor producing material commodities, from the fabrics turned out by the early power looms in the late eighteenth century to the cars and washing machines that rolled off assembly lines in European and American factories in the second half of the twentieth century. And then in the form of all the other types of labor that emerged alongside that primary model: in the countryside, in commerce, in services, but above all—as intellectual labor but labor as commodity nonetheless—in public apparatuses, in the professions, in the running of companies. An endless buying and selling of labor. The production of commodities by means of commodities— only one of which was truly irreplaceable: human work.[2] Labor as toil and as emancipation: the labor that shaped the social classes and gave form and substance to lives.

The beginnings of this period coincided with those of the Industrial Revolution in the last decades of the eighteenth century. But their appearance had a complicated and nonlinear antecedent that takes us further back, to that age of passage—between the Italian Renaissance and the French, Dutch, and English seventeenth century—that was already a "new age" and yet still not genuinely "modern."[3] A season of intermittent potential, grandiose and fluid, when Europe's history displayed paths of ideas and experiences that are now uncommon or lost, but which should not be forgotten, all the more so when they seem very distant from the outcomes that we would then know.

The structure of the new labor—its material conditions of existence, its legal and cultural regime—began to take form at the very outset of this complex transition. Indeed, it represents one of the key features of the new epoch, together with the birth of the state (and the thought that enabled its foundation) and the leap in technological growth, after a deadlock of more than a thousand years. A trinomial—state, labor, technology—that entirely encompasses, together with a fourth element of which we shall speak shortly, the conceptual-historical horizons of what would become the full maturity of the West.

The history of modern equality is wholly inscribed within this frame.

Freedom of labor was the real engine of European revival and was thus the first—and decisive—freedom of the moderns, no less important than the "republican self-government" of Italian cities in the twelfth century: ever since its appearance in the manufactories, trading houses, and guilds of the urban centers blossoming again in Lombardy, Veneto, and Tuscany.[4]

Ancient labor, in Greece and Rome, had largely been a labor without culture or history.[5] The abundance of slaves and the poverty of technology gripped it in a relentless vise. Besides this, and making the picture even more narrow and restricted, was a deep-rooted contempt for manual toil, perhaps a consequence of the antimaterialistic turn in ancient culture spoken of earlier, responsible also for technological stagnation, or perhaps of even more remote origin.

If shuttles wove by themselves there would be no need for slaves, Aristotle had written, grasping the connection between the lack of machines and the presence of slavery with an image that was also—we can truly say it—a kind of counterfactual premonition of the Industrial Revolution (in power looms the shuttles would in effect weave "by themselves").[6] The idea of the slave as a simple instrument subjugated to the designs of another mind, of the slave as automaton—which ran through the whole of ancient thought—reflected precisely this intrinsic simultaneity: the slave in the role of a machine—of an "instrument"—that was otherwise nonexistent; the machine—unrealized due to a lack of technology—that took the living form of a human being reduced to a thing: a piece of property, in the language of Aristotle; a person under the dominion of another, according to the classifications of the Roman jurists.[7]

The new labor, on the other hand, was dense with history from the start: it represented the very weave of the building of modernity—less visible and fainter before the Industrial Revolution, evident and very strong in the centuries that followed.

At the base of it lay a subtle but crucial formalism, already invented by Roman legal thought, though used only marginally in that world due to the massive presence of slaves.[8] It was the distinction between the worker as person and their estimable capacity for labor—or labor-power, as it would later be called. Only the latter was effectively for sale and could figure as the object of exchange (labor for a wage); not the entirety of the figure of the worker, whose wholeness remained in any case outside of the relationship. And the supply of the labor itself took place on the basis of a contract, not of a bond of dependency crystallized into a status, or of any other apparatus of coercion: relations founded on a formal equality of law (we shall speak of this), not on the subalternity of an unmodifiable and discriminated condition.

Without a doubt, it was a difference that could also prove hard to clearly discern, above all in the case of manual labor, where there was a crushing imbalance in economic and social power between the buyer and seller of labor. And which, above all, did not protect the seller from every kind of exploitation and abuse. A difference that, in certain historic conditions, could even—and on many occasions did—turn into mechanisms of blatant oppression and genuine expropriation. Whole generations of laborers lived "from hand to mouth," as John Locke said around 1690, using a chilling expression that was merely intended to be nakedly descriptive.[9]

Nevertheless, the separation between the laborer who remained free and the labor-power that was sold, and hence passed under the control of the buyer, marked a point of no return: the labor time—of any work, however performed—belonged in principle to the supplier, and to them alone. It was at their sole disposition, like anything directly linked to their own body or mind: "Over himself, over his own body and mind, the individual is sovereign," John Stuart Mill would write in the middle of the nineteenth century, summing up conclusively, and certainly not in neutral language, a long journey.[10] After all, Locke had declared, almost two centuries earlier, that "every man has a property in his own person. This no body has any right to but himself. The labour of his body, and the work of his hands . . . are properly his."[11] Those capacities, those aptitudes, could be ceded—even on iniquitous terms—but their original ownership, as it were, remained unerasable. For Locke, they pertained to the very constitution of the human. And this was enough to bring about enormous consequences: the whole of modern labor freed itself by being available only in the form of commodity.

* * *

The historic specificity of labor as commodity would culminate in the conceptual paradigm of labor as such, without further determinations; in the notion, that is, of labor as "invariable standard," developed by classical political economists from Adam Smith to David Ricardo, and essential for the latter's theory of value.[12] It was the point of departure adopted by Marx for the definition of "abstract human labour" (where English economic science and German philosophy were linked), and for his theory of value.[13] Labor as human energy always uniformly equal to itself, an infinitely divisible, pure, and homogeneous quantity; equal labor of individuals rendered equal by the production process; a projection at once ideal and real of the historic formation of large masses of workers, who, in workshops, factories, and then in industrial manufacturing systems, all performed the same tasks together through the endless repetition of the same actions.

Such aggregations of humans and machines, besides producing goods, also determined a particular and previously nonexistent bond between workers, equal and horizontal, because capitalist production does not just create goods but also social intercourse. A network of relations forged from discipline, sweat, skills, and solidarity ties that would deeply impact the lives of entire generations, and would have unparalleled consequences.

* * *

This mode of transforming reality and creating wealth with a previously unknown efficiency inevitably calls to mind the structures and events that had made it possible. And, above all, the formation of specific markets where labor-power was acquired in ever-larger quantities and directed toward the incessant production of goods. That same labor-power accumulated by demographic growth (the population of Europe doubled in less than a hundred years) and concentrated together following new processes of urbanization that had changed the face of Western cities between the seventeenth and eighteenth centuries.

The world of capital—a word used by Ricardo before it was by Marx—was coming into being.[14] The one we still live in today, and which more than ever before is its world: because while the labor that accompanied it for centuries is now finished, and nothing can bring it back, capital is not. It continues to unify the planet, albeit passing through the most important of its metamorphoses; and this disparity of destinies points to a dissymmetry that is dictating the shape of our future.

Prior to being a conceptual abstraction, capital is, as we said, a social relation—a structured set of connections—with its own paths and transformations. It was already present in Europe between the seventeenth and eighteenth centuries, like labor, in a particular and until then unknown historic modality, namely, that of industrial and no longer just trading capital—even though, at least until the end of the eighteenth century, the latter continued to perform an essential function: just think of the Low Countries or Venice, or even the role of the great English and Dutch trading companies. Of capital, that is, increasingly engaged directly in the production of goods destined for exchange. Or at least, of capital available for reinvestment in production, trading, and speculative circuits, instead of being transformed immediately into land property, as had happened in the past, from antiquity to the Middle Ages. And it was in this highly novel way—labor in the form of commodity, sold in exchange for wages; capital in the form of industrial capital, remunerated through profit—that this dual presence, at once united and bitterly conflictual, would mark Western history. Neither could do without the other, however high the reciprocal tension. It was the effectual truth—reflected in philosophical thought—of dialectics and contradiction as the authentic and specific form of modernity.

Only the new national bourgeoisie, however—especially in an early phase, let's say until the second half of the nineteenth century—would have the means, abilities, opportunities, and planning capacity to control the overall course of the production processes, and to direct not just their narrowly economic outcomes, but also the social and, in a certain sense, even the political ones. The labor of the direct producers, every time it appeared, would always be—at least until the end of the nineteenth century—enveloped in the shadow of the capital that permitted its existence, and of its economic and power relations, in a crucial but nonetheless subaltern role.

The ancient world—above all, Rome—also experienced concentrations of capital, sometimes of considerable proportions, and an economic performance of some note when compared to that of the European nations before the Industrial Revolution.[15] But these clusters of capital were purely commercial and did not even have an adequate banking system to sustain them—like the one, for example, already present in the late medieval Florence of the Bardis and the Peruzzis. They were confined exclusively within the sphere of circulation, admittedly of a certain size. In other words, they were never used to take large-scale control of production, which remained mostly slave-based, or to transform its time and quantity through continual and widespread investment in plant, technology, and organization. Instead, as soon as possible, these accumulations of capital were diverted toward the acquisition of land—the only form of wealth that really counted in that world, as it did in medieval societies, at least until the twelfth century.

The capitalistic mode of production thus belongs to modernity alone; just as the event that definitively formed it was only Western: the first genuine industrial takeoff in human history—which marked its triumph, as it were, and at the same time entailed the apotheosis of modern labor. Certainly not just of manual labor. Indeed, coming to the fore in an increasingly evident manner was bourgeoise labor: invariably intellectual, remunerated differently, socially esteemed, and at any rate in a different substantive relationship with capital itself, though it too was treated as a commodity. And the ethic of work, production, and gain, the particular inclination of the relationship between labor and life that it suggested, even in the sense of moral life—around which Calvinist and Puritan thought developed, and a vast literature flourished, from Defoe to Dickens, to Flaubert, and Thomas Mann, celebrating its definitive bourgeois form—soon became a standard of the new classes. A way of being to proudly set against the remnants of the old aristocracies— especially the French ones described by Proust in the last hour of their final decline, in a blaze of the sky at sunset—always accustomed to identifying the economic basis of their existence with nothing other than property income.

The Common and Human

The turn in the history of Europe had also been made possible by a profound cultural transformation that began with Italian humanism, the features of which are no less essential for defining what is known as modernity. The so-called medieval roots of the change are not in doubt, but no continuity, however significant—no "long Middle Ages"—can dim the importance of the shift.[16] The same applies to those who refuse to ascribe any periodizing value to the category of the Renaissance itself.[17]

A new vision of nature, centered on the full valorization of its materiality, was at the heart of the change. It involved the discovery of a world of bodies, whose statics and movement responded to mechanical rules, knowable through the language of mathematics and geometry ("Extension—namely in length, breadth, and thickness—makes up the real Being of that corporeal substance which we call the 'world,'" as Heidegger put it in a note about Descartes).[18] The insuppressible density of matter—intuited 2,000 years earlier by Ionian physics—linked now to the unlimited repeatability of the experiment ("relating to the sensible world and not to one on paper," in Galileo Galilei's damning criticism).[19]

It was the elaboration of these new perceptions that founded the naturalism—however steeped in Platonic echoes with an evident anti-Aristotelean function—of a lot of Renaissance thought, from Cusano to Campanella, to Bruno, and, later, to Spinoza, and the radical dualism between *res cogitans* and *res extensa* so powerfully apparent in the philosophy of Descartes—"an armistice of sorts between the established religion and the emerging science."[20]

In a mental framework that had changed greatly with respect to the ancient tradition (and in large part to the medieval one as well, dominated by an almost invariably scholastic and dogmatic reading of Aristotle— the same one rejected with such vehemence by Galilei), the place of the human being changed no less drastically.

The gaze of the literati, philosophers, historians, and jurists who had rediscovered the inexhaustible mine of Justinian's *Corpus iuris* now found a new way of living, no longer dictated by an organic rootedness within family networks or civic bodies agglutinated by hierarchies of status, of community bonds, and of the strength of kinship relations; a condition that eluded the closure of a society of orders and ranks—like that of Aristotle and Cicero, say, and, in their wake, of a great deal of medieval treatise writing.

The new outlook no longer encountered rigid, fixed, and largely non-economic social grids, but fluid, mobile clusters in which the influence of the economy and its abrupt accelerations began to impinge with increasing evidence. The present appeared above all in the form of a liberating disaggregation, bearing the promise of opportunities and new paths. The eye could now linger on the singularity of each life, facilitated also by a reconsideration of the Christian conception of *persona*—which we have already touched upon and that would return forcefully in the philosophies of the Reformation.

The emerging mentalities tended now to concentrate on the infinite, particular nuances of the relationship between action and life, work and results, industriousness and destiny: a crucial node, for example, in the thinking of Machiavelli. Humans appeared in a previously unobserved and, as it were, molecular dimension, as had already been anticipated by Dante—late thirteenth-century Florence was this too; and this too was the definitive end of the ancient age.

The highest task in the new perspective was now to transform nature and the environment through action and toil. Without activity there is no pleasure, argued Giannozzo Manetti around the middle of the fifteenth century, on the threshold of the authentic work ethic of which we have just spoken—a feature of the new world and the focus of endless reelaborations.[21]

To know so as to modify, and not just to contemplate, as was already being said by Francis Bacon, who as a young man in Paris listened to Bernard Palissy—once an apprentice glassmaker—lecturing on agriculture, geology, and minerology.[22] A few decades earlier, in his masterpiece, Rabelais did not hesitate to include regular visits to technicians and artisans in the educational program of the adolescent Gargantuan.[23] We are in the heart of the sixteenth century, and everything was acquiring shades and outlines that had never been observed before. The reappraisal of the "mechanical arts" would soon lead to Descartes's mechanism: between work that transformed, intellect that elaborated, and machines that executed a relationship was being forged—inconceivable in antiquity—which would decide the history of Europe.

※ ※ ※

It is in this ambit that, albeit in quite a lateral way, a new thinking began to develop about equality.

It lay on a dual plane, which somehow seemed to replicate the original polarity discovered earlier in classical Greece, between the position of Antiphon and that of Pericles as recounted by Thucydides.

In part—in truth, the weaker one, which would lead to fewer developments—the new reflections were associated with the reality of the city republics and its intellectual reverberations, and were entangled with the ideas of freedom cultivated within them; in the other part—much richer and pregnant with future—those ideas seemed to ignore (at least for the moment) any direct relationship with politics, developing in a more markedly universalistic direction.

In some respects, the first orientation really did appear to evoke the democratic thought of the ancient *poleis,* without forgetting the peculiarity of the doctrines that were now being advanced, and the far from univocal relationship between the extolling of freedom and pro-popular attitudes in Italian culture between the fifteenth and sixteenth centuries. We need only consider Guicciardini and his dispute with Machiavelli ("one should not give the people power in any important matters"), and the oscillating position of the latter, who even in the *Discourses* did not hesitate to make a connection between corruption and inequality ("corruption and slight aptitude for free life arise from an inequality that is in [the] city"—he was speaking of Thebes but thinking of Italy).[24]

In the same vein, Francesco Patrizi's *De institutione reipublicae* (composed between 1465 and 1471) has a chapter on "equality between citizens," even if the view that "the best form of republic is the one where every kind of man is mixed together" basically does not seem to be accepted.[25] While Leonardo Bruni, in the *Oratio in funere Nannis Strozae* (1427–1428), had already written that "the hope of attaining public honor, of building a career thanks to one's own efforts, is the same for all"; and "as soon as the possibility of rising to public honor and to seek power is made available to free people," this "has the effect of stimulating their talents"—we can really hear shades of Pericles in these words (indeed, Bruni was citing Solon).[26]

On various occasions such motifs filtered into "northern" humanism as well (Josse Clichtove or John Heywood, for example, at the beginning of the sixteenth century), and reached out to touch the thought of Erasmus.[27] But Thomas More's *Utopia* (1516) is certainly the most notable document, where Platonic echoes (the so-called communism of the *Republic*) were drawn on in the imaginary construction of an egalitarian symmetry of urban spaces, architectural volumes, and human lives that would leave an enduring and even iconographic trace in the English literary tradition all the way through to Bentham and Orwell. It was a dream that accompanied elements of precocious and moralistic criticism of the sloth of the nobility and of the more violent and ruthless traits of precapitalistic accumulation in early sixteenth-century England.

The other line of thought on equality, instead, developed the theme from a more general point of view, linked less—or not at all—to political visions.

The "republics," or at any rate the civic institutions, were not in question here, but rather the universality of the human, just as in the original Greek intuition, and then in the tradition of the Stoics and the Severan jurists or of proto-Christian thought. And even if the motifs proved to be internal to that brusque distancing from antiquity, relived only from the perspective of the detachment and the criticism of the texts, which was one of the signs of the new mentalities ("The classical past was looked upon, for the first time, as a totality cut off from the present"), at least one aspect of this thought that combined philosophy, law, and theology seemed to be conserved: the nonpolitical nature of its conception of equality.[28] As if having assumed a global point of view should at any rate remove any concrete meaning from those reflections, excluding and that every practical, operative projection from the start.

They were ideas intended as a simple philosophical-anthropological statement of facts, entailing no consequences at all for the authors' stance on society and the powers of their time. Not just that. It was as if—at least in some cases—they could coexist in a quite untroubled manner with full acceptance of points of view entirely in favor of the perpetuation of a social world dominated by all kinds of inequalities.

We should not allow ourselves to be too bedazzled by this kind of continuity with the ancient, and to exaggerate its significance. Of course, as we said, they were completely sterilized thoughts from the point of view of politics. But immediately discernible in those observations lying between humanism and very early modernity is something that had never come to light before and was entirely unknown to classical cultures. A web of concepts, resonances, and experiences was forming that presupposed contexts where, thanks in part to the newly emerging forms of social organization (times, spaces, subjects), ties with the mental pictures of the past had broken; settings where a perception of life was developing which, if still far removed from the individualistic fragmentation of the more fully realized modernity, was no less distant from the rigidities and status dependences of the Greco-Roman world and much of the medieval universe.

In other terms: we are in the presence of an already-changed and original representation of the human, albeit different and very far removed from what would then be imposed by the bourgeois triumph—when the trajectory of modernity familiar to us had not yet been fully mapped out, and several alternative paths seemed to be opening on the horizon. Spinoza would stand at the peak of this condition—at once of openness and uncertainty—historically suspended between two epochs: a moment that will require close attention. Hegel, instead, arrived when the die was cast—but more about that later.

The point of departure had been the reflection on what was then beginning to be described as the "dignity of man"—*dignitas hominis*: a well-known and widely studied theme that runs through the whole of Italian humanist thinking in the fifteenth and sixteenth centuries. Giannozzo Manetti's *De dignitate et excellentia hominis* dates to 1451–1452; the *Oratio de hominis dignitate* by Giovanni Pico della Mirandola appeared in 1486 and was devoted entirely to the "supreme marvelousness of man."[29]

A long tradition has accustomed us to read this movement of ideas through the lens of what would become modern European and American individualism, from the late eighteenth century onward: as a kind of precocious anticipation and establishment of it, in an overly close connection between humanism and enlightenment.[30] In reality, in those orientations the emphasis on the singularity of human beings—on what would later be called their "individuality" or their "personality"— appears rather fuzzy and shadowy compared to the light with which another aspect is bathed; that is, the discovery and valuing of a shared legacy of thoughts, feelings, and even carnalities that unite rather than distinguish human beings, and make them recognizable as such irrespective of their subjective specificities.

The emergence of this "common and human"—a very marginal and yet not completely absent theme (though from a different perspective) in antiquity—was the basis for the nonpolitical rediscovery of equality. It took the place of the community- and status-related organicism associated with the classical vision of life (and, though with some variants, of the medieval one too); of a conception of human singularities completely integrated within force fields dominated by cohesion and reciprocal recognition. And it came to represent a new canon of identity of the human condition and its civilizing process, founded on the search for a measure that, while evoking the Stoic tradition, nonetheless constituted a profoundly renewed interpretation of it.

It no longer had any antimaterialistic leanings in it; instead, the naturalness of the human being was posited as an essential component of a harmony and balance that formed the point of arrival of an impassioned search. Above all, unlike what happened in ancient thought, the new vision did not dissolve the singularity of lives, previously held in no account outside the context of powerfully structured relations (the family, citizenship, the web of one's own social order) that transcended particularity. On the contrary, it was given value precisely by the autoptic gaze onto the interiority of the I that was recognized as the only way of illuminating the shared part of the human.

The foundation proposed for this profound layer was an unusual one for us: where a synthesis—the significance of which would then be lost—was sought between subjectivity (later called "individuality") and the human community, between the particularity and finiteness of life and the totality of the human. Between *humanitas* (a word used in ancient Latin almost exclusively by Cicero, and which now returned with a greatly enriched spectrum of semantic meaning) and the inner world of each human being: a motif already familiar to Petrarch, then reprised, stretched, and explored, in the "civic humanism" of the following century.

It was Platina's "common utility of men"—rightly stressed by the Italian philosopher Eugenio Garin; it was the *divina voluptas*—indissoluble weft of nature, life, and sensibility—of Valla, indicated in order to elude the *quantum naufragium de genere humano,* the possible catastrophe of humanity.[31] Even more than the dignity of each man, of each *persona* (in the sense between law and theology that we glimpsed earlier—but Valla himself criticized Boethius on a key point in the use of the notion by the ancient philosopher), it was the value of the human as a whole, its privileged status in the reality of creation, however vast and boundless it was, that was emphasized and highlighted.[32]

❊ ❊ ❊

Taking shape, as can be seen, was the same strand of reflections that we encountered in Montaigne at the beginning of our story: although in many ways he was already beyond the narrowly humanistic experience, and moving within a horizon enriched by a broader, more versatile, and sometimes dramatic range of themes and demands—the history of Europe was traversing one of its most fruitful but also most critical and tormented periods.

The investigation of interiority—"It is my own self that I am painting"—was for Montaigne, as we observed, the privileged path to discovering the closeness of those before us—however dissimilar they might at first sight appear.[33]

> I once saw among us some men brought by sea from a far country. Because we did not understand their language at all, and because their ways, moreover, and their bearing and their clothes were totally remote from ours, which of us did not consider them savages and brutes? Who did not attribute it to stupidity and brutishness to see them mute, ignorant of the French language, ignorant of our hand kissings and our serpentine bows, our deportment and our bearing, which human nature must take as its pattern without fail?

> Everything that seems strange to us we condemn, and so every-
> thing that we do not understand.[34]

This comes from the *Essais,* where the other is represented in the most historically extreme form of those who (probably) came from across the ocean, and the estranging impact with the New World was displayed in all its force.

Montaigne was writing just a few years after the Peace of Cateau-Cambrésis, when the new powers—Spain, England, France—had begun to project their nascent statehood beyond the boundaries of Europe: cartography was turning into geopolitics, the Mediterranean was declining to become a local sea, and the space to circumscribe, measure, and divide was beginning to coincide with the dimensions of the globe itself.

He was certainly aware of the heated debate about the nature of Native Americans that had been raging throughout the sixteenth century. In one line of argument (embraced by Juan Ginés de Sepúlveda in his famous discussion with Bartolomé de Las Casas, the author of an extraordinary pamphlet in defense of the indigenous population) the thesis had begun to gain ground that the Native Americans should not be considered completely human ("one could barely detect any trace of humanity [in them]") and that they were destined to slavery "by nature"—Aristotle returns here.[35]

But the author of the *Essais* declared firmly that wherever one went, human beings all resembled each other, and that anything else was prejudice or deception. This takes us beyond any Stoic or Senecan reelaboration, to the acute—and empirically grounded—perception of the existence of a feature of irreducible impersonal unity of the human, which appears here—perhaps for the first time—in all its force.

The same thinking can be found in a virtually identical form, and in the same period, in Giordano Bruno (not dissimilar views also appear in Campanella, who unquestionably read *Utopia,* which served as inspiration for his *Città del sole*), even though it is impossible to establish any connection between Montaigne and Bruno.[36] Men are all equal because they are made of the same matter, the latter held: there is almost an echo of the lost voice of Antiphon and his physics. And even the Native Americans—exterminated by the Spaniards and Portuguese—were just like the Europeans, because "everywhere there is a single soul, a single spirit of the world" and "every land, in fact, produces all the animal kinds."

However (Bruno continued) the equality of men does not stop them from becoming different. This difference is the result of their activity though, of the ability of each man to construct his own life, rather than of a material or spiritual diversity inscribed in nature. But that did not stop him fearing the arrival of a moment in which "subjects, wishing to be superior, and the ignoble equal to the noble, come to pervert and mix up the order of things, so that at last there comes to be a certain neutrality and beastly equality such as is found in certain desolate and uncultured republics."[37] Politics was finally evoked, but only as a threatening ghost that carried with it the risk of a dramatic overturning of the natural order of things.

Individuals

Politics was, in the late sixteenth century and then for the whole of the seventeenth, much else besides, and this path leads us to an idea of equality as well.

In a Europe dominated by the Reformation and the Catholic response, still devastated by the wars of religion and the open wounds they had left, politics appeared to consist above all of the irresistible though sometimes tortuous construction of the new states and their fiscal, administrative, judicial, and military machinery.

It was Machiavelli who introduced the word *state* in its new meaning: "All the states, all the dominions that have held sway over men," he wrote in the famous opening to *The Prince*.[38] It designated something unknown to classical antiquity, as it was to the medieval order, barely and only partially sketched in the final phase of the Roman empire, and immediately swept away by the ruinous crisis of that world.

Politics and its theory—this too for the first time—were, moreover, an initial elaboration of human singularity in terms of a clear option for a subjective particularism that would have to identify, without other boundaries and without further mediation, the new dimension of citizen-subjects. A choice projected toward the individual, as it would soon be called: a solution that was also, as we have seen, unknown to the ancient world, and beyond humanistic conceptions as well, through to Montaigne himself, who was in search of a different equilibrium between singularity and human totality.

A path opened that would enable the West to embark on a process of self-identification as the locus par excellence for an unparalleled individualistic radicality. Holding great force and appeal, it developed in successive waves—the last, exceptionally intense, one began at the end of the last century and is still under way.

The phenomenon is of incalculable significance (here we have the fourth constitutive element of modernity that we spoke of earlier)—and central, as we shall see, to every representation of equality. And it is certainly no less important than the formation and consolidation of nation-states themselves, even if historians have often underestimated its significance, almost as if it were an obvious—somehow neutral—consequence of modernity, and the form of the individual was an obligatory construction, the only one capable of fully expressing the singularity of the human being. Instead, it was just one possible elaboration—and not without alternatives even in the decisive age in which it became established (more will be said about this as well). It is a model that therefore needs to be historicized if we are to get to the bottom of the aura of ineluctability that still surrounds it today, and which is unjustified, despite its exceptional success as one of the biggest driving forces the universe has ever known.

❊ ❊ ❊

The profile of these two figures—the state, the individual—both newly arrived on the historical stage, and both magnetically attracted to each other within the same field of events and ideas, was the outcome of the joint coming to a head of many lines of development.

In the process of state formation, a big part was played by the centripetal and by and large national concentration (this too was new) of political power, constituted—and at the same time theorized—as sovereign power, following the final disintegration of the medieval order. The space of states came into being, as happened in Spain, France, and England (Holland would follow a partly different path); while Italy and Germany—the latter above all after the Peace of Westphalia—were for different reasons excluded from this current.[39] Weight was also carried in that process by the need of the main European powers to aggregate more substantial critical masses—demographic and territorial—in order to secure the armies and resources required for the new geographic dimensions in which they were now operating, and for the enormous opportunities for conquest that were opening up across the oceans.

In turn, the genealogy of the paradigm of the individual contains elements that are no less complex. Economic conditions contributed above all: increasingly oriented in a capitalistic way, they pulverized old community contexts, breaking down traditional bonds. Overlapping with the remnants—often very resistant, as in France and in England itself—of these were polarities and ties induced by the new forms of labor division (an immediate focus of attention for the nascent economic science), which tended to emphasize the role of single human beings in production, businesses, trading companies, and consumption. There was a shift from the family to the company; from the countryside back to the urban agglomerates, now regenerated by a concentration of industry completely unknown to the ancient cities—which had been places of property income and consumption rather than production. Labor, supplied in the form of commodity, created a previously unexperienced perception of subjectivity, in the most segmented form possible: exalting on the one hand its transformational power, and on the other nailing it down to the pure essentiality of each single existence, the bestower as such of that Promethean force. It was a connection already perfectly grasped by Hegel in his *Lectures on the Philosophy of World History* (not to mention the *Elements of the Philosophy of Right*): "The industrial principle was imported from England, and industry itself contains the principle of individuality: for in industry the individual understanding is developed and becomes the dominant power."[40]

A union thus began to develop between the new labor and the emerging figure of the human individual, which would spread in an ever wider and deeper manner until it became a full-blown anthropological model. The features of the modern European class societies were beginning to emerge into the light, acquiring form and definition.

＊ ＊ ＊

No less decisive, in the early shaping of the paradigm, were the strategies of political power, which, as we said, also tended to pulverize feudal hierarchies and barriers, and to suppress any obstacle between the sovereign's command and the final receiver: each subject—each citizen—reached and framed in the individualized nudity of their isolation. This representation could thus become the overall reference for all the forms of subjectivity—legal, political, economic—that were beginning to fill the new social spaces.

These two profiles, the individual—continually desiring and expressing needs, in an incessant and implacable self-narrative, and at the same time planning, working, producing, consuming—and the state—disciplining, reassuring, controlling, pacifying, watching, punishing, engaging in wars—would occupy the stage of politics and of the philosophical and legal thought that interpreted modernity as it unfolded.

Their common ground consisted of a crucial problem, both practical and theoretical, that arose after the crisis of the late sixteenth century; namely, how to protect, how to immunize the fragile but exuberant subjectivities that were emerging through the transformations of the new epoch, from the violence and destructive fury of devastating lacerations triggered by the abrupt crumbling of many restrictions of the past, by the atomization of social life. The conflicts had just appeared historically in the form of ferocious religious clashes, but the issue was more general, and was immediately perceived as such.

With a previously unknown impetus, the economic and cultural processes of human individualization brought onto the stage of history the full creative force of diversity, the constitutive value of differences multiplied by every single life, the significance of the irreducible specificity of each human being, exalted by the lighting up—as had never happened before—of the finiteness of their particular existence, together with the unlimited potential of their social actions.

So how was it possible to reconcile the contrasts that could grow in this tempestuous ocean of differences that was forming for the first time, offering a glimpse of the future of civilization, with an indispensable principle of order and pacification? That could save its vital richness without annihilating it in a general and disastrous conflict of all against all, conducted by each individual in the name of competition and of the boundless valorization—civil, economic, intellectual—of one's own singularity?

Under the wing of the nascent capitalist organization of the Western European societies, and after the division of the Christian tradition in France, Holland, and England, a crucial question was being raised about order and liberty, sovereignty and autonomy.

This is how the two figures, the individual and the state—standing large before each other in their shared newness, but also inscribed one within the other—came to dominate the intellectual horizon in the century from Hobbes to Rousseau, and then immediately afterward, through to the American and French Revolutions. Meanwhile, barely visible off to one side, like a solitary giant, was the shadow of Spinoza.

* * *

A binding force in this entanglement was the doctrine of natural law as developed from Grotius to Kant. Almost all the attempts to build a theory—political, legal, economic—of the relationship between the two new entities was situated within it. On one hand, the state—the Leviathan of Hobbes, but also the enlightened prince described by Kant, who says, in a desperate attempt to reconcile criticism and absolute power: "*Argue* as much as you will and about whatever you will, *but obey!*"—as a concentrate of sovereignty.[41] And on the other, a shattered but extraordinarily productive form of human finiteness—the form of the individual: an empty mold, minimal and flexible, in which to pour the result of those processes of disarticulation and atomization, but at the same time of liberation and creation, that the new labor, the new classes, the new ideas, and the new social circuits, especially urban, were imposing as the sole reality with which to engage.

In its multiple versions, the doctrine of natural law basically became the only available mental frame within which to conceive and rationally comprehend the changing world—and it would remain so, almost un-challenged, until the American and French Revolutions.

It drew on ancient motifs—from the Stoics, the Christian tradition, and Roman legal thought from Gaius to Ulpian. It also picked up on elements from a very rich medieval strand, including Thomism, skipped over here in order to link the ancient and the modern directly and so as not to lose sight of the axis around which our reconstruction revolves. But it reworked them in a totally original way.

The idea that nature is a kind of zeroing of history, to look to in order to rediscover a sort of primary genealogical truth which might also possess an intrinsic prescriptive value, was ancient: an Archimedean point from which everything had originated. And it was at least in part ancient the idea that naturalness meant universality, and therefore had to be looked to in order to detect general and eternal principles of social conduct; as if it were an original layer of the human shared by every civilization.

But what was new was the tendency to link this vision to a particular figure of subjectivity, the one comprising the form of the individual, and to connect it to the genesis and the regime of statehood, in order to derive functions and structure. In a word, to make it the common language to link the two protagonists of the new age—the individual and the state: the field in which to discover the ordering structure of their relations.

And above all what was new was the attempt to turn this philosophy, with its many variants, into a general theory of rights and prerogatives associated with the figure of the state (and of the sovereign) in its regulating, repressive, and pacifying mission, and with that of individuals-subjects-citizens, in their drive to exalt their own singularity: to define, that is, the political and civil coordinates of the European scene.

What we call modernity would be the outcome of this path: in fact, the individualistic and basically postabsolutist curvatures (both fully visible in Kant)—open to constitutionalism and then to democracy—adopted and reaffirmed by the doctrine of natural law within the more radical Enlightenment, defined the fullest and most enduring representation of the new era. We are still moving within its orbit today.

❋ ❋ ❋

As we have just seen, Renaissance culture had already emphasized the role of the singularity and particularity of every human existence, compared to the hierarchy of values in the medieval world. Also presented in that thinking, though, and with no less force, was the discovery of a "common and human" and its dignity as a constituent feature of the "new age." And while certainly not yet representing full recognition of a universal principle of equality, and still less so of its political consequences, it did offer a powerful interpretative key that was beginning to move in that direction.

But then the indication was abandoned, overwhelmed by strong forces intent on extolling to the greatest possible degree differences and competition as a constitutive element of a new civilization. The great building site of European statehood, especially in France and England, and the movement of ideas that fed it—accompanied by the social consequences of the increasingly capitalistic form of the different national economies—seemed to demand and render obligatory such a change in direction. And this combination of elements was irremediable. After Spinoza, "the common and human" would almost vanish from the more direct range of visibility of politics, before it had even really entered it.

The great issue now was how to control the individual diversities, and at the same time enable them to be completely free; to allow differences to emerge from the network of medieval restrictions, and yet impose on them an order with which they could identify without being suffocated by it. Religious thought, especially the strand culminating in Calvinism—in whose idea of God's crushing sovereignty over human creatures it is not hard to detect significant traces of politics masquerading as theology, as was the case with the papal absolutism theologized by the Counter-Reformation—accentuated even further the push toward total individualization in the image of life. The picture was substantively confirmed by post-Tridentine Catholic doctrine as well, which gave rise to a specifically

Italian version of this individualistic pressure (the "particular" spoken of by Guicciardini).[42]

The features of secularization and religious thought thus became blurred on this essential point, overlapping in a highly effective mixture where the different components were almost indistinguishable. By the time Defoe wrote *Robinson Crusoe*—again an island, like that of *Utopia,* but an island that for a long time would have just one inhabitant, imprisoned by a totally reflective relationship with his labor, but also exalted by the solitary omnipotence of an ego that saw nothing beyond himself: an extraordinary metaphor of the world that was being built—the fusion was complete. The secularized conception of the individual and the Calvinistic one whereby each creature—each *persona*—was submitted in their solitude ("in the secrets of a solitary heart") to the grace dispensed by the inscrutable majesty of God and could only trust in an extremely demanding ethic of responsibility, professionalism, and work, was now consolidating a common space of proven solidity.[43] They had assumed, at least on this point, the same guise: a mix combining features of explosive emancipation, but also limitations that would become an unsustainable prison. A duplicity that we have still not been able to unravel; not even now that the anthropological mechanism of the individual as the paradigm just of the West has been transformed, almost without exception, into the overall form of the human on the entire planet.

Between State and Nature

The cause of men's fear of each other lies partly in their natural equality, partly in their willingness to hurt each other. . . . Those who have equal power against each other, are equal; and those who have the greatest power, the power to kill, in fact have equal power. Therefore all men are equal to each other by nature. Our actual inequality has been introduced by civil law.

Thomas Hobbes wrote these words in the opening chapter of *On the Citizen*.[44] It was 1641, and the philosopher had taken refuge in

Paris following the crisis of the English monarchy and the first signs of civil war.

They were difficult years: the situation in England was deteriorating, the Thirty Years' War was reaching its height, while in France, the religious conflict having abated, an increasingly bitter struggle was underway over the concentration, organization, and administration of absolute power—a constant feature of the country's political history between Louis XI and Louis XIV.

In the previous year, in his *Elements of Law* (not published until 1650), Hobbes had already argued that:

> And first, if we consider how little odds there is of strength or knowledge between men of mature age, and with how great facility he that is the weaker in strength or in wit, or in both, may utterly destroy the power of the stronger, since there needeth but little force to the taking away of a man's life; we may conclude that men considered in mere nature, ought to admit amongst themselves equality.[45]

What stands out in the text, as paradoxical proof of equality among men, is the insistence on how easy it is for anyone to kill whoever was in front of them, however superior the latter—probably an echo of the long string of bloody events that had punctuated the religious wars in the previous century, memories of which were certainly still very vivid.

A decade later, still in Paris, Hobbes returned to the theme in the thirteenth chapter of *Leviathan:*

> Nature hath made man so equall, in the faculties of body, and mind; as that though there bee found one man sometimes manifestly stronger in body, or of quicker mind then another; yet when all is reckoned together, the difference between man, and man, is not so considerable, as that one man can thereupon claim to himselfe any benefit, to which another may not pretend, as well as he. . . . And as to the faculties of the mind . . . I find yet a greater equality amongst men, than that of strength. For Prudence, is but Experience; which equall time, equally bestows on all men, in those

things they equally apply themselves unto. . . . For such is the nature of men, that howsoever they may acknowledge many others to be more witty, or more eloquent, or more learned; Yet they will hardly believe there be many so wise as themselves: For they see their own wit at hand, and other mens at a distance. But this proveth rather that men are in that point equall, than unequall. . . . From this equality of ability, ariseth equality of hope in the attaining of our Ends. And therefore if any two men desire the same thing, which neverthelesse they cannot both enjoy, they become enemies; and in the way to their End . . . endeavour to destroy, or subdue one an other. . . . Hereby it is manifest, that during the time men live without a common Power to keep them all in awe, they are in that condition which is called Warre; and such a warre, as is of every man, against every man.[46]

The legacy of ancient thought—not Antiphon's pronouncement, which had not yet been found, but certainly the Stoic and Christian tradition, and that of the Roman jurists—was unquestionably very much in Hobbes's mind, as was sixteenth-century treatise writing and the reflections of Grotius: *Di iure belli ac pacis* is from 1625, and it too appeared in Paris.

But the English philosopher only drew on the doctrine of equality—accepted and corroborated by new arguments—in order to overturn its meaning. Moreover, for Hobbes the ancient world was often a place of contradiction and paradox: just consider the dedication of *On the Citizen,* and the use Hobbes made in it of the history of Rome.[47]

There was no question that men are all naturally equal, he affirmed, and this is true both from a physical point of view and that of mental capacities. However, while for the Greek philosophers and Roman jurists, and for Christian thinking too, this was considered to be the result of the attainment of a higher, or, if one wishes, a deeper perspective, to which history and law proved unable to adapt but which nonetheless remained a reference for thought and action, for Hobbes it represented the ascertainment of a pure negativity, of an unbearable and unhappy condition.[48] It was just a point of departure to correct—as in fact had happened—in order to avoid worse evils.

The condition of original equality had brought out, unchecked, all the consequences of that kind of negative anthropology—men are only appetites and power—of which Hobbes was in no doubt, and which also pushed him far away from any form of democracy. A conception in which there was not just the pessimistic outcome—shared by Machiavelli—of a deep delving into the heart of politics. Nor was it just the recent and terrible memory of the wars of religion that weighed on him. Or perhaps other things as well, as has been supposed:[49] from readings about the conditions of Native Americans to reconstructions of late feudalism.

Visible in those extremely harsh images—evident and unconcealed—was the reflection of the hardness of the present, of the English society that Hobbes saw before him (not much different, though worse, in this respect, than what had already troubled Thomas More a century earlier). Pietro Costa is right to say that what the philosopher presents here as being prior in time is just the projection, stripped to the bone, of what seemed to him to underpin his age, in London as in Paris.[50]

For Hobbes, then, the state of nature—without sovereignty, without order—really was "a domain of werewolves," as Carl Schmitt would later observe.[51] Any organicism descending more or less remotely from Aristotle was swept away definitively from the start. Instead, as it was put in *On the Citizen*, "mutual fear" arose of being attacked by one's neighbor, of being destroyed or oppressed out of a thirst for gain (the specter of the present) or the need for security.[52] Or, as he specified in *Leviathan*, a craving for "reputation."[53] There was no way out. Equality was a condition that could arise without state—but also without civilization.

Inequality therefore needed to be introduced: a necessary, beneficial, and perhaps even salvific condition of human civilization—"of civil doctrine" (as in *On the Citizen*).[54]

Present straightaway in the most elementary cell of society, for Hobbes, was the individual, preformed as it were, and grasped in the fullest extent of their isolation (this too was an echo of the age). For him, the first "civil" sociality—barely past the level where there was just mortal strife and constant fear, in a "solitary, poor, nasty, brutish, and short" life—was already marked by unequalness: it was inequality that brought peace, and enabled property; because from a purely natural condition—we could even say pre-civil—it followed inevitably "that there be no property, no dominion, no *mine* and *thine* distinct; but only that to be every mans that he can get; and for so long, as he can keep it."[55]

A single thread connected in this way what for Hobbes was discernible inequality and the genealogy of human civilization itself, a primary foundational act of that "peace" without which "there is no place for industry; . . . no culture of the earth; no navigation, . . . no commodious building."[56] Inequality was for him the weft of human history—as was property, in an openly apologetic representation of it—and it coincided with the development of reason itself ("Reason is no less of the nature of man than passion, and is the same in all men. . . . There can therefore be no other law of nature than reason, nor no other precepts of natural law, than those which declare unto us the ways of peace, where the same may be obtained, and of defence where it may not," as he had written in the *Elements of Law*).[57]

The immense force of the state would do nothing other than take the defense of the growing articulation of the differences—of the inequality—on which every civilization was really grounded. The connection between subjectivity and subjugation—discussed by the Italian philosopher Roberto Esposito (we will return to his thought in Chapter 5)[58]—and the Hobbesian use of the category of person between theology and law are entirely functional to the full affirmation of this logic of inequality.[59]

❄ ❄ ❄

For Locke too, the natural equality of men was a primary and uncontestable given: "there . . . [is] nothing more evident, than that creatures of the same species and rank, promiscuously born to all the same advantages of nature, and the use of the same faculties, should also be equal one amongst another without subordination or subjection," we read at the beginning of the second chapter of the *Second Treatise,* published in 1690,[60] "at the time of the rise of joint-stock companies, the Bank of England and England's mastery of the seas," as Marx would later write.[61]

Then, in the sixth chapter, Locke clarified:

> Though I have said . . . "that all men by nature are equal," I cannot
> be supposed to understand all sorts of equality . . . [but] the
> equality, which all men are in, in respect of jurisdiction or do-
> minion one over another; . . . being that equal right, that every
> man hath, to his natural freedom, without being subjected to the
> will or authority of any other man.[62]

It was the end of the seventeenth century, and the language and theoretical framework of the doctrine of natural law appeared fully deployed, with the asserted priority of the individual in relation to every
type of society, and freedom associated immediately with equality. As
in part had happened also in Hobbes, what was just the result of a
recent historical change—the social atomization at the dawn of modernity—was projected indefinitely backward like an original fact,
at the basis of every further development. The theoretical viewpoint
transformed into a presupposition—into a fictive point of departure—
what was instead the result of a long and complex journey. Philosophical genealogy took the place of real history. The beginning in the
concept was confused with the beginning of a historically determined
process.

But the equality here was no longer Hobbes's; it was not just a negative phenomenon, and its existence did not preclude the forming of
sometimes very significant differences. Locke was very clear on this
point:

> There is, it is visible, great variety in men's understandings, and
> their natural constitutions put so wide a difference between some
> men in this respect, that art and industry would never be able to
> matter; and their very natures seem to want a foundation to raise
> on it that which other men easily attain unto. . . . Amongst men of
> equal education there is great inequality of parts,

he wrote in *The Conduct of the Understanding,* which appeared in
1706, after the author's death.[63] Indeed, his was an equality that existed

only in relation to freedom, as the complete and common absence of bonds of subordination ("in respect of jurisdiction or dominion one over another") for all human beings.[64]

A distinction began to take shape, which would prove very influential in subsequent thought and lead to important developments not just for the history of ideas. It was between an equality whose efficacy played out on the plane of rights alone, a reflection of abstract parity in freedom as an original condition of subjects within the state of nature; and an equality that tended instead to come about on the terrain of facts and of social life, which was plunged into crisis by the emergence of an ever greater plurality of differences between individuals; and which was dimmed by the figure of the individual as the supreme locus of specificity and of the particular. The distinction, in other words, was between an equality that would subsequently be fully defined as formal, linked to the abstract subjectivity of human subjects as such; and a substantive— but denied—equality connected to the life of individuals in the economy and in society. A difference that would soon become, as we shall see, a genuine fracture—a systemic polarity—from which two contrasting histories seemed to unfurl.

Unlike Hobbes, according to Locke the emergence from the state of nature was neither abrupt nor disruptive. For him too equality should only be interpreted as an initial condition, destined to be superseded by the advancement of civilization. However, the transition appeared to him to be gentler and less unsettling, along a more gradually shifting plane, which also made it possible to abandon almost all the negative anthropology that so evidently distinguished Hobbes's viewpoint. Human inclinations are complex and cannot be shoehorned into the scheme of a single pessimistic representation.

And it is here that, for Locke, labor appeared for the first time as a protagonist of grand philosophy: the time was ripe for this now in European—and especially English—history.[65]

The theme came up in relation to another topic no less essential for the philosopher, again connected to the superseding of the natural condition: property, to which Locke devotes the fifth chapter of the *Second Treatise*: "It is allowed to be his goods, who hath bestowed his labour upon it, though before it was the common right of every one."[66] Labor and property, bound together around the figure of the individual and their freedom, shaped the horizon of the new age.

In the same chapter, we also read:

> God, when he gave the world in common to all mankind, commanded man also to labour, and the penury of his condition required it of him. God and his reason commanded him to subdue the earth, i.e. improve it for the benefit of life, and therein lay out something upon it that was his own, his labour.[67]

Property, then, stems from labor; the genetic link was destined to shatter, according to Locke, and it was the introduction of money that broke the original proportionality between the amount of labor expended and the amount of property (of land). He did not grasp, or at any rate did not express, the force of the potential and perhaps already indistinctly glimpsed conflict between the two elements—labor and property; but the derivation was inerasable, marking an underlying connection in the universe he had presented.

The individual was defined in no other way than through a primary act of acquisition regarding the individual's own body: "By property I . . . mean that property which men have in their persons as well as goods."[68] This has been referred to as "possessive individualism," a controversial expression when it was first proposed.[69] There is no need to discuss the issues concerned here, though it must be said that it does not seem at all inappropriate. And it is hard in any case to deny that for Locke the philosophical and historic construction of human subjectivity leads back to a kind of solidly constituted quadrilateral, comprising a single social-political construct: individuality, rights, labor, and property.

In this design, equality acquired a specific position sketched on two levels. One, relating to the reality of facts, in which it tended increasingly often to vanish, crushed by the weight of differences; and the other, in which it remained clearly present, but within the limits of a purely abstract dimension, of equality between subjects represented in their reciprocal freedom, insofar as they were the possessors of equal rights.

It was an extraordinary portrait in motion, in its own way rigorous and precise, of the bourgeois world that was being born—and also of its first, lacerating contradictions.

The Romans Return

The model of the individual that economics, philosophy, and theology was constructing in the growing shadow of the great European states with the force of an authentic anthropological structure—the real center of the anthropology of modernity—required another feature for its image to be complete; a characteristic that pointed, once again, to the history of equality. It required a political-legal shield to protect its profile just as the new creature was thrown onto the social scene of an approaching age.

On the more narrowly political side, the first contribution came from English thought and constitutional praxis, starting with Locke and the "Glorious Revolution"; then the French Enlightenment, with its various components; and finally, definitively sealing its genealogy and rootedness, the revolutions in America and France. As for the legal side, its solidity was largely ensured by the return of Roman law.

The great reentry of the *Corpus iuris civilis* into the laboratory of modernity took place in large part under the deceptive guise offered by the concept of natural law. It was under this name, in fact, that ancient law presented itself to European culture: as *ratio scripta*—as the transcription of natural law and reason, already carried out, once and for all, by Roman thought, and passed down thanks to Justinian's codification.

It was above all having built what we defined as the "formal equality of law"—an order where all the subjects involved appear as abstract figures positioned on a plane of complete parity with respect to *ius*—that constituted, in the eyes of the new interpreters, the greatest merit of the ancients. This point of view, already clearly distinguishable in Pufendorf (*De iure naturae et gentium* appeared in 1672), became explicit in Thomasius (the *Institutiones Jurisprudentiae Divinae* came out in 1720), when he took *aequalitas iuris*—the equality of law constructed in the *Corpus iuris*—as the fundamental principle which any legal order must have as its starting point.[70]

It is certainly true that the revival of Roman law was largely a continental episode, linked in particular to the strengthening of French national statehood, and to historic events in Germany. While in England, especially after the local Church's split with Rome, the influence of Roman law was undoubtedly not so directly evident.

However, Roman law established a significant presence in that setting too, and it did so by offering a mental frame of reference within which to conceive English law, if not the very idea of law as a specific form of social regulation endowed with an intrinsic autonomy of its own, together with some fundamental categories of legal reasoning.

Signs of this can be traced as far back as the thirteenth century, at least to the text associated with Bracton.[71] The same happened in Scotland—where the custom of resorting to Roman law was always maintained—in particular through the Court of Session, which in many cases used the *ius commune,* or thanks to the chairs of civil law in the country's leading universities.

Likewise in England, through the contribution of the Court of Chancery, which applied what would later be called equity, through the Court of Admiralty, and, again, through the teaching of civil law and, later, of jurisprudence, at Oxford, Cambridge, and then University College, London, the radiation of Roman law never ceased to be projected onto the developments of national juridical culture, despite the tendency of common law to be closed and isolated in nature. The success of *De usu et auctoritate iuris civilis Romanorum in dominiis principum Christianorum* (1653), written by the jurist and member of parliament Arthur Duck, which discusses the importance of Roman law in Christianity and was partially translated into English with the title *On the Use and Authority of the Civil Law in the Kingdom of England,* is a significant example of this.[72]

We can but acknowledge, then, that the history of law in Great Britain was touched to the core by the Roman experience, even though British culture has almost invariably found it hard to admit. And without taking account of the legacy of ancient law, any genuinely exhaustive history of common law and the results it achieved would be inconceivable.

※ ※ ※

It is to the French and German (and in part Dutch) world that we must look to really grasp the importance of what was happening. While the very close connection with natural laws, especially on the plane of legal equality, was being stressed, the revival of Roman law was accompanied in these areas, at least from the time of Grotius's work, by a subtle and crucial process of translation—though a better word would be shifting—of its body of prescriptions into the terms of an order such as the ancient world had never seen. An order, that is, essentially centered on the person and on the rights of subjects. In other words, a law sharply oriented in an individualistic and Christian sense, which could figure as the most adequate completion of the great transformation underway on the European political, social, and intellectual stage.

It was a falsification—or rather, a serious historical misunderstanding— with incalculable practical consequences: through a subtle and very effective reelaboration of ancient materials, it provided a legal framework, especially in the field of private law, for the societies of the new Europe— directly so on the continent, in a more mediated but equally influential way in England.

The result was achieved by way of two gradual adjustments, with one basically following on from the other, even though they were pursued in different philosophical and historic contexts—still the doctrine of natural law in the first case, in the political horizon that opened up around the years of the Peace of Westphalia and the Europe of the nation states; romantic historicism in the second, in the age of the bourgeois triumph.

The protagonists of the first adjustment, in the seventeenth century, were two prominent French jurists, Jean Domat and Robert-Joseph Pothier, together with the legal thought of Leibniz (no less important than his philosophy) and of Pufendorf. The second, essentially nineteenth-century one, was principally German, fruit of the work of Friedrich Karl von Savigny and Rudolf von Jhering—two of the leading academic jurists of their time; and then of Theodor Mommsen, and of the school, which again flourished in Germany but had significant Italian developments as well, of the so-called Pandectists. Both, with their orientations, made possible, and influenced, the most important European codifications: in Austria, France, Prussia, and later in Italy and in the finally unified Germany.

❋ ❋ ❋

We have already seen how the Roman legal order reflected in the thought of its jurists had never adopted the point of view of subjects in any particularly privileged way, nor had it ever built or presupposed a theory of legal personality, still less of subjective rights; nor had the ancient doctrine of natural law ever gone so far either, for reasons that have been explained.

At the center of the formal framework of Roman law there were statuses, not subjects. The equality machine that it had constructed drew its formalizing force precisely from the estranging objectivity of its practice. It measured ("calculate[d]," to use Savigny's apt metaphor) the quantities of *ius* relating to given positions in given situations; it did not define categories of holders of subjective rights. And the figure of the *paterfamilias* had prominence because of his status, his being the linchpin around which the whole Roman system of kinship relations revolved—the throbbing heart of that world and with specificities absent from other ancient societies; and not as a single person, far less as an archetype of the individual in the modern sense of the word.

The seventeenth-century reinterpretation erased this setup, on the basis of several main nuclei of misunderstanding. One of the most important concerned the notion of *persona* itself. As we saw, it opened Gaius's classification of *ius,* proposing an arrangement, as has been observed, of "illusory simplicity" (even though the seventeenth-century jurists did not know the text of the *Institutiones,* discovered by chance at the beginning of the nineteenth century: but they did come into contact with many of its contents through the *Institutiones* of Justinian, which drew extensively on the work of the ancient jurist, besides the fragments contained in the *Digesta*).[73]

It was a model that, aside from its Justinian fortunes, was never again directly adopted by any great Roman author, restricting it to a strikingly marginal position in relation to the main lines of thought. Without mentioning once again that even within it the use of the category of *persona* had no founding value with regard to any legal subjectivity: it only described a field of *ius,* on the same plane as *res* and *actiones,* things and trial actions.

Instead, on the basis of the assumption that Roman law, in order to fully reveal the natural rationality that it expressed, had to be reordered within a more mature systematic framework than the hodgepodge of the *Corpus iuris*—an idea dear both to Domat and Leibniz—the term *per-*

sona was not just reconfirmed in its systematic function, but basically changed meaning as well: "In the examination of the several matters treated of in the body of the law, and in particular laws, we must always consider the persons whom the said matters and laws relate to," writes Domat in the opening of the *Lois civiles*.[74]

The word became something very similar to the *persona* of Christian theology (Domat was a fervent Jansenist, a friend of Pascal, and certainly influenced by Descartes and his philosophy of the subject as well).[75] A notion emerged alluding to the irreducible specificity of every human being, and their role, in their own singularity, as the center of the potential attribution of rights: in relation to both private and public law, even though the latter did not, in Domat's view, tend to express natural law—but this was not the case for English thinking, more advanced with regard to constitutional politics.

It was, in short, the figure of individuality that, in England, France, and Germany, was transplanted into the world of law (and politics) under the Christian-bourgeois guise of the person-individual.

The transposition had been successfully completed. Roman law was at once distorted (in its historic truth) and exalted (in the possibility of modern reuse), in a new life that also marked the end of its historic determinacy. It took on the appearance—which it would retain for a long time and which even now has not completely disappeared—of a timeless form: pure juridical reason at the service of the societies that were coming into being. And this is exactly how it was seen, as a kind of natural and eternal syntax of the juridical dimension of the human mind (of the legal state of the soul, to paraphrase Hillman), by that line of interpreters: from Domat to Pothier, to Leibniz, Pufendorf, and still further, through to the French and German Enlightenment, and then to the Historical School of Savigny and Gans.

In this way the machine of equality built with such care by Roman thought—the formal equaling of positions within the sphere of law—could be directly related to the new figure of the individual person elaborated by modern culture. "Although the Roman laws own a sort of equality which the law of nature establishes among all men, yet they distinguish persons by certain qualities, which have a particular relation to the matters of the civil law, and which make that which is called the *state of persons.*"[76] This is Domat again, and in his writing we can sense the tension he could see, but which ancient thought had never been in a position to grasp, between the equality recognized by the civil law—that is, by Roman law as equal law—and the differences induced by the various personal statuses: both those of Roman law itself (free men and slaves, for instance) and the now increasingly eroded figures of the French law of his time: nobleman, bourgeois, servant, vassal, professed religious, and so on, and which only the Revolution would erase.

Of course, with Domat it was still the jurist of the *ancien régime* speaking, capable though of juxtaposing ancient and modern differences of state—those which his own age had inherited from the medieval and feudal past—and encapsulating them within a single Roman-French mechanism of discrimination. But outside, and unresolved, there was already a pressing contradiction between those remote differences and an equality that, once related directly to the new subjects—to individuals— was potentially capable of expanding without limit, and of sweeping away any obstacle in its path.

The whole of Roman private law—understood as the universal natural law of private dealings, including those of labor—was reorganized, both by Domat and by Pothier, around two notions that, in the light of the new social relations being forged, seemed essential.[77] One was the idea of the contract based on the consent of the parties concerned, which regulated the mechanisms of capitalistic transactions, beginning with the increasingly decisive exchange of wages for labor. The other was property (a particular focus of Pothier's attention), constitutive of individual identity itself as possession of one's own body and labor (they were, as we have seen, Lockean terms). Both figures had already been constructed by Roman thought, but in a less clear-cut, unitary, and consequent way. They were positioned within a different overall legal regime and another normative order: not subject to the pressures of a nascent capitalistic organization, but related to a much less mobile society, with a much less expansive and dynamic economy, enclosed within insuperable barriers.

By contrast, the outcome of the combination between the—totally modern—figure of the individual person defined by its isolation and by its labor, and the Roman one of legal formalism would soon prove explosive. In addition, and making the impact even more powerful, there were the first results of the English constitutional setup, and the guarantees it offered to subject-citizens in the face of the sovereign's powers, against the backdrop of a reiterated affirmation of the natural equality of human beings. A welter that set in motion immense social energies, released also as a consequence of this coupling.

The Excluded

The individual that was helping to shape modernity, and filling its historic space, was genderless. No explicit sexual determination defined it as such. And yet it had an evident male connotation, never called into question and seemingly taken for granted in every circumstance. This tacit attribution oriented the social and political positioning of its image, coloring, as it were, its stereotype, giving it reality and concreteness.

The quintessential worker and producer of wealth was male. The buyer and trader of the "immense collection of commodities" characterizing the new economy was typically male.[78] And the figure who (in England) elected their representative in parliament could not be any other than male. And while a female could certainly stipulate a contract or own commodities, even in the field of private law the holder par excellence of subjective rights recognized by the regulatory order was undoubtedly male.

In short, both public and commercial law always talked about men, even if the gender specification was only implicit at times. The woman—when she appeared—represented in any case an exception. A space apart always opened around her at once—like a tear in the compact fabric of sociality and norms, which had to be closed quickly. The order of political and legal discourse, and so too that of the new economy, was shaped by men and made for addressing other men.

Contributing to the renewal of this implacable excluding device on the threshold of modernity—the attitudes of classical antiquity had been no different—was a combination of elements, some of long duration: genuine morphological features of a mental frame that had condensed over thousands of years through histories of materiality and culture.

But in establishing a male face as the profile of the new subject—in attributing a gender to the victorious form of the individual—two components carried very particular weight.

The first can be described as being of an anthropological-historical type. It was the presence, dominant in so many ways in the elaboration of the new paradigm, of the virtuous model of the Roman *pater-familias*—the head of the family so often idealized in the stories and descriptions of Cicero, Livy, Plutarch, the jurists, and transplanted into the new age. But stripped, as it were, of the burden of the kinship relations that connotated its original profile, reducing it to the pure abstraction of autonomy, of responsibility, of judicious social prudence, while remaining unmistakably male; a man—solitary and in command, at least of himself. In essence, a perfect individual: both in the pessimistic, Hobbesian version of *homo homini lupus,* of man wolf to another man; and in the benevolent, optimistic one found in so much natural law thinking, through to Domat himself, of *homo homini Deus,* of man recognized by the other as a divine creature.[79]

The second component was, as it were, theological: and it was determined by the Judeo-Christian representation of God as a rigorously individualized being—albeit articulated in three persons according to the trinitarian dogma—and with features that are also unequivocally male, as expressed in a millenary iconographic tradition. A God individual, and, as a male, father: of a son who, in becoming human, also chose to be a male. And father also of all the individuals comprising the human species now and forever.

Due precisely to its personalism, this narrative would horrify Spinoza, but it exerted an undisputed magnetism that would prove irresistible, radiating down innumerable paths in the history of the West—including the one about which we are speaking.

If the first person, from which everything proceeds ("I am the Lord your God"), was unequivocally identified with male images—and likewise his son, the savior of the world—even the model of his pale copy, the fragmented and abstract form of the human, the individual person thrust onto the stage of nature and history, could not but assume the same imprint, and also be presented with a definite gender specificity.

So when the formal equality of Roman private law was combined with the model of the individual that was taking shape, what it linked to was not a pure abstraction of the human, but a paradigm impressed—through both a theological and secular genealogy—with an indelibly male seal. The consequences have not ceased to concern us.

❊ ❊ ❊

There is one further aspect that needs to be emphasized in describing this epochal juncture between the form of the individual, acknowledgment of equality as the natural condition of human beings, political constitutionalism, and formal private law on the threshold of modernity: namely that, at least in the first part of its history, this new age would coexist without too many problems not just with the differences of status associated with surviving medieval elements in the *ancien régime*—later swept away by the Revolution—but also with the most significant discrimination of all, which went directly back to antiquity and Roman law: the presence of slavery.

In Western European societies slavery in the narrow sense had already ceased to exist by the late Middle Ages, even though, especially in the countryside, forms of subordination persisted that were very similar to it in substance. But it survived in the colonies—from the Americas to Africa, parts of Asia, and in particular North America, where it would play a key role in the formation of that society—becoming a constitutive fact of a whole world. Indeed the slave trade flourished, for a long time transforming the Atlantic into a sea of slaves, plied by ships sailing continually in a triangle between Europe, the African coast, and the ports of the Americas. Voyages in which the largest possible number of transportees had to be combined with the smallest possible number of deaths due to hardship and illness, in a chilling optimization of available space and the positioning of bodies during the crossing—the Nazis had nothing to invent for the interiors of their camps.[80]

Without doubt, the culture of the ancient world—from the Stoic tradition to the thought of the Roman jurists, and on to early Christianity—had already reconciled the defense of slavery and the idea of the natural equality of men. But now the construction of the economic-political-legal paradigm of the person-individual—unknown to antiquity—made the coexistence still more difficult, transforming it into a genuine contradiction.

Yet the racist radicalism of the European conquerors would have the better of this unsustainability at least until the French Revolution; and beyond the Atlantic, for much longer. The same doctrine of natural law that nurtured the ideals of the American Revolution would be unable to resolve the problem in that country, leaving the whole question, like an open wound, for the generations that followed the Founding Fathers. It was a laceration of proportions that were hard to underestimate, as, soon after, Tocqueville would understand perfectly. In the 1790s more than 700,000 slaves were living in the fledgling republic: around 20 percent of the entire population of the thirteen states.[81] Ideological prejudice and economic calculation—slave production and capitalist organization could coexist on the edges of the new system—had created a deadly mix, destined to impact deeply the origins of the democratic modernity of the West.

· II · REVOLUTIONS ·

History and Equality

We see their houses and lodgings tolerably furnished, at least stuffed well with useful and necessary household goods: even those we call poor people, journey-men, working and painstaking people do thus; they lie warm, live in plenty, work hard, and (need) know no want.

These are the people that carry off the gross of your consumption; 'tis for these your markets are kept open late on Saturday nights; because they usually receive their week's wages late. . . . And, in a word, these are the life of our whole commerce, and all by their multitude: their numbers are not hundreds or thousands, or hundreds of thousands, but millions; 'tis by their multitude, I say, that all the wheels of trade are set on foot, the manufacture and produce of the land and sea, finished, cured, and fitted for the markets abroad; 'tis by the largeness of their gettings, that they are supported, and by the largeness of their number the whole country is supported; by their wages they are able to live plentifully, and it is by their expensive, generous, free way of living, that the home consumption is raised to such a bulk, and well of our own, as of foreign production.[82]

We are in 1728, and Daniel Defoe was describing the soaring domestic demand of the working masses in contemporary England—though it was mainly London he was picturing—and its social consequences. It was the "invisible hand" of the market, described a few decades before Adam Smith's famous essay; but in 1714 Mandeville had already published the first edition of *The Fable of the Bees* (the second would appear in 1729), which probably inspired this text in part.[83]

Defoe's tone was overly optimistic, and his account has what we might describe as a Hogarthian coloring, far removed from the cold but realistic observation of Locke—who adopted an entomologist's gaze—about the lives of multitudes consumed entirely by the toil of labor and the struggle to feed themselves. It is possible that Defoe confused the classes deliberately, and that the well-being projected onto those that he himself called "poor" referred to the new bourgeois orders, including the petty bourgeoisie, rather than, in general, the laboring masses of the nascent working class. He was after all exaggerating on purpose because he wanted to emphasize the economic advantages of pursuing a policy of high wages (relative to the time, of course) as a means of promoting widespread consumption. But at any rate there was a basis of truth in his account; albeit in an emphatic way, it captured a genuine mutation, an effective change in lifestyles, at a time when servant girls in inns "could be mistaken for ladies of condition, being very neatly dressed," as an amazed traveler wrote, again in 1728.[84]

Just a few more decades and the great leap would have been made. In 1760 England imported for its cotton manufacturing industry—the cradle of the change—no more than 2 million pounds of raw materials;

only one generation later, in 1787, two years before the beginning of the Revolution in France, that figure had risen to 22 million—a volume on a completely different scale to any previous magnitude. The takeoff had begun, and capitalist organization was becoming the backbone of the whole of modernity.[85]

Eleven years earlier, in 1776, Adam Smith had published *The Wealth of Nations,* inaugurating the classic period of economic thought that now, together with political theory, comprised the two social sciences of the new age: a genuine epic of productive labor (the title of the first book is "The Productive Powers of Labor"), which features in it as the real protagonist of the transformation that was underway—a primacy that would not be lost until the very recent past.[86]

Before Smith, Rousseau in France had also written about economics, though in a more traditional way: in fact, the entry on this theme in Volume 5 of the *Encyclopédie* was his, and appeared in November 1755, the same year he published his *Discourse on the Origin and Foundations of Inequality among Men,* penned in Paris between the end of 1753 and the first few months of 1754—the work that opened the great season of modern reflection on equality.

Around a century would pass between the maturity of Rousseau and that of Marx. *The Contribution to the Critique of Political Economy* came out in 1859, without the *Introduction,* composed in 1857. In both Rousseau and Marx, the critique of the present—a youthful but fully formed capitalist and industrial society for Marx; its immediate prelude, already bourgeois and already under the aegis of business and money for Rousseau—is by far the most dominant feature. As if a harshly critical gaze on that world was in some way an integral part of its very birth and proceeded in step with its early consolidation.

In each of those views—in Rousseau no less than in Marx—the theme of equality acquired a centrality it had never previously had; though only in Marx was it closely linked to the theme of labor. Above all, for the first time in the history of Western culture, it was no longer just a problem of philosophical coherence, legal technique, religious vision, or ethical rigor, but an inescapable social and political issue—a total perspective, through which to rethink the entire history of human civilization.

In that period of around a hundred years the West had seen the onset, and in large part the completion, of the age of revolutions following the English one of 1688. In America in 1776, in France in 1789, both contemporary to the industrial one of the final decades of the century; and then the uprisings in 1830 and 1848, from Paris to Berlin to Budapest. A season dotted with great books: the European mind was giving the very best of itself, striving for (self-)understanding and (self-)criticism in a way that would remain unparalleled in the whole itinerary of the West, with the possible exception of the golden century of classical Greece. Kant's three *Critiques* appeared between 1780 and 1790; Hegel's *Phenomenology* in 1807 and his *Elements of the Philosophy of Right* in 1821 (*The Science of Logic* had come out between 1812 and 1816); Ricardo's *Principles of Political Economy* in 1817; *Democracy in America* by Tocqueville between 1835 and 1840; and the first book of Marx's *Capital* just a little outside the hundred-year span we are considering, in 1867.

What came to light in those writings was the conceptual anatomy of their epoch, of a modernity glimpsed in all its potential: at times in a forcefully apologetic way, sometimes as if suspended between vision and disenchantment; elsewhere in a mercilessly antagonistic manner; but always, as it were, conducted live. And in almost each one of them, though from different angles, the connection between individuals, labor, and equality emerged as a strategic node, the authentic measure of the changing West.

❀ ❀ ❀

The *Discourse on Inequality* can be seen as a dazzling opening to this age of thoughts and events. Stylistically, it is almost perfect. In composing it, Rousseau discovered, as has been observed, "sa grande manière":[87] an inimitable mixture of rationality and fury, research and denunciation, in which every word vibrated with a restrained but absorbing emotion.

The topic was in the air, stirred by the social transformations of late eighteenth-century France, and it fueled the more radical positions of part of the Paris Enlightenment, with the criticisms it leveled at contemporary society. As François Furet, an important French historian to whom we shall return, clearly saw, in the absence of other channels of communication between society and state, intellectuals—*philosophes* and literati—had become the most authoritative representatives and the real guiding force of the new orders arising from the increasingly capitalist-driven economic transformation.[88] Their esprit was winning over the nascent public opinion, in large part made up of professionals (especially lawyers) and businessmen from the ascendant bourgeoisie: the "Third Estate," according to the nomenclature of the constituted order, after the nobility and clergy.

The Académie de Dijon, which had chosen the theme for one of its competitions, was not therefore inventing anything new: it retransmitted a signal that was already arriving clearly and perceptibly.

The points of view did differ though. Supporters of drastic social reform moving in an egalitarian direction were opposed by much more traditional and moderate positions. A few years later, Voltaire himself, taking issue with the work of Rousseau (who he immediately detested), wrote with evident sarcasm: "Not all peasants are rich, nor is it necessary that they be so. There is a need for men who possess their arms alone" (perhaps an echo of Locke); and "Equality is thus at once the most natural and the most chimerical of things. . . . Every man has the right to believe himself, at the bottom of his heart, entirely equal to all other men," we read in the *Philosophical Dictionary*.[89] Voltaire inhabited another mental universe, and the Enlightenment revealed the multiple spirits that inhabited it.

The attitude toward the English model with its parliamentary and classist monarchy was a genuine demarcation line—a kind of litmus test. The admiration of moderates—from Voltaire himself to Montesquieu—contrasted with the criticism and skepticism of the more radical wing, first and foremost of Rousseau.

In certain respects, it was as if the reflection on equality had become an irremissible sign of being part of the age. The new urban concentrations and the faster and more dynamic life that they encouraged—Paris had around 650,000 inhabitants, and London was up there too—were giving greater visibility to differences previously diluted by distances and by the lower density of contacts, and were now creating genuine short circuits between heterogeneous social layers sharing almost the same spaces.

But what also carried considerable weight, in making these issues so topical, was the attention and persuasive capacity of staunch and polemical intellectual minorities, soon to become truly revolutionary avant-gardes, in which the criticism of absolutism, no less than of the new appetites of the bourgeoisie, acquired a tone and color that ended up affecting the whole structure of society. In these contexts, pushing up from beneath the increasingly fragile and cracked shell of the monarchy and its old civil order, though still within the *ancien régime,* were the new class structures—broad bourgeois groupings and the first nuclei of the working class—that rendered manifest old and new privileges with an evidence and incisiveness that had never previously been experienced.

It was due to these currents of thought that, for the first time, in the heart of the eighteenth century, the theme of equality among all men— of the universal equality of the human species—began to emerge from scholarly constructions and disputes, or from the heaven of a religious doctrine with neither political nor social consequences, to become an idea capable of enflaming passions, mobilizing energies, fueling projects and hopes.

❊ ❊ ❊

In Rousseau's writing there returned, bright and invasive, the state of nature, though viewed from a different perspective to that of Hobbes or Locke. It no longer described a real historic condition, to be placed in a determinate time, however remote, but rather a kind of conceptual archetype, an ideal model of coexistence among men:

> For it is no such easy task to distinguish between what is natural and what is artificial in the present constitution of man, and to make oneself well acquainted with a state which, if ever it did, does not now, and in all probability never will exist, and of which, notwithstanding, it is absolutely necessary to have just notions to judge properly of our present state,[90]

we read in the preface to the *Discourse on the Origin and Foundations of Inequality Among Mankind*. And, a little further on:

> Let us begin, therefore, by laying aside facts, for they do not affect the question. The researches, in which we may engage on this occasion, are not to be taken for historical truths, but merely as hypothetical and conditional reasonings, fitter to illustrate the nature of things, than to show their true origin, like those systems, which our naturalists daily make of the formation of the world.[91]

Rousseau was keen to stress what seemed to him to be the deep morphology of the human, beyond its actual existence in a given historic moment; and which, above all, appeared to him to be entirely independent and antithetical with respect to the establishment of any form of civilization.

Between the "nature of things" and their effective historic "origin"—between morphology and genesis—a divarication opened up that had never been conceived by the tradition of the doctrine of natural law. The historic search for genuine beginnings became irrelevant; what counted was to identify, in the shaping of subjectivity and its essential behaviors, a basic structure unaffected by the changes wrought by civilization.

This kind of degree zero of the human, not historic but morphological, was seen by Rousseau as the sole locus of perfect equality, and of the most complete happiness. But in the description of this state, the form of the individual and the form of property, held together in the English tradition from Hobbes to Hume, became drastically disassociated, with significant consequences.

While the first—the figure of the individual—was substantially accepted as the quintessential figure of the human, projected toward perfectly defining the state of nature, the second—that is, the proprietary model—appeared to be shifted entirely on the side of civilization—and so, for Rousseau, of corruption. The complete constitution of individuality did not in his view entail any significant acquisitive or competitive element; instead, it could be realized in the void of a sociality deprived of any element of systematic conflict.

Compared to an ideal condition of absolute harmony and equilibrium, history as process of development and articulation of society was thus viewed as the supreme enemy, because it inevitably brought with it increasingly serious and insuperable dissymmetries and imbalances. Its course turned into a graph of the progressive and unstoppable prevalence of inequalities.

> Such was, or must have been the origin of society and of law, which gave new fetters to the weak and new powers to the rich; irretrievably destroyed natural liberty, fixed forever the laws of property and inequality; changed an artful usurpation into an irrevocable right; and for the benefit of a few ambitious individuals, subjected the rest of mankind to perpetual labor, servitude, and misery,

we read in the second part of the *Discourse*.[92] The beneficial and positive relationship, not just between individual and property, but also between individual and labor, established with such emphasis by English thought—but Rousseau, unlike Voltaire, had no fondness for England, its revolution, or its conquests—was overturned at its roots:

> The first man, who, after enclosing a piece of ground, took it into his head to say, *this is mine,* and found people simple enough to believe him, was the real founder of civil society. How many crimes, how many wars, how many murders, how many misfortunes and horrors, would that man have saved the human species, who pulling up the stakes or filling up the ditches should have cried to his fellows: Beware of listening to this imposter; you are lost, if you forget that the fruits of the earth belong equally to us all, and the earth itself to nobody![93]

The silent antipathy Marx would have for a position like this, despite any superficial resemblance to his own, can clearly be grasped. For him, history was everything, and communism was to have been its culmination rather than its annihilation: the outcome of a thousand-year journey, not the rediscovery (which must have seemed to him ruinously regressive) of a lost or latent position. So the more the antiproprietary invective of the *Discourse* should have appealed to and seemed akin to his own views, the more it ended up seeming false and mistaken. This was not the path to take: nothing could go against history.[94]

For Rousseau, on the other hand, the reproposition of a state of nature of the kind he imagined was the Archimedean point to play on for a devastating critique of the present, an age where "everything, being reduced to appearances, becomes mere art and mummery; honor, friendship, virtue, and often vice itself, of which we at last learn the secret of boasting." Where, as a result of always "asking others what we are, and never daring to ask ourselves, in the midst of so much philosophy, humanity and politeness, and such sublime moral codes, we have nothing but a deceitful and frivolous exterior, honor without virtue, reason without wisdom, and pleasure without happiness." And where, finally: "a handful . . . gorge themselves with superfluities, while the starving masses lack the barest necessities of life"—as he writes in the dramatic conclusion to the *Discourse,* in which the distance of contemporary society from the ethical order and civil customs turned abruptly into a direct and explicit critique of its economic structure.[95] "That word *finance* is a slave's word," Rousseau would write in the *Social Contract:* therefore "it is unknown . . . in a state that is really free."[96]

Moreover, from the very beginning he had posited the issue of equality in terms that prompted him to address the social heart of the matter. He distinguished, in fact, between two kinds of inequality: a "natural" or physical one, which is:

> established by nature, and consists in the difference of age, health, bodily strength, and the qualities of the mind, or of the soul; the other which may be termed moral, or political inequality, because it depends on a kind of convention, and is established, or at least authorized by the common consent of mankind. This species of inequality consists in the different privileges, which some men enjoy, to the prejudice of others, such as that of being richer, more honored, more powerful, and even that of exacting obedience from them.[97]

Where Rousseau says "moral or political" we should understand "social," because this is effectively what he is discussing. But that adjective, present in ther very title of the *Contract,* where the expression "social state" can also be found, is not used in the *Discourse.*[98] In fact, Rousseau does not distinguish here between economic inequality—let's also say in social condition, dependent on differences in power and wealth—and a more narrowly political inequality in the field of civil and constitutional rights. The two aspects still seem to him to be too closely intertwined to yield two different levels in the calculation of inequality.

Nor, on the other hand, did the struggle for political rights that was beginning at that time, at least in England—the vote, habeas corpus: in a word, the parliamentary constitutionalism that came after Locke and the "Glorious Revolution"—have such value for him as to modify a condition that was in any case compromised. Rousseau is very explicit on this point. In the *Social Contract,* he writes:

> Sovereignty cannot be represented for the same reason that it cannot be alienated; it consists essentially in the general will, and the will cannot be represented; it is itself or it is something else; there is no middle ground. . . . The English nation thinks that it is free, but is greatly mistaken, for it is so only during the election of members of Parliament; as soon as they are elected, it is enslaved and counts for nothing. The use it makes of the brief moments of freedom renders the loss of liberty well-deserved.[99]

It is a point to which we shall return. But it should be said straightaway that the weakness of Rousseau's alternative proposal, whose undisputed fragility has attracted a flood of not always disinterested critique, has meant that the acuteness of his criticism has long been overlooked. He was thinking, of course implausibly, of a kind of direct democracy, realized through the deus ex machina of an unexplainable unanimity, by a people still formed of individuals presented in their unsurpassed particularity, ideally reunified in a continual and always concordant deliberative assembly, in the name of a metaphysical "general will" (we will come back to this as well).[100] But his objection to the mechanism of representation raised an issue that cannot be eluded, which touched on the very essence of the idea of popular sovereignty.

The whole new world, as it was unfolding before his eyes, was thus being affected by the violence of the controversy, even before it really reached completion. The Industrial Revolution would not begin in England until two decades later, and the European liberalism that many would see as the true heir of the French Revolution, at least of its early phase, did not take shape until the beginning of the new century. Yet the two main economic and political institutions of the order that was coming into being—capital in its industrial and bourgeois form, and parliaments in their liberal form—were already emptied of any sense of emancipation and progress, even before they became fully established. "Give money and soon you will have chains," Rousseau wrote in the *Social Contract,* adding, in the same page, "the deputies of the people, then, are not and cannot be its representatives."[101] From the outset the entire political and social system was hit by a backlash of condemnation of utter injustice. It was readying itself to be nothing but the triumphant realm of inequality and false appearances.

Significantly, in this early reckoning even the construction of individuality—the individual as value—was ultimately called into question, albeit in a less direct and explicit way. In fact, the model, elaborated by Rousseau in the *Social Contract,* of the recognition of the general—sovereign—will of the people as the only possible democratic and egalitarian barrier to the overwhelming drift of history inevitably plunged into crisis the principle of individuality as the central figure of the social order. In the indistinct ocean of a collective will which, in its absolute and nondelegable sovereignty, could only be centered solely and always on itself, every trace of complexity, every space of diversity, every possible differentiation among the singularities comprising it, vanished.

The imprisoning abstraction of money, the illusion of parliaments, and the blind self-referentiality of bourgeois individualism, which never became the general will of the whole people: these very same points would be identified a hundred years later, though with much more powerful analytic tools, in the research of Marx (in the meantime there had also been Hegel and Ricardo), who, above all, was dealing with a much more developed capitalist society. But before that circle closed, a century of history still had to run its course.[102]

America

We have said that Greek thinking and practice about democracy left an essential question hovering around its constructions, without ever directly formulating it: how much effective equality did a democracy need to survive and function in the best possible way?

The age of revolutions would tackle this issue openly, with a view to resolving it once and for all.

In truth, Montesquieu had already anticipated an answer in his *Esprit des Lois,* surprising in relation to his better-known views, and very exacting. "Love of the republic, in a democracy, is love of democracy; love of democracy is love of equality," he wrote in the third chapter of Book V, in a context punctuated, as was his wont, with continual references to classical antiquity.[103] And then he added, probably thinking about the solidity of Rome in the first centuries of the republic, at least as it was idealized by ancient historiography:

> Love of democracy is also love of frugality. As each one there should have the same happiness and the same advantages, each should taste the same pleasures and form the same expectations; this is something that can be anticipated only from the common frugality. . . . Although in a democracy real equality is the soul of the state, still this is so difficult to establish that an extreme precision in this regard would not always be suitable. It suffices to establish a census that reduces differences or fixes them at a different point; after which, it is the task of particular laws to equalize inequalities . . . by the burdens they impose upon the rich and the relief they afford to the poor.[104]

And he concludes, finally: "Every inequality in a democracy should be drawn from the nature of democracy and from the very principle of equality."[105]

The *Esprit* was first published in Geneva at the end of 1748, eight years before Rousseau's *Discourse,* but the author had worked on it intensely at least since 1734. This long sedimentation is reflected in the layering of the ideas sustained in it, traces of which remain even in the handwriting of the manuscript.

For Montesquieu the republican form of government was not the best (he identified three—the monarchy, the republic, and despotic government, a distant echo of the Herodotean, Platonic-Aristotelean, and Polybian classification); nor was the democratic variety the only possible kind of republic (the other option was the aristocratic one). He saw it as only being achievable within the boundaries of the "small State," a far cry from the present, with the large and weighty structures of the modern states. For these, despite some oscillation in his viewpoint, the monarchic form seemed preferable, tempered by a rigorous division of powers—an English kind of setup, which received its consecration with him.[106]

And yet, notwithstanding the limit of nonactuality, Montesquieu's description of republican democracy in the *Esprit* betrays a deep and evident sympathy and participation, revealing an interest and passion—to use a word dear to the author—cultivated over time. The democratic republic was quintessentially a place of virtue: no other model taken into consideration was appraised in such a way.

But democracy meant nothing if not equality: Montesquieu did not have the slightest doubt about making this equation, so loaded with implications. And for him equality was not just about political rights or legal forms, as in ancient Greece or in England. It had to extend to the social and economic condition of citizens, and to cover the entirety of their lives. In a democratic republic it would have been the delicate task of the state and its legislation—emanated according to the sovereignty of the people, a commonwealth of virtuous citizens—to constantly intervene to preserve a basic equilibrium in the distribution of wealth. Without it, the whole construction would collapse.

An unexpected convergence emerged on this point. The democratic fabric imagined by the "moderate" Montesquieu ended up being close to, if not exactly the same as, the one conceived by the "radical" Rousseau in the *Contract.* For both, the democratic condition was total, leaving no room or margin for compromise: achieving it presupposed a continual adjustment of individuals' lives to a virtuous measure and action with which each person would have to identify and find fulfillment, erasing their singularity. The best of all possible worlds equated to the most egalitarian and solidaristic one.

It was a kind of unconscious announcement, containing two words that would soon be the subject of much talk: republic and equality.

It is true that the revolutions which erupted a few decades later in America and France were broadly unexpected, with a form—imagined by no one in advance—that only became delineated as they occurred; and that the European Enlightenment of the eighteenth century—in England, France, and Italy—seemed more oriented toward pathways of reform than abrupt and radical ruptures. But in many respects a point of no return had now been crossed in the criticism of political and social reality, and though the future protagonists themselves were only dimly aware of it, a season of great turmoil was creating many of the premises and conditions of revolution.

In effect, the final quarter of the eighteenth century—between the English factories, the streets of Paris, and the British colonies in America—would change the history of the world. And the idea of equality, in its relationship with politics and with labor, would occupy a crucial position in it.

⁕ ⁕ ⁕

It would be completely mistaken to isolate the American Revolution and consider it a separate case to what was about to happen in France and Europe. This tendency, rightly criticized by a significant strand of English-language historiography, to which this book owes a great deal, from Robert R. Palmer to Henry F. May, through to the recent research of James T. Kloppenberg and Jonathan Israel, results in the loss of an overall view that must be maintained at all costs if we are to fully understand the unprecedented originality of the picture that would emerge on both sides of the Atlantic over the long term.[107] A scene marked by the political articulations of a now industrial and capitalistic West, in its crucial relationship with the construction—and limitations—of modern democracy.

This unitary perspective had already somehow been presupposed in the thinking and studies of Alexis de Tocqueville. On the other hand, it was immediately and forcefully contested by a strand of conservative thought, both European and American, that had in the German diplomat and writer Friedrich von Gentz one of its first and most significant exponents, and which tended to carve out a chasm between the two revolutions—saving the limited and, as it were, defensive American one, and condemning the confused and aggressive French version. It is no accident that Gentz's work was admired and translated by John Quincy Adams, a leading proponent of republican moderatism in America.[108]

I do not really know whether the term "Atlantic revolution," which proved very popular, especially in America, and has now been revived by Jonathan Israel to describe the force of the connection between events in America and France, is completely acceptable.[109] Or whether—by overestimating a purely political and intellectual perspective of history—it blocks out a network of (especially) social differences that were indisputably macroscopic, and which were continually stressed by Hannah Arendt, albeit from a psychological and sociologizing perspective that I feel unable to share or to propose as an acceptable interpretive model.[110]

In any case there is no question, adopting all due caution, that a global view is the most appropriate for understanding what happened. And I will go further: we must also look elsewhere if we really want to come up with a unitary picture for that period. Besides the political revolutions in America and France, I believe we should also include in our perspective the no less explosive onset of the Industrial Revolution in England in the same years. Its short- and long-term intellectual and social consequences were of great importance in shaping the "Atlantic" picture opportunely referred to by Anglo-American historians. What we need to keep sight of here is a more complicated triptych that cut across and restructured the culture, economy, institutions, and society of the West; and not with a sharp polarity between just two series of purely political and intellectual events in France and America.

Our survey cannot be limited to maintaining a steady gaze on this combined vision—especially now that we can examine the whole age of the great political revolutions retrospectively following its definitive conclusion, and now also that the epoch ushered in by the Industrial Revolution can be considered to be over. Neither must it prevent us from seeing with equal clarity the whole spectrum of specificities manifested in that context, and the many different, though linked, planes on which the effects of the three revolutions—in America, France, and England—unfolded. It is the essential task of the historian to draw connections without generating confusion, and it is the only way we have of addressing the complexity of investigated phenomena.

Of course, how can we think of comparing the outcomes of the Revolution on the agrarian history of France with that of American Independence on the rural landscape of the United States between 1780 and the Civil War? Or the dynamics of the revolutionary involvement of the humblest strands of the Parisian population with that of the less well-off inhabitants of Philadelphia or Boston?

Care must also be taken not to bring forward to the end of the eighteenth century a cultural and political division between Europe and America that did not open up until the middle of the nineteenth century. Not before, that is, the European revolts of 1848–1849, the heightened conservativism of American politics and intellectual debate in the following decade, after the Mexican-American War; and, on the other side of the Atlantic, the publication in Germany of the *Manifesto of the Communist Party*. The latter can be considered a genuine watershed between Europe and America, because the thought of Marx and the birth of the socialist movement—specifically European consequences of the Industrial Revolution—though of the utmost importance, concerned almost exclusively the Old World: a sign of the "exceptionalism" of the continental part of Europe (I am rather provocatively overturning the use of a word customarily applied to America) with respect to a now defined industrial and capitalist mainstream which, between England and the United States, was acquiring an increasingly marked Atlantic dimension.

The fracture between the two continents would persist for a long time. It would only begin to close with the Second World War (as Jonathan Israel rightly observes),[111] but fifty more years would elapse before it was really overcome: with the end of the Cold War, the collapse of the Soviet empire, and the withering of the socialist ideal; and then with the unexpected crisis in the functioning of democracy almost everywhere in the West. When, like it or not, everyone ended back up in the same boat, facing the same unknown sea.

* * *

Due above all to French Enlightenment thinking, the eighteenth century had witnessed, as we saw, strong and unexpected pressure for a repoliticization of the notion of equality, which had never been so much at the center of attention since the brief Greek parenthesis between the fifth and fourth century. This revival was the result of many convergences, some short lived, others of a longer duration, which contributed to determining its features and substance. Among these, significant weight was undoubtedly carried by the connection between individuals and labor developed in particular by thinkers from Locke to Hume in the shadow of the nascent English capitalist organization, and the emancipatory—if not directly egalitarian—impulse that accompanied it, then further dilated by the Industrial Revolution. This was the social, legal, and philosophical construction of the individual as a primarily working subject who, by working, defines themselves and at the same time produces and acquires wealth (becoming its owner). It was not a figure of equality, but certainly of a renewed sociality, however problematic: and in any case a profile and an image that, in France and in other respects in America, would end up slipping toward an egalitarian idea of the human condition. English economy, American sociality, and French thought. After all, the minds of a good deal of the Parisian intelligentsia were across the Channel in those years (and in some cases in America), more so than in their own country; and that constantly generated a curious sense of dystopia.

In the politicization we are discussing, a key role was also played by the definitive conceptual surpassing of an old split within the tradition of the ancient doctrine of natural law and early modernity. This was between the affirmation of the universality of equality on a purely ideal and theoretical plane, or (from the Christian creatural perspective) before God in the kingdom of heaven; and, on the other hand, the drastic reduction of that principle—if one moved to the actuality of institutions—

within the boundaries of a minority of citizens enclosed in a rigidly exclusive *polis*. A disassociation that had marked the whole of classical experience through to the Roman jurists.

Now, the universalism of the doctrine of natural law—and to a certain extent even the Christian one, especially in its Lutheran and Calvinistic version—integrated within incomparably more open economic structures, more lively and dynamic social environments, and a critical thought ready to grasp and reelaborate these new occasions, could aspire to fully transform itself into an immediately political perspective. To directly nurture a constitutional model—a tendency running through the whole of the more restless and critical wing of the French Enlightenment, and a significant part of the Italian "reforming eighteenth century" too,[112] from Filangieri—known and read in America,[113] and who corresponded with Franklin—to Beccaria.

The American Revolution stored up and amplified this impetus, giving it a concrete outlet for the first time in an extraordinarily favorable political and social context. This rendered possible a kind of constitutional process of nation building from scratch, in a barely shaped society, without any real structure or order, nor classes (without misery, said Hannah Arendt, simplifying: "It is as though the American Revolution was achieved in a kind of ivory tower into which the fearful spectacle of human misery, the haunting voices of abject poverty, never penetrated").[114] A world with less than a century of history, surrounded by virtually unlimited spaces with immense resources: an unthinkable scenario in Europe, which made what was happening there in many ways unique and unrepeatable.

Here, in the peculiarity of its genesis, lies the legacy of the irrepressible and, as it were, congenital radicality of the American experience, over and above any differences between moderates and extremists, between followers of Locke, of Montesquieu, and of the English-style "mixed" government and those—à la Paine—of Rousseau and Condorcet. In this can be found the epoch-making character of the rupture that it brought about, which emerges, intermittent but powerful and inerasable, to bind together and give meaning to the entire history of the United States. This was somehow intuited, around a hundred years apart, by Tocqueville and Arendt—the two great European interpreters of the

New World, both of whom had unresolved issues with the idea of revolution.[115] We can see it in the willingness to take out human universality not just from philosophy and religion, right in the middle of an incandescent intellectual debate, but also to place it—with an unprecedented choice—in the heart of political institutions, within an act of national foundation. And of having done all of this under the aegis of equality.

Without a doubt, this universality was immediately and dramatically contradicted, in the very moment in which it was affirmed. Jefferson owned no fewer slaves than Ulpian, or a fourth-century Christian bishop in Carthage or Antioch.[116] And there was a lot of truth in the sarcastic observation made much later by Lincoln, that this equality, though greatly emphasized, was only valid provided one did not include "negroes and foreigners and Catholics,"[117] and, we might add, women: to have any hope of fully enjoying it one had to identify as male, white, Protestant, and a native English speaker.

And yet, once that message had been carried into the field of political action and institution building, once it had descended, as it were, from heaven onto earth, its limitations became, as such, a contradiction that was also wholly political. They became conflictual and contestable; the pole of a dialectic; and no longer, as had been the case until then, dependent on an unmodifiable difference of planes between principles and history, heaven and earth, and therefore outside of any possible social and political conflict.

✽ ✽ ✽

Nothing can help us more in understanding this shift than to refer to a famous text:

> When in the Course of human events, it becomes necessary for one
> people to dissolve the political bands which have connected them
> with another, and to assume among the powers of the earth, the
> separate and equal station to which the Laws of Nature and of Nature's God entitle them, a decent respect to the opinions of mankind requires that they should declare the causes which impel them
> to the separation.

We hold these truths to be self-evident, that all men are created
equal, that they are endowed by their Creator with certain unalienable Rights, that among these are Life, Liberty and the pursuit of
Happiness.—That to secure these rights, Governments are instituted among Men, deriving their just powers from the consent
of the governed,—That whenever any Form of Government becomes destructive of these ends, it is the Right of the People to
alter or to abolish it, and to institute new Government, laying its
foundation on such principles and organizing its powers in such
form, as to them shall seem most likely to effect their Safety and
Happiness.[118]

The celebrated opening of the Declaration of Independence of the
thirteen American states, which immediately prompted the futile sarcasm of Jeremy Bentham—who only later turned into a staunch defender
of freedoms across the Atlantic—can be regarded as the start of an epoch:
that of republican democracy in Western history: the age of democratic
modernity, as Jonathan Israel would write.[119]

Two elements made it explosive. The first, evident from the very first
words, is the direct and unmediated relationship established between
people and institution, between people and state we might say. The
"people" which, indicated straightaway as the real subject of the whole
political-institutional process, are transformed immediately afterward
into one of the "powers" of the earth, with the right to "separate" and
"equal" treatment. Sovereignty thus belongs directly to the people, and
it is enough to establish the state: it is this entitlement that transforms it
into "power," without the need for any regality, without the interposi-
tion of any other figure. The republic, as yet unnamed, already dominated the scene, creating a political and constitutional situation without
precedent in modern times.

In this context equality is mentioned for the first time: as parity between "separate," independent "powers," dictated by nature and by its
God—we can almost hear a Spinozian echo in this nondistinguishing
distinction (completely missed by Bentham, even though he focused on
the passage).[120] The God of nature appears above all as the God of
equality.

Immediately afterward, the equality of the "powers" (of states, in the international order) becomes, with a strongly resonant symmetry, the equality of the human beings who form them; not of men as citizens, but of men as such. This is what is "self-evident": the equality of all men as such, because they are the creatures of the same Creator—in a perspective, that is, which combines the doctrine of natural law and theology. And this is the second explosive point of the text.

In itself, the affirmation was not at all revolutionary despite its universalism: Christian thought had established it very early on. And as we have seen, although from within a different culture, Ulpian, a jurist with world government responsibilities, had said no different 1,500 years earlier: according to natural law, all men are equal.

Those declarations had, however, now become the center of a political project, the point of departure for a never previously described constitutional consequentiality, unthinkable for any ancient culture. Its elements were perfectly articulated: all men are equal; equality translates into unalienable rights like those of life, liberty, and the pursuit of happiness; governments are established to guarantee such rights, and when that does not happen, the people can legitimately change or abolish them.

In this journey, which is at once logical and historical, the people—the whole people—insofar as they are sovereign and constituent, are identified as a community of equals. If equality is violated, it is the people's right to restore the conditions of it by any means.

The state, therefore, could not have been anything other than republican. And the form of the republic nothing if not essentially democratic. Many of its features could potentially be discussed, as in effect happened: just consider the texts gathered together in the *Federalist*,[121] which would accompany the passing of the American Constitution, in 1778 ("there is no better book," in Jefferson's judgment, precisely because, despite the variety of views, there was finally a shift from theory to practice— "Descending from theory to practice").[122]

There was no question that modern politics had begun the final stage of a complete transformation, long prepared and destined to explode in less than two decades, while in England, "the unbound Prometheus," the transformative power—social, intellectual, economic—of mechanical and capitalist industry gave the first sudden display of its impetuous force.[123]

It really was, and literally so, an age of revolutions that was commencing—even if this word, first used in astronomy by Copernicus, originally alluded, in its metaphorical transposition into the sphere of politics, more to a restoration than an overturning projected into the future.[124]

❋ ❋ ❋

As we have already observed, the American Founding Fathers had no modern examples on which to draw. Their upbringing dictated that they turn to the ancient republics, and classicism was a kind of constitutional necessity, soon projected onto the architecture of buildings and the names of places.[125] English culture throughout the eighteenth century, especially during the reign of George III, had already been deeply traversed by republican idealizations and values, albeit a constitutionally and politically innocuous republicanism, at least on the surface, combined with an equally indisputable loyalism to the crown. And the love for classical antiquity had nurtured that thought, providing stories, citations, and antityrannical examples: not just a political-ethical but also an aesthetic background.[126]

In continuing that tradition, republican Rome, much more than the Athens of Pericles, immediately became for the Americans in revolt the source of a multitude of references. But there was probably something more, and different, in that classicist background. The effort to find at any cost a precedent for what America was building, and to trace it so far back in time, also served—though not always consciously—to dampen the perturbing force of the new that was emerging, to smooth the sharper edges; to somehow bring the present, despite its disruptiveness, into the furrow of the already-happened, within the aura of ancient truths that had always been known to human beings.

The Roman republic had also been a slave society, and had an aristocratic basis, without anyone having thought that those features could diminish the untainted value of its protagonists. One could therefore perfectly well be virtuous and a slave owner; perfectly well be virtuous and cultivate aristocratic and perhaps even oligarchic tendencies. The equality spoken of in the Declaration of 1776 therefore needed to be read with caution, and once again ringed by barriers and exclusions, beginning with slavery, the racial foundation of which could not be called into question. The American Enlightenment—like that of France and Europe—contained many variants, and its description is hard to fit solely into the contraposition between "moderates" and "radicals"; and certainly, the distance separating the positions of an Adams from those of a Jefferson clearly reflects the extent of these gaps. We are in the presence—in Europe as in America—of highly complex movements of ideas, in which the common motif of the elaboration of the new developed in a discontinuous, nonlinear way, and in which the theme of equality was the crucial point of all the divisions.[127]

As always in history, in the American case the public use of the past was not neutral. Behind it, and the rhetoric that often fueled it, there unfailingly lay, if we know where to look, the outlines of a reality which, by evoking that past, there was the intention to cover over, or erase, or even to fictitiously construct.

France

The contrast between different impulses, already perfectly visible, albeit with less lacerating outcomes, in the American Revolution, erupted dramatically in France, in a setting marked by much more serious conflicts. "Thought became violence where it was faced with the positive as violence," Hegel would write in his *Lectures on the Philosophy of World History*, with precisely the events of those years in mind.[128] And equality—which by now had already become a political matter thanks to the French philosophers and the American founders—was at the heart of the clash.

The two most important historians to have recently studied the revolution in France, François Furet and Jonathan Israel, present reconstructions so far removed from each other as to have readers wondering at times whether they are talking about two different events. This is, after all, the beauty of writing about history: the uninterrupted regeneration of the story. Our relationship with the past is quintessentially unstable, and it takes nothing—the breeze of an idea, the surfacing of a hidden detail—to reverse, sometimes drastically, perspectives, luminosities, textures. Of course, facts exist, in their unequivocal nakedness: the death of Louis XVI, or the outcome of the Battle of Valmy. But each of these, even the most insignificant, once it has happened, produces all around it, in the thread of relations connecting it to other events situated in the same web of space and time, such an indeterminable spectrum of oscillations and displacements—like a frothy wave of alternative compositions—that choosing a single trajectory within it is as difficult as it is often arbitrary. Indeterminacy, perhaps, is the only way for our intelligence to perceive and reelaborate in the final analysis the reality that forms and envelops us.

❋ ❋ ❋

Furet was writing at a time when the Soviet Union was still standing, and the socialist perspective in Western Europe, though it had taken some hard knocks, continued, however nebulously, to be among the possibilities of history: the Eurocommunist alliance, shared by the Marxist leaders of France, Italy, and Spain, had just been forged, and seemed to be opening up, despite everything, new possibilities for renewal and action. The relationship between the French Revolution of 1789 and the Russian one of October 1917 (What continuity between the two? What references? What symmetries? What steps forward?) was still a matter of incandescent ideology, the subject of impassioned debate with evident political overtones. This climate, strongly felt by the French historian, gave his work an almost militantly historiographic quality, polemically revisionist with respect to what he judged to be the dominant Marxist vulgate, powerful above all in French and Italian studies.

Israel's research appeared on the other hand when the system of socialist states had collapsed in Eastern Europe over two decades previously, and almost no one talked about Marxism any longer, at least in the West. The connection between the two revolutions—French and Russian—appeared in a completely different light. The history of the world had changed: the issue had suddenly cooled off, and the political clash which had involved it had slipped from prominence. The mutation undoubtedly permitted a more detached bird's-eye view, which we too need to exploit as best we can.

The point where the divergence between the two authors is most evident touches on an essential theme: the appraisal of the final phase of the French revolutionary trajectory, between 1793 and 1794, dominated by the Reign of Terror and by Robespierre's lacerating presence. For Furet—Hegelian in this, in his own way and without knowing it (I believe)—that period was the inevitable consequence of the process begun in 1789.[129] For Israel, it was instead a dramatic deviation—a genuine and ruinous betrayal—with respect to the intrinsically republican and democratic revolution that had begun four years earlier, culminating in the draft constitution drawn up by Condorcet in February 1791.[130]

The issue directly impacts the question of equality, at the center of the turn in 1793: its quality and its quantity, in relation to the other two cornerstones of the revolutionary action: the liberty of single persons and the sovereignty of the people.

As early as the "Declaration" of August 1789, largely written by Mirabeau and Sieyès, the word "equals" appeared in a very prominent position right from Article 1.[131] But it was immediately accompanied by an important specification, absent from the analogous American text of 1776, which the inspirers of the French document—above all Mirabeau and Condorcet, no less than Mounier and Sieyès—clearly had in mind (from it they probably drew the intention to prepare a declaration of principles as a guide and program for revolutionary action), and the vocabulary of which they employed without hesitation when it seemed appropriate (for example, in the reference to "happiness," which bounced back from Rousseau himself).[132]

The equality that in the French text was shared by all men from birth (as in the American declaration, though this contained Christian overtones absent from the document of 1789) concerned "rights"—especially those indicated immediately afterward in Article 2: liberty, property, security, and resistance to oppression—and these alone.[133] Because then immediately, in the second sentence of Article 1, with a counterpoint pregnant with significance, mention was made of "social distinctions," the existence of which, alongside natural equality, was fully legitimated (though an even more drastic version, located in another article, was then removed from the final draft).[134] However, it was immediately added, they "may be based only on considerations of the general good."

What did that formulation mean exactly? What were the positive, acceptable distinctions, as it were, and what were they set against?

In reality, what was being outlined here, at the end of a long debate, was a primary separation of fields, absent in the American text: with law and politics on one side, and economics on the other. The first indicated the space where the (natural) equality of men was achieved, while the second was characterized by diversity and the unequal.

Let us begin with the latter. Distinctions "based only on considerations of the general good"—the wording was revealing—could only be those induced by the smooth functioning of the economic machine, as portrayed by its numerous apologists in late eighteenth-century Europe—not just in England—between physiocratic thought and precocious praise of the market, at the dawn of classic economic science in the time of Quesnay and Smith.

The key elements underpinning this vision were all, moreover, already present in France as well. The mass social division of labor, especially in relation to the development of industrial factories and the intellectual professions—but also in the countryside, where the agrarian aristocracy of the *ancien régime* had long since embarked on significant modernization; the increase in consumption; the widespread presence of capital in the sphere of production and no longer just in the traditional one of trade; a markedly unequal accumulation of wealth, such as to facilitate productive reinvestment. In brief, the backbone of the capitalistic organization of society—rendered even more evident by the contemporary Industrial Revolution in England—was beginning to display its already formed profile, and to impose its compatibilities. From the now fully "bourgeois" viewpoint of that transformation, and of the (especially English) economic doctrines that accompanied and supported it, the inequalities stemming from the economy necessarily appear to be fully justified, precisely because they were functional to the common good, to the growing increase in overall wealth. The same was true of the right of property, not mentioned in the American declaration, but referred to twice in the French text: in Article 2 as "natural" and "imprescriptible," and in Article 17 as "inviolable and sacred," and hence "no one may be deprived thereof."[135]

Economic inequalities were not the only ones that had to be taken into account. The reference to distinctions "founded . . . upon the general good" also evoked the presence of other imbalances of a different provenance, which could not adduce the same economic legitimation. Tracing them was simple. They related to the whole apparatus of discriminations, gradations, exemptions, and privileges that had survived from the ancient feudal system, which the Revolution was preparing to abolish at a stroke. Those were the bad distinctions, as opposed to the diversities founded on the "common good," and they no longer had any reason to exist; "unjust, odious, and at odds with the supreme end of every political society" (according to Sieyès, in a text from those years).[136] The conclusion was obvious: the social divisions—of class—induced by the good functioning of the new economy were entirely acceptable; those of status, a legacy of the old order, were on the other hand inexorably condemned. Rousseau was neglected in the name of Smith and Mandeville—or, if we wish, of Voltaire.

Opposite, in a space apart—the space of rights—there lay, as we have seen, the domain of equality, however tempered—but this limit, at least in part, was not destined to last long in the revolutionary age—by the separation of citizens into two distinct spheres, on the basis of income and of social standing and gender.[137]

On one side were the "active" (whose income, position in society, and gender authorized them to fully exercise their political rights). On the other were the "passive" or "inactive"—servants, the propertyless, vagabonds, women—who possessed, like everyone else, the rights of liberty and security but not the political ones enabling participation in public life. Equality was above all parity before the "Law": "it must be the same for all", "all citizens, being equal in the eyes of the law . . ." (Article 6): juridical equality, then, from which there derives both political equality ("All citizens have the right to take part, personally or through their representatives, in its [the law's] making" (Article 6), and that which concerns the appropriation of assets (everyone can be the owner of everything: Article 17).

The two parts of Article 1—the first sentence about equality, the second about difference—sketched out two distinct if not contrasting worlds, described for the first time with great Cartesian clarity: which, however, had a supposed compatibility if not perfect harmony. It was already the picture of the bourgeois world, foreshadowed, albeit in a rough form, by at least a century of English history—constitutional (since the age of the Glorious Revolution), intellectual (from Hobbes to Hume, and to Smith), and economic (with the long lead-up to the Industrial Revolution).

Positioned symmetrically to the equality of rights in the text of 1789 was the other great declaration of principle and the generator of the revolutionary process: that of freedom.

It was, par excellence, the freedom of each "individual," isolated as "man" and "citizen," subject solely to the command of the "Law." With the dissolution of all the feudal restrictions and stratifications, society appeared in an already completely atomized form, determined by economic dynamics alone. It was in this context that equality was to have unfolded; and where, above all, the "general will" (Article 6) had to be attained, without which the sovereignty of the nation (Article 3) could not manifest itself and that found its highest expression in the "Law"; and the mechanism of politics could not move—a politics relating entirely to the intentions of the people.

As long as that equality remained on the plane of rights alone—of a parity of subjects before the law, like the one conceptually elaborated for the first time by the Roman jurists—it could well be realized within a society of the kind that was being prefigured. But what might happen if—as would very soon be the case—there was a shift to an equality that impacted the social conditions of each individual? How could it be achieved—what would its regime have had to be like—if every life presented itself only in the fragmentation of its individual specificity, lost in an ocean of differences?

Emerging into full light, already in the bare formulations of this text rich in destiny, was what François Furet acutely described as the greatest dilemma of the eighteenth century: how was it possible to conceive of sociality—and, I would add, the link, the connection, the sharedness indispensable for lifting equality out of a purely formal shell—by starting solely from the individual, from singularity, from the solitude of the fragment?[138]

We could go much further in outlining the difficulty. Because what we are pointing to here was not just (as Furet seemed to think) a crucial issue for the culture of the French Revolution, as it had been, moreover, for Rousseau's thinking. It was the insurmountable contradiction that 1789 bequeathed to the following century, and which then came down to us through the unfolding of many events. Marx and the European socialist movement would try in vain to overcome this obstacle—by appealing to a previously unconsidered element—but ended up disastrously crashing against it.

❁ ❁ ❁

A feature intrinsic to revolutionary processes—found in America, France, Russia, and even in the English industrial takeoff—was the sensational acceleration of historic time that developed within them, and the force of projection onto the future. In the space of a few years centuries of the past were burned up, and whole swathes of the future anticipated—an aspect already perfectly clear to Robespierre, when he wrote, though with some exaggeration, that "the present Revolution has produced in a few days greater events than the whole previous history of mankind"; not to mention Lenin.[139]

In France, at least three distinct revolutionary impulses—or perhaps it would be better to say three distinct revolutionary "moments"—overlapped and became intertwined between 1790 and 1794, in an unprecedented contraction of intervals, accompanied by a proportional velocity in the rhythm of events (the "irresistibility" of which Arendt wrote).[140] One can be described as liberal parliamentarism, of the English kind: bourgeois in its social content, and from a constitutional point of view still fundamentally promonarchic, at least at the beginning.

Another was openly republican and democratic, and is given particular value in Israel's perspective, for whom the constitution of 1793 was "the world's first democratic constitution"; a judgment perhaps due also to the fact that this model resembled most closely the American Revolution, as he himself described it.[141]

Finally, there was a third politically exceptionalistic moment, with the suspension of constitutional guarantees on the grounds of the dangers faced by the Revolution, and socially (at least in the intentions and declarations) very interventionist. A kind of vertiginous and visionary anticipation of socialism, but still without an idea of socialism, and without even a genuine working class (there was, however, a magmatic Parisian multitude, on the cusp between the early modern class nuclei and the still plebeian groupings of the *ancien régime*). A situation that immediately slipped into despotism and the Terror, dominated by the obsession with internal enemies, and the omnipresent shadow of the aristocratic conspiracy—the point on which Furet focused, while Israel proposed a definition that in my view is misleading and unacceptable, seeing in it a kind of prefiguration of fascism.[142]

* * *

The question of equality was the true dividing line in the acceleration of this *prestissimo*.

In a frenetic jumble of social doctrines and political practices, an increasingly strong conviction gained ground, through a continual short circuit between urban masses and revolutionary avant-gardes: the paradigm of equality envisaged in the Declaration of 1789, that of Mirabeau and Sieyès—parity of rights (albeit within two types of citizenship) and inequality in the economy and society—could no longer be sustained. In other words, the reduction of equality to a purely formal matter—the great invention of the Roman jurists—was poorly suited to the multiplication of centers of "democratic sociability" and the correct functioning of a democracy conceived of as increasingly demanding, inclusive, and consequent.[143]

On the contrary, the view began to be taken that the formation of a strong political will, shared by the whole people, and the development of a truly virtuous citizenry necessarily required an equally significant reduction in social and economic inequalities, if not their complete elimination. It was the dream of a total change in the existing state of things that had by now been injected—after Rousseau—into the spirit of French (and German) intellectual radicalism and would run through to Marx.

"Wealth and poverty were equally disappearing under a regime of equality," reads a decree of the *commune* of Paris dating to November 1793,[144] and "There must no longer be rich or poor. Opulence is a disgrace," Saint-Just would say in the same year.[145] Full democratic participation in the life and decisions of the republic could not be achieved without first drastically reducing existing social imbalances. Montesquieu and Rousseau—in agreement on this point—were right, then. Democracy, to be effective, needed an equality that went beyond the plane of rights alone, touching on the substance of citizens' material lives. The question left hanging by the ancients saw the confirmation of a very challenging modern response.

Before proceeding, clarity is required on an essential point. In advancing this solution, revolutionary discourse remained completely and solely ethical-political in nature (as Rousseau's had effectively been in his *Discourse*). It did not venture into the sphere of the economy as such or lead to any attack on the mechanisms of capitalistic production; nor did it touch the field of sociability, which continued to be viewed as wholly constructed around the individual.

The issue was simply that of redistributing in an ethically and politically correct manner—that is, with a basic parity—a wealth whose primary creation remained totally outside the range of revolutionary action; far less did it become the object of a critique pushed beyond the level of a moralistic attack on luxury and corruption that inevitably followed it. Not even the model of a sociability of "individuals" was called into question, just as it had not been in the Enlightenment tradition, which had contributed to its crystallization. Babeuf and his "society of equals" never really crosses these thresholds either. Everything remained within the confines of a redistributive action, though it was imagined as being significant and resolutory.

Nothing more was seen. The will of the law sufficed to level things up. And effectively, the impetuous development of the revolutionary process, which appeared to its very own leaders as miraculously self-fueled and self-supported (program after program, popular revolt after popular revolt) had not just rapidly radicalized those elites, self-hypnotized by the speed with which continually changing scenarios were absorbed and elaborated. But it had also (and disastrously) persuaded them that there were no limits to what could be imposed by politics. And that, in its solitary omnipotence, anything could be asked of it, provided it was sustained by a determination and clarity proportionate to the objectives. It was what Marx would call "the illusion of politics," opportunely recalled by Furet in the analysis at the heart of his famous study.[146] And it would be exactly this lack of awareness of limits—this omnivorous and totalizing, almost metaphysical, idea of political action—that generated the Terror and took the Revolution down a blind alley (here I gauge the importance of the previously mentioned interpretation and at the same time my distance from it).

I believe that it was the idea of holding limitless and concentrated power thanks to the revolutionary exceptionality of the moment (limitless precisely because it was concentrated) that wound up multiplying in the groups in command the phantasmatic perception of the presence of the enemy, its ubiquity, and therefore the constant fear of conspiracy and of networks of possible alliances. The omnipotence of politics was not just contiguous to but the very cause of the delirium that saw an aristocratic conspiracy lurking and spreading everywhere, and not—as Furet seems to suggest—directly the idea of equality: even though the attempt to achieve it in that context ran into no less serious problems.

Let us return now to the radicalization surrounding the notion of equality. Without a doubt, the intention to go beyond a purely and rigidly formal conception, restricted to the legal and political sphere, stemmed from the intuition of a genuine difficulty, which anticipated, as we shall see, at least two centuries of Western social and political history. We can try to articulate it in these terms.

The more the equality of the kind envisaged in 1789 (which did not affect the material conditions of the subjects involved at all) was posited as inclusive of the whole social body to which it referred—that is, the more it connected to a democracy, as happened in France from at least 1790 onward—the more it tended to be rendered vain in reality. The economic differences that it encompassed would hinder or even impede the exercising of those rights—political ones first and foremost—for the guaranteeing of which it had originally been affirmed. Expressed differently, beyond a given threshold, class distances got the better of formal unification. Unequal quantity (of subjects) outweighed equal quality (of form), crushing it.

To restore sovereignty to the people—to the whole people—it was necessary to inject a different kind of equality into the system, one that eliminated the substantive obstacles that were effectively preventing those recognized as possessing certain rights from enjoying them in full. But though the problem really did exist—and it would be the great theme of European social history between the nineteenth and twentieth century—the solution was tragically mistaken.

It was in fact thought that the matter could be resolved simply by fortifying with political power—unprecedented power—a revolutionary avant-garde that had convinced itself it was acting on behalf of the whole nation and, through its authority, imposing politics, and the will it expressed, as the total principle of life, outside of which there could not be any scope for salvation, any autonomous projection of the human. The question of whether such a vision was compatible with the existence of an already capitalist economy, a sociality linked exclusively to the form of the individual, and critical thinking largely oriented in other directions (and, moreover, forming a public opinion) was not even raised.

In the effort to move forward, the experiment therefore had to be accompanied by such a degree of coercion, such ethical overdetermination, as to quickly make the costs unsustainable.

When Robespierre declared that "everything which is necessary to maintain life must be common good and only the surplus can be recognized as private property," or "the most sacred of all laws, the welfare of the people, the most irrefragable of all titles, necessity," he was uprooting the whole structure of formal law, and hence every equality derived from it, without being able to replace it, in that context, with anything equally structured—economically, socially, or culturally.[147] He just waved the flag of a substantialism more ethical than legal, whose only support was the primacy of a political will that no longer recognized any limits to its action. A position that he lucidly saw as the outcome of a clash without any possible mediation between "forms" and "principles." "We invoke forms because we lack principles."[148]

The attempt would end in disaster, as we well know. Facts took their revenge on ideas that did not recognize their sharp-edged hardness. And the Restoration would, in the ultimate analysis, still be a small price compared to the dimensions of the failure.[149]

But the trajectory of that path, like the wake of an incandescent meteor, would continue to inflame the Western skies. It left behind a triple, not unambiguous signal, destined to weigh upon the history of the world: that modern politics could be conceived and practiced as a total institution; that to achieve a full democracy, based on genuine popular sovereignty, any purely formal conception of the rights of citizens had to be surpassed in the name of a more markedly substantialist vision of equality; and that one could forge a strong and virtuous sociality in terms of solidarity and bonds (the revolutionary "fraternity") without calling into question the individual as the dominant figure of the human.

At least in part, we are still within this horizon of contradictions.

Figures of Equality

The revolutions in America and France had managed to transform the question of equality into a political issue (something which, at least partially, had already happened in the Greek *poleis*), and to do so without forgoing—in principle at any rate, and this was an absolute novelty—a universalization of it: all human beings have the right to be treated as equals.

What is more, they also believed they had indicated a way to combine the glorification of individuality as the exclusive form of the human, with the construction of a paradigm of equalness able to create a bond between those involved in it; that is to say—as we recalled, citing Furet—thinking of the social by starting from the individual.

The chosen route had been to clearly separate two distinct figures of equality. One—purely formal—effectively taken from Roman thought, where it had first been invented and applied, consisted of isolating the abstract profile of the considered subjects, reduced to possession of a predefined and calculable quantum of rights, and of reserving for it the sphere of the law (first private, then public as well) and of politics.

The other, which concerned the social condition of the subjects concerned, presupposed, though again starting from the individual, a more substantive leveling up in the distribution of wealth or at least of life opportunities and was associated with a markedly democratic notion of politics. The separation between the two profiles—the formal and the substantive—less clear, at least initially, in the American experience, more visible in the French one, for reasons relating to the radically different history of the two countries, led in the latter to a dramatic rupture in its revolution, and the attempt to tread a hard, unrealistic path of reunification that ended in open violence.

This failure would bar for almost a century any possible connection and slippage between the two models in European political experience, paving the way for the liberal route toward democracy. And while the former would lie at the center of important theoretical investigations, contemporary to and after the two revolutions, which would mark the trail from Kant through to Weber and Kelsen, the latter would become the pole star for the thinking of Marx and the European socialist doctrines that began with him, eventually culminating in the October Revolution.

Between the two paradigms—tracing a partially different trajectory—was the equality of American democracy, reflected in the memorable mirror built by the dazzling thought of Tocqueville.

* * *

The echoes of the French Revolution in German philosophical culture—especially in the Enlightenment circles of Lessing's generation—were many and varied. In a context politically frozen by absolutism, however mitigated by Prussian reformism, and economically much less developed in industrial and capitalistic terms than England, and even France, Kant's appraisal of the Revolution was always bravely and generally positive, despite its "miseries and cruelties," as he wrote in 1797, and notwithstanding the horror provoked by the execution of Louis XVI.[150] He saw in it—at least the part between 1789 and 1791—a decisive step, of which Germany and the rest of Europe had not been capable, in the process of legal formalization and rationalization and of the edification of the rule of law that seemed to him one of the high points of human civilization.

Kant's youthful sympathies for Rousseau ("the penetrating Rousseau,"[151] as he wrote in 1771), though they subsequently cooled in the light of the formal totalization that constituted the backbone of his reflection, did nonetheless leave an important trace. And Kant always shared with him a certain antipathy for England and a significant part of its thinking—for its policy of interfering in French affairs and for its constitutional order—in addition to a solid link with the theory of human rights. "The rights of man are more important than the order and tranquility . . . based on general oppression. While disorder, which arises from the desire for justice, passes," he would write in one of his anthropological studies.[152]

In his philosophical universe, dominated by the presence of the cognitive and moral a priori and by his self-centered formal structure, a markedly individualistic reading of the human ("a rational valuing of one's own worth and of the calling of each individual to think for himself"),[153] taken in full from the Enlightenment tradition no less than from the Lutheran-Christian one, was combined with a powerfully abstract (and hence unifying) construction of subjectivity, seen as the foundation—transcendental, we might say—of the modern political and juridical order. In this respect, Kant was perhaps (together with Leibniz) the most significant modern continuer of the thinking of the Roman jurists, or at least of its most important invention—the conception of law as a world of forms. It is no accident, in fact, that the greatest expert of ancient law in the first half of the nineteenth century, Friedrich Carl von Savigny, was firmly Kantian, even though the philosopher himself never had much truck with the strand of conservative—if not actually reactionary—historicism that had a certain following in Germany at the time, and of which Savigny was indisputably the key player.[154]

It was within this framework that Kant constructed his theory of equality. The mechanism developed through the combination of two end points. On the one hand he reaffirmed the existence of an equality founded on a naturalistic datum, which cannot be obscured. In 1777 he wrote:

All human beings on the wide earth belong to one and the same natural species because they consistently beget fertile children with one another, no matter what great differences may otherwise be encountered in their shape. One can adduce only a single natural cause for this unity of the natural species, which unity is tantamount to the unity of the generative power that they have in common: namely that they all belong to the same phylum, from which, notwithstanding their differences, they originated, or at least could have originated.[155]

At the other end of the line was equality as determined by the abstract construction of the subject, "external (rightful) *equality* within a state is that relation of its citizens in which no one can rightfully bind another to something without being subject to a law by which he in turn can be bound in the same way by the other."[156]

Opening up between the two, as if in parentheses, is the universe of the unequal:

This uniform equality of human beings as subjects of a state is, however, perfectly consistent with the utmost inequality in the degree of their possessions, whether these take the form of physical or mental superiority over others, or of fortuitous external property and of particular rights (of which there may be many) with respect to others. Thus the welfare of the one depends very much on the will of the other (the poor depending on the rich), the one must obey the other (as the child its parents or the wife her husband), the one serves (the day labourer) while the other pays, etc. Nevertheless, they are all equal as subjects *before the law*, which, as the pronouncement of the general will, can only be single in form, and which concerns the form of law and not the material or object in relation to which I possess rights. For no-one can coerce anyone else other than through the public law and its executor, the head of state, while everyone else can resist the others in the same way and to the same degree. No-one, however, can lose this authority to coerce others and to have rights towards them except through committing a crime. And no-one can voluntarily renounce his rights by a contract or legal transaction to the effect that he has no rights but only duties, for such a contract would deprive him of the right to make a contract, and would thus invalidate the one he had already made.[157]

Kant presents his thinking in the framework of what he calls the "civil state" (*constitutio civilis*) of a society, which he saw as being founded on three a priori principles: the freedom of each person as a *human being*—the human being as ultimate end and absolute value; equality as a *subject*; independence as a *citizen*.[158] In this universe of individuals— from time to time, on the basis of their formal determination, simply "human beings," each of whom is "a being capable of possessing rights," especially of property; or "subjects," or, again, "citizens"—equality appears completely enclosed within the relationship between form and law ("concerns the form . . . and not the material").[159] The uniformity of the human—a motif by no means absent in Kant—is overwhelmed by its individualistic fragmentation, by the autonomy of single wills as the founding principle of practical reason ("Kant's fundamental principle is to claim the categories for self-consciousness, understood as the subjective 'I,'" Hegel would later say).[160] Stretching out all around is the field of the unequal, whose proportions are without limit. The nonconflictual coexistence between the different planes—and therefore between formal abstract equality and inequality in "the degree of . . . possessions"—is deduced solely from the a priori nature of the distinction, and as such is removed from any empirical conflictuality. The reality of labor, such a strong presence in English writers, is only barely evoked compared to the force with which property is referred to, and what is more in an outdated manner ("the day labourer"). It is the triumph—but a triumph resulting from separation and scission—of logic over historic actuality, of abstract intellect over the positivity of contradiction. And at the same time—against the light—it is the definitive codification of the two equalities in European thought. The drama of the French Revolution is evoked and simultaneously negated at its roots. The formalism of Roman law—though integrated into an incomparably more conscious and complex conceptual framework: the transcendental structure of pure practical reason on one hand, the new order of "public law" on the other—thus becomes the spirit of modern rationality itself, not just legal but political as well (abstraction of the proprietary subject, and formal abstraction of equality) and finds here its fullest and highest celebration.[161]

Between State and Theology

The French Revolution, which for Hegel had its "origin and its basis in thought," was in turn translated by him into philosophy.[162] And we cannot but observe how that sentence—even if the "thought" mentioned in it had a broader and more complex meaning than a simple reference to a specific movement of ideas—seems to coincide almost literally with the result of Jonathan Israel's work, when he concludes his formidable research by declaring that "Radical Enlightenment was incontrovertibly the one 'big' cause of the French Revolution" (but I do not believe Israel ever had that page from Hegel in mind).[163] The coincidence does, however, offer further proof of the extraordinary weight philosophy has carried in the course of European history.[164]

In relation to the issue of equality, Hegel's views would be completely different—as for many other themes—to those of Kant: they represent a kind of complete upending of them.

Although the image of Hegel as a theorist of the Restoration periodically comes to light, after the studies of Eric Weil, of Ritter, Riedel, Ilting, and, in Italy, Biagio de Giovanni and Remo Bodei, it no longer seems possible to seriously call into question the philosopher's strong relationship with the French Revolution, one of the great axes around which his thought revolved.[165]

I do believe, however, that we should not obscure one far from marginal aspect of his thinking, and that it helps to explain the stubborn reappearance of an interpretation that moves Hegel to a conservative if not openly reactionary position. I am referring here to the existence of a gap, like a continual shift or superimposition of planes, visible above all (but not just here, to tell the truth) in the more directly political-historical works.

On the one hand, taking shape and looming large before our eyes is the extraordinary speculative force deployed by that philosophy, with all the metaphysical richness of the proposed solutions: a structure that showed itself increasingly to be the most coherent attempt by Western thought to get to the bottom of the scission between subject and object, mind and body, concept and substance—the lacerating dualism of Descartes and Kant—and at the same time to save the restless finiteness of single lives and of the historic world by integrating the power of the infinite that transfigures them. (I must add here that in this respect I consider de Giovanni's recent reading of Hegel's crucial relationship with Spinoza to be of great importance; we shall return to it in due course, also to clarify and circumscribe my sole but not insignificant point of dissent from this very acute interpretation.)[166]

On the other hand, and complicating matters, there is an incontrovertibly powerful reduction of the Hegelian perspective when attention shifts from metaphysics and from a space dominated by concepts to the elusive actuality of historic events and the role played in them by the present. When, from the dazzling identity between logic and ontology, from the constructive power of the double negation—the negation of negation—as the way for the thrilling and dramatic recognition of the infinite productivity of the finite, capable of exceeding, in this mediation, mediation itself, we move into the gray area where the concept encounters, determining itself, the accidentalities of the present ("the subject of philosophy is the present, that is, the real") and implies a judgment of them and of the institutions of the time as they appeared in Europe and America between the 1810s and 1820s.[167]

The impression, then, is of a rigidifying and ossifying of Hegel's analytic powers, of a contracting of his theoretical breadth within an evaluative device not without a certain mechanicalness (a critical point touched on lightly by Löwith).[168] In short, that theory, impoverished, took a step back and retreated in the face of the proliferating facets of the present containing it, and of its limits: almost as if a fully deployed historicity was exacting its revenge on a metaphysics that had transcended it with such impetus and promise (an observation that is close, while not entirely taking it on board, to Marx's remark in the *Critique of Hegel's 'Philosophy of Right,'* when he writes that Hegel's "sole interest . . . is that of recovering the Idea simply, the logical Idea in each element . . . and the real subjects . . . become their mere names. Consequently, there is only the appearance of a real understanding, while in fact these determinate things are and remain uncomprehended because they are not understood in their specific essence").[169] It is as if the un-limited accidentality and creativity of the finite, irrespective of the gen-eral form (logical and ontological) that includes and explains it—"the objective logic thus takes the place rather of the former *metaphysics*"—were the real stumbling block, an insuperable point of crisis.[170] The sign of the persistence of something profoundly unresolved in the relation-ship between historicity and metaphysics, between the full structuring of processes in history and their ontological foundation. Something which, on occasion, brought Hegel very close to an interpretative ship-wreck, rendering possible divergent and even antithetical (though not entirely grounded) readings of his thought. And it should also be added in this respect that if the *Logic* lies completely outside (or above) this risk, neither the *Philosophy of Right* nor the *Philosophy of History* are immune to it, as they are closer to matters of historic understanding and evalua-tion of the present; while the *Phenomenology*—intrinsically suspended between morphology and historicity—is positioned, as it were, halfway between.

> In the Christian age, the divine spirit has come into the world and taken up its abode in the individual, who is now completely free and endowed with substantial freedom. This is the reconciliation of the subjective with the objective spirit. The spirit is reconciled and united with its concept, in which it had split in the direction of subjectivity, the end of its first genetic process deriving from the state of nature,

says Hegel in the *Lectures on the Philosophy of World History,* published posthumously by his pupil Eduard Gans in 1837 but delivered at the University of Berlin in the 1820s.[171] And in the *Encyclopedia*, he writes: "It is true that God is necessity, or, as we may also put it, that he is the absolute Thing: he is however no less the absolute Person."[172]

If there were still any need to verify the weight of Christian theology in crucial junctures of Western thought, these texts would feature prom-inently in the demonstration. We are in the presence of a decisive step here, which would radically condition Hegel's idea of equality.

The articulation of the trinitarian dogma—the God-person that gen-erated the son that became man—is, in Hegel's thinking, the route to the definitive consecration of the individual as the noble and privileged form of the human, of the "substantive" (and hence noncompressible) freedom that it realizes, and of its place in history—a result that could not have been achieved in any way without Christianity.

What individuality though? Certainly not a fragmented, split figure lost in its own isolation; not, in a word, the atomized individuality that was emerging increasingly clearly in the ideas and reality of modern societies, especially in England: the same one foreshadowed in the for-malism of the Roman jurists—and then built with much more powerful analytic tools in the thought of Kant—and heavily criticized by Hegel.[173] But rather a form that could reveal itself to be the place of reconcilia-tion, through the concept, between subject and object; while previously it was merely nailed down in terms of a scission represented by the side of subjectivity.

Such an individuality, if we can express it like this, no longer has anything unilaterally "subjective" about it, but is profoundly affected by the impersonal, by the substantive, by the "objective," which runs throughout it. It preserves nothing, that is, of the bad subjectivity re-sulting from a dualism, which can be overcome precisely through uni-fication "in the concept." This joining together is only possible thanks to the human incarnation of the divine, of the infinite that became person and history ("absolute Thing"—namely, absolute substance—and "absolute Person," as Hegel writes: Subject that encompasses the infinite), finally reconciling "subjective spirit" and "objective spirit," subject and world. Without Christianity—without its mediation, without the im-manence of transcendence (as de Giovanni rightly says)—there is no conceivable way, according to Hegel, of escaping the scission and con-ceptualizing the relationship between the absolute and the finite; al-though the impression is that the theological structure acts at once as a way of criticizing the individual, but also as a block on a complete settling of matters with this figure, precisely due to the presence of the God-person.[174]

There was space, then, for a difficult mediation. The device of the person-individual remained in place, but insofar as it was regenerated through the rediscovered unity—an individuality that no longer spoke in the first person, because it had acquired a now firmly incorporated experience of the universal—it could not have much to do with the figure of the modern individual built with such effort, and with numerous oscillations and variants, in thinking from Hobbes to Kant. Nor, even less so, with the representations of the multitudes of producing and consuming individuals created by the capitalistic dynamics that were redesigning modern societies according to the new economy, those alluded to many times in the sections on property and civil society in the *Elements of the Philosophy of Right*. Instead, it was an individuality that could only rediscover itself—reconciled with itself—by starting from the place where the universal came together, in present time, with the rationality of history ("reason is present," wrote Hegel in a note for his course on the philosophy of law in 1824–1825).

This place—literally the place of reason—is, for Hegel, the state.

What state, though?

A state for Germany, first of all, which it did not yet have—not identifiable with any of the models offered by contemporary historical experience. Which, to start with, had nothing to do with English constitutional praxis, as "this inherently incoherent aggregate of positive determinations has not yet undergone the development and transformation which has been accomplished in the civilized states of the Continent, and which the German territories, for example, have enjoyed for a longer or shorter period of time"—a judgment that would scandalize Norberto Bobbio, though the reasons for it can be well understood (if not actually shared).[175] And not even with the young American democracy, or at any rate with any republican paradigm, bearing in mind that "North America cannot yet be regarded as a fully developed and mature state, but merely as one which is still in the process of becoming; it has not yet progressed far enough to feel the need for a monarchy," as Hegel says in his *Lectures on the Philosophy of World History*.[176] But also very different, finally, from France's post-Revolution constitutional experience, where, as a consequence of the "democratic, indeed anarchic, principle of isolation," "the citizens appear as isolated atoms, the electoral assemblies as unordered and inorganic aggregations, and the people as dissolved in a multitude."[177]

In paragraph 260 of his *Philosophy of Right,* Hegel wrote:

> The state is the actuality of concrete freedom. But *concrete freedom* requires that personal individuality and its particular interests should reach their full *development* and gain *recognition of their right* for itself (within the system of the family and of civil society), and also that they should, on the one hand, *pass over* of their own accord into the interest of the universal, and, on the other, knowingly and willingly acknowledge this universal interest even as their own *substantial spirit,* and *actively pursue it* as their *ultimate end.* The effect of this is that the universal does not attain validity or fulfilment without the interest, knowledge, and volition of the particular, and that individuals do not live as private persons merely for these particular interests without at the same time directing their will to a universal end and acting in conscious awareness of this end. The principle of modern states has enormous strength and depth because it allows the principle of subjectivity to attain fulfilment in the *self-sufficient extreme* of personal particularity, while at the same time *bringing it back to substantial unity* and so preserving this unity in the principle of subjectivity itself.[178]

And, just before, at the opening of Section 3 of the third part of the *Elements:* "The state is the reality of the ethical Idea—the ethical spirit, understood as the substantial, *manifest,* and self-revealed will, which thinks and knows itself, and accomplishes what it knows and in so far as it knows it."[179]

The modern state was, then, for Hegel, the realization of the universal. Its presence was to enable particular and personal individualities—the same ones founded by Christianity in their "absolute" value, and then exalted, albeit only as smashed identities, by the modern philosophy and economy, and which had burst into politics with the American and French Revolutions—to recognize the universality (the "absolute") within them. In this way, it was possible to go beyond ("pass over") the unilateral nature of the scission that had tied them down to their atomized condition. They could thus find genuine freedom in this decisive step; not that of subjective will, but that of the universal "substance" active in each of them, the same one that the state expressed through the form of the law, which Hegel set against the will of jurists and any purely jurisprudential law. And it was for this reason that "the state is the reality of the ethical Idea": because, by obeying it, each individual could be reunited with their own universality and their own substantive freedom.

❈ ❈ ❈

Hegel's thinking regarding the specific institutional features of the state paradigm thus identified oscillated on several occasions. Certainly it was a monarchy; certainly a constitutional monarchy capable of guaranteeing the civil rights enshrined in the French Declaration of 1789; certainly it envisaged the existence of some form of representation, perhaps corporative, perhaps even "national" along French lines, or perhaps both; and it is certain, finally, that there was to be room in its articulation for intermediate social formations able to piece together, from the bottom up, the atomized dust of civil society. But it certainly did not coincide with the Prussian state in which Hegel lived and worked, especially after the conservative turn of 1819.

Revealing in this respect is the bitter dispute the philosopher engaged in during his Berlin years, with jurists in general and the Historical School of law in particular, especially its leading exponent, Friedrich von Savigny (also a professor in Berlin, a member of the State Council and, after Hegel's death, a minister of Frederick William IV from 1842 to 1848).

"Juristic law" ("juristische Recht," as he says in the *Encyclopedia*),[180] entirely distinct from public law (that is, "domestic state law," as he writes in the *Elements*),[181] was in Hegel's view almost exclusively private law: property and contracts; and it was a law—in a Germany that did not yet have a codification—largely based on Roman law, albeit reelaborated in the modern and mainly French, German, and Dutch tradition (a "system of modern Roman law," as Savigny would later write).[182]

But Hegel considered it to be a minor order, with no capacity for tasks able to move toward the universal. This unfitness had distant origins, stemming from its Roman roots. His appraisal of ancient law was in fact very severe, and completely at odds with the prevailing view, in particular that of the Prussian jurists. He wrote in the *Elements* (and what he said probably contributed to the book's disastrous reception in German academic circles):[183]

> In this realm [the Roman empire] differentiation comes to an end with the infinite diremption of ethical life into the extremes of *personal* or private self-consciousness and *abstract universality*. This opposition, which begins with a collision between the substantial intuition of an aristocracy and the principle of free personality in democratic form, develops into superstition and the assertion of cold and acquisitive power on the one hand, and into a corrupt rabble on the other. The dissolution of the whole ends in universal misfortune and the demise of ethical life, in which the individualities of nations perish in the unity of a pantheon, and all individuals sink to the level of private persons and to *equals* with a formal law, who are therefore held together only by an abstract will of immense proportions.[184]

And earlier, again in the *Elements:*

> That logical consistency which Leibniz praises [speaking of Roman jurists] is certainly an essential characteristic of legal science, as of mathematics and every other science of the understanding; but this logical consistency of the understanding has nothing to do with the satisfaction of the demands of reason and with philosophical science. Apart from this, however, the very *inconsistency* of the Roman jurists and praetors should be regarded as one of their greatest virtues.[185]

The historically strained and simplified judgment of the Roman empire is quite evident, not just in relation to our knowledge and interpretations but also to those in Hegel's own time: Gibbon would not have agreed with a word of it. But that is not the point. Rather, it is that, in Hegel's view, the chief merit of the thought of the ancient jurists, the invention that had made their knowledge the cornerstone of all modern law—formalism—became instead the greatest limit of their practice. Hegel correctly linked equality and formalism: but for him this connection led to the decadence of individualities, "held together only by an abstract and arbitrary will"—evidently that of the ancient prince, identified as a tyrant.

Compared to previous thought, to the European legal-political tradition through to Kant, the perspective was completely reversed. Hegel opened—or tried to—a new horizon that envisaged moving beyond all formal law to build nothing less than a new figure of the human. Moreover, he had already written in the *Phenomenology,* in the section on the "rule of law": "The universal is splintered into the atoms of absolutely multiple individuals; this spirit, having died, is an *equality* in which *all* count for as much as *each* and where each and all count as *persons*."[186]

Formalism—and the equality deriving from it—could not, therefore, have been the genuine completion of the individual. Instead, it was its negation—an *"abstract universality,"* as he again says in the *Phenomenology,* or its "decadence," as in the *Elements.*[187] It contained something that would have been irremediably destructive, if it had not been capable, on its path, of tapping into another presence, the field of action of a different force, which redeemed its limits and unilaterality in a higher mediation. His was a false universality—the universality of an abstract and fictitious equalness—useful solely for the purposes of private law, of the realization of a provisional equality, suited only to promoting economic exchanges. It would instead be the full and deployed presence of the modern state and of the ethical totality it embodied—an organically organized totality—finally achievable in the present ("reason is the present") that could open up to the individual the path of authentic universality, just as only the Christian embodiment of God—Person in a person—had enabled the infinite to enter into the finiteness of historicity and give it substance.

It is not necessary here to see how Hegel actually constructed his theory of statehood in the final part of the *Elements,* and how the forms he introduced—the immediate focus of a precocious and very acute critique by a youthful Marx—reflected and reproduced in thought real figures of the political and economic dynamics of the first European capitalist societies (the "point of view cannot be concrete when the object of the point of view is abstract," as Marx put it).[188]

What is important to bear in mind here is that a key node in Hegel's reflection was the proposal of a philosophical and political relation between individuality and universality that was not centered on the formalism of equality, that did not delineate the individual in terms of what he considered the bad abstraction of formalism. It was based on a different connection between the individual and the universal, not quantitative but qualitative. It therefore neither destroyed nor weakened the specificity of single personal figures, in which the universal did not consist of the abstract equality of the subjects involved, but their relationship— not necessarily egalitarian, indeed tending toward the hierarchical— within a strongly and powerfully structured totality: the people of a state and of a nation. The truth of individuality, of each person, was to be found in the universal force of this connection, not in the atomism of the singularities (of the "multitudes") that the new economy seemed to be imposing as the highest spirit of the age, and the new politics assuming in an entirely acritical way.

We can express this in different terms: for Hegel the polemic directed at the Roman jurists was just an extension of his anti-Kantianism; the formalism of law and of politics—and their equality—were not the true destiny of individuality in the historic era of modernity. A decisive protrusion still remained, not covered by that outcome.

And yet in this surpassing, no possibility of a higher and more complete human equality took shape. Hegel's dissatisfaction with the "law of jurists" did not lead to an egalitarian conception of the universal: although all of the finite had been equally traversed by the presence of the divine—of the infinite that became history; and although it was possible to identify uniformly with the unfolding of the state.

At least, that did not happen in relation to the form of politics imagined by Hegel. Indeed, this is, as I said earlier, one of those more problematic points of juncture between the ontological vision (the logic and ontology of the modern state) and the empirical historicity involved in it. As if the figure delineated by Hegel were marked by the presence of a dual register: on one hand the metaphysical power that defined its profile in relation to the idea, and on the other the contingent historicity of its social and constitutional structuring.

* * *

In this play of mirrors, the reference to the theme of labor occupied an essential role. What the modernity of the latter represented had already been clarified by Hegel in a famous passage of the *Phenomenology*, which has been the subject of endless comments and seems to move powerfully beyond the Aristotelian view referred to earlier:

> The master relates himself *to the servant mediately through self-sufficient being*, for it is on this very point that the servant is held fast. It is his chain, the one he could not ignore in the struggle, and for that reason he proved himself to be non-self-sufficient and to have his self-sufficiency in the shape of thing-hood. However, the master is the power over this being . . . the master thus has . . . the other as subordinate to him. The master likewise relates himself *to the thing mediately through the servant*. The servant . . . relates himself negatively to the thing and sublates the thing. However, at the same time the thing is for him self-sufficient, and, for that reason, he cannot through his negativity be over and done with it, cannot have eliminated it; or, the servant only *processes* it. On the other hand, to the master, the immediate relation *comes to be* through this mediation as the pure negation of the thing, or as the *consumption* of the thing. Where desire had failed, the master now succeeds in being over and done with the thing, and he achieves satisfaction in his consumption of it. . . . The master, who has interposed the servant between the thing and himself, as a result only links up with the non-self-sufficiency of the thing and simply consumes it. He leaves the aspect of its self-sufficiency in the care of the servant, who works on the thing. . . . This satisfaction [of the master] is itself only a vanishing, for it lacks the *objective* aspect, or *stable existence*. In contrast work [of the servant] is desire *held in check*, it is vanishing *staved off*, or: work *cultivates and educates*. The negative relation to the object becomes the *form* of the object;

it becomes something that *endures* because it is just for the laborer himself that the object has self-sufficiency.[189]

I consider this text to be an authentic philosophical epiphany of modern productive labor; in some way of working-class labor: the kind which, in being exercised on objects, becomes their form. Hegel explains why the relation—viewed from the side of the master, as in Aristotle—can only be immobile, tied down on itself (as it appeared to Aristotle). The master is stiffened in his mastery, observes Alexandre Kojève, the unparalleled twentieth-century exegete of the *Phenomenology:* the relation cannot surpass itself, change, progress.[190] But the master, who does not work, creates nothing fixed outside of himself; he only destroys the products of the servant's labor. He lives in the condition of a sterile short circuit between desire and consumption: in an "existential impasse," Kojève again notes.[191] Instead, history germinates and develops entirely on the side of the servant who works. Hegel looked at his activity with the perspective of one who is able to gauge all the power contained in the sociality of modern labor, where the ancient fracture between intelligence and the materiality of doing had been overcome, and the explosive force of the self-emancipation of producing, of "giving form" to objects, was becoming established through the construction of the new European civil society. As if in a flash, at least three centuries of history are condensed into this writing, which fully renders, in the space of a few lines, all the distance separating the ancient and the modern.

In the second section of part three of the *Elements,* devoted to "civil society," Hegel returns to the theme from another point of view. The direct object of his analysis now is the free labor of the moderns, and no longer the "dependent" kind of the servant:

> The universal and objective aspect of work consists, however, in that [process of] *abstraction* which confers a specific character on means and needs and hence also on production, so giving rise to the *division of labour.* Through this division, the work of the individual becomes *simpler,* so that his skill at his abstract work becomes greater, as does the volume of his output. At the same time, this abstraction of skill and means makes the *dependence* and *reciprocity*

of human beings in the satisfaction of their other needs complete and entirely necessary. Furthermore, the abstraction of production makes work increasingly *mechanical*, so that the human being is eventually able to step aside and let a *machine* take his place.[192]

Here there is already, tested as if in a first experiment, the language of Marx—that inimitable mix of German philosophy and English political science, also read with attention by Hegel—but still without Marx of course. And there is the relationship—crucial and full of consequences—between the abstraction of labor (real abstraction, not only of the concept) and its unlimited fragmentation and mechanization. And there is also the discovery of the relationship between the abstraction of labor and the "*reciprocity* of human beings"—and hence a step away from the identification of the consequences, inevitably political as well, of the social nature of modern production and its class structure.

Hegel stops here though. A few paragraphs further on, again in the same section, his focus reverts to the individual with respect to labor:

> The individual attains actuality only by entering into *existence* in general, and hence into *determinate particularity*; he must accordingly limit himself *exclusively* to one of the *particular* spheres of need. The ethical disposition within this system is therefore that of *rectitude* and the *honour of one's estate* [*Standesehre*], so that each individual, by a process of self-determination, makes himself a member of one of the moments of civil society through his activity, diligence, and skill, and supports himself in this capacity; and only through this mediation with the universal does he simultaneously provide for himself and gain *recognition* in his own eyes and in the eyes of others.[193]

Instead of classes, there are "estates." Instead of conflict, of the negative, of movement, of struggle, the vision of a harmonic, hierarchically ordered totality, where each person, "through his activity, diligence, and skill"—i.e., his labor—becomes "a member of one of the moments of civil society"—of an organically organized totality—and "supports himself

in this capacity," thereby entering into "mediation with the universal"—
that is, taking his place in the ethical totality of the people and of the
state, of a people that had become state.

Once again, unavoidably, the question we raised earlier returns: what
state was Hegel talking about? How is it possible to reconcile the structured and totalizing organicity to which he alludes constantly with the
necessary pluralism of the democratic forms that America was already
producing, and which would soon become known in Europe too? Those
same forms that some were already beginning to see as the future of the
world?

Put differently: what exactly was the path being indicated here? And
in it, would the destiny of equality just be tied to its formalism—to the
formalism of equal law and the "rule of law" that presupposed it? And
that of the individual only to their permanence in the different "estates"?
Again, and above all: how could the common articulation in the universal of single individuals not have posed the problem of their equality—
including political equality—besides the diversity of "estates"? The impression here is that Hegel was aware on the one hand of the limits of
the individual as a pulverized figure of the human and was trying to get
to the bottom of it; and on the other that he clearly realized how the atomization of individuals was an unavoidable result of modern societies, which could not be set aside. He therefore attempted a composition—
however weak—in the name of "estates," of a hierarchical-corporative
structuring of society, in which he sought to reconcile an individualistic
foundation with an organicist mediation.

In any case what is certain is that metaphysics and history seem to part
company here, with the reason of the thing—the ontology of modernity
with its integration between the finite and the infinite—far removed from
its actual history, at least for a long epoch. And that the increasingly
Atlantic history of the West—a history marked by the two revolutions—
was embarking on another path.

American Democracy

But this august dignity I treat of, is not the dignity of kings and
robes, but that abounding dignity which has no robed investiture . . .

that democratic dignity which, on all hands, radiates without end from God; Himself! The great God absolute! The centre and circumference of all democracy! His omnipresence, our divine equality! . . .

Then against all mortal critics bear me out in it, thou just Spirit of Equality, which hast spread one royal mantle of humanity over all my kind! Bear me out in it, thou great democratic God![194]

It is Herman Melville writing here, in *Moby Dick,* published in New York in 1851 (he is outlining the physical and moral qualities of Starbuck, the first officer of the *Pequod*). And the democratic and egalitarian God he invokes is without doubt an American God.

Between the Constitution of 1787 and the Civil War, the political paths of the United States would develop in anything but a linear manner, and there were many in that period who sought to separate the republic from democracy. In their view, the former would differ "more widely from a democracy than a democracy from a despotism," as Fisher Ames—an eminent lawyer and representative from Massachusetts—said at the beginning of the century.[195] The version they proposed was openly conservative, if not exactly oligarchical (I believe it is indisputable that what might be described as an aristocratic feature—sometimes more explicit, sometimes almost entirely submerged—runs through the whole of American history). And yet it would be hard to doubt that the United States appeared to European eyes and was widely regarded by American public opinion as the first great example of democratic government in modern times.

The government adopted here is a democracy. It is well for us to understand this word, so much ridiculed by the international enemies of our beloved country. The word democracy is formed of two Greek words, one signifies *the people,* and the other the *government* which is in the people. . . . My Friends, let us never be ashamed of democracy!

declared Elias Smith, a well-known religious preacher of the time, in 1809.[196]

Democracy from the American viewpoint, implied equality: in his invocation, Melville put "democracy" and "divine equality" into the same image, establishing an almost synonymic connection between them. Returning, in the crucible of that reality, in the fervor of the transformation that had completely erased the old colonial and monarchic face of American society, was the crucial pair that had already emerged in ancient thought, and to which, as we saw, a part of the eighteenth-century European Enlightenment had returned. It was the experience of the age that was reflected in Melville's impassioned rhetoric: and Gordon Wood is therefore right when he says that "within decades following the Declaration of Independence the United States became the most egalitarian nation in the history of the world."[197]

And this is exactly how—as the most egalitarian nation in the history of the world—it appeared to the curious and restless gaze of Alexis de Tocqueville when, on May 9, 1831, he disembarked the ship that had carried him from Le Havre to Rhode Island together with his faithful traveling companion Gustave de Beaumont.[198] The president at the time was Andrew Jackson, who had succeeded John Quincy Adams in 1829—a democrat of humble origins, not a member of any elite, and the inventor of the government spoils system.

The two volumes of *Democracy in America*, published in Paris in 1835 and in 1840—the fruit of that unforgettable journey—are an absolute masterpiece of European historical, sociological, and political thought. A memorable, engaged, and revealing portrait—the "way we were" of America in the early 1830s—that has remained unequaled.

Tocqueville immediately reversed the customary perspective, deploying a theatrical masterstroke with an extraordinary prophetic effect: the United States was not still a childlike society waiting to acquire more mature European characteristics (as Hegel had said in relation to the monarchy); instead, it was anticipating with all the force of its youth the inevitable future of the Old World. Observing it—for anyone arriving from the other side of the Atlantic—was a leap into the future, not an exercise in pedagogy.

In Tocqueville's portrait the element dominating the scene was equality. In the very first sentence, he writes: "No novelty in the United

States struck me more vividly during my stay there than the equality of conditions," before continuing, on the same page:

> I soon realized that the influence of this fact [equality] extends far beyond political mores and laws, exercising dominion over civil society as much as over the government; it creates opinions, gives birth to feelings, suggests customs, and modifies whatever it does not create.
>
> So the more I studied American society, the more clearly I saw equality of conditions as the creative element from which each particular fact derived, and all my observations constantly returned to this nodal point.[199]

Equality, then, as the "creative element" generating the whole of society. Nothing of the sort had ever been seen in Europe: it was something only possible in a country almost without a past. And once again we must ask ourselves: what equality?

At this point there is a second novelty in Tocqueville's thought.

In fact, he tended to close the divarication—opened, albeit in different ways, by German philosophers from Kant to Hegel, and, even before them, by continental legal culture and English political thought—between formal equality before the law and the state, and substantive equality from the point of view of social conditions—a divergence dramatically borne out by the events of the French Revolution, at least according to the (generally conservative) interpretation that drastically separated 1789 from 1793.

Tocqueville instead cast the different aspects together in a unitary paradigm, precisely the one he perceived as active—though never theorized—in American life. In this sense, his description seemed to tie in more with Rousseau (whose work he certainly knew and to which he was strongly attracted) than with Hegel, who he probably never read (although, in truth, certain pages in Democracy do seem to contain some echoes).[200]

He believed that in America "the equality of conditions" was what he defined as a "social state": a category which, by creatively mixing theory and empirics, enabled him to integrate within a single descriptive mechanism legal forms and matters of fact, norms and mentalities, already unified in the real processes of the society he was observing. "The social state is commonly the result of circumstances, sometimes of laws, but most often of a combination of the two. But once it has come into being, it may itself be considered as the prime cause of most of the laws, customs, and ideas which control the nation's behavior; it modifies even those things which it does not cause," he wrote at the beginning of chapter 3 of volume 1. Before then adding, immediately afterward, as a conclusion: "the social state of the Anglo-Americans is eminently democratic."[201] In referring to America, he also used—just as we saw Melville do—democracy and equality almost as synonyms, though it should not be forgotten that Tocqueville attributed various meanings to the word "democracy"—no fewer than eleven have been counted—and there has even been talk of a particular "iridescence" to his vocabulary.[202]

What he saw at work in the United States was a powerful and totalizing democratic mechanism (following Tocqueville, I am giving "democracy" both the meaning of form of government and that of a "social situation of increasing egalitarianism," as Luciano Cafagna writes in an illuminating essay).[203] A condition in which political equality—the principle of universal suffrage, though restricted just to white males, was an acquired right from the second half of the 1820s, and this was an absolute world first—became the motor of a more penetrating and more invasive parity, which, though not the prelude to a leveling up of wealth—that would have been unthinkable in America—did appear profoundly different from a purely abstract equivalence, from a simple legal form. It was a deep cultural structure, a genuine egalitarian mentality capable of turning into social fabric and institutional body, of becoming, as it were, substantial: equality in life opportunities and occasions; equality in not excluding anyone from anything; equality in holding that every individual situation could be modified, even radically, in a short space of time.

The cultural and social condition described by Tocqueville was therefore a strong response to the question we have referred to on several occasions: how much equality, and of what sort, does a democracy need to function at its best? And the answer—implicit but crystal clear in his analysis—was very exacting, as had been the one already given both by

Montesquieu (who had had a determining influence on Tocqueville) and (in his own way, and even more) by Rousseau.[204] American democracy in its nascent state survived and gained strength because it rested, far beyond just the recognition of political rights, on a "social fact" inside which the self-government of the people—its sovereignty—was integrated into a network of incisive and rebalancing equalities that enveloped the whole of community life.

Only the birth and continual reproduction of this condition—at once the presupposition and the result of the effective enjoyment of political rights and legal parity—permitted the democratic fullness of the national reality. It was (we would say) only the material constitution underpinning society as a whole that permitted the full and correct unfolding of the formal constitution that represented its highest legislative point of reference.

Tocqueville laid great stress on the theme of popular sovereignty: "Any discussion of the political laws of the United States must always begin with the dogma of the sovereignty of the people," he wrote at the start of chapter 4 in volume 1, affirming that it was, "from the beginning . . . the creative principle of most of the English colonies in America. . . . The American Revolution broke out. The dogma of the sovereignty of the people came out from the township and took possession of the government; every class enlisted in its cause; the war was fought and victory obtained in its name; it became the law of laws."[205]

The force of his own description led him then to brush up against the problem (very familiar to Rousseau, as we have seen) of how that principle could be realized through a representative democracy (the expression had first been used by Hamilton in 1777, precisely with regard to the American Constitution), in which, that is, legislative power was held by the representative of the people and not directly by the people themselves. Tocqueville circumvented the obstacle by pointing to the existence, in America, of a great closeness between people and representatives, guaranteed by universal suffrage, by the frequency of elections, and the continual control exercised by public opinion over the elected. "Sometimes the body of the people makes the laws, as at Athens; sometimes deputies, elected by universal suffrage, represent it and act in its name under its almost immediate supervision."[206]

The image of the Athenian square overlapped as if by magic with the neoclassical one of Capitol Hill in Washington, in an effort—conceptually very weak, in truth—to erase any distance between the two democracies: the direct, ancient, and the representative, modern.

> In America the people appoint both those who make the laws and those who execute them; . . . the people *directly* nominate their representatives and generally choose them *annually* so as to hold them more completely dependent. So direction really comes from the people, and though the form of government is representative, it is clear that the opinions, prejudices, interests, and even passions of the people can find no lasting obstacles preventing them from being manifest in the daily conduct of society,

wrote Tocqueville at the opening of the second part of volume 1.[207] The House of Representatives was not similar, therefore, to the English Parliament: Rousseau's criticisms (not evoked but certainly present in the background of this page, and wholly concentrated in that "though" which introduces the reference to the representative form) would have had no reason to exist here.[208] In America, representation did not cancel out democracy, but simply made it possible where vast spaces and large numbers existed. The problem was put to one side for the time being, not because it had really been theoretically overcome, but because the American reality—the actuality of its institutions—seemed to have resolved it concretely, having built a constitutional model where representation did not prevent the people from exercising a direct and continual power.

It was thus possible, according to Tocqueville, to close the essential and very tight circle between equality and democracy, between the sovereignty of the people and the social condition of individuals, which he saw at the core of American political life. The tension of that relation produced an unlimited energy that became one of the driving forces for the whole of society: "Democratic institutions awaken and flatter the passion for equality without ever being able to satisfy it entirely. This complete equality is always slipping through the people's fingers at the moment when they think to grasp it, fleeing, as Pascal says, in an eternal flight," he wrote in chapter 5 of the second part of volume 1.[209] It was translated, that is, into a border that was always shifted forward, in a never predeterminable limit, into a whirl of absolute—the "eternal flight." Here Tocqueville probably had in mind, transfiguring it into his writing, the American frontier myth that was then taking shape, transferring it from the plane of physical movement, of a journey of conquest and adventurous challenge, to the somehow metaphysical one of the attainment of an ideal, of the impossible and therefore always missed achievement of a definitive state of grace; in other words, of perfection.

Five years later, in volume 2, Tocqueville returned to this point—which, with Hegel, we might say is that of the finite that contains the infinite—in one of the densest and most beautiful passages of the whole work, where his empathy for America and its people turned into a genuine and powerful projection of the philosophy of history. The theme is again that of American equality, and its effects and consequences:

> Equality puts many ideas into the human mind which would not
> have come there without it, and it changes almost all the ideas that
> were there before. I take the concept of human perfectibility as an
> example, for that is one of the chief ideas which the mind can con-
> ceive and which by itself constitutes a great philosophical theory,
> a theory whose effects can be seen at every moment in the conduct
> of affairs. . . .
>
> When citizens are classified by rank, profession, or birth, and
> when all are obliged to follow the career which chance has opened
> before them, everyone thinks that he can see the ultimate limits of
> human endeavor quite close in front of him, and no one attempts
> to fight against an inevitable fate. It is not that aristocratic peoples
> absolutely deny man's capacity to improve himself, but they do not
> think it unlimited. They think in terms of amelioration, not change;
> they imagine that the conditions of the societies of the future will
> be better but not really different; while admitting that humanity
> has made great advances and may be able to go still further, they
> assume in advance certain impassable limits to such progress. . . .
>
> But when castes disappear and classes are brought together,
> when men are jumbled together and habits, customs, and laws are

changing, when new facts impinge and new truths are discovered, when old conceptions vanish and new ones take their place, then the human mind imagines the possibility of an ideal but always fugitive perfection. . . . Thus, searching always, falling, picking himself up again, often disappointed, never discouraged, he is ever striving toward that immense grandeur glimpsed indistinctly at the end of the long track humanity must follow. . . .

I once met an American sailor and asked him why his country's ships are made so that they will not last long. He answered offhand that the art of navigation was making such quick progress that even the best of boats would be almost useless if it lasted more than a few years.

I recognized in these casual words of an uneducated man about a particular subject the general and systematic conception by which a great people conducts all its affairs.[210]

"The ultimate limits of human endeavor"; "when men are jumbled together"; "immense grandeur"; "a great people." The stylistic emphasis becomes dense and revolves around a single point: equality as the result of total engagement among human beings, not enclosed in predetermined hierarchies (an echo of Hegel?), and capable in turn of setting in motion the infinite potential of the human—revealed by a people that had just embarked on a previously untrodden path in the history of the world. Equality as a mechanism capable of freeing unthinkable resources of intelligence and initiative, of becoming the reference for a new common sense (the anecdote of the "American sailor"), which had made the unlimited progress of science and technology an undisputable truth able to guide the choices of an entire civilization.

Of course, it should never be forgotten that the equality spoken of here was still and at any rate a restricted version, which excluded a very significant proportion of the American population. It did not concern women—who were soon to embark on a long and hard journey to securing recognition of their parity. It did not concern Black people, both those crushed by slavery—in Tocqueville's eyes, "the most formidable evil threatening the future of the United States," with a truly prophetic intuition—and those who were free, but deprived in effect, to almost general approval, of rights to which they were legally entitled by the law.[211] The dark picture that Tocqueville paints of the rights of Black people is merciless in its realism:

> In almost all the states where slavery has been abolished, the Negroes have been given electoral rights, but they would come forward to vote at the risk of their lives. When oppressed, they can bring an action at law, but they will find only white men among their judges. It is true that the laws make them eligible as jurors, but prejudice wards them off. The Negro's son is excluded from the school to which the European's child goes. In the theaters he cannot for good money buy the right to sit by his former master's side; in the hospitals he lies apart. He is allowed to worship the same God as the white man but must not pray at the same altars ... So the Negro is free, but he cannot share the rights, pleasures, labors, griefs, or even the tomb of him whose equal he has been declared; there is nowhere where he can meet him, neither in life nor in death,

he wrote in chapter 10 (the whole of which is a harsh and memorable fresco) of the second part of volume 1 of *Democracy*.[212]

Nor did equality in any way concern the Native Americans, whose oppression and desperate pride were already described forcefully and at times with great feeling in the notes Tocqueville later published in *Journey to America*.[213] Finally, it did not concern many of the first-generation immigrants—the plebs of the big cities on the east coast.

These restrictions were certainly not just an American problem. Indeed, America was undoubtedly the country where parity within the human condition—setting slavery to one side for a moment—was in many respects the most open and widespread.

In reality, the genuine universalization of equality—whatever meaning we choose to give to this word, from the most formal and restricted to the most substantial and comprehensive—its full reference to the human in general, and not just to specific and more or less broad categories of subjects, was the great unsolved problem of the nineteenth century on both sides of the Atlantic. We shall have occasion to discuss it later.

❀ ❀ ❀

Tocqueville looked at America with extraordinary powers of observation, but with part of his mind continually directed toward France, just as Arendt would do in thinking about Germany and Europe. *Democracy in America* must therefore be read with his other great book, *The Old Regime and the Revolution* (written in the 1850s), constantly in mind. His intelligence grappled here with a comparison between the two revolutions—the triumph of American democracy and the catastrophe of the French aristocracy—and their different outcomes. He believed they would have a common destiny, the spread of democracy worldwide as the real sign of the century: "the century is primarily democratic. Democracy is like a rising tide; it only recoils to come back with greater force. . . . The immediate future of European society is completely democratic," he wrote in 1833, shortly after his return from the United States.[214] But their paths were divided for now. In America the democratic experiment had been achieved, as it were, in vitro, in a society almost without history—and this rarefaction, this absence of weight, would literally enchant Tocqueville, who was accustomed to the millenarian stratification of European history. In France, the Revolution had run up against old and entrenched patterns—the conformation of the agrarian landscape, the construction of the state structure, the history of classes—and its novelties continually had to reckon with accumulations of the past which it proved impossible to shake off.

This previously unseen lightness explained (in his eyes) why American democratic egalitarianism took root quickly and without difficulty: "The Americans have this great advantage, that they attained democracy without the sufferings of a democratic revolution and that they were born equal instead of becoming so," he wrote at the end of chapter 3 of the second part of volume 2, evidently thinking of the revolution in France.[215]

And it was again with French events in mind—where it had violently broken down—that he discussed the relationship, rendered crucial by European history, between freedom and equality. "It is possible to imagine," he wrote in volume 2 of *Democracy*, "an extreme point at which freedom and equality would meet and blend," granted that "men cannot be absolutely equal without being entirely free, and consequently equality, in its most extreme form, must merge with freedom."[216] The formulation is almost literally Marxian, but it should not surprise us in Tocqueville, who liked to look far ahead and was not afraid to combine the play of abstractions with historic and sociological analysis of a society or an epoch—a form of historical practice not far removed from that of Marx ("I speak of classes, they alone ought to interest history," he sustained in *The Old Regime and the Revolution*).[217]

It is hard to say though whether for Tocqueville that "extreme point" coincided with a precise moment, however far projected into an indeterminate future (and in this case it would in all probability have been a moment in American history), or whether it was just a metaphysical place, illuminated by the power of the concept but that could only lie outside history. Naturally, for him the attainment of democracy—built as it was to combine from the outset, as its very condition of existence, the impetus toward equality of conditions with the tendency toward complete popular sovereignty—could not consist of anything other than the reaching of a point of equilibrium where the maximum degree of self-government was combined with the maximum degree of social parity; and where the maximum freedom coincided with the maximum equality.

And yet history continually disturbed this relation, introducing pressures that altered it:

> Democratic peoples always like equality, but there are times when their passion for it turns to delirium. This happens when the old social hierarchy, long menaced, finally collapses after a severe internal struggle and the barriers of rank are at length thrown down,

he wrote, again in the second volume of *Democracy*.[218] When the perspective was shortened, then, things became complicated. The diversity of different histories resurfaced. And returning with them was France and the Terror: the period in which the link between freedom and equality had touched its most critical point, becoming dramatic and at the same time revealing the full extent of its problematic nature, as never before; and the attempt to achieve the maximum equality had turned into a "delirium" that had led to the death of freedom. The powerful memory of that tragedy is what drove Tocqueville to see in all democracies the tendency to tip the balance between the love of freedom and the desire for equality in favor of the latter, with all the risks that such an imbalance might entail—a danger to which in his view America itself was not completely immune.

In the category of "extreme equality"—which probably derived from Montesquieu—he condensed all the negativity of this drift: a dark evil that in his view threatened the development of every democracy.[219] Returning here—though shifted a long way forward—is the problem that is now very familiar to us, reelaborated but not overcome: where should the limits of equality be set to ensure that its pursuit is not transformed from an indispensable prerequisite for the functioning of a democratic system into a mortal danger to its survival? And given that in any case the equality under discussion did not imply a leveling out of riches available to individuals—the American model certainly did not move in this direction—what exactly were the limits that could not be exceeded?

With a perceptive though perhaps not entirely conscious intuition, Tocqueville linked this problem somehow to that of the consolidation of "individualism" in American society (a word that, when he was writing, had just entered the refined French lexicon).[220] The four chapters on the relationship between equality and freedom and on individualism follow one another in the opening to the second part of volume 2 of the *Democracy*.[221] America is not directly mentioned, as was often the case in the second volume, written when the most vivid impressions of his trip had softened, and Tocqueville tended instead to use the United States as an implied model to construct a kind of general theory of democracies; but it is nonetheless America about which he is speaking.

Individualism—"the individuality of character," as William E. Channing had written in 1829—was certainly already by then an important trait of American society, and it would remain so in a basically definitive way: a long-lived feature in the cultural and social history of that world.[222] And Tocqueville was not wrong to emphasize it.

He did, however, exaggerate in seeing in it a specifically "democratic origin": condensed within that attitude—the exaltation of the individual form of the human—was a cultural and social tradition that, as we have seen, had very remote roots.[223] It was a legacy that had been shaped by the new English bourgeoisie, if anything filtered through the Lutheran and Calvinist experience, and only emphasized by the peculiar environmental conditions of the New World. But Tocqueville hit the mark by establishing a contiguity between the consolidation of that attitude—whereby all folk "owe no man anything and hardly expect anything from anybody. They form the habit of thinking of themselves in isolation and imagine that their whole destiny is in their own hands": a magnificent portrait of the people of the West—and the specific American way of reconciling freedom and equality.[224]

In that context, in fact, the reinforcement of the individual, with the inevitable valorization of personal diversities—capacities, talent, even of fortune—acted as an antidote to any radicalization of equality, instead producing a combination of different, even antagonistic, pressures, which, while it lasted, gave rise to a society without comparison in the West—and it was an essential element of the "American Dream."

At the heart of it there was what we might describe as an elastic and empirical idea of equality, which could stretch, but without vanishing, to include sometimes very significant differences. These were given space in the name of the irreducible particularity of each person, provided there was no undermining of the recognition that humans—or at least those accepted as being fully so—possessed a common quality and dignity. It was a kind of primary right to sharing, which rendered possible and legitimate any social ascent; a community bond acquired by being born and maintained through behavior able—in the common view—to preserve and enhance it. This was the same tie that by 1791 prompted Jedidiah Morse to describe New England as the place where "every man thinks himself at least as good as his neighbors, and believes that all mankind have, or ought to possess equal rights."[225]

Although Tocqueville had a certain perception, however nebulous, of these balances, he continued to see great risks in democratic individualism, which appeared to him as the "isolation of each man from the rest": to the point that "not only does democracy make men forget their ancestors, but also clouds their view of their descendants and isolates them from their contemporaries. Each man is forever thrown back on himself alone, and there is a danger that he may be shut up in the solitude of his own heart."[226] In this appraisal, there was perhaps a tinge of regret for the ancient forms of aristocratic solidarity of the old systems in the *ancien régime,* capable of acting both vertically—from the top down—and horizontally, between equals. Nor was there any awareness in him of what—in more strongly industrialized contexts—were beginning to be the new forms of workers' socialization.

These aspects of closure and nostalgia did not prevent him from also objectively recognizing the antibodies that American society had managed to put in place to curb excessive fragmentation. First among them was the construction of a system of "local liberties" that drove each community to collectively deal with their own administration; and then a powerful vocation for associationism, for combining forces to achieve clearly determined micro-objectives: "Americans of all ages, all stations in life, and all types of disposition are forever forming associations," Tocqueville wrote, again in the second part of volume 2. Shortly after, he added: "Thus the most democratic country in the world now is that in which men have in our time carried to the highest perfection the art of pursuing in common the objects of common desires and have applied this new technique to the greatest number of purposes."[227] Individualities and ties: a difficult pair, like freedom and equality. A democracy could only strengthen itself by holding together many opposites, mixing them with skill. An extreme and almost impossible task.

❊ ❊ ❊

The difference in the specific weight of the past between American and European society—which certainly measured an objective state of affairs irrespective of Tocqueville's perception of it—also accounts, at least in part, for an essential difference between the two worlds as they appeared in the heart of the nineteenth century. *Democracy in America* did not address this theme directly (it would probably have been too soon at the time), but, as we shall see, it would soon have very important consequences.

The impetuous industrial development in the United States, as it did not take place in an already highly structured society but started, as it were, almost from zero, in barely outlined social contexts, never led, unlike in Europe—in France, in Germany, then in Italy and Spain, and, first of all, in England—to the forming of rigid class structures. Far less did it provoke the spread, if not in an episodic and marginal way, of forms of worker consciousness informed by the idea of struggle and conflict as a key element of their vision. It is almost as if the relationship between capital and labor acquired a completely distinctive configuration in America, less divisive and contradictory; and what in Europe proved to be a conflict charged with tension was, across the Atlantic, a much less essential aspect in the dynamics of the entire society.

This difference has more than one explanation.

Besides the lack of past that we have already mentioned, another similarly important element emerges. In the United States, a vertiginous mobility—from the bottom up, but also vice versa—and the proliferation of opportunities that continually ran through every single existence, every barely formed individuality, prevented the stable aggregation of classes around a particular social condition determined by the position occupied within productive structures, and by the difference between manual and intellectual labor. On the contrary, it continually pulverized it into fluxes of perennially changing personal situations that did not crystallize into a defined and lasting configuration. No rigid formations were created with set profiles, but rather social clouds whose components mutated continually. Nor did the consciousness of an unmodifiable hierarchy dictated by the economy form within them; instead, the cultural trait of those aggregations was solely the incessant drive for change. Rootedness did not appear except in a residual way, in extreme and marginal contexts; in its place were movement and flight.

Put differently, before the contradictions of class had time to weigh on and mold individual subjectivities, the latter changed position, dispelling those conflicts from their horizons, while other multitudes succeeded one another in the same roles. The speed of change, in short, was a factor in reducing the force and radicality of the contrast between capital and labor, or at least its principal effects on forms of consciousness, creating an environment where classes did form, but in a fluid and discontinuous manner.

Tocqueville himself had already had a perception of this extreme mutability: "Among democratic peoples new families continually rise from nothing while others fall, and nobody's position is quite stable. The woof of time is ever being broken and the track of past generations lost," he wrote in volume 2 of *Democracy*—and the generalization ("democratic peoples") makes it no less certain that he was thinking of America.[228] Social contradictions there did not, as it were, have time to land on lives and mark them, because the reference points changed too quickly.

The exact opposite was beginning to happen in Europe, where big industry, taking shape in much "stickier" contexts, defined by long-term stratifications and with much less internal mobility (fewer opportunities, fewer spaces, fewer resources), became the producers of much more stable social formations, where contrasts and contradictions had plenty of time to settle upon consciousnesses, and to cut into the living flesh of the relations that were built.

This difference would contribute strongly to determining two distinct histories in the common capitalistic development on both sides of the Atlantic, and from then on would yield very different ways of conceiving of equality, diversifying paths that started together from a shared Enlightenment and protocapitalistic matrix. France, Germany, Italy, and the whole of the European West on one side, for which, already from the mid-eighteenth century, that idea would begin to be identified with the experience of class struggle and its prevalent political and cultural forms—that of socialism and Marxism. On the other side, the United States, where the word "socialism" would never really enter the political lexicon, but where the only equality conceived by their culture was made to coincide with the genuine fulfillment of their democracy. Between the two lay England: closer to the French and German side than to the American one, but with a completely specific variant of its own.

Class Struggle

In Europe, after 1848 and the end of the Restoration, the spread of the Industrial Revolution was shifting the propulsive centers of the national economies—above all in England, in northern France, and in Germany along the Rhine and the North Sea—from the countryside to the cities, where the establishment of big factory systems and the settling of large masses of workers had completely transformed the urban landscapes in comparison to the previous century.

Becoming more clearly delineated were what we have just described as the class profiles of the new societies: the first in history for which it is possible to use this formula appropriately. In the absence of a mobility even distantly comparable to America's, fundamental social distinctions, determined by the capitalist economy and inscribed, unlike what was happening in the United States, in contexts already stratified by previous hierarchies, acquired features that rigidified them into enduring morphologies. Environments in which the new divisions—operating for the first time in their full force—overlapped and blended with barriers and distinctions consolidated over centuries. Paris between Stendhal and Proust, or the London of Engels and Marx—or, if we wish, of Dickens and Trollope—offer a very vivid and realistic picture of this teeming social and mental interweaving of old and new.

I just said: for the first time. I am convinced, in fact, that the arbitrary dilatation of the paradigm of classes and their (eventual) forms of consciousness, to the point of making it a kind of universal key for historical interpretation, has been (and remains) one of the worst failures that the absorbing of a simplified Marxism has produced in twentieth-century Western culture. A mess that prevented one of the most radical novelties in European history from being grasped for what it was: the specifically capitalist birth, in this part of the world alone, of authentic class societies.

This configuration—if we do not simply give "class" a generic and metaphorical meaning that sweeps away any rigorous definition in terms of social analysis—pertains in fact to only some of the societies arising from the Industrial Revolution, and is limited to their history alone. All the more so as "class struggle," which in certain respects was a great generator of almost two centuries of European events, identifies a specific model of conflict and collective subjectivity, the scheme of which cannot be transposed outside its historic times and places: neither back into the past (ancient or medieval, for example), nor forward (to include the present, for example).[229] Still less can we dilate it in a spatial sense. Part of Asia has always been outside it, to say nothing of almost all of Africa, and of the particular position of America itself—whose peculiarity we have already spoken of and to which we will return.

The history of the idea of equality between the nineteenth and twentieth centuries is, on the European side, indissolubly linked to this specificity: the birth, however integrated within the frame of previous formations, of societies constructed entirely on the basis of relationships of conflictual cooperation between capital and labor—and hence marked by the class struggle that developed in particularly complex contexts.

The novelty we are describing entails a drastic change of scenario for our story. The idea of equality, which had already become a prominent political issue thanks to Enlightenment thought and the revolutions in America and France, and which in the United States, by becoming entwined with a new republican form, had led to the most democratic material—and not just formal—constitution ever produced, was now once again transformed in Europe, taking on the appearance of a great social question capable of involving entire peoples.

It became, as had never happened before, a theme linked to the centrality of labor—especially working-class labor—for the recognition of its dignity and its rights: often raised with a view to radically changing the whole of society. The expansion of capitalistic organization broadened in a proportional manner the productive bases of the most developed national economies—in England, but also in France, in Germany, in the Low Countries—and this rendered manual labor, for the first time in history, a mass phenomenon, the dimensions, importance, and visibility of which were clear to all.

Worker cooperation in the main industrial plants, made necessary by increasingly advanced production techniques, created a new tight-knit, pervasive, and compact sociality that went beyond the factory walls and became the constitutive element of previously unseen models of ethics and life, and of a working culture marked more and more by class consciousness.

Equality—which the final phase of the French Revolution had already transformed, though ephemerally, into a relatively widespread sentiment—became almost naturally a banner for this new sensibility. Ever broader demands by workers and rural peasants, fueled by the bitterness of labor relations not mediated by American democratic counterbalances, was turning it into an idea-force capable of orienting and mobilizing almost unlimited energies, both through new socialist-inspired parties and thanks to the consolidation of the first union organizations. This situation would persist, through many changes, until the final decades of the twentieth century.

Equality, in short, was becoming the ideological icon of the contrasts, but also of the capacity for emancipation, liberation, and social struggle of an entire epoch. In the harshness of the conflicts, its dual profile, which in the European setting now had a consolidated tradition behind it—equality in rights, and equality (or less inequality) in wealth and social standing—often blended together. And the conflict pursued in its name took on the character—more generic and more radical—of the struggle for an overall emancipation of the subaltern classes, for the emergence from a position of inferiority in which ancient exclusions were interwoven with more recent subordinations.

❈ ❈ ❈

There is no doubt that the marked economic liberalism which characterized European countries following the Industrial Revolution strongly encouraged both the radicalization of the labor question and a development based on profit margins such as to generously finance the growing technological innovations associated with the use of machines.[230] A self-propulsive and expansive circuit with very high social costs was set into motion, the features of which would soon become familiar.

It is always difficult to identify regularities in the course of history, and there is often the risk of falling prey to sometimes glaring tricks of perspective. Yet if we compare the early phases of the European industrial takeoff with the much more recent ones of the great technological transformation that, in the final part of the twentieth century, put an end in the West to the epoch of big factory systems and paved the way for deindustrialization and the new economy, an unignorable symmetry emerges: between the original lack of political restrictions in which the capitalist impetus of the time operated, and the return, at the end of the twentieth century, of a no less powerful, and entirely unexpected, neo-liberalist wave.

It is as if, in order to come about and take root, both technological leaps needed a shared and peculiar lack of restrictions externally imposed by politics, compared to the autoinduced tendencies of the economic process. Freedom translated inevitably into a lack of protection of the weakest subjects, on whom the cost of the transformation fell almost entirely on both occasions. Then it was the newly formed working classes; now it is the many who are excluded from the rarefied and fleeting world of the new jobs producing immaterial commodities with a high technological and financial density.

It is in any case incontrovertible that throughout the nineteenth century the European working masses—in England, France, Germany, Austria, then later in Italy and Spain—paid a very high price for the capitalistic modernization of this part of the world. Their capillary exploitation—whose indispensability with respect to the overall functioning of the system has always been, from the point of view of economic theory, an open issue (we shall return to it)—was, in historic terms, a painful truth that has been amply documented and proven. Whole generations carried the signs of it for their entire existence.

Against such a background the idea of equality became indissolubly tied to the class struggle—we can now use this expression in its proper sense—that had turned into one of the motors of the continent's history, at the center of a long sequence of events commencing with the insurrections of 1848 and culminating in the October Revolution of 1917 and the subsequent establishment of communism in Russia. The latter brought to an end the age of revolutions in Europe and in turn had a dual epilogue. First with the death of Lenin in 1924; and then, almost seventy years later, with the collapse of the Soviet Union in 1991.

This whole season was largely conditioned, perhaps even dominated, by the hegemonic presence of an explosive new theory presented as a genuine doctrine of equality, completely different from anything previously seen. A thinking that would take on a role of absolute importance in the events of a century at least, confirmation (to reiterate the point once again) of the crushing weight of philosophy in the history of Europe. A system of ideas that seemed able to weld together—as never before—facts and concepts, science and passions, Being and Ought, and which spread rapidly around the world, offering a formidable backbone above all for the European socialist movements and then those of the entire planet. A philosophy that we are forgetting, but which impacted the history of the world in a way unprecedented for any form of thought—except Christianity—profoundly modifying its perspective and features.

To try to understand, it is necessary to go back and look at where it all started: at the reflection of its undisputed founder. At the heart of the studies of Marx.

※ ※ ※

We can consider that thought to be the greatest intellectual epic of modern labor—of industrial mass labor—ever conceived. A kind of extraordinary cathedral in honor of what Marx regarded, probably rightly, as the absolute protagonist of modernity: a judgment whose precedents we have seen surfacing, one after another—the increasingly pressing theme had already been in the air for some time—against the background of the gradual establishment of the capitalist economy in Europe through to the English industrial takeoff. A motif that had passed from Renaissance thought to Locke, to the classical economists, to Rousseau, to Hegel's affirmations from the *Phenomenology* to the *Philosophy of Right*.

But Marx completely changed the horizon of vision compared to every predecessor, because he considered the protagonism claimed for modern labor as a disavowed and betrayed primacy; a protagonism in chains, as it were: and not due to the perfidy of human beings, but the objective laws of history. The task he set himself in his research was therefore to reestablish the truth, an indispensable condition if the human labor constructing the modern world—that for which "the wealth of societies in which the capitalist mode of production prevails appears as 'an immense collection of commodities'" (the celebrated incipit of *Capital*)—was to break its bonds and take the place it was due, and that was made for it alone.

His theory of equality was therefore also a theory of liberation, and was linked to a kind of palingenesis, of reestablished superiority. It was intended to be the theory of labor, which finally rediscovered itself.

❉ ❉ ❉

Let's start from a fact that is often denied or concealed, though it might at first sight appear paradoxical.[231] Marx was never a political scientist or theorist. A huge distance separated him from Machiavelli or Hobbes, for whom politics was everything; as it did from Rousseau or Tocqueville, or even from Gramsci.

That does not mean he did not contribute important reflections on the topic: sometimes short, penetrating notes; in other cases, long pages of analysis, for example in the brilliant *Eighteenth Brumaire of Louis Bonaparte,* which opens with the famous comment about history repeating itself twice, the first time "as tragedy," the second "as farce."[232] But politics—the great magnetic field that attracted so many great minds interested in capturing the secret of its forms, rules, and dynamics—never truly interested him as an independent object of study. His mind, more than seeing it, continually went through it, like stepping through a wraith: an attitude which (as we shall see) had its own reasoning and would be dense with consequences. In some moments of his life, he tried to practice it directly, rather than thinking it: without any great success, in truth, but that is another matter. His intelligence chose to focus on different objects: logic and metaphysics; economics, naturally; history, above all.

And yet Marx's success was first of all—and it could not have been otherwise—sensationally and intensely political. For almost a century his image summed up the ideological iconography of the age, and it appeared almost impossible to disassociate the name and the teaching of the exile from Trier from the passions, rhetoric, arms, and blood—that too—of large masses of women and men engaged in a struggle from one end of the planet to the other.

This singular asymmetry has always created serious problems for Marxists. And in their best years, many of them—Engels and Lenin to the fore—devoted a great deal of energy to trying to fill the lacuna and to attribute a fully rounded body of political thought to the master, in harmony with his theory (at least as it appeared to them) and above all compatible with what in the meantime was happening in the world. This effort was particularly prolonged and perspicacious in France and Italy, where it continued until the second half of the twentieth century and engaged some remarkable minds.

In reality, with his silence Marx behaved in a perfectly consistent way. And the political fortune that his thinking would enjoy was entirely understandable, without adding a jot to his writings. From his youthful years through to his final texts, these had in fact developed according to a very particular and totally original project.

His work was always conceived by the author as the only possible path not just to a scientific understanding of historic reality, but above all to its direct transformation. An instrument at once of knowledge and action: just as the natural sciences had become for the physical world after Bacon and Descartes. Essentially, a weapon, in its own way intrinsically and powerfully political, without the need for further steps. The *Manifesto of the Communist Party* was composed wholly in this conviction. It was intended as an explosively political document—the ringing announcement of a new science of society and of history with the ability to change the destiny of the human race—but it did not present itself in the slightest as an essay on political theory.

Marx had himself already said so, right from 1845, in his unmistakable way, at once impassioned and concise, in a text that would soon become famous and which was known as the *Eleventh Thesis on Feuerbach*: "The philosophers have only *interpreted* the world in different ways; [but] the point is to *change* it."[233] To understand, then, in order to change; expressed differently, to be capable of producing and putting into play a transformative knowledge.

The connection would appear with the same intensity—albeit from a very different perspective—around half a century later, at the foundation of Freud's analytic framework: in his case, to understand in order to cure. For both, it was the final end point of classical philosophy from Kant to Hegel. The same one that would return—in a perspective changed once more—concealed at the heart of theoretical physics in Germany at the beginning of the twentieth century, from the Einstein of special relativity to the Heisenberg of the uncertainty principle: nothing is known that is not changed by the very act of knowledge. Subterranean traces of the most powerful nucleus of classic German philosophy.

* * *

How did Marx believe he could indicate the way to transform the world?

His conviction started from a fixed notion. Politics on its own, in the ways that had been tried until then, which had found their democratic highpoint in the French Revolution, had proven utterly incapable in the face of the task, whatever its aims and programs. There was nothing for it but to acknowledge this failure once and for all.

It was therefore necessary to go beyond the horizon of its movements and figures, and to appeal to something more solid and compact. The modern world had made it a trap: the pure reflection—admittedly precise, given the ability to decipher it—of a reality that stood behind it and which, remaining within its borders, it was never possible to touch, far less to change. The first thing to do, then, was to unmask this condition of subalternity and distance, and fully grasp it.

Marx's mistrust was total and included the rejection—but I should say contempt—of any form of heroic subjectivism, even the most noble, and which opened a chasm with respect to the choices made by every kind of Jacobinism, under whatever guise it appeared. Movements hopelessly doomed to end badly in the blind exaltation of the omnipotence of revolutionary will, mystified as being capable of overcoming any obstacle through the simple accumulation of ethical tension. In a word, in the pointless adventure of Robespierre.

Against them, Marx never tired of asserting the insuperable hardness of facts—social relations, the physical production of wealth and the power of the forces determining it, the tendential regularities of history, as heavy as rocks: in short, what would be called his original and harsh realism.

The possibility of transforming the world and making it a world of equals had to be sought elsewhere. There was the need for a genuine cognitive leap: toward a peculiar strategy of analysis, where different strands of knowledge could be combined, capable of piecing together what capitalistic modernity had deliberately broken, separating the earth of the economy from the sky of law and politics. A state of affairs that Marx saw mirrored with extraordinary acuteness in Hegelian philosophy, which he engaged with throughout his life, in an attempt to give the revolutionary perspective an objective, scientific, and irresistible impulse.

This was the core reason that prevented him from becoming a political theorist: for him science could not be constructed from what was just appearance, a separate and deceptive space: an alternation of abstract forms imprisoned by contents and determinations that controlled them from afar, without ever joining together with them. "Political life in the modern sense is the Scholasticism of popular life," he wrote in his *Critique of Hegel's 'Philosophy of Right,'* composed between 1841 and 1843 but only published in 1927. And just after he added: "The abstraction of the state as such belongs only to modern times because the abstraction of private life belongs only to modern times. The abstraction of the political state is a modern product."[234] Modernity, then, condemned politics in the very moment in which it constituted it as a separate sphere around the abstraction of the state.

Paradoxically, the more a political result was sought, the sooner it was necessary to abandon that treacherous field, in which the "view" cannot be concrete when its *object* is "abstract." And right then—Marx thought—the occasion was presenting itself for the first time (in him, as in Hegel, there was this glaring overestimation of his present).

The social and intellectual developments of the time made it possible—he believed—to conduct revealing research. To open a new chapter in human knowledge, able not only to render visible the authentic reality of capitalist societies—the backbone of modernity: in this he was not mistaken—and to bring to light that anatomy already glimpsed, but in an apologetic manner, from Hegel to Ricardo, but above all to decipher their destiny. Which, sooner or later, would be to disintegrate, destroyed by the irreconcilable antagonisms produced ever more devastatingly and unstoppably by the course of their own development. Over the ashes of the old system a new world could then be built, the perfect and complete overturning of the previous order: a solidaristic society of the free and equal.

To this new science, to the critique of political economy, as he decided to call it, echoing Kant, Marx devoted his entire life. In his perspective, every exclusively political horizon had gone. He believed that he was expressing a doctrine that presented itself, at one and the same time, as a scientific description of the capitalist reality and as a no less grounded prediction of its overcoming.

An analysis capable of demonstrating how the social character of wealth production—which was concentrating ever vaster masses of men and women in the workplace, creating a dense network of ties between them but constraining them at the same time within a lacerated and subaltern condition, expropriating a decisive part of their labor time—inevitably ended up clashing with the opposing private nature—economically dominant, though increasingly restricted and socially asphyxiated—of the means by which wealth was produced, above all capital.

"At a certain stage of development"—he wrote in the preface to *A Contribution to the Critique of Political Economy* of 1859, "the material productive forces of society come into conflict with the existing relations of production or—this merely expresses the same thing in legal terms—with the property relations within the framework of which they have operated hitherto. From forms of development of the productive forces these relations turn into their fetters. Then begins an era of social revolution."[235]

The capitalist form of production, beyond a certain historic moment, would no longer have had any functional reason to exist, except to preserve worker exploitation: and hence a bourgeois privilege that, "at a certain stage," would lack any positive role. The contradiction it expressed—and which, as it were, put society head down ("in this form of production everything appears upended")—would lead to the symmetrical overturning of its elements: with the producers—the workers—finally in a dominant position, ending with the complete disappearance of the private ownership of means of production, and of the class—the bourgeoisie—upon which it was founded.[236] "No social order is ever destroyed before all the productive forces for which it is sufficient have been developed, and new superior relations of production never replace older ones before the material conditions for their existence have matured within the framework of the old society," we read, again in the preface to the *Critique*.[237] The problem, then, was not political, but one of historic development, and of a scientific critique of the capitalist economy.

His theory of equality, therefore, had a wholly historic-economic, not political, nucleus. At the heart of the capitalist way of producing was a structurally unequal exchange: between labor and salary, the dissymmetry of which permitted bourgeois profit. To overturn its functioning meant reuniting workers to the entirety of their labor and its products, which had been taken away, "alienated,"[238] at the very moment in which they agreed to grant their labor-power as a commodity like any other.

In the first book of *Capital*, while illustrating—in relation to the American Civil War—the difference between the slave's labor and that of the free worker, Marx wrote:

> In slave labour, even the part of the working day in which the slave is only replacing the value of his own means of subsistence, in which he therefore actually works for himself alone, appears as labour for his master. All his labour appears as unpaid labour. In wage-labour, on the contrary, even surplus labour, or unpaid labor, appears as paid. In the one case, the property-relation conceals the slave's labour for himself; in the other case the money-relation [i.e., the wage] conceals the uncompensated labour of the wage-labourer.[239]

To set up his comparison, Marx employed the concept of surplus labor, the difference, that is, between the overall quantity of labor supplied by the worker over a given time, and the quantity contained in the commodities consumed by the worker in the same period, both as wages and in other ways.

There is no need here to recap the debate about the relationship between this analysis and the so-called theory of value (the exchange relations between commodities, in a balanced market, are equal to the relations between the amount of labor contained in the commodities themselves), nor to return to the uncertain possibility of scientifically demonstrating the structural existence of a "capitalist exploitation."[240] It will suffice to reaffirm that for Marx all production revolved around a fundamental inequality, concealed by the formal parity of the exchange. Without cancelling this primary imbalance, labor could not be reconnected with the subjects who had provided it, and no equality could come about, if not through the construction of false appearances—exactly the task of modern politics. The theory of equality coincided, then, with the science that revealed the actual functioning of capitalist society, unmasking its fallacies and deceptions.

❋ ❋ ❋

How was the turn toward communism to be achieved?

In truth, Marx never gave the matter much attention. He possessed a utopian and visionary streak, fueled by different sources: Enlightenment traditions, buried echoes of early German Romanticism, perhaps even traces of genuine Jewish prophetism. There are pages describing the future—anticipating communism—that are incomprehensible without supposing a complex intersecting of influences. I believe however that he was acutely aware of the treachery of such terrain, and the risks of an attraction that would have led him, if he pursued it to its end, far away from the certainties of scientific reasoning (or what he considered to be such). And I believe that this tension between a truth that he saw as being linked to the study of the concrete capitalistic present alone, and the temptation to represent a tomorrow that already appeared half visible, upside down, in the signs of today—a kind of unresolved polarity between criticism and prophecy—is one of the most important codes of his writing.

There would of course (he predicted) be a phase of transition dominated by open conflict between the classes in the struggle: with a proletariat strong enough to firmly grasp the reins of the initiative, and a bourgeoisie in difficulty but not yet defeated. And it is in this context that he speaks—in truth in a very brief passage—of a "revolutionary dictatorship of the proletariat": a phrase exaggeratedly gnawed at by critics, at the foundation of innumerable subsequent theoretical constructions—and unfortunately not just theoretical—to which history would later give a sinister meaning, associating it by antonomasia with the years of Stalin.[241]

But they are just a few pointers that did not occupy Marx's reflections at length. And it is understandable—to him they must have seemed details of modest significance. Without a doubt, the transition would not be pain free: he linked it to a physical conflict as well, probably with Germany in mind, or France. How could he really have imagined otherwise, just after the bloody repression that had put an end to the Paris Commune, a few decades after 1848, and less than a century on from the Terror?

At any rate, if he really had to look to the future, he preferred to direct his gaze further ahead: to the first construction of the new society, with the gradual dissolution of the bourgeois state and law (to be clear, the ones theorized from Hobbes to Montesquieu), the functions of which would be reabsorbed by the collectivity of producers able to regulate themselves, where "all the springs of cooperative wealth flow more abundantly," and the quantification and distribution of labor would take place on the basis of a kind of social keeping of "accounts" (he uses precisely this word in *Capital*), and democracy and economy would finally come together again.[242] A definitively recomposed way of life would be established, a perfect and harmonic universality of equals: it was the return of Eden. It was communism.

Thinking in this way, Marx reproduced—probably without even being aware of it—distant scenarios, with even folkloristic backgrounds. The image of the fullness of the times as the result of a total overturning of the existing order, of the opulence associated with a complete shake-up of the world, did in fact have remote origins in European culture, in an overlapping of places and traditions, and with jumbled layers of both popular and much more refined motifs. But he managed to regenerate it, placing it beneath an (apparent) light of modern scientificalness with such force as to render it almost unrecognizable. And even when he seemed to be abandoning himself to the pleasure of a pure visionary fantasy, his intellectual self-control immediately brought him back toward other poles: and precisely in places where it might be said that he was alluding in a less guarded way to the future of communism, he succeeded in producing some of the most acutely perceptive pages on the relationship between legal equality and social inequality, among the most penetrating ever written on this topic.

* * *

Communist society would function without state and without politics. For Marx this deduction was in some way necessary, and an indispensable condition for the achievement of equality. Those two figures were just the reflection of the capitalistic division of labor and of the class structure of the modern world, which required a rigid separation between "civil society" and the sphere of the state, as Hegel had conclusively demonstrated (at least in Marx's reading). The tasks that they performed related solely to this contrived fracture. With the advent of communism, it would inevitably be overcome.

In a recomposed social universe, there would be no reason to distinguish "citizens" and "producers"; politics and economy. We would only encounter—if I can put it like this—whole human figures, reintegrated into the totality of their natural and historic essence: with complete freedom as regards their needs and gratifications, previously violated continually by capitalistic deformations.

In this regenerated environment, politics would serve little purpose. And for a simple reason: the new communist production of wealth, no longer imprisoned by old abstractions—commodity, money, state: forms with functions of dominance—would suffice to harmoniously hold up all of society, without the obligation to resort to successive mediations, to the artifices of any legal construction.[243] We would enter the realm of immediacy and concreteness: but not as happened in primitive life, or in Rousseauian fantasies of the good savage. But rather as the outcome of a hard and tiring civilizing journey that had experienced the frozen wastes of formalism and abstraction (I am stealing an image that Theodor Adorno takes from Benjamin) and had managed to traverse them, joining together in a higher synthesis—communism—humanism and technology, productive power and economic and social equality.[244]

We come now to the crucial juncture.

The assumption of the entire analysis was that there existed—or better, that there could exist, if certain conditions were realized—an

economic form (in the original language: a combination between production relations and productive forces) antithetical to the capitalist
world, capable of spontaneously and virtuously creating and maintaining, without the resort to any political intervention, the most complete and substantive equality among human beings. And that all this
should happen in an exactly specular manner with respect to "bourgeois"
societies, where the economic cycle, once set in motion, reproduced in a
similarly spontaneous but perverse way just exploitation and inequality.
The magnetism of this symmetry—the image of a total overturning—
dominated the whole of Marx's thinking.

It was a completely implausible hypothesis, though: on the current
state of our knowledge—both historic and theoretical—an evident and
glaring mistake.

It indicated the point where the validity of much of the critique directed at the capitalist reality of his time turned into the unrealism of
prophecy. We shall return to this shortly. But first we must say that it
was Marx's absolute faith in the scientific correctness of his analysis that
made it entirely pointless in his eyes to have a (political) doctrine of democracy in the perspective of communism.

This omission—which, viewed from outside, even seems paradoxical
in someone who had made democracy taken to its extreme consequences
his very raison d'être—was not a problem for him. It was the obvious
consequence of a viewpoint judged to be scientifically impeccable.

In fact, there could be no other possibilities. Either democracy assumed its bourgeois guise, parliamentary and representative, let's say
of the English kind (Marx did not consider America, as we shall see, despite talking of the United States as the "most modern form of bourgeois
society");[245] and thus could not be anything other than a deception, because concealed beneath the false appearance of formal equality (legal
and political) lay economic exploitation and social inequality; and so any
theory of it would have ended up being grist to the mill of a colossal
fraud. Or it was achieved in the only true way, the communist one: but
here too its attainment had no need of a separate theory. In this case, it
would finally acquire flesh and blood, becoming, so to speak, substantive, within an economic regime that would produce it in an entirely
spontaneous manner, developing it among individuals already made

equal by the fact of their all being, in the same way, producers with full mastery over themselves, and completely free citizens.

There remained the phase of transition: of the open passage from one way of producing and living to the other. But Marx imagined it as being relatively brief, and at any rate determined by the maturity of the capitalist crisis and the circumstances of the moment. Clearly, he believed, it would in any case be a period of struggle, violent even (he mentions weapons: and nothing suggests it was a metaphor).[246] In that phase, the problem would not be to guarantee democracy (and of what kind?), but to win, and quickly, in the name of a revolution that, for the first time in history, would have the reasons of science on its side, besides those of justice and passion.

Unfortunately, this deduction had no legs either, exactly like the idea on which it rested. What is more, both—the economy of equality and communist democracy as its inevitable result—constituted a disastrous sequence. The failure they were heading toward—serious and irremediable—would give rise to the start of the catastrophe.

Historicity and Metaphysics

Marx chose to stake everything on the dramatic divarication between the two paradigms of equality that he inherited from the European philosophical tradition, obtained by juxtaposing, as it were, Hegel with the English thinkers and Rousseau. On one hand a formal equality, merely legal and political, which reproduced in its separate abstractions (law, the state) the truly abstract character of capitalist societies (equality as a central category in the capitalist abstraction of money and commodity). On the other—without there being any possible connection between the two moments—a substantive and effective equality, determined not by politics and rights, but by the communist economy.

The second of these—the one that really counted—could not be achieved via the path of political decision, tried in vain during the French Revolution, but could only be obtained as the necessary and happy outcome of a complete overturning of the productive process. An event that could be realized, in turn, in specific historic conditions: not invented by the temerity of revolutionary leaders, but scientifically ascertained in the material reality of capitalist development.

What pushed him in this direction?

Once again, we are back where we had already arrived. Underpinning everything was Marx's absolute conviction that there existed—that there could exist—an economy of equality opposite and symmetrical to the intrinsically and irremediably unequal economy of exploitation and alienation distinguishing capitalist production; and that, once established, it could succeed in functioning without forgoing any of the conquests of industrial modernity: indeed, that it was the only one that could enable unlimited development. In other words, that it was possible to build an economic form able to generate equality from within its own dynamics; from the bottom up; and without slipping into any primitivist reveries (no Rousseauian reconquered "state of nature"), but, on the contrary, as the sole solution for fully achieving the productive power of modern times.

In the new reality, the functions of the state would be completely incorporated into the intrinsically democratic framework of the communistic production process: and while awaiting that moment, the critique of the capitalist economy could already occupy the place taken away from it by the bourgeois theory of politics.

The entire construction was the result of Marx's long and fascinating game of intellectual chess with Hegelian logic (recently discussed in a short but invaluable book by Biagio de Giovanni), to the point of becoming trapped in a relationship between ontology and history that completely pressed the latter down onto the former; and imagining therefore to be able to deduce the historic plausibility of a whole social universe, sustaining it solely on the correctness of a figure of Hegel's "objective logic": the negative of capitalist alienation and its unequal exchange which, overturned, was transformed into the positive of the communist recomposition.[247]

Despite appearances, it was still metaphysics, and not historic thought: grand metaphysics, up there with Spinoza and Hegel, beneath the garb of materialistic laws of historic development. And what we have already pointed to in Hegel as a problematic relationship between ontology and history, between metaphysics and present, became, in Marx, the acceptance of an industrialist utopia put on stage as the final completion of civilization.

The groundlessness of this passage stripped Marx's predictions of all credibility. It dug a definitive furrow between the truth of the critique and the implausibility of the prophecy.

❋ ❋ ❋

At the root of everything lies a crucial misunderstanding, historical and not theoretical. Marx imagined that factory labor—of the capitalist factory he could see, which already foreshadowed Fordism and Taylorism—was, from a social and technological point of view, an already perfected form destined to last limitlessly. He projected its presence into an undetermined future, as the only possible model of all modern labor. Outside it was nothing but Rousseau's fancies.

For him it was the linchpin—solid in its immutable nature—upon which the whole of society was to have pivoted in its revolutionary subversion and was to have constructed the world of communism. What had to change were the social and economic relations that lay around it—surplus value, exploitation, commodities, money—not the material conditions and the structure of its existence. This was fixed in a definitively established scheme: great masses of human beings clustered around ever more complex systems of machines; in short, the England of his own time, as he himself explicitly stated in the preface to the first edition of *Capital* in 1867:

> The physicist either observes natural processes where they occur in their most significant form, and are least affected by disturbing influences, or, wherever possible, he makes experiments under conditions which ensure that the process will occur in its pure state. What I have to examine in this work is the capitalist mode of production, and the relations of production and forms of intercourse that correspond to it. Until now, their locus classicus has been England.[248]

That such a combination between human beings and machines assumed the demoniacal features of a total expropriation of workers, or instead became the occasion for the free growth of personalities and minds in the now liberated and communist world, depended solely on the configuration of the economic and social relations built around them. Marx repeated this continually: capital is a social relation, not a thing: "political economy . . . is not technology."[249] It is not identified with machines as such, far less with the physical reality of the factory and of the worker's labor:

> The historical conditions of its [capital's] existence are by no means given with the mere circulation of money and commodities. It arises only when the owner of the means of production and subsistence finds the free worker available, on the market, as the seller of his own labour-power. And this one historical pre-condition comprises a world's history. Capital, therefore, announces from the outset a new epoch in the process of social production.[250]

The critique of political economy and the science of history thus blended together into one form of knowledge, the real key to understanding the present.

For anyone familiar with his thought, it never ceases to be striking how on a number of occasions Marx was on the point of taking the fatal step, which would have enabled him to grasp the whole precariousness—or at least the extreme relativity—of his notion of communism. At various points we find exceptionally acute observations about the infinite resources of science and technology as productive and social forces capable of transforming from within

> the creation of real wealth [which] comes to depend less on labour time and on the amount of labour employed than on the power of the agencies set in motion during labour time, whose 'powerful effectiveness' is itself in turn out of all proportion to the direct labour time spent on their production, but depends rather on the general state of science and on the progress of technology, or the application of this science to production.[251]

He seems to be a hair's breadth away from intuiting the abyss that opened up just after. If things were like that, the worker's labor could not be considered the unshakable pillar around which the history of the world revolved: indeed, in a more or less distant future, it ran the risk of literally melting away into nothing. So the very idea of communism—that presupposed its total pervasiveness, and, what is more, in the form existing at a particular historic moment—could not hold up, revealing what it really was: just the fanciful overturning of the contingent reality of the factories of early capitalistic production; a utopia linked to the age of the initial establishment of large-scale machine industry.

But Marx always stopped. He sensed that the increasing rise of the technological threshold would relegate workers' living labor to no more than a secondary role in the ways of creating wealth. However, from it he drew a completely contradictory and ungrounded deduction: that the growth beyond a certain limit of the productivity of labor was the final point of capitalist development, and that any more could only be obtained by exceeding its limit; but without ever doubting the unmodifiable permanence of an industrial structure entirely similar to what he had just seen taking shape before his eyes.

The universality of the working class thus remained an untouchable fact for him: he did not see it as being at risk from technological transformations despite intuiting their magnitude. That the very centrality of the factory—as it was configured in his time—was just a phenomenon, albeit grandiose, destined sooner or later to disappear socially and technologically in the most advanced countries, and that the whole system of large-scale industry represented just a transitory phase in capitalist development, never appeared to Marx as a conclusion already implicit in the most powerful pages of his own analysis.

Thus immobilized, working-class labor was transformed into something similar to an ontological category: the foundation—metaphysical, or metahistorical—of communist society.

We can therefore grasp the origin and degree of plausibility of what would prove to be the most disastrous of his thoughts: the idea of an economy of equality, of an equality that was finally to become substantive in the world of producers, without the need for political mediations. It was the imaginary—and entirely unjustified—outcome of the socialization of labor, of the material uniformity induced by co-operation between workers, of their productive community, rendered universal by the growth of development itself—but no longer with capitalist dominion and the unequal exchange on which this was founded. No longer with anything looming large to distort and crush them. Free, finally to acquire their form: that of self-government and democracy.

Marx projected in this way the material conditions dictated by large-scale machine industry into an aura of necessity and irreversible definitiveness, as a point of arrival of history. He was unable to conceive of any other productive activity and described communist society as an unlimited extension of the factory structure, entirely gathered together in its shadow. He pictured, in an entirely fictitious way, a one-dimensional social universe generated solely by worker cooperation: his idea of equality betrayed a simplification that sought to exalt but actually distorted the sense of modernity. It was the pure projection onto the social plane of the automatic seriality of the barely established capitalist production: a concept that smelled of coal and steam. Industrialist metaphysics and egalitarian utopia—scientistic positivism and revolutionary mythology—bound together in a single embrace.

* * *

Without a doubt it is only the weight of history and the knowledge of what would happen later—the irresistible force of hindsight—that makes our criticism conclusive. Only by having witnessed the decline of working-class labor in the West during a transformation comparable to the Industrial Revolution itself can we truly grasp how deceptive Marx's perspective is. He could not have known it yet—at least in these terms; nor could he have anticipated a century of history. And we must also acknowledge that as long as working-class labor remained at the center of capitalistic production, his hypothesis did seem able to hold up.

This does not however detract from the fact that his hyperevaluation of the factory system and the associated working class, transmuted from historically determined reality to fixed motors not subject to any change, contained, already in relation to his own times and even to the most advanced strands of his thinking—"that knew no other science than history"—something hopelessly disconnected and forced.[252]

I would describe it as an arrest of historicity in the face of class: a consequence of the overturning (imagined as a definitive point of arrival) of the relationship between life and forms, between living labor and the abstraction of capital, which Marx had placed at the center of his analysis, and perhaps also, if de Giovanni is correct, as the result of an intermittence—of a point of obscurity—in his interpretation of Hegel.[253] Almost as if the moral requirement to redeem the working-class condition from the extreme harshness imposed by capitalist production in Europe in the second half of the nineteenth century (and how can we deny that this was justified?) pushed him to transfigure it into a kind of universal principle of salvation of the human race (workers who, by freeing themselves, freed the whole world): like in a sort of announced secular resurrection, following the capitalist crucifixion—once again, a ruinous slide from critique into prophecy.

That is not all. Pursuing the same thread, it can be said that the belief in the overthrow of the capitalist system, immediately giving rise to an opposite world, was also once more nothing but another metaphysical hypothesis. Concealed within it was the persuasion that the overturning of bourgeois society was not just a possible event in history, but that it must carry genetically inscribed within it—simply by virtue of its coming into being—the whole reality of a new world, already ordered and composed. In other words: that the form of the movement—the dialectic of overthrowal—could transmute directly into the substance of the now-reversed thing; that the negation already carried with it all the determinations of the positive destroyed by overturning it. The same danger that Hegel had circled around time and time again, but without falling into it completely.

It suffices merely to evoke the ghost of real history—of any hypothetical European history between the nineteenth and twentieth century—for a gulf to open up straightaway between the transition described by Marx and any plausible prefiguration of the facts. How would it have been possible to reduce to the scheme of a single simultaneous overthrowing—however disruptive—all the historic and social complexity of any European nation, in Germany, France, Italy, or even in England? How was it conceivable that a single event would be enough to bring about an irresistible and automatic socialization of all power from the bottom up, capable of rapidly overcoming any obstacle?

Nor is it any good objecting that the perspective was not intended to represent a future history, but merely to fix the paradigm of a turn: to build a model of revolution, not to anticipate the concreteness of a scenario. Even in this case, it should have been evident just how problematic the relationship was between the new socialized economy and the construction of an institutional framework capable of supporting it.

The fact is that, for Marx, this junction did not exist at all. Or rather, it did not exist outside of a complete identification between the two elements in play: the communist economy was already a politics and a constitution—that of democracy and equality. It incorporated a state within it. And it is precisely the figure of this identity—I was about to say mystic—that betrayed its prophetic background.

A prisoner of his own hypothesis, Marx condemned himself to an iron determinism when speaking about communism. And it is almost incredible that it was precisely him—who in his analysis of the societies of his age and their prior vicissitudes managed to avoid any mechanicism, and to take account with great acumen of the inexhaustible imagination of history—who forgot everything in an instant when picturing the communist future. No alternative possibility would be given in it. There would be no space for any variable. The economy self-regulated by producers would in any case have delineated the highway—which would also have been the only possible one.

* * *

One other and very important thing did not add up in Marx's prediction.

He took it for granted that individuality was the dominant form of the human in his time. "Individuals producing in a society, and hence the socially determined production of individuals, is of course the point of departure," he wrote at the beginning of the *Introduction* of 1857. Before adding, soon after:

The further back we trace the course of history, the more does the individual, and accordingly also the producing individual, appear to be dependent and to belong to a larger whole. At first, the individual in a still quite natural manner is part of the family and of the tribe which evolves from the family; later he is part of a community, of one of the different forms of the community which arise from the conflict and the merging of tribes. It is not until the eighteenth century that in bourgeois society the various forms of the social texture confront the individual as merely means towards his private ends, as external necessity. But the epoch which produces this standpoint, namely that of the solitary individual, is precisely the epoch of the (as yet) most highly developed social (according to this standpoint, general) relations.[254]

And what is this "solitary individual"—the "bourgeois" point of arrival of a millenary history? It is a figure that, while recognizing the presence of the universal within it—the presence of God according to the Christian Hegelian tradition well known to Marx—could not, while the private, namely, capitalist, nature of production, and the "nonshared" quality of labor persisted, have relations with others if not through produced things and their value as commodities, and hence only through the abstractness of their labor.

But if this framework were shattered, and the labor of each person became, having gone beyond the capitalist organization, "shared labor," a simple part of overall social labor—that of a communist society—their situation would change. They would finally be able to recognize themselves as being integrated into a whole ("where work is shared, the relations between men in social production are not represented as 'value' of 'things'").[255] They would be able to recognize the universal within and around themselves, without being constrained to project it into the kingdom of heaven (according to Christianity: the essence of the human being is God), or to discover it only in the face of Hegel's state (the earthly place of achieved reconciliation).

Marx does not seem to realize that this mundane and direct reappropriation of the universal would have required a change that could not just concern relations of production, just the world of labor, no matter how crucial this was. It would have involved casting into doubt the very figure of the individual—and its archetype in the Christian person—and in any case it would have no longer been the only conceivable form of the human.

Something much more profound than the dissolving of the individualistic bourgeois "I" into the collectivist "we" of the Jacobin and socialist tradition (and perhaps formerly Rousseauian), which juxtaposed individualities without really going beyond them. It would at least have demanded a question about whether and how much the modern form of the individual was capable of incorporating within it a completely humanized universal, no longer confined in heaven or the state; and of opening up on the basis of this to a complete equality, without exceptions and without reservations.

Marx, though, had a humanistic-materialist tradition behind him (according to Lucio Colletti's valuable observations), which did not lead him in this direction: and the form of the individual—the human being as a "natural species-being"—also basically seemed to him to be a point of no return, exactly like class and the factory, perfectly compatible with the socialization of labor that would produce communism.[256] A critical point, and just how problematic it was would become apparent when the moment came to really try to build communism.

Capitalistic Rebalances

For the purposes of our account, it is sufficient to have identified some points of rupture in Marx's thought, which (as we shall see) would prove crucial in subsequent events. Other errors in his doctrine, no less serious in terms of their historical consequences but less closely related to the thread that we are pursuing, have long been known—and are again linked to its egalitarian and prophetic aspects. For example, how the different formulations of the "crisis theory" overlapped without reinforcing each other, deferring hopeless incongruences, and without even resolving the doubt about whether the definitive capitalist collapse would come about due to the irresistible power of an unbreakable law (the tendency of the rate of profit to fall, or insurmountable problems of return in situations of overproduction, or whatever else), or whether it would depend—at least in part—on the actions of the key players, leaving open the possibility of more uncertain outcomes, and a greater unpredictability of history. A tenuousness shared by almost all the purely economic demonstrations of the *Grundrisse* or *Capital,* none of which really held up, including the crucial one of capitalist "exploitation," as late Italian Marxism had already clearly shown.[257]

And yet, however many lacunae and missteps we manage to detect in that thought, and however much it appears implicated in the tragedies that would come, it is still impossible to do without it today. Something remains at the core of his thinking which should not be lost: a capacity for analysis that is part of our modernity itself. And I believe that, for this reason too, anyone who devotes themselves professionally to studying the past cannot refuse to acknowledge their debt to those interpretations.

The incomparable capacity to historicize the world, to discover history and that alone, where others stubbornly saw (and would continue to do so) the presence of unmodifiable "natural laws" of economy and society, is still an exceptional lesson—in method prior even to the results.

Similarly unparalleled is Marx's talent for giving to historic investigation schemes and categories able to integrate in a single connection events and structures; to hold together economic facts, institutions, politics, culture, and mentality within a unitary picture. Approaching his books is a memorable experience, now more than ever: and until a few decades ago it had the flavor of a revelation. The mix of intellectual passion and moral life pulsating in almost every page still reawakens deep emotions: echoes that fortunately are not fading away.

The capitalist society he criticized really was traversed by lacerating contradictions, which make it appear, in any nonapologetic retrospective view, as a system able to build (also) mechanisms for a preestablished, crushing power, through to the existential annihilation of entire classes: anyone wishing to gain an idea of this will find it vividly expressed in the "factory journal" of Simone Weil, written at a time when the original violence, though less harsh, had not entirely abated.[258]

That exploitation, whose theoretical demonstration—as an intrinsic rule of the capitalist mode of production—did not assume the appearance of necessity, was, from the historic point of view, an evident and extremely burdensome reality. The conviction—brazenly displayed by some today—of the progressive triumph of a universally rosy market economy is among the silliest falsifications of our age. A hundred years of working-class pressure have played a key role in correcting the initial state of affairs in Europe. And in America too, not everything would work out for the best, and significant reforms would be required (we will say more about this later).

Without Marx such an impulse would certainly not have been produced. The rapid spread of his thinking all over the world had an irresistible objective convergence behind it: like no one else, he managed to transform into concepts—and into ideology—the incandescent matter of social conflict in the very act of its coming into being—and to give it a form: in this sense, it would be hard to imagine a more penetrating influence, even when it only seemed to be a remote inspiration, an unaccepted proposal, barely distinguishable in the background, as in the case of America.

The history of the capitalist mode of production in the West ended up absorbing large doses of it: and if European societies became, in the course of the twentieth century, very different from those studied by Marx, to a significant degree this is due to the effects of his presence. Without him, Schumpeter or Keynes, and even the New Deal, would have been inconceivable. His progressive outdatedness has been—in many respects—also a result of his success: he enabled history to change.

※ ※ ※

The great process of capitalist rebalancing in a way favorable to the working class in the countries to the forefront of economic development encapsulates one of the most powerful meanings of the twentieth century and—it seems to me—has yet to be fully studied. We shall return to this in the following chapter.

It should be said immediately—without underestimating in any way the weight of Marx's thought on all subsequent events through to the end of the twentieth century—that the readjustment would not always follow the path of a conscious class struggle led directly by Marxist-oriented movements: a model whose expansion—though important—has probably been inflated, in particular by Italian and French historiography (to say nothing of the Soviet one).

In reality, the combination between social conflicts and Marxist organizations (between history and class consciousness, as an unjustly famous book puts it) has fully manifested itself in the West just in particular situations.[259] With singular regularity, we only find it in cases in which there had already been revolutionary precedents against *ancien régime* structures: where, that is, there was already a tenacious collective memory of a relationship between revolution and people, as in France—or where, for different reasons, the *ancien régimes* had lasted longer and been particularly slow to crumble. And, at any rate, always in the presence of strong antiliberal forces that continued to survive, or of particular resistance to liberal-democratic assimilation: in Germany, in Austria, then in Italy and Spain, briefly (and dramatically) in Russia. But not in England, led by a crown and a nobility precociously reformed at the school of a peculiar liberal and bourgeois, and then openly democratic, compromise: here, despite having the oldest and most robust workers' organizations in the world, and in a rigidly classist society, social tensions never turned into head-on confrontation, and Marxism never became a mass doctrine.

And, above all, not in the United States. A country literally without an *ancien régime,* and with a republican aristocracy that, although significant, had no history behind it; a society in which there had immediately taken root—as an original condition—a democratic mentality without equal in Europe, England included.

I will not venture to propose a more precise delineation in this correspondence, nor to hazard the reasons for it. History develops underlying constants, something similar to tendential laws of development: but the analysis of their status, and above all the expression of their mechanisms of action is a delicate and difficult task. I only feel able to say that in the path of the West between the nineteenth and twentieth centuries it seems possible to discern a kind of inverse relation between precocity in the liberal-democratic reform of states and social bodies, and the spread of class struggle through the cultural and organizational apparatus of Marxism. As if the rooting of the latter, in short, was always and in any case linked to a kind of dissymmetry or delay in civil and political transformation—in the material constitution of society in a democratic sense, we would say—with respect to pure economic development.

If this were well founded, it would sensationally undermine Marx's thesis regarding the complete irrelevance of political democracy compared to the essential terms of the working-class condition in capitalist societies in the first 150 years after the Industrial Revolution. The exact opposite would be true: that the political and legal correction of capitalistic exploitation, accompanied by alternative mechanisms of social integration—though implemented in different ways in the two oldest democracies in the world—was able to produce effects such that, from the outset, and forever, and precisely in the most advanced places of development, history did not go down the road of a head-on opposition between the classes, imagined by Marx as the only possible path. If he had given greater consideration to America and Tocqueville, he would probably have seen new possibilities for his reflection. Perhaps, despite a number of declarations to the contrary, and Marx's intermittent perception of some features of American modernity, his view was clouded by the persistence of a certain colonial prejudice, determined above all by the lingering presence of slavery in the Southern states.

The fact remains, however, that the dynamic of class conflicts, even where it would play out in terms closer to the theoretical predictions made by Marxism (in France, for example, or in Germany, or later in Italy and Spain), would never lead, in any country even remotely advanced in economic terms, to a revolutionary settling of accounts.

The only place where this occurred—Tsarist Russia—had long constituted a classic example of backwardness and underdevelopment, in a setting where neither capitalistic growth nor class struggle had become rooted in a widespread manner. And the revolutionary event did not present itself as the epilogue of an irresistible historic necessity, but, on the contrary, just as the fortuitous outcome of a coup de main made possible by the circumstances of the moment.

Marx's errors could have remained confined within his books. The prophetic aspects of the doctrine might at most have been a nebulous frame for the critique of capitalist injustice and for the gradual social-democratic integration of the European working-class masses, in Germany, France, even in Italy, to say nothing of England (but we shall return to this). They pointed to a basically inexistent horizon, but useful, with its undoubted appeal, to mobilize forces, stir minds, and to obtain victories on the terrain of rights and social protection, which, if they certainly did not achieve the total equality spoken of by Marx, did attenuate the most unbearable imbalances.

Between the end of the nineteenth and the beginning of the twentieth century, it really seemed that the history of Europe had clearly taken this latter direction: that it was acting as a careful and intelligent filter, capable of separating and distinguishing. The reequilibrium of capitalist societies was only just starting, without question: and the majority was still to be done. But the path seemed to have been outlined, and everywhere it indicated that even in the realities where Marxism had been accepted by workers' movements as a crucial point of reference—Germany is a case in point—there was a tendency to propose an ever less radical version of it. It was an interpretation that Lenin would later describe as that of "renegades," certainly not faithful to the spirit of the master, but carefully evolutive, which bent doctrine to the conditions of the time, and transformed what originally was to have been a breaching weapon into a formidable machine for a long and slow war of position.[260] The aim of communism was moved far into the future, making way for a "revisionist" strategy of realistic and immediate conquests, to be patiently and forcefully wrenched from the class foe, without prefiguring apocalyptic outcomes to the conflict.

But the destiny that was beginning to take shape was very different. And as what would happen is closely connected to the success and the errors of Marx's thinking, I believe it is opportune to interrupt for a while the temporal thread that has shaped our account, in order to immediately explore the development of this matter.

"A Revolution against *Capital*"

Everything began with the precipice of the First World War: an event not glorified by time but enveloped in a shadow of livid irrationality: sudden as well, and so all the more devastating.[261] It was the heat of war that reopened the season of revolutions, like in a chain reaction. One after another, in a deadly connection, the paradigms of "nation" and "class"—the two great figures of thought and social-political engineering of the twentieth century—abruptly presented an unexpected check, about which there has not been sufficient reflection: a whole generation would pay it with the almost complete destruction of itself. We have already talked about the idea of class. As for that of nation, its intrinsically antiegalitarian and antiuniversalistic nature has already been clearly highlighted by historians.[262] In late eighteenth-century Germany, it was a notion primed to fill up with those elements of blind exclusivism that subsequent history would soon provide.[263]

If for brevity we were to condense the story into a formula, I would say that the turning point can be described as the birth, in different contexts, of a new relationship between people and state, induced by the total nature of the modern war mobilization, never tested until then: a kind of short circuit containing an unknown force. For the first time, millions and millions of men on both sides of the war fronts were integrated into the same mechanism of discipline and command—a space at once physical and mental, where all subjective independence was erased or suspended in a kind of immense leveling from above—and they all concentrated on a single objective, identical for all: the annihilation of the adversary.[264]

The exceptionality of the experience crystallized almost immediately in the magnetism of a model, projected from the war to politics, and used to a very similar degree by opposing forces. Less touched by it were only those countries in which liberal and democratic institutions and mentalities had become established with fewer contrasts, and which possessed greater resources for tackling the novelty: once again, Britain, America, and in part France. But where the national assimilation of the peasant, working-class, and petit bourgeois masses was still precarious or entirely incomplete with regard to the frame of democratic sociality, very different instruments now took shape for realizing an alternative model looking in a very different direction.

There was suddenly a whole new climate, still inconceivable only at the beginning of the century. Political democracy appeared isolated and unsuccessful outside of its traditional strongholds. Quite abruptly, its procedures seemed old and ineffective; its solutions and relative truths blurred in the face of the demands being made by societies hungry for ideology, exhausted by the war or by defeat, and anxious to place their trust in new regimes of salvation. Mobilized by arms to politics, masses of individuals cut loose from their original environments and cast onto the stage of "nation" or "class" (or both together) suddenly found themselves willing to enter into an unprecedented social contract based not on citizenship but on ideology.

A delegation of sovereignty that identified a leader—a commander in the field, surrounded by a small loyal group—invested with total consensus, granted in exchange for a promise of recognition and liberation, felt to be all the more reliable and authentic the more it was offered outside the context of any formal guarantee, on the basis of a more global and profound emotive correspondence—a sort of unquestionable primary identification. Returning in this way—but in very new forms—was the classic relationship between tyrant and people: the old nub of the ancient republics, re-presented in a frame of mass dimensions, of the manipulation of consensus, and of incomparably more powerful and effective opportunities for control.

At the same time there returned—inevitably—the idea of revolution, the great protagonist of Western history between the eighteenth and nineteenth century, in crisis after the legalistic choices of the socialist parties: it was like this in Germany, in Italy, in Russia itself, which had stronger impediments to, and delays in, the democratic transformation of social bodies, in contrast with the dramatic speed of their military integration.

Without a doubt the colors of the new scenarios had little to do with the Marxist tradition as it had taken shape until then, except for the critique of bourgeois democracy; instead, they remixed, in an explosive and unstable combination, many elements of the ancient hostility of the antiliberal reaction to the rules of the parliamentary orders.

Here I do not even want to touch on the discussion—though we will return to it—surrounding the concept of "totalitarianism": a category that should be able to explain in a unitary way communism, Nazism, and, in part, fascism itself (to whom we owe the invention of the word).[265] I am convinced that some of the objections made to the line of thought running from Arendt to Furet are not unfounded.[266] And I also believe that the abuse of the term can lead us to lose sight of both the genetic and functional peculiarities of the different systems, which we need to grasp if we wish to understand.

But no reservation can hide a series of evident facts. First, that in the emerging triptych of the European tragedy—Germany, Italy, Russia—the social bases of democracy seemed weaker or almost inexistent; and this condition, combined with the effects of the war, was crucial in all three cases to the opening up of subversive perspectives.

Secondly, that in two of these countries there was a shift, in a very brief lapse of time—a decade for Germany, much less for Italy—from the possibility of a socialist revolution (how effective need not concern us here, the point is that it was experienced as such) to a fascist and Nazi outcome, with by no means marginal displacements in popular consensus— the middle orders, intellectuals, but also the working class—from one hypothesis to the other (in Italy this swing would see a second important movement, in the opposite direction, from fascism to communism, in the final phase and at the end of the Second World War).

Finally, that in all three situations, what we might define as the nascent revolutionary state—both in the fascist and Nazi form, and in the Soviet one—reelaborated and fused together some common elements of far from secondary importance: criticism of democracy and the excesses of "bourgeois" individualism; criticism of the irrationality and spirit of capitalism; permanent ideological mobilization of the masses, under the guidance of a revolutionary avant-garde bound together in a party, which in turn had already identified a charismatic leader, immediately offered up to popular visibility and emotions.

※ ※ ※

Precipitating its appointment with destiny, the October Revolution— that began with the war still underway—immediately chose to bring back into play the most dangerous Marx: not the implacable critic of market injustices, but the prophet of a world that, once upturned, was to have been miraculously straightened up.

The extraordinary success obtained by Lenin—a speculative talent of the first order, as his *Philosophical Notebooks* clearly demonstrate— opened onto a perspective both unexpected and boundless.[267] The victory, in the way it was achieved—a crushing triumph in Russia, but for now only in Russia—invested the victors with an immense task: to build—on their own—the first communist society in human history; to transform the revolution—the history that came after—into a figure of reason. Immediately before and during the brief period of the struggle for power, Marx's critique had returned, in the hands of the revolutionaries, to being an assault weapon, to reinforce the hegemony of the party, to extend the alliance among peasants, soldiers, workers, students, and to temper their firmness to the extreme.[268] But once this phase was over, that part of the doctrine became unusable for the first time. It was no longer a question of unmasking and condemning, but of building: nothing less than erecting communism.

A very widespread view, almost a vulgate of the European left, has long tried to separate the judgment of the ideas—Marx and Marxism, especially the Western kind—from the degeneration of the facts—the reality of the Soviet Union—determined by the adversity of the situation, not to mention the perversions of Stalin. There is no need here to trace the origins of this interpretation: certainly not far removed from the perspective adopted by Khrushchev in 1956, when he denounced the crimes of the recently dead dictator to the party.[269] Suffice it to observe that, paradoxically, the thesis of a basically identical totalitarianism in the Nazi and communist incarnations ends up—in the apparent radicality of the condemnation—actually supporting this essentially justificatory reading, at least for the theory: a risk that Arendt's famous book—so dazzling in its acuteness and fervor—is unable (it seems to me) to elude. If Nazism and communism were almost completely equal, that means the opposing sides in the doctrinaire and ideological content of the two systems—universal equality against Aryan racism—ultimately counted for little, or were entirely disregarded, at least on the communist side. What would prove decisive was just the totalitarian form of the ideologies, and the terroristic outcomes that would ensue, in Moscow as in Berlin. Marxism, therefore—at least as a conceptual system—did not, on this view, come into it much: to each their own.[270]

But that is not how things stand. I believe instead that Marx's thought carried crucial weight in the course of what happened, right from the beginning. And it is the dynamic of this entanglement between thought and events—never previously realized—that needs to be explained.

From the very start, it was Marxism alone that made the Revolution I would not say possible, but identifiable—that is, to consign the Revolution to itself—enabling it to be thought and represented—to display its significance and the spectacle on the Russian and world scene—in the very act in which it was taking place, or rather, even before it did.

Before then, no political upheaval had enjoyed such an extraordinary privilege. Now, instead, Marx offered the protagonists a double and converging profundity for their presence: that of theory and that of action. As if, through them, history and the philosophy of history—facts and reasons—were finally coinciding. Not even the Enlightenment in relation to the French Revolution had been capable of so much, even if, in a certain sense, that link had acted as the midwife for this later one, more than a hundred years later.

The fever of such an exceptional conjunction—of the illusion of having produced it—consumed Lenin after 1917: when he began to sense that things did not add up, he was crushed.

Of course, according to the canons of Marx, Russia in the age of the Romanovs was neither the time nor the place. We can intuit that if the contest had been lost, such a sensational incongruence would have branded Bolshevism forever. But it did not happen: Russian history, the ongoing war, and the fragility of the adversaries—a kind of dying feudalism and a still unrooted capitalistic structure—provided sufficient help: and the victory definitively cemented that anomalous alliance between nonconverging facts and ideas, which had contributed to making it possible.

* * *

The Russian Revolution still awaits its Tocqueville, or at least its Furet. As has been repeated many times, it was a product of circumstances, and represented the quintessence of that "Jacobin" triumph of politics—deprived of any economic necessity—which was the exact opposite of Marx's hopes and predictions. In this sense, it was certainly "a revolution against *Capital*" (to draw on a celebrated expression), destined to repropose for the whole century the myth of the conquest of power as a pure act of force and will: virtue plus good fortune—calculation and occasion.[271]

Notwithstanding this, precisely while the revolution was taking place and belying Marxism in the process, it declared—I should say shouted from the rooftops—with an extraordinary concentration of dramatic tension, that it was being carried out in the name of Marxist thought, and as an exclusive function of the goals it indicated, first and foremost the achievement of a complete political, social, and economic equality. The more radical the contrast with reality, the more resolutely it was proposed.

Was such behavior contradictory? Certainly, but it amplified the force of the revolutionary cause, immediately attributing to it a universal value: the final emancipation of humankind had begun. The revolution of 1789—with its whole symbolic horizon—could be drawn fully into the new orbit: the work left undone for over a century before the walls of the Bastille was finished in front of the Winter Palace. The theory did not coincide with the context, but it was used with such determination as to retroact upon it, to the point of creating totally new conditions, which would not have existed—or would not have been perceived as such—if the protagonists had been moved by a less deep conviction. The bare facts of the revolution—the circumstances of history—and the affirmations of the doctrine were not sequences flowing on distinct planes, separated by their reciprocal incompatibility. On the contrary, the very rhythm of events arranged them, albeit in an illusory and fleeting way, within the same frame: and the theoretical presuppositions—though entirely inappropriate with respect to the reality of the situation—were continually transformed into parameters, objectives, and propaganda of revolutionary action.

In turn, the political success reflected onto the theory, enriching it with a completely undeserved prize, but no less effective because of it. Truth of theory and truth of the facts seemed to reaffirm each other. The communist victory confirmed that Marx had seen things correctly: at the end of the history of capital there really was a total upheaval. Russia was just the first step: where exceptional and fortunate circumstances had made it possible to change the delay of history into anticipation of the future. The weakest link had been transformed into the heart of the blaze. Soon, very soon, the rest would follow.

It has been said on various occasions that—at least until the end of 1920 and, intermittently through to 1923—the Russian communists believed they were the avant-garde of a world or at least a European revolution.[272] After Russia, it would be Germany's turn, finally hitting one of the cores of the world capitalistic organization. Such a firm conviction further reduced—in the years of the conquest of power—the perception of the gap between facts and theory. The revolution was in any case a world process—just as Marx had seen—called upon to destroy the old national borders. Its "internationalism" did not lie just in the values it disseminated—the liberation of all human beings, the community solidarity of the workers—but in the capacity to propagate, playing on contradictions and needs that were much stronger in the rest of Europe than in Russia itself.

This universalistic aspiration was crucial for the course of events. Marxism was its essential key, in turn reinforced to an extraordinary degree by the use that was made of it: day after day the laboratory of history seemed to confirm its scientific value and predictive capacity.

In this way, from the beginning, "revolution" and "equality" appeared to be an irresistibly evident synthesis. Naturally, the equality in question was no longer that of the French Revolution, and it did not refer to Rousseau, far less to the theorists of German socialist revisionism, or to some of the European democratic traditions. It was strictly that of Marx: the announced and inevitable effect of the soon to be established communist economy. A decisive restraint was thus created. On the one hand, the revolution—thanks to Marxism—managed to fully tap a historic juncture of modernity, which political democracy had not been capable until then of resolving at the root, and not even to tackle in an acceptable way outside of America and (in part) England: the demand for recognition and attention raised by the masses who had entered the scene with the industrial transformation, the capitalist takeoff, and now the war—and through them, by the humiliated of the earth, no nationality, religion, or skin color excepted. On the other, the more effectively it interpreted this need, the more the answer it offered was dogmatically bound to the rigidity—and errors—of the doctrine that had however enabled the link to click into place.

※ ※ ※

The correspondence between the radicality of the image it presented of itself and the depth of the hopes it aroused immediately prompted a wave of sympathy for the revolution outside of Russia: a favor that would last even when, in what was by then the Soviet Union, all enthusiasm for it had already completely drained away. Without Lenin's victory, Marxism would never have attained so much. But the revolution, without Marxism, would not even have been conceived. And the success it obtained would obscure right to the end the fact that Marx had become a weapon in the wrong hands—merely to give force to a coup de main—and, what's more, a weapon that would prove to be mortally defective.

The situation began to deteriorate when the moment came to pass from a universal equality promised in the heat of battle—with the prospect of moving on rapidly at least from Moscow to Berlin—to an equality to be built in the Soviet Union alone. It was then that, as the impossible could not be realized, in its place came tragedy.

The revolution had taken place in a total void of political thought. The lacuna, as we have seen, had remote origins. The theory whose truth was invoked every day had made this lack a point of honor. In *State and Revolution* Lenin again demonstrated his firm conviction that communist democracy presupposed the extinction of the state and the end of its separations.[273] His prediction was condensed into the famous announcement that a cook could go directly from the kitchen to the government—confirmation of the achievement of authentic equality.[274]

The weight of this absence has been underestimated. It made possible the conceptual and ethical uncoupling of the revolutionary elites from any democratic reference and practice, except for an initial and chaotic phase of assemblies dictated by the circumstances, already exhausted when attempts were made—outside the Soviet Union as well—to elaborate an outline of it from a constitutional point of view.[275] Democracy just meant building communism and defeating its foes. A movement with some wholly Jacobin features, which generated an enormous voluntarism, found itself thus legitimized by theory to act outside of any restriction on the means: exactly when it was affirming its wish to destroy the primacy of politics for good, it became the most exalted expression of it.

Moreover, unlike the French Revolution, the Bolshevik one was not linked—and knew it full well—to any underlying tendency active within the society it proposed to transform: besides the political desert there was the effect of a drastic historic isolation, which, however, soon gave the illusion of an unlimited freedom of movement, even if it was to build a world of sand. It would take eighty years to fully realize the poverty of the results. Closed within itself, centered on its own image, overwhelmed by its own speed, the revolution, to survive, could do no other than flee even further forward, in the direction of its own utopia. It was therefore necessary to immediately address that economy of equality—that complete overthrowal of the existent—which for Marx was the solution to all problems.

Naturally there was no question of building equality from the bottom up, dissolving the functions of the state in the self-organization of producers according to the original design. The model was so unrealizable it was pointless to test it, and no attempt was even made. However, this obviousness became apparent to the communists only in an indirect way. The impracticality of the paradigm did not seem to them to be the result of an intrinsic inconsistency, finally demonstrated by facts, but just a consequence of the particular conditions in Russia in the 1920s: where, due to the backwardness of the country, the working class was not yet able to perform its functions as the "universal liberator," according to the scheme delineated by Marx.

The delay could not however be used as an easy alibi: if it had not previously seemed a sufficient reason for stopping the communists from imposing a lightning acceleration on events, it could not now be adopted as justification for renouncing their objectives. And if they had stopped, what would have happened? Who might have taken advantage of the immobility? After all, it was not an experiment that was being conducted, but a war.

The decision was thus made—and the responsibility fell once again to Lenin, who would be devastated by it—to invert the direction of travel, with a variant of a strategic nature. If it was not possible to attain equality from the bottom up, starting from the unlimited extension of the socialization of labor prophesied by Marx—from the community of all producers—it would in the meanwhile be imposed, so to speak, from above, through the apparatuses and powers of a rigidly centralized government. This gave rise to a previously unseen state economy controlled by the workers through the party, founded on the hypothesis of a dramatically unequal alliance between the factory proletariat and the peasant masses.

It was a serious derogation, but it was also the only way to keep the continually evoked doctrine from falling apart: ultimately, the Marxian vagueness about the theme of the transition justified the view that the shift was not inappropriate, while the void of political thought left enormous scope for improvisation. Communism was still the undisputed end goal. But if Russian society was not yet mature enough to generate it spontaneously, from within its own productive base, a start would be made on achieving it through state direction of the economic process— in factories and the countryside—and the tendentially egalitarian distribution of social wealth, removing market inequities and erasing the antagonism between capital and labor.

The revolution remained a figure of science and reason, though it would not transmit its powers to the body of a liberated society, but into the hands of the state, run by the party: which became, in this way, the cornerstone of the entire system. Instead of the death of politics, a supremely powerful form of it crystallized: the concentrate of revolutionary action, which required a pervasive and absolute discipline. The socialization of labor did not open up any effective practice of equality; and the new collective structures compressed and suffocated, but did not destroy, the previous forms of individual lives or microcommunities.

Economic backwardness therefore ended up performing a dual function of screening and concealment. On the one hand it justified the inversion in the direction of travel: from society to state; and on the other, it masked the unrealizability of the theory, hiding it behind a problem of social development: ultimately a contingent difficulty, superable with an intense program of industrial modernization.

A picture thus formed with all the elements that would lead to the tragedy. Enormous concentrations of political power, instead of its grass-roots diffusion. The impossibility of linking the generalized abolition of capitalist profit and private ownership of means of production, coercively established, to the birth of anything even remotely resembling an economy of equality, without constantly passing by way of rigid state control. Enormous difficulties—again resolved in an authoritarian way—in reducing the whole of social and productive life to the measure of the socialization of labor alone, and in overcoming through this the previous individualistic forms.

The economic "accounting" self-managed by the producers—about which we have seen Marx fantasizing—transmuted, upon impact with reality, into the hypertrophy of a state and a party acting as global distributors of collective wealth. Market functions were replaced not by the liberated spontaneity of communist democracy, but by the rigidity of a social taxonomy arbitrarily decided by the party through the state, and expanded to the point of enveloping the whole civil universe in its meshes, without retreating in the face of its most remote fold; while the calculation of resources and needs became lost—as was inevitable—in the hierarchies of an asphyxiating, omnipotent, and irresponsible bureaucracy, deformed by the carrying out of an impossible task.

❋ ❋ ❋

Where did the Russian revolutionaries—and Lenin himself—get the idea of exchanging society with the state, leaving intact the dogma of a fully grounded communist paradigm: the universality of the working class, the economy of equality, the democracy of producers? I believe we can identify a tangle of impulses.

Above all, it was, in many respects, another consequence of the faith placed in Marx's conceptual frame. If the end point was the construction of an economy of equality, and this could only be achieved through a strong dose of coercion—after all, Marx himself never precisely indicated how the political transition was to be effected or the institutional profile of the new democracy—the state seemed the only acceptable way to keep realism and coherence together.

Then there was, undoubtedly, a perception of the weakness of the Russian working class, unable to perform by itself the role mapped out by Marx in relation to a mature capitalistic society that simply did not exist in Russia. And in the face of a fragile society, the symmetries elaborated in specular fashion by Hegel and by Marx himself could only compensate for it by prescribing the construction of an invincible state. Naturally, the other aspect of the question passed completely unobserved: that the recourse to an iron-fisted government would at any rate be necessary—and not just in a situation of backwardness—in order to try to implement something of Marx's program, because it would in any case be the only way to discipline the social complexity inherited from the previous mode of production, and to impose the forced distribution of wealth in place of the unrealizable self-managed division of resources and products. Later, in fact, wherever the communist countries became industrially less backward—in the Soviet Union itself in the 1960s and 1970s, or in the leading Eastern European countries— the modernization of production never led to a reduction in the invasiveness of state control of the economy and society: if anything, exactly the opposite.

Finally, weighing on that choice, irrespective of Marxism, was what might be called a certain spirit of the age, to which we will return. An attitude that was in the air from the 1920s: a propensity to view the primacy of the state as resolutory for any problem of social engineering— shared by left and right alike—steeped in finalism, and markedly interventionist in the face of the capitalistic disorder of the period.

In the countries with a more deep-rooted democratic tradition, this orientation would be expressed in Keynesian, Labourite, socialist, or, in America, New Deal policies. In contexts exposed to greater risks, it would take on openly illiberal features—the economic crisis was putting democracy on the defensive everywhere—favoring the birth of totalitarian regimes (if we wish to use this controversial word). In Russia, it facilitated the statist solution, helping to make it familiar and acceptable: a necessary phase (it was said) of the transition toward an authentic communist society.

The Jacobin character of the Revolution, having crystallized into a form of state, rapidly turned into despotism, following a classic pattern well known to French history itself: and the metamorphosis was definitive. As in revolutionary France, despotism became the condition of equality. But now, it was of the communist version of equality, which lacked any theory of liberated subjectivities—or of the overcoming of individualistic forms of life and consumption different from that of the socialization of labor (as we have seen, there was nothing else in Marxian thought); capable only, in the Soviet interpretation, of exhausting the potential wealth of the original concept in a pure operation of economic leveling outside of the market, conducted in a granular, authoritarian manner.

It was an entirely inevitable outcome, following Marx. Both the unlimited concentration of power, and the dominion of the planning state were responses made necessary by the errors of the theory. The first sought to impose, through an institutional prolongation of Jacobin violence, that overturning of the capitalist order which in the original hypothesis was to have been brought about by the ineluctable thrust of deep, structural agents, only barely helped by a short revolutionary phase. The second tried to replace, with the effects of planning from above, that economy of equality which, for Marx, was to have developed from within society, transformed into a rational community of producers thanks to the end of capitalist oppression. In short, wherever the theory—erroneously—predicted the presence of a liberated sociality, it was propped up by substituting the myth of democratic spontaneity for the reality of the regime's coercion.

Despotism thus showed itself to be the very essence of communism, in its complete dependence on a groundless theory: it was its very substance, not a simple accident created by subjective choices and circumstances. There could be no "real" communism if not in a rigorously authoritarian form: accepting the omnipotence of a devouring politics, and the bureaucratic imposition of an otherwise unachievable social leveling. Of course, Soviet history was not just this. Stalin cannot be understood if we remain within the horizons of Marxism, and very soon the despotism induced by Marx's glaring errors would be combined with the much more ancient one deriving directly from Russia's autocratic past.[276] But of the two components—the communist form and the Eastern form of despotism—it is the first, the newest arrival, that explains and founds the other, having completely drawn it into its field; not vice versa.

It was communism that, to survive, had to disarticulate to an incredible extent the society it was itself in some respects modernizing—to the point of not even being able to establish a true party aristocracy, but just a "nomenclature"—in order to maintain a level of planning and forced wealth distribution such as to keep alive the ghost of equality. It was communism that had to replace the impossible one-dimensional character of a society of worker-producers with a universe of total standardization, where any diversity became deviance. Finally, it was communism that had to devise a capillary social practice of untruth to assimilate to the world described in the theory the one constructed in facts, which was just a spectral stand-in of the errors contained in the idea whose name it bore.

We have arrived, then, at the conceptual thresholds of the new Terror and of the gulags: when authoritarian political command and social control, exercised in contexts broken up by the new economy and by old backwardness—the conditions of communist equality—came together at the extreme point of mass annihilation.

We know full well that in terms of the methodical destruction of human life, similar or even worse abysses were reached in the twentieth century starting also from different ideas and places. Yet this does not mean we should strain the resemblance between the points of origin to the extent of confusing them. It only means—and this is perhaps one of the lessons left to us by the century—that the omnipotence of political command, whatever the content and inspiration, combined with the power of technology, can lead to hell.

Every path has its history. And Marxism's was full of risks from the start: even though it was not written beforehand where it necessarily had to end.

Starting from Marx, it might have been possible to arrive somewhere else, as in effect did happen. Certainly, as we shall see, at the Western social democracies and laborisms; but it might also have been possible to venture in directions destined to remain unexplored.

In Italy, for example, the conceptual premises at least existed for an entirely different development of Marxist thought. I believe, in fact, that Gramsci's writings from the prison years contained all the elements for a drastic revision of the legacy left by the socialist tradition. The *Notebooks*—in the original order of their thoughts—have a conceptual framework that is basically already outside the European Marxism of the 1920s and 1930s, even though they concede little to the classic version of democracy. They should instead be related to the orientations encompassing realism, historicism, and materialism of an important strand of Italian culture running from Machiavelli to Vico and to Labriola (not to mention Leopardi, despite Gramsci's aversion to him), much more than Engels or Lenin, and contain elements of a theory of democracy that are entirely heterodox in relation to Marx's thought.

❊ ❊ ❊

How long would real socialism be able to resist in the Eastern countries?

The story of the protracted, unstoppable crisis of the Soviet state—in terms of structure and consensus—and the astounding inefficiencies—to the point of complete breakdown—of its economy is not among the aims of this book.

I believe, though, that the explanation for its sudden collapse—an irresistible and total disintegration that recalls, grotesquely reversed, the end imagined by Marx for the capitalist mode of production—should not just be sought within those events, however tragic.

Instead, the coup de grace came from outside: and it was inflicted directly by the extraordinary capitalist transformation, which from the second half of the 1970s changed the face of the planet. The new revolution killed off the previous one, precisely as, paradoxically, it achieved one of its original objectives: to shift the axis of history from politics to the economy, though on the side of capitalist production and certainly not of communism.

Even a barely in-depth analysis would take us too far. Here I wish merely to establish a connection between the two phenomena. Overwhelmed by change and incapable of adapting, communism had suddenly become a dated and obsolete figure: the new capitalist setup behaved with that construction as a biological form does, when, having made a crucial evolutionary leap, it renders everything surrounding and preceding it archaic and destined to die out.

The petrification of an industrialist myth could not survive the end of the epoch that had produced it. The metaphysics of working-class labor could not hold up anymore, if in the most advanced part of the planet the social weight of the working class was beginning to disappear.

The resources and energies for adapting to the transformations were not available in Soviet society, if not at the cost of denying itself completely. The system, as such, suddenly had no future: just as Marx had imagined for capitalist society.

It could have exacerbated even further its repressive aspect, shutting itself off like a besieged fortress without any entrances, or attempted a military adventure. But both would have been desperate solutions, demanding terrible sacrifices. The evolutive success had been manifested entirely elsewhere: and it was an irreversible phenomenon, destined to change the world and to commence an extraordinary transition in reverse—from communism to capitalistic organization, the exact opposite of the one conceived by Marx—subsequently realized in some way by China as well, albeit in a different political context.[277]

All that remained was to acknowledge it.

CHAPTER FOUR

NEVER SO EQUAL, NEVER SO DIFFERENT

The Twentieth Century in Four Acts

Democracies under Threat

We can now pick up the temporal thread where we left it in order to bring together in a single sweeping view the vicissitudes of Marx's thought and the attempt at building communism that derived from its fortunes.

It is to the beginning of the twentieth century that we must return, to the opening of an age in which the story we are telling reached its culmination, and at the same time its epilogue and point of greatest contrast. Only in the 1900s, in fact, did the theme of equality become a problem without borders: indeed, in certain respects, the real problem of the planet.

The twentieth century was the first that truly unified the world: with wars, commodities, migrations, customs. And it was the age in which what we have called the individual form of the human—propped up by the impetuous growth of consumption and communication and the increasing uniformity of lifestyles, especially among the young—turned into an immense mass individualism, developed from one corner of the globe to the other: from Shanghai to Berlin and London, from Moscow to Tokyo and Los Angeles. A phenomenon full of hopes, but also contradictions, because the universalization of individualism somehow destroys it, compromising its exclusivist foundation.

For the West, the twentieth century was the age of equality in a wholly particular way. Its theoretical foundations, largely drawn from the eighteenth- and nineteenth-century tradition, were not renewed. It was, however, possible to empirically construct a model of it endowed with a great expansive force. As a result, for the first time the idea of equality—in a version whose meaning was not just transferred outside of the world—became a value capable of being projected, from the end of 1940s, onto the entire universality of the human, albeit precariously and incompletely.

Appertaining to no lesser degree to the same century was the brief yet tragic season of the most complete modern negation of that principle and of the history lying behind it—chasms of denial that erased the very right to exist of those viewed as different. Millions of women and men reduced to corporeal things or to reified, depersonalized bodies that could be annihilated without exception: the demoniacal face of the two rounds of civil war that devastated and fatally wounded Europe. An outcome with distant origins, casting a shadow over the very meaning of modernity: an epilogue with which we have not fully come to terms, in a thickening of contrasts whose consequences still envelop us and which requires, to explain it, a cognitive force that we do not yet possess.

※ ※ ※

The affirmation of the idea of equality took two routes during the century, in different versions that were both heirs to the thinking of the 1800s and 1900s. Paths that proved bitterly alternative, though they would intersect at various points, especially in Europe; while events in America would develop along an independent curve, largely due, as we have already observed, to the precocity of its democratic practice.

On one hand, there was the way outlined by the Marxist movements, by the socialist revolution in Russia and the building of the first regimes arising from it—we have just spoken of this. On the other, the road that would lead, often following bitter class struggles, to the complete democratic transformation of the parliamentary systems inherited from the nineteenth century. This continued right through to the constitution-alizing of equality as a notion that was not just formal, in the achievement of which the power of the state was directly engaged, though without ever calling into question the capitalistic setup of the economy and of society.

In this second variant, almost invariably advanced by Labourite and social-democratic reformism, the principle of equality appeared together with other experiences that contributed to defining its content and pro-file. Also inherited from the 1800s, they acquired a greater expansive force in the new century: mass democracy; the social protection of labor as affirmation and liberation; and the defense of individualities, speci-fied by gender difference.

What emerged was a kind of political complex of Western emanci-pation, basically shared on both sides of the Atlantic though with dis-tinct trajectories: democracy, labor, equality, individuality, gender, its components arranged in a broad but unstable web that had never previ-ously been tested. A connection that would manifest its force and ca-pacity to spread on many occasions, helping to define the very image of the West, and which filled with its colors and tonalities the horizon of an epoch.

※ ※ ※

The journey was not, however, progressive and free from mishaps. And only in the last three decades, since the crisis of the Eastern European communist regimes and the beginning of the technological leap, have the Western political systems—where all the features just indicated were present in some combination or other—established themselves as a vic-torious and solitary paradigm: as democracy par excellence, without qualification; a sort of necessary path (at least in ideological declarations and manifestos) of human civilization; and the (democratic) discourse on democracy has turned into a political grammar claiming to be uni-versal, a background music that has accompanied us ever since.[1]

Equality and democracy—in their European version—were actually at greatest risk in the course of the 1900s, after having initially gained ground at the beginning of the century, largely as a result of the class struggles of the previous decades. They were contested in the Old World—especially between the two world wars—by opposing sides, both theoretically and on the plane of political reality.

Powerful and antagonistic forces, fueled by the same nineteenth-century thought and generated by the same social fractures, moved in fact in totally opposite directions. Sharing a symmetrical faith in the omnipotence of politics, after a paradoxical but explainable antidemocratic convergence, they would arrive at a conflict that is still revealing, retrospectively, the depth of its significance; but always preserving traces of their common birth.

Fascism above all (a strictly Italian invention) and Nazism, together with the thinking that nurtured it: the proposal of a model of society completely integrated into the antiegalitarian hierarchies of a total state, built on an ideology of "racial" supremacy (the notion of "race" was commonly used at least until around the middle of the century) radicalized to the point of paroxysm, and on a will to power developed through a permanent activation from above of masses already nationalized by war.[2]

On the opposite side stood Soviet communism and the European Marxist parties, these too, at least until the 1960s, implacable adversaries of liberal democracy: insofar as they upheld a completely different and, in their view, much more effective idea of equality and popular sovereignty. Objectives that were both presented as being in the process of realization, at least in some parts of the world, after the October Revolution: along an itinerary that succeeded in appearing—deceiving even its most hardened critics—as an alternative hypothesis of progress and civilization, capable of interpreting in the very best way the sense of history, and the authentic spirit of the time. In 1942 Joseph Schumpeter—one of the leading economists of the age—considered the global victory of socialism to be inevitable;[3] and as late as 1970, Paul Samuelson, another prominent scholar, predicted that in the final decade of the century—actually that of the communist catastrophe—the Soviet economy might overtake the American one.[4]

The twentieth century would develop in depth, and dramatically, all the themes of this triple engagement between fascism, communism, and liberal democracies, which revolved above all around different ways of interpreting—through to their complete negation—equality and individual liberty. A challenge articulated first in an alternative between democracy and antidemocracy; then in an antifascist alliance that saw Western democracies and communist regimes taking sides together; and finally, in a clash between the democratic West and communist East.

The different positions would always be defined through great ideological constructs that penetrated them completely—the twentieth century was also the century of ideologies—in which there was a kind of constant political mobilization of nineteenth-century philosophical thought: rigidified, underinterpreted, and, so to speak, sent into battle.

In the center lay in any case the crossroads represented by Hegel, in opposing readings. From Hegel to Marx and Lenin, who had studied him in depth in the *Philosophical Notebooks*. Or from Hegel to Nietzsche: to the discovery of the force of the unequal grasped in the boundless exaltation of isolated subjectivities in their will to power ("life itself recognizes neither solidarity nor 'parity of rights' between the healthy and sick parts of an organism: the latter need to be *cut off*, or the whole perishes"—though it would be senseless to encapsulate in one citation a body of thought with a highly complex tension between life and the unequal, which, however, lies outside the scope of this account).[5] And to Heidegger, to Schmitt, to the jurists who built the Nazi state, or, differently, to Gentile. Or finally, once again commencing somehow from Hegel, toward the full constitutionalizing of the pluralist structure of modern civil society, in the shape of a completely formed welfare state: toward Weber, Keynes, and beyond.

Surfacing once again, then, was the unitary but fractured nucleus of Western metaphysics and of the whole European intelligence: that lacerated community of thoughts which transformed into civil wars the conflicts between the continent's powers. The three readings of Hegel just mentioned rested on three ways of interpreting the very same figures of modernity: the historic task of recomposing universality and the destiny of the modern state; the dialectic between finite and infinite in the formation of the human, especially in reference to the role of Christianity; the crucial relationship between individuality, equality, and labor.

The oppositions that would stem from them shattered the history of the Old World even more than the wars of religion had done in the sixteenth century. Like in a periodic return of an uncontainable drive to self-destruction on the European stage, at the beginning and end of its parabola; the reproduction—centuries apart—of the immense power of the negative, which would then be projected onto the whole world, establishing a definitive threshold of nonreturn.

The aphorism according to which the academic dispute between the Hegelian right and left would end on the battlefields between Moscow and Berlin therefore contains a terrible, albeit partial, truth; to which must be added the acknowledgment that even the side that emerged victorious would soon head toward a no less complete and irremediable defeat.

Those two paths were both dead ends. As for the outcome of the third, we will speak of that later.

✸ ✸ ✸

In what has proved to be a very successful book, the English historian Eric Hobsbawm defined the twentieth century—having lived through almost all of it and recounted it with undeniable talent—as a "short" century.[6] He singled out two dates—1914 and 1991, the Great War and the collapse of the Soviet empire—as the start and end of a more limited arc than the one fixed by the calendar.

Despite having his own good reasons for this definition, I must say that I have always found it questionable and ultimately rather superficial. From the point of view of the intensity of events and changes, rather than simple chronology—of the particular density of its historic time— the twentieth century was interminable, probably the longest in history, at least for the West. It opened with carriages and oil lamps (cars were rare and unreliable) and ended with internet and transoceanic jets.

Even aside from these incredible leaps, the incessant accumulation of events entirely out of scale with respect to any precedent had the effect of stretching rather than restricting the passage of those decades, transforming their duration almost as if they were entire epochs. Simply recalling the most important facts takes the breath away. The long civil war of Europe, marked by two world wars; Fascism, Nazism, and the unprecedented horror of extermination; the advent of communism in Russia and its bloody course from science to gulag, through to its inglorious and unexpected end. Then the start of a technological revolution unequaled in history, which put paid to the age of labor, preceded by the shift of the center of the world to outside of Europe. And finally arriving at the global spread—we do not yet know if and how deceptive—of the Western version of democracy, held up almost everywhere, at least in programmatic declarations, as the universal figure of politics, and the only acceptable paradigm of every constitutional order.

If we take the fortunes of this last model as a point of reference, we can distinguish four main blocs in the century.

The beginnings, until 1914. Then the years of the wars between 1914 and 1945, which would lead to the revolution in Russia and the two world conflicts, pushed to the extreme of genocide. And then, from the end of the 1940s, the age of the Cold War and the bipolar division of the world, ending abruptly in the early 1990s. Finally, the period between the collapse of the Soviet Union and September 11, 2001 (the real end of the twentieth century). A decade that marked—with the explosion of the technological revolution, the decline of the industrial age and its associated forms of labor, and the start of an unexpected cycle of international disorder—the entry into a new epoch.

The third person—historical perspective of all possible outcomes, a disparate

The Vote and Representation

Mishap of puzzle pieces put together for final evaluation, immediately

We have spoken so far of a Western figure of democracy, as if it were a *outdated as* single object. In reality, while the scene was continually changing all *soon as it* around, European and American—let's say Atlantic—democratic prac- *arrives,* tices had not stabilized into an unvaried paradigm either. The models *The* in place at the end of the twentieth century were not those of its begin- *first* ning, still less so in America, though elements of continuity did at first *person* sight seem to prevail there. Instead, they had undergone significant *withholding* transformations, precisely in relation to the regimes of equality incor- *the* porated within them. The changes were induced both by the social strug- *my seam* gles and mass movements that had developed in the different national *of*

preserved rising only to be mostly forgotten & leaving

contexts, and by the modified relationship between state and economy following the adoption of policies more or less involved in what has been called by Michael Sandel—in reference to America between the late 1930s and early 1960s—"the Keynesian revolution."[7]

To bring this history to light, we must try to observe the twentieth-century democratic paradigm and its variants from another point of view: that of its stratigraphy, of the deconstruction of its constituent components.

In it we can find above all the deposit of an experience that we have already come across: on the one hand, American republicanism, and, if we wish, that of revolutionary France around 1791 and 1848; on the other, the English and then European parliamentarism of the second half of the nineteenth century (the Third Republic in France, and then Italy and Germany following their national reunifications)—the original features of which were far from democratic, with its elitist and restricted character only subsequently softening to take on more openly popular shades.

In this mix we can in turn see two essential elements deriving from different sources: the vote, and its gradual extension; and representation, in relation to the effective exercising of popular sovereignty.

The vote has always been consubstantial to the idea of democracy, ever since its birth in ancient Greece. Alongside it, the possibility of lots was also envisaged when choosing magistrates. The two mechanisms were not at odds. Both were informed by the same persuasion, namely, that the citizen electing a magistrate or deliberating on the text of a law might do so on the basis of information allowing him not only to express a sensible opinion, but also, if the occasion arose, to directly carry out a public function.

In any case the vote involved a count.[8] If everyone did not share the same opinion, this entailed the formation of a majority—and their view prevailed with respect to a minority whose opinion no longer carried any weight in the matter. The Greeks came round, not without difficulty, to accepting this conception, that is, to numerically counting voters, attracted by a unanimist and in a certain sense totalitarian vision of collective will: a motif destined to resurface both in the medieval and modern ages—we saw it in relation to Rousseau.

Once adopted, however, the majority principle would constitute a fixed point, a pillar of (not just democratic) politics in the West, a sort of primary element. It would underpin the device whereby that which, before the counting of the votes, was only a part, was transformed—after having prevailed numerically—into whole; and could therefore legitimately behave as if—though still only a fraction—it had become the totality: a part wishing and positing itself as the whole, taking away space and visibility from those outside.

It was the democratic metaphysics of quantity, which took shape and became an irremissible rule. A criterion that, following a long tradition largely extraneous to democracy—from the medieval Church to the first modern representative assemblies—has become familiar to us; emphasized by the assumption "one person, one vote": by the principle, that is, of the equality of all voters—a not undisputed canon, moreover, that has historically had many derogations. Antonio Gramsci wrote about it beautifully in his *Notebooks,* still in the heart of the twentieth century, to circumscribe in some way its most mechanical and arithmetical meaning, and thus to defend the increasingly democratic parliamentarism of his own times from its openly reactionary critics.[9]

And while it is certainly true (as he wrote) that votes can never really all be equal and carry the same weight, because they are an expression of opinions, and there are those who create and spread them, and those who simply share them, the validity of such analysis does not undermine the credibility of another consideration. That we are always basically faced by an (effectively undemonstrated) equation between quantity and truth; between quantity and reason, so to speak: which seems to reflect a kind of democratic postulate, at the basis of everything else: that quantity is—in the field of politics—in itself an absolute value.

* * *

Ancient democracy presupposed, as we have seen, small numbers and small spaces. According to a very well-known adage, a city (including its surrounding countryside) choosing to regulate its affairs democratically had to be of a size that every citizen could leave his house no earlier than dawn, take part in the assembly, and return home no later than sundown.[10]

If that framework was to change, an epochal and cultural shift was required. It was necessary to insert into the configuration of the democratic form—entirely within a direct relationship between people and power—an element that had historically been extraneous to it: that of representation.[11] The idea and the device—somehow paradoxical— whereby the people, in order to exercise democracy, had to divest themselves of the power it conferred upon them, and to separate themselves from their own political will—what modern thought now called sovereignty—ceding it to a restricted group of representatives selected through an electoral procedure. It was the latter who were entrusted with the power to legislate and to attend to the governing of public affairs.

A representative parliament linked to an electoral mechanism existed in England from at least the seventeenth century. Its function was to build, in relation to the Crown, an articulation of powers more attentive to the freedoms and rights of single persons, and to produce a system with greater equilibrium founded on checks and balances and the separation of roles.

This situation had given rise to a constitutional model that had nothing in common with the democratic paradigm—either the ancient version or the one that would then be theorized by Rousseau and the radical French Enlightenment—and in particular it had nothing specifically popular about it: either in England, or in the other European countries where it would then be adopted (France, Germany, post-unification Italy).

It was in fact an inherently classist and aristocratic system, in which the principle of representation was used in a powerfully selective manner.[12] The will of the people was never evoked, substituted by the will of the nation, in turn interpreted solely by its ruling classes. In the English case (that became an example) it tended to form new and basically professional political elites, rather than creating an authentic popular sovereignty or extending political equality among citizens; indeed, it was rebuffed, sometimes through harsh repression, for much of the nineteenth century. A few hundred votes often sufficed to be elected to parliament, encouraging widespread corruption, with interminable and continual legal disputes: the novels of Anthony Trollope paint a vivid picture.

Not even in the United States immediately after Independence did the system of representation immediately have the properly democratic and egalitarian meaning that it would subsequently acquire—as was quite clear in the early political thinking of the new republic. In Europe it founded the parliamentarian tradition, with, at its center, the separation and balance of powers: the subjection of the state and the sovereign to the authority of the law and of juridical form—the rule of law; the guarantee (albeit with some limits) of political pluralism and personal freedoms. In short, Locke and Montesquieu, not Rousseau. A state of affairs such that even just the formal equality of all citizens—though now perceived, after the revolutions in America and France, as a clear political objective—remained a distant destination, beginning with England itself.

The conditions would change drastically with the extension of the right to vote. An initial turning point came with the introduction of universal male suffrage: achieved early on in America, making it in Tocqueville's eyes a genuine political laboratory; and later in Europe, between the middle of the 1800s and the early years of the new century. A transformation completed in the space of a few decades, with the admission of women to the vote, obtained above all thanks to the combativeness of important women's movements in Europe and America.

The quantitative increase in voters provoked an abrupt qualitative leap in the structure of representation and in the organization of consensus, and therefore in the political weight of suffrage itself, conferring on it the egalitarian tonality that belongs to mass democracies. The vote, universalized, modified the profile and consistency of politics, which acquired a social base that it had never previously possessed. All citizens were now, at least potentially, electors; and equality in key political rights no longer had, even if just formally, any limitation.

A transition was taking place from the old and restricted parliamentarian orders to contemporary mass democracies, which presupposed a different and much more exacting regime of equality. Here, consensus could no longer form and be managed within narrow circles; it required the establishment of large organizations: the new mass parties—genuine protagonists of democratic political life—and the large trade union federations, which in Europe were almost all of socialist inspiration, established to defend working-class labor.

The egalitarian extension of the right to vote brought for the first time the circle of representatives close to the universe of the represented. And this happened just as the relationship between people and state, and hence the form of the state itself, was changing as a consequence of the war; and while, in the same years, public administrations were forging a new role in the economy and society: an innovation shared, irrespective of appearances, by all the countries that emerged from the First World War, independently of their political regime. It would concern Fascist Italy no less than Nazi Germany, or Roosevelt's America, the Great Britain of the trade unions and the first Labour Party successes, or the France of the Popular Front. To say nothing of Lenin and Stalin's Russia, where the party-led state had become the supreme protagonist in the establishment of socialism.

* * *

It was a change of great importance. Unfolding from the late 1920s onward was what we might describe as the age of the Second Leviathan: the social refoundation of the modern state, after its political birth; with Lenin, Roosevelt, and Keynes instead of Machiavelli and Hobbes.

The laissez-faire model of the "minimal State," which had accompanied the start and consolidation of the Industrial Revolution in a vacuum of rules that favored investment and innovation, and left the management of economic processes entirely up to private individuals and the market—to the spontaneity of civil society—gave way to the project for a different relationship between public structures and capitalistic production. Through interventions impacting both demand and supply, the state became a key player in national economies. It generally performed the function of offsetting the sharpest points of capitalist inequality through social rebalancing and redistribution. Whether this authentic regeneration took on the democratic guise of France, England, or the United States, or the neoreactionary and totalitarian one of Fascism and

Nazism, it displayed common features that cannot be ignored. While even in Russia the state machine—instead of being abolished according to the Marxist prediction—became the driving force of economic transformation on the path of socialism.

At the center of this drastic change of perspective was the same answer to the same need: that politics, through the state and its instruments, had to assume the burden of problems, conflicts, crises, and changes brought about by the new complexity of the postwar societies, and by the vertiginous intensification of industrial production arising from it. And that this new role should be performed even when the mode of production itself was overthrown.

Whether the answer was a rigidly hierarchical and supremacist order, with the colors of the authoritarian modernization of Nazi-Fascism; or the utopian-despotic-egalitarian one of Soviet communism, ready to slide into the crushing power, violence, and privilege of a party oligarchy; or finally, the more and more openly democratic setup—though firmly retaining a capitalistic structure—of the Atlantic West, is naturally of decisive importance from the point of view of historic and moral judgment, but should not prevent us from seeing the common traits uniting these apparently divergent experiences.

Surfacing in all of them was the shared need of state which we have just mentioned, induced by the relationship that had been developing between masses, industry, and labor, which would last right through to the mid-1970s. In the Soviet Union, it would lead to the unprecedented construction of a state socialism quite different from anything predicted by Marxism. In the West, the impetus would result in a more balanced renegotiation of the social pact—interpreted by modernity until then in substantially laissez-faire terms. An agreement that might even be openly authoritarian, provided it guaranteed a certain social promotion of labor, accompanied by some degree of solidarity for the less well-off, albeit within a rigid hierarchy of inequality and subalternity.

The path opened by Fascism and Nazism ended in the unspeakable horror of extermination. That of the Russian Revolution would revive the Reign of Terror, without even displaying the furious ethicality of its origins, giving it mass dimensions bordering on genocide, through to a final catastrophe more grotesque than grand.

But the Western democracies were beginning the season of the Great Rebalancing—the culmination of civilizing labor.[13]

Citizens and Workers

The two equalities, as they had been fixed in the interpretation stretching from Hegel to Marx, continued, at least in European developments, to be two distinct worlds—all the more so after the instauration of the first socialist economy in history. On the one hand, the formal equality invented by the Roman jurists, then extended to the constitutional plane and that of public law, which found its fullest expression—its real truth—in the abstractions of capitalist society—labor, commodities, the state—assumed by Hegel (especially the third), and radically critiqued by Marx.

On the other, the substantive equality in the distribution of income, political power, and life opportunities, first theorized by Marxism, which then became the most important programmatic point of the October Revolution.

Yet the extension of political rights to all citizens, followed, thanks to the effects of new state policies, by the introduction of significant social rights—regarding education, health, and then, though less strongly and cogently, the environment, work, housing—was creating a new sliding plane between the two figures in some European democracies, particularly evident after the Second World War.

This juncture seemed able to mitigate—if not exactly heal—the fracture opened by the French Revolution with the turn of 1793, later theorized by Marx, between a formal and a substantive idea of equality. It was the most visible result of the social-democratic and Labourite strategies that had renounced the revolutionary aspect of Marxism, but taken many of its lessons on board, in the belief that inequalities could be corrected from within, perhaps with reforms that were decisive but did not question the foundations of the capitalistic mode of production. A celebrated sentence by Keynes in an essay from 1933, written as Roosevelt was being installed as President of the United States and the first New Deal was already being conceived, clearly embodies its spirit:

"Capitalism . . . is not intelligent, it is not beautiful, it is not just, it is not virtuous—and it doesn't deliver the goods. In short, we dislike it, and we are beginning to despise it. But when we wonder what to put in its place, we are extremely perplexed."[14] We will need to return to the attitude expressed here later.

So, between the 1930s and 1950s, what might be called an intermediate and revisionist paradigm of equality came into being: revisionist with respect to Marxist thought, but also to any laissez-faire dogma. Though not underpinned—as we have already said—by any genuinely new theoretical framework, it experimented, politically and socially, with a flexible and expansive way of being equal; concretely breaking down the barrier of formalism, but without injecting excessive doses of coercion into society (simultaneously protecting itself, as Walzer later said, "against the modern tyranny of politics"), and without subverting its economic foundations.[15] And taking care not to violate any fundamental liberty being constructed on the plane of history but placing at the core of the political initiative the valorization of a new figure of citizen worker, able to create through unions and parties the fullness of their civil role.

At the center of the new context was the institutional, social, and cultural forging of a close tie between politics, democracy, and labor. This was founded on the idea that labor was a unifying and intrinsically egalitarian anthropological experience, a distinctive human characteristic (we might say: the category founding the transcendental and historic unity of the species). Not the communist overthrow of the bourgeois universe to liberate labor from capitalist bonds, but its integration within a democratic politics that acknowledged it in a wide range of ways, and favored a better distributive relationship between labor income and capital income, with the consequent overlap—to the point of almost total identification—of the figure of the worker and that of the citizen.

It was the Western response to the challenge posed and rendered fearfully realistic by the mere presence of the Soviet Union and its socialism. And it was the pragmatic but effective response to one of the questions accompanying the journey of the democratic system in the West, which not even the experience of the Russian Revolution seemed to have solved: namely, how far one should go, in building equality, beyond the mere recognition of political rights and parity before the law.

The founding of citizenship around the figure of the worker was an attempt to get to the bottom of the problem. The capitalist structure was not in question; but, to offset its imbalances, action was taken on the side of distribution—through fiscality and public spending—in the form of wage increases, public services, and, finally, a social safety net and individualized economic support.

The choice did have an important consequence. All the democracies—especially in Europe, but in many respects the American one too—ended up linking their rebalancing policies to a historically determined paradigm of labor—the large-scale production of material commodities—which was mistaken for a universal and immutable form, a kind of tipping point for what was then called human progress (which did nothing but repeat the error made by Marx). As if that mass socializing experience, with a powerful egalitarian value, to which a large part of white collar, and even intellectual, labor was also tied in—sucked into the orbit of directly productive labor—were a kind of definitive acquisition of civilization.

The full deceptiveness of this fundamental error would later become apparent. But in the meantime, it did enable the culture of equality to reach its high point in Europe and, in the second half of the twentieth century, perhaps in the whole of the West. Political and legal formalism remained a decisive conquest. But the democratic destiny of the West did not end there. In the praxis that was taking shape, though the relationship between individuality and equality remained unresolved, the other key question, which had also emerged in the most incandescent core of the revolutions—the conflict between freedom and equality—seemed at least to have been circumvented. More equality could be introduced. Or, to put it better: equality could be injected into a greater number of different fields, going beyond the horizon of formalism alone, without significantly compressing the spaces of freedom. The issue was not solved theoretically, but an empirical solution was envisaged that at the very least seemed to make it less unsurmountable.

* * *

The Italian Constitution of 1948—a culturally advanced text, albeit now dated and wanting in some parts—is, from a legal point of view, perhaps the most limpid and shining example of what I would call the constitutionalizing of a median and flexible view of equality, even if conceptually not entirely determined.[16]

It was conceived and drafted almost in the same period as the Universal Declaration of Human Rights, which was inspired by the Western powers and adopted by the United Nations in Paris in December 1948, with forty-eight countries out of fifty-eight voting in favor: a text that can be regarded as the first attempt, on the back of the victory over Nazi-Fascism, to politically universalize the principle of equality, and in a nongeneric formulation no less, conferring on it a meaning akin to a full-blown legal norm (albeit sanction free) referring without exception, like an unbreakable decree, to all human beings (Article 1).[17]

For its own part, the Italian constitutional charter reflected, with greater legal conciseness, the same spirit found in the Declaration; and the very idea of a median form of equality that was proposed in it with great and detailed clarity had a number of—admittedly generic—correspondences in the statements made in the UN document (for example, in Articles 22–26). But the Italian Constitution did not stem from a social-democratic world, far less from settings close to American democracy, but rather from what was for once a happy compromise between popular Catholicism and Marxist culture, in the particular version elaborated by the communist leader Palmiro Togliatti and by a new generation of Christian Democrat politicians and intellectuals headed by Alcide de Gasperi.

The constitution starts by establishing, in Article 1, that "Italy is a democratic Republic founded on labour." Here, straightaway, is the idea of the citizen worker taking shape, because even the form of the state is founded on labor. Then, the first part of Article 3 states that "all citizens have equal social dignity and are equal before the law, without distinction of sex, race, language, religion, political opinion, personal and social conditions"—and this is the formal—legal and political—equality, affirmed, however, with a particular emphasis on "social" (the word recurs twice very close together). And finally, the second part of the same article declares that "it is the duty of the Republic to remove those obstacles of an economic or social nature which constrain the freedom and equality of citizens, thereby impeding the full development of the human person and the effective participation of all workers in the political, economic and social organisation of the country."[18] And here, once again, is the exchange between "citizens" and "workers"—truly the sign of an epoch and of a culture: French Revolution, industrialism, and working class. And, above all, there is the bridge between the two equalities: formal parity, though complete, was no longer enough. It needed to be flanked by a continual striving on the part of the state to remove obstacles, justified by setting against the principle of the formal equality of citizen workers, the "fact" of its impediment for reasons of "an economic or social nature." That is, a program was envisaged for a genuine public (re)construction of society through the redistribution of resources and power, with the aim of rendering effective a parity that might otherwise remain confined in the realm of political rights without any tangible consequences for the actual lives of the masses.

Just how far the Italian Republic really moved in this direction, to what extent the norm enshrined in the constitution really became a rule applied and translated into government action and binding directives for the public administration, is another matter. But certainly the welfare state built in Italy between the 1970s and 1990s—with the active collaboration of a communist party that had effectively become, uniquely in the West, the social-democratic mass organization which the country had never had, and of a small but bold and combative socialist party—can rightly be considered one of the freest and most advanced in the world, despite the persistence of significant structural imbalances, and the congenital fragility and inadequacy of public institutions.

* * *

Throughout the century the course of equality in the United States had a different character to that found in Europe, both in timing and content. The precocious experience of democracy and the extraordinary social mobility guaranteed by the abundance of resources and opportunities— for those in a position to take advantage of them—had created an entirely peculiar situation right from the start. Much sooner than in the Old World, they had helped to build an egalitarian paradigm in which the two aspects—the form of equality, and its actuality from the point of view of the naked concreteness of each life—so distant in the mirror of nineteenth-century European thought, appeared on the contrary to be much less disconnected. It was as if at least some of the results obtained with such difficulty in Europe—often after hard social struggle— were attained sooner and with much greater ease in America by going down a distinct though partially convergent path: as the consequence of a democratic practice that was much more penetrating from the outset. The same one that would later give rise to a society with an affluence and well-being capable of conquering the world, of creating an "irresistible empire," what with the rationalization of blue-collar labor, big pay increases (the revolution of the five-dollar daily wage announced by the Ford Company on January 5, 1914), the development of the large-scale retail trade, mass consumerism, accentuated individualism, and an egalitarian mentality (though the latter had many exceptions), in a tendentially unstable yet highly resistant equilibrium.[19] Between 1913 and 1948 this led to a marked reduction of income distribution inequalities— the most significant in the whole of American history. In the 1910s and 1920s—as Piketty observes—the richest 10 percent of the American population accounted for up to 40–45 percent of national income, while at the end of the 1940s that figure had dropped to 30–35 percent, a fall of about 10 percent.[20]

The crisis of 1929, the New Deal, and the "Keynesian revolution" represented a turning point, ushering in a new phase lasting, after the war, until the early 1960s—more or less until the presidencies of Kennedy and Johnson. When it petered out, under pressure from cultural and social forces that could no longer be contained within what was still basically a Rooseveltian framework, there would be important consequences on the plane of ideas as well.

These were the years of the youth movements that seemed to be rocking the United States from Berkeley to Chicago to New York; of the Vietnam War—the end of America's ingenuous view of empire—and of the struggles for the emancipation of minorities, starting with Black people, who were taking decisive steps forward in mobilizing to claim their rights.

And it was in this climate—of grand expectations, no less than of strong impatience and radicalization—that a new strand of thinking about equality developed unexpectedly in America, capable, at least from a conceptual point of view, of opening previously unexplored paths, and certainly one of the most important American contributions to the culture of the century.[21]

As we have already said, the twentieth century had not seen until then, not even in Europe, important novelties in this sense: nothing comparable to the great tradition between the eighteenth and nineteenth century. Nor would the thought that developed around the student movements of the late 1960s—with the partial exception of France—ever contain anything that really changed the intellectual scene.

In general, the political practices of the European 1968 placed emphasis instead on the liberation of subjectivities, particularly the historically weaker ones: women, minorities, the excluded, and thus on the fulfillment of individualities—in some cases making decisive contributions to the modernization of the respective countries (in Italy, for example, this aspect was prevalent)—rather than on that of equality, which was left to the initiative of the traditional left-wing parties.

From a theoretical point of view, Western political philosophy remained substantially stuck on the alternative between the socialist model and bourgeois democracy: in other words, on the acceptance or rejection of the Marxist perspective, which in turn was being articulated with remarkable richness in different orientations: from the Soviet orthodoxy, based on a dogmatic adherence to Leninism, to the various Western Marxisms, among which the French and Italian versions stood out.

In a certain sense, it was as if the conceptual density of the issue had been entirely cancelled out, on both sides of the Atlantic, by the immediately ideological-political dimension of the conflict that commenced straight after the Second World War: which left scope for little other than to take sides. And even outside of this reduction, the most important figures in the twentieth-century debate, at least until the 1970s—from Weber to Croce, to Gentile, or from Husserl to Heidegger, or, again, from Lukács to Benjamin, Sartre, and Merleau-Ponty—cannot be regarded as thinkers of equality. A case apart—due also to the exceptionality of her story, between Europe and America—is Hannah Arendt, who we have referred to several times and will do so again. Another is represented by the French thought of the second half of the century, to which we shall return.

And there is something more to add regarding Europe: the impression—though the point would merit much greater study—that the relationship between metaphysics and politics, especially in German and Italian philosophy in the years around the two world wars (but the same might apply, with some distinction, also for France and for England itself) represented, and perhaps even exacerbated, the same difficulty that we identified earlier in Hegel's thought. Namely, the creation of a gap between the speculative force of ontology and the shortening of his gaze, full of misunderstandings, when he tried to include the reality of the present in order to deduce tendencies and evaluations: and, moreover, in an incomparably more serious and dramatic historic situation than the one in which Hegel lived. The consequence was the repetition of a kind of short circuit in the face of the extreme criticality of the passage: the riskier it was, the more penetrating the force of the thought in play. A kind of intermittence of philosophy before the hard opacity of history, precisely in the moments in which that very same philosophy seemed to be acquiring a decisive weight in the course of events. I believe it is a condition that holds true for Heidegger no less than for Gentile, for whom one might even say that Nazism and Fascism in some way represented what, for Hegel, was the blinding presence of Napoleon on the battlefields of Jena and Austerlitz.[22] And the thread of these considerations may lead further still, to the point of thematizing the existence of an overall problematicality in the relationship between philosophy and democracy in the great European metaphysics of the twentieth century—with its holistic and totalizing background—and to pushing the difficulty all the way back to Hegel, albeit within a different framework. But this is not a path I intend to venture down here, though I believe it will be necessary sooner or later to come to terms with this aspect of Europe's history as well.

An exception regarding the weight of equality in his thought could be Gramsci, whose political doctrine and vision of democracy are coming more and more clearly into focus with time.[23] They are basically far removed from the main strands of European Marxism in the 1920s, within which they were long constrained for reasons of party orthodoxy.

His ideas of "hegemony" and intellectual and social "organicity" have other sources relating to different traditions, also deeper within Italian thought. But immersing ourselves in his world with any degree of originality would take us away—I fear without sufficient advantage—from the perspective we are pursuing, and so with some regret I will refrain.

Even social-democratic and Labourite revisionism—after an initial season of fervor in the decades preceding the First World War—had no genuine conceptual framework to sustain them, but rather the fortunate invention of a series of empirical solutions. These were guided, in the economy, by choices of more or less direct Keynesian inspiration, and by the general conviction that the democratic state had to be socially committed and play a key role in redistribution policies for the benefit of the less privileged.

※ ※ ※

All the more important, then, was the wave of new American thought, which seemed to set aside the European alternative between socialism and bourgeois society—though the worldwide presence of the socialist camp was still clearly discernible within it—in the effort to arrive at an analytical objectivity shorn of ideological dross: an indispensable condition for attaining a point of view hoping to present itself as universal.

We can consider the most famous book by John Rawls—*A Theory of Justice*, published in 1971 but drawing on studies begun at the end of the 1950s—as the most significant seal on this change.[24] In his perspective, the question of equality was related back to the classical terms of the rational foundations of a theory of justice with clearly neo-Aristotelian elements, thereby opening the last great public discussion on this theme in Western thinking.

In reality, beyond the veil of rigidly formalized communicative protocols, it is hard not to detect in this work an evident trace of the times, and not to recognize in it a lucid democratic passion, however well concealed behind the cold (and sometimes even rather dull) style customarily employed in the English and American analytic tradition. If we pay attention, it is possible to hear in it all the anxieties, disappointments, hopes, and tensions that were already a part of the America of Kennedy and of the "new frontier"; and then of Vietnam and the racial and civil rights struggles; and, at the same time, of the standoff with the Soviet Union, interpreted as a global challenge to civilization.

We can see reflected in it, hidden and yet clearly perceivable, a country and its intellectual elites that were by now profoundly different—more mature but also more shaken and uncertain—to those of Roosevelt and of the New Deal. Though from an openly radical perspective, just two years after Rawls's work appeared, James O'Connor in *The Fiscal Crisis of the State* would display a not dissimilar attitude.[25] In those years it seemed to many that America had reached a point of no return, and new paths needed to be sought out.

The background to Rawls's reflection was a dramatically open American problem, though he did not thematize it directly, in line with a strategy of apparent avoidance of the present which remains one of the most interesting facets of his writing. It was not about the incisiveness of equality, nor of the fields touched by it. The question did not concern the "equality of what," as Amartya Sen would write in 1979, but rather inclusion.[26] Not the economic depth of the equal, but its horizontal political widening—as would be retrospectively well observed by Robert Dahl in 2006.[27] Above all, in the structure of the new American thinking about equality, there was this: a strong and urgent demand for inclusion.

The point was not to give greater penetration and substantive consistency to a merely formal provision of parity. But rather to decide if and how to make the American model of equality—which almost from the beginning had already been a web of formal rights and material opportunities, but which had been conceived in a similarly precocious manner as burdened by heavy excluding mechanisms—a conquest effectively within reach of all citizens. If the time had come to finally put to the test a democratic frame without preconstituted exclusions regarding marginalized minorities, as had happened right from the time of Independence: for the Native Americans, for last-generation immigrants, and, above all, for Black people—now free, but heavily discriminated against in every field: the wound that had never healed, left as an inheritance by the slave system of the eighteenth and nineteenth centuries. That is to say, whether to really make what had been called, not without grounds, "the American dream"—freedom, (a certain) equality, consumption, and opportunities—a dream that could really be dreamed with some degree of realism by all Americans. In other words, whether to make citizenship, as it had been being historically configured not just in the United States, a completely inclusive tie.

> First: each person is to have an equal right to the most extensive scheme of equal basic liberties compatible with a similar scheme of liberties for others.
> Second: social and economic inequalities are to be arranged so that they are both (a) reasonably expected to be to everyone's advantage, and (b) attached to positions and offices open to all.[28]

Here, Rawls is presenting his "two principles of justice." Later in the same work, he reformulated the second of these as follows, with an even more marked and direct egalitarian connotation: "Social and economic inequalities are to be arranged so that they are both (a) to the greatest expected benefit of the least advantaged and (b) attached to offices and positions open to all under conditions of fair equality of opportunity."[29] And finally, a third, conclusive version, where the phrase "consistent with the just savings principle" was added to (a).[30] The progression reveals the effort made to achieve a formulation that was as "fair" as possible, but at the same time broad and comprehensive enough to take account of every determination considered indispensable—an endeavor he continued to pursue in his *Political Liberalism* of 1993.[31]

The goal was ambitious: to outline the conceptual model of a new social pact, more solid and, above all, less excluding, in an age in which the invisible hand of the market and the consequent relative casualness of the natural and social lottery—accepted until then, together with the legacy of slavery, without too much difficulty by the American democratic tradition—were beginning to be judged as no longer structurally sufficient, despite the corrections of a generally effective state interventionism (rightly observed by Fred Hirsch and Salvatore Veca).[32]

The philosophical frame within which Rawls was operating was that of a strongly felt neocontractualism, which took as its points of reference Locke (the *Second Treatise*), Rousseau (the Rousseau of the *Social*

Contract), and Kant (*The Metaphysics of Morals*), against a perceptible neo-Aristotelian background, in a return of ethicality—if we wish, of tension between ethics and economy—that stood in clear contrast to Hume, Bentham, and any eminently utilitarian perspective.

Rawls's justice was in fact an explicit redistributive justice, which required direct, incisive, and continual intervention by public institutions in the economic process:

> The main problem of distributive justice is the choice of a social system. . . . The social system is to be designed so that the resulting distribution is just however things turn out. To achieve this end it is necessary to set the social and economic process within the surroundings of suitable political and legal institutions.[33]

And here too we are well beyond the New Deal and, it seems to me, a long way beyond any specifically American political or intellectual tradition; a long way beyond the leveling up of opportunities and the democratic mentality which—albeit within the limits noted above—were now inscribed within republican customs.[34] Instead, the European social-democratic and Labourite vision was being implicitly evoked: a large public presence aiming to build and maintain a genuine welfare state not far removed from what could be found in the Scandinavian countries or in Great Britain between the end of the war and the 1960s. In elaborating the ideas at the heart of his research it is possible to discern in Rawls the formulation of doctrines that tapped into the experience of the European West, and Marxism itself, though he projected them into an analytic frame that seemed to do completely without them.

Just over a decade later, this perspective would be rendered more explicit, and probably more accentuated as well, in an important work by Michael Walzer, *Spheres of Justice*. Published in 1983, it openly positioned itself, with notable differences of thought but inspired by the same ethical commitment, in the space opened up by Rawls's work. Almost at the end of his book, Walzer wrote:

> The appropriate arrangements in our own society are those, I think, of a decentralized democratic socialism; a strong welfare state run, in part at least, by local and amateur officials; a constrained market;

an open and demystified civil service; independent public schools; the sharing of hard work and free time; the protection of religious and familial life; a system of public honoring and dishonoring free from all considerations of rank or class; workers' control of companies and factories; a politics of parties, movements, meetings, and public debate.[35]

It was a hypothesis that went further than the northern European social-democratic viewpoint itself. It arrived at the threshold of a full-blown socialist humanism, in which the capitalistic character of production might no longer have been untouchable, even though Walzer continued with great acumen to point out the social advantages of a market-based economy.

As the author himself declared,[36] *Spheres of Justice* made considerably greater use—and with notable mastery—of history and anthropology than Rawls's great book, which was more attuned to economics and behavioral psychology. And the concept of complex equality articulated in it ("no citizen's standing in one sphere or with regard to one social good can be undercut by his standing in some other sphere, with regard to some other good") was a sophisticated attempt—more advanced than Rawls's in some respects, and less reliant on seventeenth- and eighteenth-century sources—to combine economics, sociology, and political theory in a paradigm of equality better suited to the complexity of the contemporary world.[37]

In both works it is possible to detect, clearly and palpably, a similar intellectual attitude. Something that I would describe as a need to move beyond—if not a genuine dissatisfaction with—the American democratic tradition and the political praxis reflected in it until then. The awareness that—however great and irremissible the achievements thus far—its legacy was no longer enough, and that it could not just be continually updated. In some way—perhaps more openly in Walzer, less evident in Rawls—the idea that transpired, in a more or less declared fashion, was the need to look once again to Europe and its experiences: not in order to repeat them, but to open up a new horizon. In certain respects, even a book like James Meade's *Agathotopia*—the last of the great economists of the Keynesian circle—which appeared in England in 1989, can be regarded as confirmation of this reciprocal moving

closer.[38] The gulf that for around a century had separated the two sides
of the Atlantic was beginning to close.

Equal Individuals?

It is not our task here to chart the long and intense debate sparked—
especially in the United States—by Rawls's hypotheses, which in a certain
sense has never entirely subsided; far less is it to examine all the "egal-
itarianist" positions that surfaced in American legal-philosophical debate,
from Dworkin to Nagel and Scanlon.[39] Suffice it to observe how, until the
end of the 1980s—until the full explosion of the technological revolution
in the West, and the collapse of the Soviet Union and its communism—
this discussion took place entirely in the shadow of the (uncontestable)
existence of an alternative to the capitalist mode of production and of
organizing society which, almost in a flash, literally vanished.

Since then—despite the multiplication of the contradictions surrounding us—it is as if dialectic—or even simply just the taste for and
value of alternative thought—has disappeared from the great history of
the world. Wherever one looks it is impossible to see anything but the
looming figure of new capital, and the power of its protean presence. And
wherever politics is conceived (except, in part, if we look at China),
nothing else takes shape, at least in the declarations of the key players—
the facts are another matter—if not a flesh-stripped version of the Western
form of democracy. While the only social model that seems to attract
consensus and interest—everywhere, this time including China—is a
mass individualism, acquisitive and consumerist, which has become—
at different levels of articulation and development, sometimes very rough
and barely shaped, in other cases more sophisticated and aware—the
universal paradigm of any human coexistence.

＊ ＊ ＊

This loss of multiplicity—like a one-dimensional contracting of
history—has played a crucial role in the way of thinking equality; and the
change concerns America no less than Europe. A book like Amartya

Sen's *The Idea of Justice,* which appeared in 2009 and is dedicated to Rawls, despite an apparent continuity in the debate, reveals on almost every page that it is the child of another age (reflected also in his intriguing—though I am not sure how truly successful—attempt to introduce into his analysis different, non-Western traditions of thought, for instance Indian).[40]

There is, however, something more as well, which, observed retrospectively, emerges in the long discussion begun by Rawls. A motif that takes us back to a different and no less fundamental aspect of the American conception of equality, which touches on the history of the deep culture of that society and from there reaches out to the whole of the West. An issue that we have brushed up against several times, and which we must now begin to consider more closely: I am referring to the problematic relationship between individuality and equality.

If the individual remains the only form through which to conceive the human—not the indisputable singularity of the "biological roots" of each life, but its cultural and, let's say, anthropological projection on the plane of history—how can its full valorization be reconciled with an equality that goes beyond a formal parity of a solely political and legal kind?[41]

In Rawls this difficulty seems to me to be very evident. To deal with it, he has to devise an unrealistic and laborious mechanism, albeit inspired by classical sources. To presuppose—developing both Rousseauian and Kantian motifs—that it is possible to start out from an "initial position of equality," however "hypothetical," where "no one knows his place in society, his class position or social status, nor does any one know his fortune in the distribution of natural assets and abilities, his intelligence, strength, and the like."[42]

In this way individuals will be able to choose "the principles of justice" enveloped by what Rawls calls a "veil of ignorance."[43] A screening—a kind of undeclared transcendentalism—separating them from the knowledge "that would enable them to choose heteronomous principles," to adopt, that is, solutions inspired in part by respective individual advantages, orienting themselves instead "as free and equal rational persons knowing only that those circumstances obtain which give rise to the need for principles of justice."[44]

Put differently, Rawls resorts to picturing an entirely imaginary but essential condition—something halfway between a rediscovery of the Rousseauian state of nature and a purely transcendental reduction of the human—with the sole aim of substituting the concrete and actual individualities of a historically determined social universe with an entirely impersonal function, which places them temporarily between parentheses. And in fact, individuals must be supposed as "moral persons, that is, as rational beings with their own ends and capable, I shall assume, of a sense of justice"—essentially, that they stop being historically determined individuals—as the only way of realizing the base conditions for the construction of a just society.[45]

In addition to Rawls—regarding whom, on this point, Sen's criticisms appear highly pertinent, though made from within an alternative perspective—the same problem seems to me to be present in Walzer as well.[46] But in his case the response differs and is, I would say, less abstract and transcendental, more closely linked—in keeping with his intellectual style—to the effective historicity of the situations he examines.

"The establishment of an egalitarian society will not be the end of the struggle for equality," he writes in the final page of *Spheres of Justice*.[47] Before continuing, immediately after:

> All that one can hope for is that the struggle might get a little easier. . . . There is a certain attitude of mind that underlies the theory of justice and that ought to be strengthened by the experience of complex equality: we can think of it as a decent respect for the opinions of mankind. Not the opinions of this or that individual, which may well deserve a brusque response: I mean those deeper opinions that are the reflections in individual minds, shaped also by individual thought, of the social meanings that constitute our common life.[48]

Between the opinions of individuals as "moral persons" described in Rawls's conception, and the "deeper" ones "that are the reflections in individual minds . . . of the social meanings that constitute our common life" of the reconstruction offered by Walzer there are, of course, notable differences, which we must not neglect: the contractualism of Lockean and Enlightenment derivation of the former cannot be superimposed without an unacceptably forced reading over the historicized and sociologized communitarianism of the latter.

And yet we find, in both views, the insistence on the same and, in truth, decisive point: namely, that in order to establish a "fair" version of equality in a theoretically and socially correct way, it is necessary by the very nature of things—though not in a definitive manner—to jump over the barrier of the individual, or at least to circumscribe and place it between parentheses, in order to touch down in a different world, articulated around a different dimension of the human, to which one's own vision can be solidly anchored.

But where exactly?

Emancipation and Difference

The problematic relation between individuality and equality runs, as we have seen, through the whole course of modernity.

Up to a certain level of social complexity, there was no contradiction between the two terms—at least from the historical point of view, which is the only one that really counts. The determination of individuality as a value, of the irreducible specificity of each life as a richness to protect, fitted perfectly with the discovery of what we might call the human sharing of the human: the dazzling intuition of Montaigne—the primary basis for the recognition of any form of equality.

There was already this dual register—which to some extent used individuality as a path to equality—in the Christian construction of the person, specular with respect to the theological one of the Trinity. Just as there was still the same doubleness in the initial dissolving of the ancient and medieval web of ties, dependencies, kinship, and community amalgamations that, within insuperable hierarchies, erased any particular existence, making the escape into asceticism (the individual "outside of the world") the only possible means for constructing an independent self fully capable of self-recognition.

With the developments of modernity, however, things would change.

The individual, liberated and atomized through labor, and conceived as such by the new philosophy, discovered the force of the new social class ties: both of the "bourgeois" kind, and the—intrinsically egalitarian—ones that bound them into large masses of workers (a people of workers). But the individual also perceived the liberating power of differences, and the thrust toward complete self-autonomy contained in their full unfolding. Emancipation through the recognition of equality, made possible by the sociality of labor; and emancipation through the valuing of differences, made possible, especially for the bourgeoisie, by the growing development of individualities—thanks to the increase in consumption, the growth of information, and the capitalistic diversification of opportunities—thus turned into the extremes of an axis around which the sense of the whole of modernity revolved. Ever more equal, and ever more different, in a polarity becoming more unstable by the day.

The critical point of greatest contrast—and greatest power—in this duality would be expressed in the history of American democracy and society, built right from the outset on this double background: individualistic and at the same time egalitarian. Tocqueville had been nebulously aware of it, and it would have been impossible to see it any more clearly in his time. The thinking on equality developed in the United States in the 1970s and 1980s probably contained a stronger perception, but it was still too much within the world that had produced it. In Europe—where the same tension also manifested itself—everything appeared hazier and less distinct due to the heavy stratification of a more intricate and tortuous social history: but there would be intellectual outcomes here too, especially in France—and we shall speak of these in due course.

* * *

The great movements that traversed American society, especially in the second half of the twentieth century—for the rights of Black Americans and, in particular, the women's movement—were at one and the same time, almost indissolubly, struggles for equality, starting with the political kind—with respect to white people, to men, to the more privileged—and struggles for the recognition of differences: of gender, of cultural identity, of autonomy in the construction of each individual profile. The ever-variable specificity of the intertwining between equality and difference was determined empirically from one occasion to another by the type of demand that was made, by the goal that was set, and by its context.

What proved to be wholly new was, so to speak, the microphysics of the claimed equality, the actual horizon. Now it was an equality that always included difference; or an equality included in a difference: an equality, in short, achieved or traversed by the contemporary recognition of the unequal, of the multiple, of the particularized. In any case, an equality that was not the mere overcoming of difference, but which admitted the continuing existence of the unequal, though stripped of its discriminating effect. That saw diversity as a value in its own right, worthy of formal protection—the formalization of the unequal as the means to achieving a fairer equal—in the same moment in which its cancellation was requested from the point of view of the acknowledgment of this or that right, of this or that power previously denied or taken away.

The more the spaces of equality expanded—starting with politics, not formally generalized in America until the mid-1960s[49]—the more its recognition and its emancipating power split immediately into the contemporaneous emergence of a network of diversity that until then had been socially hidden, which precisely the achievement of equality allowed to come out, and which retroacted on the very configuration of the just-acknowledged equal, confirming it and denying it at the same time. An ocean of differences-equalities that were added to the, as it were, historic ones, the result of the insuppressibly individualistic basis of American society. It was the logic of contradiction and of negation—often double negation—that became life, history, social quality, the very form of perceived or dreamed justice.

＊ ＊ ＊

In this reshaped horizon, which culminated in the 1990s and also saw the spread, at times superficial and purely extrinsic, of the culture of the politically correct and its relativistic background—being able to coexist by way of juxtaposition, without the toil of really having to mediate—Europe, especially its continental and western part, would occupy a place apart.

In this corner of the world, the more or less efficient but generally acceptable functioning of the welfare states established in each nation, which enjoyed renewed impetus after the capitalistic stabilization at the end of the 1970s, following the oil crisis; a less developed culture of minorities and women's movements than in America; and finally—before the migratory waves—relative social homogeneity, seemed to render these problems—linked to a new way of conceiving equality—less acute and visible. And what we described as the sliding plane between the form and substance of being equal seemed in any case to guarantee a relatively stable platform for any future development.

It was in this context that the technological revolution which would change the social condition of the planet matured and exploded.

Changing Labor

The end of the age of labor is an event that is filling our time, and its importance, though the consequences never cease to disorient us, has not yet been fully grasped from either a historic or a conceptual point of view.

In saying this, we certainly do not wish to claim that labor has ceased to exist as a human activity.[50] It simply denotes the end of a historic way of working that constituted modernity and our manner of thinking, even for those who did not directly engage in it themselves: the kind involving the production, through capitalist industry, of material commodities destined for exchange. A mode that had been capable, with wealth created, social bonds forged, and culture radiated, of giving rise to an entire civilization: that belonged to it—retrospectively we can now say this—no less than to the formative and liberating power of capital; and of promoting a previously unknown model of emancipation.

The expression also alludes to the no less important fact that the new jobs which are replacing the old declining labor in the West cannot have, now or at any time in the future, for structural reasons quite independent of any political, legal, or ethical choice, the same function as the figure that is disappearing.

To begin to understand this, we need first of all to relate what is happening to the metamorphosis of the historic forms of capital, which depend in turn on the mutation of the technological conditions of production—the real driving force of the current revolution. It was in fact the leap in technology that projected society beyond the age of industry, of large factory systems with the mass labor force clustered around them: of "individuals posited as workers," to use Marx's limpid, succinct definition. And which put an end to the economy that had shaped modernity and marked its entire history.

In place of the industrial form, the last few decades have been seeing the construction of what I shall define—in historic terms and not those of economic theory—as the techno-financial form of capital, characterized by the ever more intensely technological production of services and immaterial commodities—or at any rate of goods in which the material component is of less and less importance in determining their market value. A model as spatially offshored as the previous one was rooted in place, which has reduced old frontiers to dust and thrown the rigid state-hoods of former times into crisis;[51] where the cloud, software, and the web have replaced steel and coal. And where the multiplication of speculative income, made possible by an accumulation of capital in the form of global financial flows, ready to be moved around on a world checkerboard in the search for the best yields, has acquired previously unimagined proportions.

We must recognize it: for the history of capital and its metamorphoses there is no single corresponding mode of wealth production, as Marx still thought; but a plurality of modes, some of them very different. Capital is a social relation and is not identified with the use of a specific technology but can encompass many. Change transforms its composition (more or less what Marx called its "organic composition") in favor of the financial and "immaterial" quota with respect to that of "physical" property (to use Piketty's terminology) and modifies its relationship with labor, penetrating to mutate its quality, without touching the private enterprise character of the appropriation of profit.[52]

✸ ✸ ✸

In the context of the situation we are now experiencing, wealth is present above all in its immaterial mode, directly connected with the dematerialization that is impacting our lives: now consisting almost exclusively of communication, information, services, virtuality presented as abstractions of abstraction (only the physicality of death—the infinite dispelling of the finite—seems to resist this process, in its irreversible materiality: which is why the culture surrounding us tends to repress it everywhere).

The novelty has enormous consequences for working conditions. The value of commodities tends to be increasingly and almost solely linked to the amount of technology present in each product unit. And as technology and innovation themselves appear in no other form than as commodities (like living labor in the old system), it follows that the commodity par excellence, the commodity from which all commodities can be produced, is no longer—or is less and less so—directly supplied living labor, but technology, in its concrete conditions of existence.

Therefore, producing commodities through commodities now basically no longer means producing commodities through labor as commodity, but through technology as commodity, which has become an autonomous component with respect to living labor in the actual course of the production process.

Naturally, every kind of technology incorporates labor—the labor required to devise and refine it—but it appears, so to speak, absorbed within its result. As it is also clear that technology in turn requires an addition of living labor in the production process; but the more such labor is integrated with advanced technology, the less it takes the classic form of the old serial and standardized labor, becoming a punctiform, molecularized labor, destructured in its classic terms, and recomposed only on the basis of the intensity and specificity of knowledge that it requires. In other words: the more technology develops, the more the cognitive quality and creative specificity of the living labor necessary to include it in the production process grows in parallel.

Unfolding, then, is what could be described as the epoch of the corporative neofragmentation of labor, which does not determine equality and does not create networks of mass social relations, still less stable class structures—paradoxically, just like the old precapitalistic labor.[53] A new age, dominated by physically lighter types of work, less socializing, less invasive, less rigid, more particularized, which will probably require increasingly less life time and more study and training time—and will also be much harder to unionize and to unify politically, because they are more separate and in competition with each other.[54] It represents the triumph of difference in the working world too, which previously appeared to be the universe of the equal—a social and cultural reflection of the real character of its former abstraction. It is the affirmation of specificity, if we wish of individuality, in the production of wealth, where all the labor that really counts is the cognitively intense kind; while prevalently manual labor is pushed to the fringes of the production process.

The production of low-tech material commodities will obviously not disappear in this new reality (just as agricultural labor did not in the old industrial world). Nor will manual or mechanically executed labor; but it is seeing a gradual reduction in numbers, replaced in part by machines endowed with artificial intelligence; it is being offshored with respect to highly specialized production; and above all it is declining socially, losing contractual power. Nothing decisive is taking place in its field for the equilibrium and dynamics of the society to which it belongs; just as, in its own time, after the Industrial Revolution, nothing socially decisive happened again in the countryside. Manual workers are being reduced to figures of little importance: their labor-power is losing weight, fading, together with the tasks that define it.

Capital, on the other hand, detached from its historic and formal reference to mass living labor, is losing its classic social bases, the ones that saw it established as industrial capital, and is become ever more autonomous from any production without advanced technological content, or which does not directly develop a new technology; it is losing any spatial or national point of reference, and is tending to accentuate to the highest degree its financial metamorphosis, which in truth was already underway at the end of the big-industry mode of production (we could say that in a certain sense the financialization of industrial capital acted as "primitive accumulation" for the new mode of production).[55]

It is this more abstract and free form of capital that is needed by technological development, which requires investment to be rapidly concentrated where innovation and the research that supports it appear most promising in terms of profitability. And it was to make this connection more evident that we spoke earlier of an interweaving of the technological and the financial.

In this system, the reproduction of capital through financial speculation is to some extent an inevitable tendency. A functional proneness to secure the resources needed to fuel innovation, which translates into an ever-increasing impetus for innovation itself, for an increasing technological richness of commodities, and hence their greater value.

But as it is technology that ultimately mediates between capital and its profits, and the latter always demands the financial transformation of capital, it is in any case destined to underpin the entire system. While pure speculation, if not plowed back into new technology, has an only apparent autonomy; its range of action is limited. If isolated as such, it indicates a functional and historic pathology rather than a physiological condition. It does not produce social wealth, but just the fictitious appearance of it, liable to ruinous collapses.

❈ ❈ ❈

The change we are living through is turning the technological revolution into a social revolution, the weight of which is hard to imagine.

In the space of a few decades, the formation of techno-financial capital has rocked the cultural and social foundations of the Western industrial societies, the product of centuries of developments, and has created a new historic form of the relationship between capital and labor. This is no longer founded on the progressive and unlimited expansion of the production base (more production, more labor, more wealth), and therefore on the quantitative and serial dimension of labor, but on the increase of the qualitative specificities of individual jobs, always measured by the amount of technology they incorporate and transform into immaterial commodities and services that can be sold on the market.

Put succinctly, we could say that we are in the presence of the end of the "abstract" labor of the classical economy, and of a recovery of its lost particularity—but with an enormously higher level of cognitive skills than any precapitalist past. This epochal change is generating new hierarchies in knowledge and skills, and new social scales, albeit more fluid than the old and now unrecognizable class structures. And it is creating around it an aura of inevitability, giving fresh significance to Marx's old warning not to regard as unmodifiable natural laws what were only historic tendencies resulting from bourgeois capitalistic organization.

Above all the new age has broken the historic relation between equality and labor: a cornerstone of modernity. The triumph of the quality of labor over its pure quantity, while opening novel and unexplored trails for the potential of human intelligence, has also marked the end of labor as the inexhaustible motor of social ties, of class solidarity, of community bonds.

Indeed, its intrinsically differentiated status is building new inequalities, adding to those induced by the economic cycle as such, and creating gulfs between one job and another that we thought had been overcome forever.

In the new configuration, classic exploitation—what Marx called the extraction of surplus value through surplus labor—is reserved only for low-tech forms of labor, where the purely quantitative aspect of work continues to prevail—its old abstract form: jobs now without protection, because they have become socially marginal, especially as nothing passes through them that is decisive for capital, and not even for society as a whole. While the more that labor incorporates complex skills, the more balanced is its relationship with capital, and the differences between their incomes tend to diminish.

The consequence is the complete devaluation of human activities that do not possess new knowledge and new technology: their impoverishment, their reduction to pure quantity, replaceable at any moment, because the seriality of labor has almost no value anymore. And given that the whole of modernity was built on the relation between individual life and labor, the result—inevitable—is that the disvalue of labor is transformed into disvalue of lives, to the point of producing savage forms of exploitation on the threshold of a neoslavery that seems to have re-emerged from the darkest recesses of the past.

Space is thus being created for new contradictions: on the one hand, the unlimited growth of individual subjectivities and expectations, made possible by the dizzying increase in information, and by the universal circulation of consumerist options. On the other, the tendency toward the crystallization of a new structure of privileges, linked to the capacity to create wealth through technology, with the marginalization of masses of citizen workers diminished by unemployment or socially irrelevant jobs.

There is another effect of this authentic social tornado: the erosion of the mass bases that enabled the birth and existence of the twentieth-century democracies—especially in the Labourite and social-democratic variant. The classes that gave substance to that background, once solid, have now disappeared—first of all the working class, but also many of the traditional productive middle classes—transmuted into shapeless pools of rancor and fear.

Their existence was in fact founded entirely on the relationship between the increasing amount of socially useful work and the amount of wealth produced, and on the consequent political representation—through universal suffrage—of equal and abstract labor as an element indispensable to the production of wealth. A role and a function now destroyed by the current form of the relationship between capital, technology, and labor, which is exposing entire generations to risks we believed had been totally averted.

The so-called populisms are a desperate cry—though their full impotence will soon become apparent—against the consolidation of the new global capitalistic aristocracy (capital income, and income from cognitively advanced jobs) which is emerging from this metamorphosis and taking shape before our eyes with increasing clarity.

It is with this reality that democracy must come to terms: a democracy that will have to reform itself if it wishes to survive.

CHAPTER FIVE

THE NEW EQUALITY

Figures of the Human in the Age of Technology

The Resurgence of the Unequal

Technological revolutions inevitably engender new forms of the human: the latter being nothing—in its biological basis as in its anthropological and cultural profile—but the result of processes in constant movement, even at their very core. As such, they are the unmistakable heartbeat of the historicity of the species.

The human changes: if its relationship with nature and the environment is modified, if the quality of relational life mutates (and every technological leap provokes such metamorphoses), the interior and social perception that we elaborate about ourselves and its projections on the plane of history are also transformed. New horizons of meaning open up. New worlds of thought are produced. It happened thousands of years ago, as far as can be ascertained, with the early development of agriculture and then of metallurgy, which led in the West to what Snell and Vernant called "the discovery of the mind."[1] It was repeated, a long time later, with the revolution in labor and industry, an authentic new "axial age" which, as it unfolded, completed the invention of the modern individual.[2]

The idea of equality is the measure of our vision of the human. An idea that we have seen growing stronger in proportion to our ability to grasp and represent the universal—the infinite, if we like—in the unlimited articulation of negations and particularities, however unsurmountable and lacerating they may appear. And the effect of proximity that can be achieved with the new technologies in relation to any place of social aggregation on the planet is making it possible for the first time for a unitary image of the human to become shared sense, albeit in a fragile and intermittent manner for now: not the intuition of a few, but the self-representation of an entire civilization. From this point of view, we cannot be anything other than optimistic. Never has the unity of the species appeared with such persuasive clarity. The biological evidence—once just anatomical (like that from which Antiphon's observation started 2,500 years ago) but now genetic as well—accompanied by the contiguity of spaces and consumption, and increasingly less dimmed by ideological prejudices, has given rise to political orientations, social demands, and even legal norms. And yet the future has never seemed so uncertain and threatening. From within the vortex of this sudden and incredible acceleration of historic time, the scale and direction of change still eludes us.[3] Its shockwave is stirring a maelstrom of dust, dimming the light in which we are bathed and making the things around us deceptive and indistinct. We are struggling to distinguish the new figures from the remains of the old, now lost, world. Shadows that seem never to have been observed before are proving to be just ruins in the final stages of disintegration; while barely formed profiles, charged with future, are hidden, still not clearly defined, beneath layers of unusable rubble.

The significance of the devastating pandemic that has turned the world upside down must also be understood in this framework of new uncertainties. It should be viewed as a signal of history: but if we can grasp its "prophetic" meaning, and act accordingly, all its ills will not have been in vain.

The COVID-19 epidemic is the first in history to have been subject (almost) from the start to total, worldwide medicalization, with, as its epilogue, an extraordinary mass vaccination campaign, and it has been accompanied by an uninterrupted barrage of information (albeit with some serious shortcomings). Nothing of the kind has ever happened before. An abyss separates it from the 1918 influenza pandemic of a century ago, which played out almost in silence despite the shocking number of deaths. These have never fully been calculated but are in the order of tens of millions.

In the crisis that broke out so suddenly, science and technology have clearly appeared for what they now effectively are: the custodians of the human, the guarantors of its very existence. Their protocols, procedures, and prescriptions have for the first time revealed themselves to be the measure of a universally accepted community of destinies. But what has likewise been evident—sometimes in dramatic fashion—is the whole contradiction between the essential value of scientific research, with the results it is able to achieve (in this case, vaccines), and the largely private nature that governs its functioning. It can therefore rightly be said that the salvation of the human—its own bare life—appears today exclusively in the form of a commodity.

Ambiguity now enshrouds the condition of equality as well, and the view we have of it.

If we squeeze the boundaries of the planet into a single shot, as it is now easy to do, we realize that in no past time have its inhabitants been so linked to each other—to the extent that everyone has quite literally become "our neighbor." The globalization of the capitalist economy brought out, even before the onset of the pandemic and in a completely unexpected way, precisely that common bedrock of the human that we have seen on many occasions at the center of European philosophy: the one nebulously detected by the ancients, and observed with masterly insight by Montaigne at the dawn of modernity. It has been transformed into the motor of a universal system of needs that underpins the network of markets on which our lives depend, permitted in turn by the ever more rapid circulation of lifestyle habits and information. It is one of the benign aspects of globalization.

In very different contexts, and not only due to economic forces, masses of women and men have, for the first time, left behind them an existence devoted solely to survival and have begun looking beyond the search for water to quench their thirst and food to stave off hunger. In a few short years, entire parts of the world—especially in Asia, above all in the large urban centers—have acquired a prominence they never had before; and those living there have succeeded, to the extent that it is possible, in taking charge of their own destiny.

Enormous blocs of humanity have, as if were, emerged from nature and entered history, in different ways and along different paths. They have encountered pieces of modernity and given themselves a fabric of identity using the only available model: that which the West, once again victorious—much more than it is able and willing to recognize, partly to escape its responsibilities—has proposed to them. They have fragmented into multitudes of individuals, in ways that do not always link the new subjects to the traditional and typically Western figures of state and nation—models too restricted to fully express the magmatic tumult of this impetuous eruption into a new dimension of historicity, dense with life and determinations. Multitudes in movement, and sometimes not just metaphorically, who are demanding visibility, a listening ear, security, commodities. In some cases, they wish to escape from violence and war—in the residual shape of atrocious peripheral conflicts—or from conditions of hardship and privation that the abrupt virtual contiguity with abundance and wellbeing make suddenly unbearable. They are discovering the allure of the capitalistic market, whose opulence is visible to them every day through borderless communication, transmuting them directly into consumers immediately charged with desires. After all, for a long time now the culture of the West has bound together individuality and consumption in a cast-iron, demanding relationship. We are accustomed to it, but it is now bouncing back at us from outside, rendered extraneous after having passed through the lens of sensibilities and backgrounds that are not ours.

These new individuals / consumers expect to be treated as equals—as equal persons. They vaguely sense that equality—at least in the primary dimension which ascribes to every autonomous fragment of humanity the right to life and to bodily integrity, the same one spoken of in the first articles of the Universal Declaration—has begun to truly enter into the order and consciousness of the world, even if very often in tortuous ways. This too is a victory of the West: to lend its face to the resurgence of what until now has been the forgotten part of the planet.

Technology connects, informs, brings closer, like the market network that it enables: while the structures of inequality have always, in vast intercontinental spaces, fed off isolation and exclusion. And that is why the need for equalness—of a human treated everywhere as equal—has never been so strong or attracted so much attention. The technological leap has brought a tight mesh of global social connectedness and has set in motion irreversible processes of mingling and increasing resemblance. The world really is becoming "flat," and fusion is the rule.[4] The big cities on both sides of the Pacific are the most extraordinary sign of this unprecedented mixing of minds and cultures.

※ ※ ※

If we look to the West, it is immediately apparent that the picture is very different and much less reassuring. Here, while the new capital is integrating the world economy into a single volume, bringing together the American West Coast and the Asian East Coast facing onto what has become a unifying sea, as the Mediterranean once was—so too unforeseen whirlwinds of inequality, no less unexpected than the new global similarities, are splintering the societies that emerged from the twentieth century, spreading a troubling sense of disorientation and danger. We have just shed light on some aspects of this.

From France to the United States to Italy—the problem seems to be affecting Great Britain and Germany less for now, but it is unclear for how long—the full extent of what Stiglitz has called "the great divide" is becoming clear, and though the crisis of 2008 is behind us the gap seems to be getting ever wider.[5] The West, which had not long since made equality a principle of the world—at least in the dimension of an abstract Ought—seems to have mislaid its meaning in its own home. A contradiction that is filling our age with anxiety, and provoking searing conflicts. The principle of offering hospitality in the name of fraternity among equals seems to be transmuting into the unjust denial of any solidaristic protection for the rights and expectations of those who in practice have to open the door—whether in Lampedusa or on the borders with Mexico. As a result, rallying cries like "America first" or "Italians first" have been garnering unexpected levels of support.

In Europe and America income from labor—especially the kind deriving from more traditional types of employment—and from capital are separating with ever-increasing speed, even in situations no longer affected by economic crisis.

The disappearance of the old class system, with its well-defined boundaries and structural rigidities—more in evidence in Europe, where the barriers left deep marks, than in America, where its architecture had always been much less solid—has replaced traditional distinctions with a new polarity, more elementary and at the same time more explosive.

At one end are relatively restricted though growing elites; at the other, an indistinct, downward drifting mass of people—described, in a successful metaphor, as "liquid"—with fewer and fewer protections: exposed, at the first stumble, to crashing falls taking them below the threshold of a social dignity thought to have been acquired for good.[6] This irresistible tendency is creating even more accentuated divergences, something on which Stiglitz and Piketty seem to be in complete agreement,[7] resulting in what Stiglitz calls the 1 percent, or even the 0.1 percent: with privileged minorities, also structured pyramidically, surrounded by oceans of other people struggling to get by if not in outright difficulty.[8] Contexts where a tiny number talk about which jet to buy, or how much noise their neighbors' helicopter makes as it comes in to land, while the rest worry at the very least about how to put together a half decent pension for their old age, or the risk of a serious and sudden illness they would be financially ill equipped to face. It marks an unforeseen return, at the heart of the West, to the society bleakly denounced by Rousseau, where the very few were awash in the superfluous, while most lacked the necessary. It is almost as if the last two centuries—and all the successes of the struggle for greater social justice—never existed.

By radically transforming, through the metamorphosis of labor, the organic composition of capital and the consequent scaffolding of classes within it, the technological leap has not just plunged into crisis what appeared to be a consolidated social setup; it has also destroyed the very presuppositions—material and ideal—upon which all the modern paradigms of equality were constructed for more than four centuries, paving the way for huge new imbalances. The migratory waves of the last few years, however contained, have merely aggravated the situation.

The current difficulty, everywhere in the West, in seriously reviving political debate about this principle, and its relationship with democracy, stems precisely from this new strategic condition: the irreversible erosion of the social and cultural background upon which the modernity of the idea of equality was built. The end of the age of labor, with the associated waning both of Marxism and of the great Labourite and (in America) "liberal" ideologies, has left a terrible void of identity in the center of the Western tradition: and it is this deficit of political intelligence and vision that is undermining the democratic force of the West, creating an increasingly pronounced imbalance between its power—still substantially intact—and its capacity to respond adequately to problems, which seems to be seriously compromised.

This is not to say that the whole of the past has been lost in the change, swallowed up in a flash, and that we need to rethink equality from scratch. That is not how history works. If a line of development winds up in a blind alley, as the link between equality and labor has, the tendency of which it was the expression should not necessarily be viewed as exhausted. It just means that a particular path, however promising it seemed, led nowhere and must be abandoned where it petered out; and therefore that conflating the figures of the worker and of the citizen is no longer a conceptually and politically useful hypothesis. The journey must continue in another direction, capable this time of opening onto the future.

Irrespective of its conclusion, the old course has left a cultural radiation—let's say, a model of critical and ethical intelligence—that goes beyond the disappearance of the foundations which enabled it, and continues to produce effects, like genealogy surviving time. And it is this last wave of efficacy that is spreading throughout the world, producing a light which is not going out.

This explains why equality is becoming a global measure, just as the West, where it began and advanced furthest, risks losing it, or is at least seeing its contraction. It is no surprise: the intrinsic historicity of the human consists of differences in level, of disconnections, of this unpredictable multiplicity of (relatively) independent planes. History is being in transformation. It does not coincide with the simple flow of time, far less with chronology, even if we are only able to perceive the changes within the structures of temporality—the reason we tend frequently to confuse time with history.

❀ ❀ ❀

It is not a question, then, of rediscovering a lost thread and retying it where it broke. That weft has been irreversibly frayed by the end of the relationship between equality and labor, and of the class struggle stemming from it (strongly present in Europe and, though less directly and in a more fragmentary manner, in America too), and by the end of labor as a determinant factor of social aggregation and collective emancipation. We just need to acknowledge it. We must, in other words, detach the idea of equality not just from every form of socialism, but from laborism and social democracy too. We must conceive it beneath another firmament, and with other guiding stars.

The great legacy of the age that has just ended—an idea of equality traversing every single life, forming bonds holding together sometimes very complex social formations and underpinning the political functioning of an authentic popular sovereignty—has not vanished, though. It is in a condition that might be described as suspended, objectively in the balance—a large construction whose foundations are suddenly being rocked—and its destiny could take many courses.

It might collapse entirely, following the fate of the structures that have supported it so far: history destroys, it does not just conserve. The fall would have incalculable consequences, yet we must have the intellectual courage to admit that a global society built solidly on a new worldwide inequality is not at all inconceivable.

Such inequality would be founded no longer on mechanisms of separation and exploitation like those of the old imperialistic structures of classic capitalistic organization, with its divisions of labor. But on transnational devices of inclusion-exclusion, or excluding inclusion, which would reproduce on a global scale those that the West is already trying out in the light of the new relations between labor and capital, and which will soon become a universal paradigm.

It is a clear possibility, and one that would reproduce, in new scenarios, ancient discriminations we believed had been overcome forever; and it would create new imbalances, induced not just by the cycle of capital in the narrow sense, but as the consequence of dramatically unequal access to technological innovations that are already on the horizon, and which will be capable of impacting the biological form of existence itself. Whole parts of the planet, having just emerged from a millenary subalternity, would once again plunge into the chasm of a no less dramatic dissymmetry. If it were to happen, the West itself would disappear, swallowed up by its negation (so much for the defense of its borders!), because the idea of equality has been the weft—at times more visible and exposed, at others submerged and almost completely hidden, but no less tenacious—of its identity, granted that one ever existed; and in certain respects, even of its very life: before even modernity, and certainly before capital.

The idea of equality might instead—and this is the other open hypothesis—be regenerated on new social and cultural foundations. It could draw on the tradition lying behind it—the extraordinary accumulation of thinking and experience crystallized over centuries of history—filter its magnitude and value, and project it into a new horizon, in the world currently taking shape, entrusting it with the historic completion of the universal human which only now is beginning to fully reveal itself to our gaze.

Above all, it might lead to an intellectual and political critique of techno-financial capital and how it functions. To a critique of the new economy, barely outlined as yet and still with no genuine theoretical framework, so as to create a system of rules for regulating and rendering transparent the mechanisms associated with the accumulation of profits (on the financial markets and from other commodities) and their reinvestment. And to a rethinking of the relationship between capital and bare human life outside labor, and the one between representation, politics, and sovereignty, which could even yield proposals for a more adequate and coherent model of democracy.

Capital, like the marketplace, is neither a natural nor an eternal form. It is just a figure, however decisive thus far, of our being in history. And when it is no longer able to control the productive and transformative power that it mobilized and expressed, it will become an obsolete way of organizing the creation and distribution of wealth, and therefore of giving form to the dominant social relations in our species—even if we cannot predict what setup will take its place, far less when such a shift might realistically occur.[9]

Going down this path presupposes in any case the resolution of at least two essential nodes.

The first is political. It relates to the need to recompose in a nonephemeral way—and certainly not just at a national level—a network of social actors (what was once called, with a term that now sounds archaic, a "historical bloc") that identifies its moral colors and its civil promotion in a refoundation of the primacy of democratic rationality over purely economic reason.[10] An alliance around which to construct government programs of capitalistic transformation, these too not limited to within single states. When Piketty talks about a global tax on capital, or when the International Monetary Fund suggests taxing the assets of the rich to offset, at least in part, the new inequalities provoked by COVID-19, and this proposal is accepted by the world's leading democracies, it demonstrates an uncontestable need for a new sense of measure and regulation that is already moving in the direction of a worldwide economic and fiscal governance.[11] This in turn requires a new discourse—theoretical and political—about the role of states and how they are articulated; about citizenship, and about the very notion of the people: themes which I can only mention here, because to explore them even minimally would go beyond the goals of this book.

The other node concerns the elaboration of a new paradigm of equality, because without one we will be unable to make any headway whatsoever in addressing the difficulties facing us. A paradigm mindful of the past, but suited to the reality of the present, which can guide us on the path that awaits us.

It is to gain at least a glimpse of the way ahead that we have made the journey outlined in this book.

New Thought

The clear trace points to the need to separate the idea of equality not just from the experience of modern labor, and therefore from any notion of socialism, but also from the historic and anthropological form of the individual, with which it has problematically cohabited throughout the modern age. To break the knot binding together the paths of the ethical and political intelligence of an entire epoch, and no longer considering individuality as the sole conceivable figure of the human, to which any development in civilization must be linked. To look no longer just at the device of the person-individual, nor to propose to move beyond it with a now-impracticable model of collective sociality, of the free association of producers, as in the tradition running from Rousseau to Marxism. But rather to consider the intrinsically objective and intraindividual unfolding of the living human in its full complexity, as the bearer, overall, of an infinite value—currently, as far as we know, unique (even if, probably, not solitary) in the infinity of the universe. A value reflected in each of its biologically self-sufficient fragments, but which should always be considered as an inseparable whole: that of the species to which they belong. To relate equality, therefore, to a different and historically more adequate and pertinent mode of conceiving the indisputable universality of the human: its bare impersonality. And to think of equality as the quintessential form of the impersonal human.

This will involve laying the foundations for a new theory of the human—the basis for a cultural, political, and moral anthropology standing alongside and shaping the revolution that has just begun, like the anthropology and theory of the human advanced by European thought from Hobbes to Hegel stood alongside and shaped, albeit with many variants, the great epoch of early industrial and capitalist modernity—the world that we have now lost.

The paradigm of the "individual" at the center of that construct was unopposed, linked by innumerable ties to the Christian concept (in the Lutheran and Calvinist version adopted by Hegel) of the "person." The bourgeois Christian person-individual—which has been described as the sovereignty of the personal—then became so overwhelmingly pre-eminent in the Western tradition that it is now identified with the form of the human itself. It is as if it were the neutral reflection of a natural fact, rather than a social and cultural construct, however extraordinarily potent: a historical product, and one which must be considered as such. Even the line of thought that tried to counter it with the model of the collective "we" in place of "I"—a line running from Rousseau to Marx and through to the successive socialist doctrines—ultimately took its basic features to be unalterable. The resulting paradox, as François Furet lucidly pointed out, was that the only way modernity could contemplate the social was by starting from the individual.

The time has come now to openly declare that this figure, however glorious and charged with the past, no longer—on its own at least—coincides with the entirety of the human or expresses all the richness and potential emerging from the transformation taking place around us. Indeed, in certain circumstances the figure of the individual can arguably be considered a regressive form, stymieing the developments we are already beginning to see. And though it is perhaps going too far to say, as Miguel Benasayag radically suggests, that the individual, especially its contemporary hyperacquisitive version, is the true enemy of the planet, it does seem that, with human consciousness on the verge of breaching the biological margins imposed by its evolutionary history, we need to move beyond this figure as the exclusive paradigm of its self-representation.[12]

This is not to say that the device of the person-individual so success-fully developed by modernity should be regarded as obsolete and that we can now do without it. Just that it is time to free the human form from the monopolistic stranglehold of that mechanism and its cultural projection (ethical, political, legal), so as to integrate it with other constructs in a complementary relationship between coexisting rather than mutually exclusive forms. Such an aim could become one of the next goals of history.

It is for exactly this reason that we are in urgent need of a new humanism: a philosophy able to give us an image and an ethics of the human that look beyond the individual. Achieving this—or at least making a start on it—is one of the crucial conditions that must be met

[handwritten margin notes: The dynamic of the "I" would be selfish of individuality rather than the sociality of an equitable lens. Do all "I" become equitable; shouldn't we look to solutions that we all can benefit from]

if we are once again to imagine the future in terms of progress and liberation, and restore a confident sense of trust in ourselves irrespective of the harsh and divisive present.

We need to consider the spread of the human, with all its differences and in its full complexity, as a unique, total subjectivity—the global subjectivity of the species, which does not say "I" but speaks only in the third person, which we must learn to recognize as the only way the impersonal can be expressed. It would be recognized in this way as the true subject of our history, as a comprehensive form of the entire universality of the human. If we are capable of it, there will be this identification and reconnection in our future.

❋ ❋ ❋

It has been impossible to detach individuality from equality until now for reasons relating to the material and cultural horizon in which modernity developed: only the atomized individuals of the market economy and the new sociality were able to relate to the equal with sufficient force, despite contradicting a part of themselves: what made each of them different from the other.

Now, however, it is no longer like that. The technological leap—which is projecting us into the economy of the immaterial—if used well, holds the possibility to separate what previously could not be uncoupled: to distinguish the two forms of the human—the individual and the impersonal—reserving for each distinct social and economic functions (we shall return to this point shortly).

To choose this perspective does not mean that individuality will somehow be erased from our future. It would be literally senseless even to imagine it. The construct of the modern individual, clad in the armor of its freedoms—to which capitalist organization, the Christian tradition, liberalism, and then democracy contributed—remains perhaps the most important conquest in a journey of emancipation to which the West devoted the very best part of itself. The mere hypothesis of doing without it conjures nightmare scenarios.

But that does not mean this figure must be presented as the only possible way of imparting ethical, political, and legal form and measure to the human: like a kind of natural datum, a necessary frame for every experience of relational life. We have seen that this is not the case. That it is the product of many convergences—theological-political, economic, social, philosophical, literary—which can in any case be historicized, and like any historical product, put into perspective, relativized, consciously integrated into a broader process.

The point is precisely this: not to do away with the form of the individual, but to place another and no less rich and fruitful determination alongside it. A configuration of the human that goes beyond the individual, not denying but incorporating it into a dialectic in which the opposite pole—that of the impersonal—has no less force, and no less expressive capacity.

If we mold the human solely on the individual, its universality—though so greatly emphasized by the modern tradition and its Christian background—inevitably fades and runs the risk of being reduced at any time to a purely abstract construction. To avoid this, two paths have been taken. The first ended up attributing to the state—as in the thinking of Hegel, who in this respect stands at the summit of Christian bourgeois modernity—such a broad, complex, and invasive role as a conciliator and producer of ethicality as to potentially lend itself, as would then dramatically be the case, even to opposite interpretations, openly totalitarian, both pushed to the point of aberration. This happened with Fascism and Nazism on the one hand, and communism on the other. Schmitt, Gentile, and Heidegger, no less than Lenin, were highly acute readers of Hegel.

The other, Christian, one shifted this need for a higher reunification beyond the plane of history, into a theologically deduced kingdom of heaven where alone can be found the fullness of truth and life.

If an alternative form of the human can be built and articulated instead, well within the boundaries of history, things change. A figure not identified either with the "I" of the individual nor with the "we" of the Rousseauian-socialist tradition, but with the impersonality of the third person, of that "one," of that "not person" which, outside each of us, enables everyone to exist and to think, and not to drown in the prison of an endless self-representation.

A different path can open out in this way. Where an earthly and de-termined polarity is established between finite and infinite—between the particular individual and the universal impersonal—wholly immersed in historicity: like between two forms facing each other on the same level, without the necessity to deny each other, or to attribute to a different function (for example, the state) tasks fraught with risk and overexpo-sure; and without even deferring the reunification to a purely theolog-ical plane.

The individual is thus left solely with the task—its alone, and by no means small—of representing the profile of particularity, of singularity, of the finite, of negation (*omnis determinatio est negatio,* according to Spinoza), of difference—including that of gender—and therefore of the unequal, in its every expression, natural and social. And entrusted to the construct of the impersonal is the enactment—political, ethical, legal—of the infinite universality of the human, of the (temporary) ne-gation of difference: with its global rationality, and its ethic of affirma-tion, conservation, solidarity, and totally inclusive identity.

And, above all, with its intrinsic equality.

❉ ❉ ❉

There is an important—however marginal—philosophical tradition of the impersonal, which indicates a different, though until now minority, itinerary in the history of thought, compared to the one dominated by the device of the individual person. In the course of our account, we have alluded to it several times, but stopped just short of discussing it, so as not to break the compactness of a discourse aimed at shedding light on the main axis along which the theme of equality was being developed.

It is the indisputable merit of a contemporary Italian philosopher, Ro-berto Esposito—to whom I gladly acknowledge my debt—to have force-fully and effectively drawn attention to this line of thought, retrieving it from the shadow in which it had been confined before the twentieth century.[13]

It is a precious legacy, concealed beneath layers of dust by the triumph of modern individualism, in its winning connection with the capitalistic organization of the West (European and American): a success which, as we saw, not even the Marxist critique and, later, the building of socialism, had undermined. Their idea of the collective, of the "we," emphasized by working-class sociality, would in fact never be able to address the solidity of the construction centered on the individual (the "we" which, according to Simone Weil, is in any case even worse than the "I": "Perfection is impersonal. Our personality is the part of us which belongs to error and sin. The whole effort of the mystic has always been to become such that there is no part left in his soul to say 'I.' But the part of the soul that says 'We' is infinitely more dangerous still").[14] Indeed, it would even end up perpetuating its effects, simply juxtaposing individualities—whose status was not seriously called into question—without overcoming them if not superficially, imagining it possible to unify the whole multitude of singularities merely through the tie of serial factory labor. A link that functioned in the heat of the class struggle, but which would prove utterly inadequate in building a new and full sociality, as soon became starkly evident.

In Esposito's interpretation, the reappraisal of thought on the impersonal is associated above all with a closely argued critique of the notion of "person," whose Roman-Christian foundations are scrutinized and dismantled.[15] As we have already said, the connection between Roman legal thought and late antique Christian theology (Tertullian, Augustine) is actually more fragile and problematic in this regard than appears in Esposito's reading; and from a historic point of view, the relationship between the original Christian idea on the one hand and the modern construction of the individual as the exclusive form of the human on the other seems to me more significant. But this observation does not detract from the force of the critique.

The next step—which forms the kernel of my proposal—moves in a direction that is not explored by Esposito. It consists of linking thought about the impersonal to the idea of equality; and of constructing a theory of equality as the primary projection of the impersonality of the human on the social, ethical, and legal plane. The point of juncture between impersonality and equality is the discovery of that "whole form of the human condition," of that "common and human model," which already moves beyond the fragmented construction of individualities, dissolving it in the impersonal inclusivity of a boundless sharedness. Exactly what Montaigne had indicated as the ultimate goal of his reflection, and which is present, through the claiming of human universality—or of the infinite that it contains and expresses—in a great deal of modern philosophy, from the humanists who informed and shaped Montaigne's own thought all the way through to Hegel at least, and then Marx, but without ever truly escaping the cage of the individual, despite on many occasions depicting all its limits.

It is a question, that is, of recognizing on the plane of history and not of metaphysics the existence of a shared bedrock of attitudes, behaviors, ways of reasoning and feeling, of cognitive and emotive potentialities, of transformative productivities, constitutive in an egalitarian way of what we might call the historic-anthropological stamp of the species, and of projecting it onto the plane of rules and of Ought. Of being able to see the unitary imprint that brings together the whole evolutive development within the design of a single complex profile: not a transcendentality empty of content, locked in the prison of the "I" (as, for example, in the Kantian model), but a universality full of history, and yet without any privilege being granted to the view of the subject. In other words, of recognizing in the impersonal the authentic place of juncture—historic, not metaphysical—between finite and infinite: between the finite that dies, and the infinite as the unlimited capacity to produce the world of history; an attitude that runs through the finite, even as it is dying.

In European thought the brightness of this vision was immediately compromised by the other great construction of modernity: that of the liberation of human singularities from the web of ties, restrictions, and accretions—parental, political-communitarian, economic, religious—into which they had been constrained by the societies of the ancient and then medieval West; and then of the explosion of their differences. By the birth, that is, of the modern individual, some of the key developments of which we have traced. And it was this perturbing and decisive presence that prevented contact between the two paradigms—impersonality and equality—marginalizing the former and constraining the other into a forced coexistence with the dominant model of the individual. This gave rise to a continual exchange only between these last figures—individuality and equality—that traversed the whole of modernity; which was reciprocally reinforcing, but also pitted one against the other in contrasts that harmed both, stopping each from fully developing their own formative capacities.

* * *

Averroes's *Commentary* on Aristotle's *de anima*—written in the heart of the twelfth century, between the intellectual fervor of Muslim Spain and the vivacity of Marrakesh—can be considered the dazzling debut of the philosophy of the impersonal, a genuine epiphany of the separate and impersonal unity of the human intellect, much more than the Aristotelean framework taken as a point of reference: even if it must be added that Greek and especially Roman Antiquity was in its own way familiar with a notion of the impersonal.[16] But this was a kind of "premodern" impersonal, still untouched by the impetuous force of the individual; and though it can be evoked today as a precious echo, it comes from another world and is of little use today.

The contribution of the great twelfth-century Arab philosopher, not by chance violently attacked by humanist thinkers from Petrarch to Valla, must be viewed as the starting point on a path to positioning the power of thought in a field outside subjectivity—and therefore to radically reducing the weight of the individual in forming the human intelligence—which would then run like an underground river through the whole of European culture. A trail that goes, admittedly in a far from linear manner, from Bruno (with his "antihumanism") to Spinoza, to Schelling to Nietzsche to Bergson (we will speak of Hegel shortly), right through to important strands of contemporary philosophy.[17] A genuinely alternative itinerary of modernity compared to the device put into place, after Descartes and the English political philosophers, by French and German jurists and philosophers of the eighteenth and nineteenth century on the one hand, and by Kant on the other—for whom we have reconstructed some salient features. By what would lead to the gnoseological, ethical, and legal construction of the modern "subject"—a word that overturned the semantic value of the Latin *subiectum* from which it actually derived, and which on the contrary denoted the subjected, in an ambiguous reversal between subjugation and subject that has been carefully investigated by Michel Foucault.[18]

The itinerary of the impersonal would largely remain, in any case, without any outlets. Powerful forces obstructed its progress. Besides the evident conflict with the winning paradigm of the individual, it was also up against the interdiction exercised by Christian thought, which saw in it an attempt to depersonalize the human that seriously undermined its most important theological-political construction: the relationship between man and God established and rendered comprehensible by the use of the concept of person. In other terms, the full force of the Christian bourgeois machine took up position against that hypothesis. The violent attack that Leibniz would launch, centuries later, against Averroes's positions in the *Considérations sur la doctrine d'un Esprit universel unique,* in reality distorting his thought to the point of charging him with having exceeded "the boundaries of reason," is an early and exemplary document of a struggle—as uneven as it was intransigent and nonnegotiable—already being waged against that thought by important strands of Italian humanism.[19]

It would be excessive for our purposes to trace all the vicissitudes of this philosophical line now—though it would make for an extremely interesting reconstruction, as yet only roughly sketched.[20] It will suffice to stop for a moment to examine its most significant juncture, which again takes us back to the heart of the seventeenth century, straight to the work of Spinoza, and the interpretation of it by Hegel two centuries later. It returns us to the crucial engagement between these two philosophies—the significance of which has been greatly stressed in recent times, though often misunderstood—now brought into focus by the illuminating research of Biagio de Giovanni, in a fine book which, while establishing a distance from it, moves within a glorious Italian interpretative tradition running from Bertrando Spaventa to Giovanni Gentile.[21]

But why them: Spinoza, and then Hegel? Because in both the effort to overcome the dualism between mind and body, between reason and matter, between subject and object—the positions of Descartes and Kant—and to find a point of connection between the infinite and the finite that could save the latter from a destiny of scission and annihilation, acquires a highly singular curvature. In fact, it translates, chiefly and sensationally, in Spinoza, but to an important degree in Hegel himself, into a process of depersonalization of subjectivity—with the latter made to coincide with the universality of substance (Spinoza) or with the objectivity of the concept (Hegel)—and into an impersonal foundation of thought and of life, which partially open up scenarios moving in the direction of that alternative to the absolutization of the individual of which we spoke earlier.

It is Spinoza who paves the way.

Here he is in a text from 1665, where we gain a measure of the distance separating him from the subjectivistic dualism of Descartes:

> Every body, in so far as it exists as modified in a definite way, must be considered as a part of the whole universe, and as agreeing with the whole and cohering with the other parts. Now since the nature of the universe, unlike the nature of the blood, is not limited, but is absolutely infinite, its parts are controlled by the nature of this infinite potency in infinite ways, and are compelled to undergo infinite variations. However, I conceive that in respect to substance each part has a more intimate union with its whole. . . . Since it is of the nature of substance to be infinite, it follows that each part pertains to the nature of all corporeal substance, and can neither be nor be conceived without it.
>
> So you see in what way and why I hold that the human body is a part of the universe. As regards the human mind, I maintain that it, too, is a part of the universe; for I hold that in Nature there also exists an infinite power of thinking which, in so far as it is infinite, contains within itself the whole of Nature ideally. . . . Further, I maintain that the human mind is that same power of thinking, not in so far as that power is infinite and apprehends the whole of Nature, but in so far as it is finite, namely, in so far as it apprehends the human body. The human mind, I maintain, is in this way part of an infinite intellect.[22]

Now let's listen to Hegel too, in the *Science of Logic,* polemicizing with Kant:

His [Kant's] principal idea is to vindicate the *categories* for self-consciousness understood as the subjective "I." Because of this determination, his point of view remains confined within consciousness and its opposition, and, besides the empirical element of feeling and intuition, is left with something else not posited and determined by thinking self-consciousness, a *thing-in-itself*, something alien and external to thinking—although it is easy to see that such an abstract entity as the *thing-in-itself* is itself only the product of thought, and of merely abstractive thought at that.[23]

And once again in the *Logic*:

But the "I" is the pure concept itself, the concept that has come into determinate existence. But the "I" is *in the first place* purely self-referring unity, and is this not immediately but by abstracting from all determinateness and content and withdrawing into the freedom of unrestricted equality with itself. As such it is *universality*.[24]

The equation whereby Spinoza stands to Descartes as Hegel does to Kant contains an element of undisputable truth, albeit in the schematism of a probably excessive simplification. The axis around which the double comparison revolves is the critique shared by Spinoza and Hegel of the subjectivistic foundation of modern philosophy: of the Cartesian *cogito,* as of the transcendental "I" of Kantian criticism. And it is for this that Hegel always regarded Spinoza as a necessary point of reference, and the privileged interlocutor of all his philosophy—an essential step toward the ontological structure he built in the *Phenomenology* and the *Logic*: "the objective logic thus takes the place rather of the former *metaphysics*," we read, once more in the *Logic*.[25]

It is again for this reason that both—first, and radically, Spinoza; then, in a more mediated fashion, Hegel—built and left open an escape route from the primacy of the individual: a trail which, however, would for a long time be little trod.

Admittedly, Spinoza lived in an age in which the affirmation of modern individualism was not yet crushingly victorious: even if the Holland of the "embarrassment of riches" (to use Simon Schama's

evocative expression) was already anticipating in some respects the salient features of the subsequent bourgeois triumph.[26] While Hegel was
faced, both through his own direct experience and what he was able to
learn about contemporary France and England, with a far more advanced reality in that respect.

Both were at one in their efforts to dissolve, even if in different ways,
the hegemonic isolation of the subject in the objective weft of a thought
that identified fully with the substantiality of being (Spinoza), or in the
very reason of the thing (Hegel); and in any case always steering clear of
superimposing the word "subject" over "individual."[27] And they shared
the attempt to build a path in which the concept (the logic) could itself
become ontological structure and form of being (I believe that on this
point the readings of Esposito and de Giovanni come together, and I
share them).

However, Spinoza inhabited a less developed environment, in a capitalistic and bourgeois sense, than the one Hegel was in time to observe;
a world where the three revolutions of full modernity—the American,
the French, and the industrial one of production and labor—could still
not even be glimpsed. The construction of the modern individual—a
word that the Dutch philosopher in any case did not use, preferring the
expression *res singularis*, the single thing, the singularity of the thing,
closer, as we saw earlier, to classical antiquity—had not taken on that
aura of necessary irresistibility that it would acquire little more than a
century later and with which Hegel would have to contend. Its political
and legal completion was still relatively far off, even if its outlines were
already beginning to become delineated (here the relationship between
Hobbes and Spinoza resurfaces).[28] As we have already said, and all the
more so for Montaigne (and a slender thread links Montaigne to Spinoza: a shared fascination for measure and proportion), other paths were
still possible then, and what we call modernity might still have developed in different ways.

The philosophy of the great Dutch thinker fully reflects this fluidity
of context with respect to the outcomes of the modern. His idea of a finite human traversed by the impersonal and the common—of a world
removed from the "blinding light of the Ego" (as de Giovanni writes),
immersed in the flow of an infinite naturalness, without subject or ends
("Nature has no preestablished end, and all final causes are nothing but

human fictions")—presents itself to us in an extraordinarily actual light.[29] It is outlined in extreme clarity, without having been subjected to the mediation of at least two and a half centuries of individualistic elaboration of sociality, politics, knowledge. We feel we are inside an intact and multiverse potentiality, not yet consumed by the harshness and fatigue of history.

Spinoza's philosophy also reflects, with no less force, a vast distance from the whole Judeo-Christian tradition—not to mention the Islamic one—without, however, involving the idea of God in the rupture, provided it coincided with that same one of an infinite nature (*Deus sive natura*). Only the image of a personal God was swept away, especially that of a God who becomes man—of a substance that becomes subject—and then dies on the cross. "As to the additional teaching of certain Churches," Spinoza wrote to his friend Oldenburg in 1675, "that God took upon himself human nature, I have expressly indicated that I do not understand what they say. Indeed, to tell the truth, they seem to me to speak no less absurdly than one who might tell me that a circle has taken on the nature of a square";[30] because, as he had already written the year before in another letter: "This I do know, that between the finite and the infinite there is no proportion."[31] It is exactly this distance that enabled Spinoza to proceed with a radical foundation of a philosophy of the impersonal, even if it ended up compromising the rescue of the finite. Symmetrically, it was the Christian theology of the God-person that made a new foundation of the finite possible for Hegel, but at the same time impeded him from taking the decisive step toward a complete philosophy of the impersonal, even though his thought contained the premises for it.

It is all the more surprising, not to say even paradoxical—at least in appearance—that it was precisely Hegel, for whom the theological-political mechanism of the God-person was an essential juncture of his system of thought, who then fully recognized the decisive importance of Spinoza's antisubjectivistic position and rediscovered in his anti-Cartesianism an indispensable premise for his own engagement with Kant.

Irrespective of sometimes very broad and significant differences, which de Giovanni's work perhaps skims over a little too hastily, there is an underlying theme that unites the two greatest metaphysicians of

Western modernity. It is the shared awareness, cruder in Spinoza, more mediated—and *pour cause*—in Hegel, that the more the power of thought tries to penetrate into the reason of the world, and to appropriate it, the more the impersonal quality of its constructive capacity emerges irresistibly, through to that limit point—glimpsed by Spinoza and elaborated on by Hegel—where the subjectless logic of the human, and its intrinsic egalitarian connotation, coincide with the very ontology of the impersonality, infinite and without ends, of the universe.[32]

Impersonality and Equality

Relating equality to the impersonal feature that traverses the human does not have to be merely a philosophical operation, limited to the field of the history of ideas. If adequately developed, it could become a primary political objective: the goal of an epoch.

To attain this on the plane of historic actuality would require an institutional and social construction of impersonality, and an ethical and legal articulation of it too—a complex undertaking that would take considerable energy, resources, and knowledge to achieve even partially.

The center of the process would lie not in subjects—persons, individuals—but in objects: not inside, as it were, but outside each of us; in the structure of reality—both natural and artificial; or at least, in that part of it shared by the human as a whole: in that portion of the world that we all pertain to insofar as we are human beings. This sphere is in continual expansion, as technological mechanisms exert ever-increasing degrees of control over nature, both within us and in the environment.

The integration between the technological revolution and new forms of capital does not necessarily generate conflict alone; it does not just produce bloated disproportion and inequality. On the contrary, if governed, the dissolution of the class structures of the old capitalist societies could set in motion previously inconceivable solidaristic unifications of the human; and it could bring out expansive elements of objective, impersonal equality with respect to any type of individual difference, or of gender.

This would enable the formation—around certain specific goods deemed indispensable in the given historic conditions—of shared spaces that aggregate islands of equality in the multiform ocean of individual inequalities. Contexts in which subjectivities provisionally vanish, no longer carrying any weight with regard to the consideration of the human as such, in its universal indetermination. Anyone coming into contact with these territories would be desubjectivized, maintaining value only as an indistinguishable fragment of humanness.

It would be—this really would be—the revolution of the impersonal: a new humanism without a subject. Bands of deindividualized life would appear, regulated by an equality that acts, so to speak, according to "punctuated equilibria" (to use the now famous expression of Stephen J. Gould);[33] an intermittent and discontinuous parity, associated only with the use of certain resources, in relation to which any personal diversity would drop away; while for everything else the criteria of differentiation and imbalance induced by nature, gender, the market would continue to prevail. Without any claim to being exhaustive, it is not hard to suggest some categories of goods that might be included in these spaces, with the recent and, above all, legal reflection on so-called common goods offering a preliminary overview.[34] First, there is human life, in its full material existence and based on the conditions determined by the existing level of technology: inviolability, food, and, above all, health (the latter in particular must be wrestled as far as possible from the marketplace and entrusted to different and structurally egalitarian distribution mechanisms, as the COVID-19 pandemic has made all too dramatically evident). Next, the entire ecosystem, the first of the common goods: air, water; the balanced occupation and transformation of the environment, its soft humanization; and the protection of nonhuman living beings. Then, access to education and information, so those with the appropriate abilities can attain the highest levels of knowledge. Finally, access to technologies capable of modifying the genetic status of the human, a massive issue looming on the horizon which will require the sharing of the principle whereby the genetic unity of the species—the evolutive result which started our history—must be considered an inviolable acquisition, meaning that any potential modification which is inheritably transmittable will only be taken into consideration if it is accessible, in conditions of equality, to the whole of humanity.

Maintaining each of these islands or points of equality requires the development of an economy of the impersonal—or, observed from another perspective, of an economy and law of common goods—whose incentivization and integration into the historic forms of the new capital would need to be one of the political priorities of the twenty-first century. It would be an economy producing use values and not exchange values, which, while certainly not liberating us either from the commodity form, or, far less, from capital—inconceivable objectives with no historic presuppositions—would at any rate represent a structural factor of equilibrium between supply and needs. Its sustainability would be a function of the general propensity to in turn transform the use values consumed into a general increase in the productivity of the entire system. A challenge for the future.

* * *

To emphasize, as we are doing, that the relation between impersonality and equality is like an axis around which there can rotate a vision of society capable of positively resolving one of the great nodes of modernity does not mean—it is worth repeating this yet again—bidding farewell to the model of the individual and the paradigm of the person.

The drastic critique of the latter—especially its inefficacy in offering any real guarantee of what have been called "human rights"—lies at the center of some memorable pages by Simone Weil, which anticipate, as has been justly noted, no less penetrating observations from Hannah Arendt.[35] It is a theme which would have important developments in the second half of the twentieth century, from Deleuze to Foucault, to Levinas, often accompanied by a rediscovery of the impersonal, prefigured by Bergson, who in turn reworked Spinoza (and significant strands—in part valorized by Foucault himself—can already be found in Nietzsche).[36] It is at any rate a matter of fact that the whole of twentieth-century French culture—not just philosophy, but also linguistics, anthropology, and even historiography—is traversed by a constant need to desubjectivize the world, which remains one of the strongest features of a long intellectual tradition culminating in many respects in 1968—a kind of radical adieu to Descartes. There is a passage by Deleuze that always seems to me to be an almost dramatic manifesto of this tendency, of a burning and never completely satisfied desire to escape from the trap of conceiving "those determinable singularities only which are impris-oned inside a supreme Self or a superior I."[37]

We will avoid pursuing the extremely varied traces of these orienta-tions: even if I cannot refrain from expressing a much greater sense of affinity with the analyses, though very different, of Weil, Foucault (the Foucault historian par excellence of the impersonal, of the formless lives of "infamous men"),[38] and Esposito, than with Deleuze and Levinas; but going into the reasons for this preference would be too far ranging a task.

It is worth stressing again, however—with respect to this line of interpretations—that the position sketched out here does not consider the paradigm of the impersonal as alternative to that of the person; and it does not regard the complete deconstruction of the latter as the only way of preparing the field for a philosophy and a practice of the "third person." We can speak instead of a complementarity between the two models, rather than a reciprocal exclusion; without even isolating too much the markedly theological-Christian constitution of the idea of person from the typically capitalistic-bourgeois one of the individual, which are actually profoundly interwoven in the paths of modernity, giving rise to a single Christian bourgeois mechanism, the outcomes of which demand our attention today.

In other words: what is at stake is not so much the historical and con-ceptual utility of the person-individual device as the recognition of its incapacity to represent the human in its every form, in particular with reference to the equal. The irreversible end of modern industrial labor has carved out an abyss between individuality and equality, definitively undermining a relation that had in any case always been difficult and precarious. Another path must be taken: equality cannot pass by way of the paradigm of the individual person.

This position, which, though removing the form of the human from the monopoly of the individual person still acknowledges its importance and significance, helps us to grasp the sometimes serious limits of that figure. The most important of these has thus far undoubtedly consisted of interposing a screen of metaphysical origin—the abstract, transcen-dent, or at least secularly transcendental figure of "person"—between every bare life and its legal, ethical, and political projection; in separating forever, that is, the subject from its body. Provoking, as a consequence, an irrecuperable fracture between rule and life, into which there is the risk that every theory of "human rights," and every attempt to "preserve men from all harm," to use the words of Simone Weil, might fall.[39]

That is not all, though. An even more serious crack is appearing in this conception. If, in the dualism between person and body that it presupposes, the latter figures as an object to master (here bourgeois thought and Christian tradition seem to come together perfectly), what happens when technological development, through an increasingly sophisticated genetic editing, puts us in a position to modify our physical and biological structure so profoundly as to alter the very form of its relationship with the "person" that should dominate it—for example, by exponentially increasing its cognitive capacities?

If, as is already happening, we take full control of our natural conditions of existence, which will end up being no longer an intangible presupposition of our lives,[40] but a historic result, the ever modifiable fruit of our choices, to what should we relate decisions about possible new genetic configurations of the human—morphologies which, we repeat, will be able to transform from within the very relation between the living body and its projection as person? To what and to whom, if everything remains enclosed in the dialectic between individual person and the state, but a state that is a long way off interpreting itself as an ethical totality?

If the person can become the object of transformation of its own conditions of existence, how can we not see that it is necessary to leave this figure behind, to find a measure capable of acting as a point of reference? And that it can only be found in the global subjectivity of the species, taken as a guide and as value? And what else is the subjectivity of the species if not the criterion of its impersonality? Of the impersonality of the human which—in a particular moment of its historic development— is elevated directly to ethical and legal norm, to a universal rule of conduct?

The point of arrival, then, can only be the search for a new equilibrium between individuality and impersonality. A balancing that starts from the bands of new equality to be constructed within the shared and equal use of common goods, including the decisive protection of the equality of the human, to be preserved as an absolute value, in the given historic conditions.

* * *

A very close connection exists between impersonality and globalization: this link creates previously inconceivable scope for the construction of new profiles of equality.

Impersonality is the authentic global form of the human: a design open to the equal, clearly reflecting the network of connections and reciprocal dependencies that now comprise the fabric of the world around us. Of course, this uniformity appears today to be inevitably flooded by the symmetrical worldwide multiplication of individualities—an unprecedented consumerist and possessive fragmentation—as the highway to self-emancipation and initial self-affirmation for the great masses now appearing on historical stage. But that takes nothing away from the force of the observation.

There is an immense and almost entirely unused reserve of power in the new communication technologies, which is pushing in the direction just indicated: the web is, par excellence, the technical basis of the impersonal, and an extraordinary vector of equality as well. It is being employed intelligently to accelerate almost limitlessly the circulation of commodities and capital, and to make the exchange of information and ideas more fluid and rapid within established fields of knowledge, with important results. But aside from these uses, we still employ it almost invariably in a way that can be described without hesitation as barbaric or crudely primitive, in the service of a backward and archaic way of understanding human society—as if everything was just about exploiting anonymity to channel drives and emotions for which we are not then held accountable, instead of using it to project ourselves toward the recognition of the deep mind of the species, whose only form is the impersonal.

In this sense, it must be said that the metaphor of the "global village," despite its immediate popularity, is actually very poor, because it gives the entirely mistaken impression that nothing other than dimensions has changed in comparison to the past.[41] Village before, village now. It is not like that. The dizzying increase in quantities transforms the quality of contacts, and over time determines their content. We are no longer in a village. We are the complexity of the world. And thanks to the web, the human as a whole has a voice for the first time: something that previously did not exist. It is an astounding novelty, which we have not yet fully realized. We must find the right thought and words to conceptualize the change and make it suitably evident. It is not easy, but we are just at the beginning. The knowledge of reality is structurally impersonal, and its egalitarian energy is very strong provided we can find the vectors, the lines of transmission, the social points of impact.

We must, however, avoid believing that everything that continues to say "I" is an expression of the old, and that everything which functions through the third person is a sign of the new. Nothing in history is ever so linear. Neither a society of the impersonal, nor, far less, the social and political foundations of the new equality, can be built through stark contrasts of this type.

Two questions in particular are essential to bring the appropriate mediations into play, and to form the indispensable framework of joins between the individual person on the one hand, and the figures of the impersonal (with its equality) on the other, so as to finally understand them, together, as the dual, irrepressible total form of the human.

The first theme is the construction of a public language of impersonality, relating above all to the contours of the new equality; just as there already are for the development of individualities (an elaboration that ran through modernity, and is still being articulated), and for the globalization of commodities and financial markets (a more recent but no less significant acquisition). It concerns the creation of a full-blown transnational lexicon of equality—and of its ethical, political, and legal projections—connected no longer to subjects, but to the objectivity of the goods within it, and to the social functions activated by their equal and shared use. A cultural development of this kind would finally put the globalization of the human on a footing with that of commodities and capital—as cannot be done by starting just with individuals, still bound by the territorial and local restrictions of different citizenships.

The second question pertains to the necessity to define—for now at least in reference to the heart of the West—a new status for individuality, as a consequence of the changed relationship between labor and life in the postindustrial age: a task that is now unavoidable but has received little attention to date.[42]

The subjectivity of the moderns was constructed (as we have seen in this book) almost entirely in the shadow of a form of labor that has been swept away by the technological revolution.[43] How could it possibly be thought that this mutation would not profoundly modify the coordinates within which the "I" has been built? And how is it possible to think that we can still speak of equality, without truly coming to terms with a change of such import?

In these pages it is only possible to sketch a broad outline of an answer. It passes by way of a crucial separation, to be executed with entirely untested means. That between labor as commodity—the labor-power sold and bought on the market—and labor as hard work and toil for the realization and fulfillment of self, of our individual self and of the impersonal one: a labor removed from the market and the commodity form and handed over instead to a sociality not determined by capital, but more and more indispensable for the full valorization of the human, in its dual personal and impersonal configuration.

This scission has been impossible until now: the technological conditions did not allow for it. All labor had to end up on the market, to permit the material survival and social dignity of entire classes, of by far the largest part of humanity. Now it is starting to no longer be like that. The quantity of labor destined for the market—directly under the control of capital—is diminishing, because a part is being replaced by technology, freeing up an increasing amount of human psychophysical energy for other purposes. This differential will inevitably continue to widen in the future, in the face of a structural imbalance between an upward global demographic trend and a reduction in labor power requirements for productive growth. The resources freed up in this way hold enormous potential. Due to an effect of cultural and social distortion, they are only seen today as a surplus of unemployed labor power, often with dramatic consequences for those excluded from production circuits. But actually they are an invaluable reserve that can finally be directed toward different functions far removed from the total reduction of labor to labor power.

This order of thoughts offers a glimpse of immense fields to explore, and might even end up telling us something about the historicity of capital. There is a need for intellectual courage, for imagination, for vision. Constructing a different way of being equal cannot do without such inquiry.

* * *

It is impossible to try to catch even a glimpse of the outlines of this new equality without once again encountering the question of democracy. We have already spoken about its at least apparent affirmation throughout the world at the end of the last century, in the version that extols a tendentially universalist formalism. Paradoxically, however, its success has been accompanied by a difficulty and a discontent manifested to varying degrees in the heart of the West. A generalized tiredness and abdication, expressed through the fraying and in some cases even the dissolution of the political parties that constituted its scaffolding; the advance of the so-called populist movements, giving voice, at least in their slogans, to ambitious projects of political de-intermediation between governors and governed; growing mistrust in representation and delegation;[44] an evident collapse in the selection of governing elites, even where, as in Great Britain and in the United States itself, this mechanism had weathered serious tests, and seemed able to resist any upheaval.

There are profound reasons for this darkening, and to explain them would lead us away from the thread of this book. The crisis affects the structure of the democratic device itself and concerns the crucial relation—now in part historically and functionally worn out—between representation and sovereignty.[45] But the inequalities that unexpectedly opened up in Western societies following the end of the industrial age, and the consequent change in the form of capital, together with the transformation of labor and the associated productive and financial globalization, have undoubtedly carried decisive weight. Democracy needs an injection of ideas. It should not be regarded as an unmodifiable conquest, "the end of history," the site of a truth acquired for all time, but just as an imperfect mechanism, the fruit of an unstable combination of two heterogeneous elements: delegation and the sovereignty of the people. And there are searching questions to be asked of politics, which can no longer just be that of Machiavelli and Hobbes, oriented solely toward what repeats itself in history, but must look at what is mutating and transforming. Most of all, it must once again view the future as a promised land.

The old, unresolved question, which we have seen hovering right from the earliest democratic thought—about how much equality a democratic system needs to function in the best way—returns with a sometimes dramatic urgency.

We can now say quite clearly that a single, complete, and definitive answer does not exist. There is no ideal proportion—a sort of golden ratio—to excogitate and put into practice, valid in every situation. We will have to satisfy ourselves with reaching a result by approximation, in relation to the forces in play, the degree of economic development, social demands, cultural processing, political mediations. This alone can be said: to conserve democracy in a specific society the degree of inequality must be no greater than that of the spirit of identity. And there is one thing we also know for sure: that if we try to break up the complexity of the bond between equality and democracy, and to confine democratic equality within rigidly formal, even if abstractly universalizing, boundaries—political rights, the parity of citizens before the law, and nothing else—we will end up down a blind alley. If democracy is enclosed in a bubble away from the concrete reality of life, as was attempted several times during the last century (nor has it stopped), we will quickly compromise the functioning of those very same formal devices that we wish to protect by isolating them. To save democracy—even its formal aspects—a much more advanced point of mediation must be found, which inserts as much as possible the fullness of life into the horizon of democratic equality, without compromising the construction of individualities in freedom that has perhaps been the greatest conquest of modern times. The welfare states of the second half of the twentieth century—with the valuing of labor within the frame of capital, the empirical compromise between individuality, freedom, and equality, and the direct intervention of public structures in orienting economic processes—provided an important response. The technological revolution and the capitalistic unification of the world have eroded the social and cultural foundations of that compromise. We must now move in a different direction: to finally untie the knot between the individual and the equal; to build an equality connected not to individuals, but to an economy and a sociality of the impersonal, based on the recognition of the common and human as the distinctive and unitary feature of the species.

The moment has come, then, to begin to conceive of a new pact of equality to save the future of democracy; a pact not limited to a single country, a single national society, but at the very least at the center of a strongly European cultural and political action that can become a kind of standard bearer of the continent: the intellectual and moral revolution of the impersonal as the final gift of the Old World to history, whose center now lies elsewhere, in the megalopolises on the shores of the Pacific. A pact of equality capable of turning into a political program (a lot of effort and study will be required), and that starts not from the parity of individuals but from the unlimited equal divisibility of things— of some things, of some goods, material and immaterial, commencing with the good that is life itself, to be shared equitably among all living beings. A pact entered into not in the name of a class, or of any subject that, to denote itself, has to exclude others from the definition—which carries within it, in other words, the sign of negation—but of the common and human as subject and as inclusive and global value. This does not mean denying space and particular rights to each individuality, not even to the egoism of the "I," which is such a powerful driving force of emancipation and achievement; but rediscovering every day with renewed vigor that each of us—*ekastos emon,* to end where we began—would be nothing, would literally not exist, if it were not possible to gaze deep into the eyes of the other, of any other on the earth, and recognize them as part of a whole, to which they also belong.

❀ ❀ ❀

Of decisive importance in the consolidation of the modern conception of individuality—even the most apparently secularized kind—was the contribution of the Christian tradition and its theological core.

In establishing the paradigm of the individual person, and then giving it such force, it carried enormous weight that this category—person—had been used to think the form of God, of the trinitarian God, and to conceptualize the incarnation of the God-person in the person of a man. This is how the circuit between theology and politics has always functioned, even outside of thought influenced by Christianity (just think of the Jewish tradition): through an uninterrupted and reciprocal exchange, which produced one of the greatest vectors of sense in the whole history of the West, and not just that—we need only recall the path of Islam.

Today the shadow of that construction is blocking to no small degree the full development of a doctrine and practice of impersonality. And it is no accident, therefore, if the two first and greatest philosophers of the impersonal—Averroes and Spinoza—were painfully extraneous to the religious orthodoxy of the cultures to which they belonged, and that the force of their thought was long viewed as an evil to be cancelled out (for their fortune Islamic Spain in the twelfth century and Amsterdam of the seventeenth were still tolerant enough places to spare them both the atrocious fate of Bruno).

It is all the more extraordinary, then, that Hegel engaged throughout his life with the philosophy of Spinoza, who considered the very idea of the incarnation to be aberrant—Hegel, the author of the *Phenomenology* and the *Logic,* who had made the God-person and man the point of encounter between the infinite and the finite that redeemed once and for all the limits of finiteness (the finite dies, and never ceases to die), without abolishing them, but overturning negativity into new creation: the infinite formative power of the finite and of the negative.

Yet there is something that has eluded the many people who, especially recently, have studied this engagement, with the exception, it seems to me, of Biagio de Giovanni.[46] Namely, that despite everything, the two positions are less irreconcilable that they might seem. And that Hegel's appreciation for Spinoza—sometimes explicit and direct, on other occasions silent but no less evident—goes precisely in this direction. Toward the shared discovery that present and active in the deepest core of the human is a charge of powerful impersonality—of impersonal and common equality, glimpsed vividly by Montaigne—that identified the very being of the species, the capacity of human thought to sever at the root the opposition between subject and object, and with it any dualism between spirit and matter. An outcome that the construction of the person, of Christian bourgeois individuality, did not erase, did not oppose head on, but put provisionally to one side, in order to then rediscover it, albeit in another place and in another time, outside of history.

For Hegel, as we have said, the place of reunification had a lot to do, on earth, with the totalizing force of the state; and this distanced him from Spinoza; not to mention from us, people of the twenty-first century, who know full well how insidious that collocation can become, and we have the means to grasp how the sociality of the impersonal is different from the majesty of the *Leviathan*—whatever figure represents it. But that does not prevent us thinking that in the dialogue between those two greats there was something more than a revelation of modernity: there was the, so to speak, ontological—that is, historical—meaning of our own destiny.

In the closing page of "Human Personality," to which Giorgio Agamben has already drawn attention for other reasons, Simone Weil positions herself without knowing it in the same theological perspective as Hegel, and asks herself if it is really true that the God-person of the Christian tradition leaves no room for conceiving of the impersonal— a question that silently runs through the thinking of the German philosopher.[47] And she concludes that no, a juncture can be proposed. In support, she cites Matthew 5:45–46: "That ye may be like the children of your Father which is in heaven; for he maketh his sun to rise on the evil and on the good, sendeth rain on the just and on the unjust," considering it to be a limpid example of the gospel allusion "to this impersonal and divine order of the universe," and therefore of the possibility that the figure of God and the figure of man can come together also irrespective of a theology of the person conceived as being without alternatives.

I believe that she is right.

NOTES

INDEX OF NAMES

NOTES

Almost all the themes touched on in this book have a vast literature. The following pages do not account for all the readings I undertook to orient myself in these stratified accumulations of thought, but just point to the authors directly referred to in the text, and to what is closely connected to the ideas and interpretations I sustain.

The abbreviations are the customary ones employed in the different disciplines to which the citations relate.

Prologue

1. M. de Montaigne, *Les Essais*, ed. J. Balsamo, M. Magnien, and C. Magnien–Simonin (Paris: Gallimard–Pléiade, 2007), 1166, in English as *The Complete Essays*, trans. M. A. Screech (London: Penguin Books, 2003), 1268–1269; trans. modified.

2. Montaigne, *Les Essais*, 1850 and, more generally, xciii ff.

3. Montaigne, *Les Essais*, 845 (*Essays*, 908).

4. Montaigne, *Les Essais*, 845: "humaine condition" (*Essays*, 908: "human condition").

5. Montaigne, *Les Essais*, 1850.

6. I am referring to the themes of the great legal humanism of Hadrian's age, as developed by the likes of Juventius Celsus or Salvius Julianus: but Montaigne, while he had some idea of Roman law, could not possibly cultivate a particularized

approach to individual ancient jurists and their thought, which was almost entirely extraneous to the culture of his age.

7. I presuppose F. Moretti, *The Bourgeois: Between History and Literature* (London: Verso, 2013), 25 ff. See also I. Watt, *Myths of Modern Individualism: Faust, Don Quixote, Don Juan, Robinson Crusoe* (Cambridge: Cambridge University Press, 1997), 141 ff.

8. "de son estre": Montaigne, *Les Essais*, 1166 (*Essays*, 1268).

9. Montaigne, *Les Essais*, 845 (*Essays*, 908).

10. Observations that move in the direction I indicate can be found in A. Compagnon, *Un été avec Montaigne* (Paris: Éd. des Equateurs, 2013), in English as *A Summer with Montaigne: On the Art of Living Well*, trans. T. Kover (London: Europa Compass, 2019), chap. 40. Regarding Machiavelli, see, for example, the memorable opening of his letter to Francesco Guicciardini on May 17, 1521, in N. Machiavelli, *Opere*, vol. 2, ed. C. Vivanti (Turin: Einaudi, 1999), 372. Machiavelli himself was, moreover, perfectly aware of these, as it were, freedoms. See his letter to Francesco Vettori on January 31, 1515: "Anyone who might see our letters. . . . But then, turning the page, he would discover that these same serious men were frivolous, inconstant, lustful, and occupied with trifles," Machiavelli, *Opere*, vol. 2, 349; see G. Ferroni, "Le 'cose vane' nelle lettere di Machiavelli," *La Rassegna della letteratura italiana*, series 6, 76 (1972): 215 ff. As for Rabelais and Aretino, there is an embarrassment of choice: for the former, just take the beginning of chapter 21 of the first book of *Gargantua and Pantagruel*, with the morning activities of the young Gargantua; for the latter, it will suffice to glance at the first day of the second part of the *Ragionamenti*.

11. E. M. Forster, *A Passage to India* [1924] (London: Penguin, 2005), 275.

12. Forster, *A Passage to India*, 275: this too was extraordinary praise of human measure, of the "spirit in a reasonable form."

13. An unsurpassed guide to the *Essays* is the now classic work of J. Starobinski, *Montaigne en mouvement* (Paris: Gallimard, 1982), which I cite from the new edition of 1993, in English as *Montaigne in Motion*, trans. A. Goldhammer (Chicago: Chicago University Press, 1985), 159 ff. Also memorable is M. Merleau–Ponty, "Lecture de Montaigne," in *id.*, *Signes* (Paris: Gallimard, 1960), in English as "Reading Montaigne," in *Signs*, trans. R. McCleary (Evanston, IL: Northwestern University Press, 1964), 198 ff. Also worth reading is the essay of M. Fumaroli, "De Montaigne à Pascal. Les humanités, la science moderne et la foi," in *id.*, *Exercises de lecture: De Rabelais à Paul Valéry* (Paris: Gallimard, 2006), 293 ff.

1. The Greek Alternative

1. Aeschylus, *The Suppliants*, vv. 370–372: "You are the city, you are the people [*demion*]. You are an unjudgeable prince, you rule [*kratuneis*] the altar . . ." (the Danaids are speaking): D. Musti, *Demokratía. Origini di un'idea* (Rome:

Laterza: 1995), 19 ff.; E. Stolfi, *Introduzione allo studio dei diritti greci* (Turin: Giappichelli, 2006), 55 ff.

2. P. Oxy. 11, 1364, F2 + P. Oxy. 3647. I am drawing on the Loeb edition of A. Laks and G. W. Most in *Early Greek Philosophy,* vol. 9, *Sophists,* part 2 (Cambridge, MA: Harvard University Press, 2016), 56–58 [translation modified].

3. See L. Canfora, "Douleuein," in *id., Una società premoderna: Lavoro, morale, scrittura in Grecia* (Bari: Dedalo, 1989), 65 ff., esp. 69–70 (previously published in *Studi Storici,* 26 [1985]: 903 ff, esp. 905–906), and *id.,* "Il soggetto passivo della polis classica," *Una società premoderna,* 73 ff., esp. 77–78 (previously in *Opus,* 1 [1982]: 33 ff., esp. 35 ff.). Still worthy of consideration is the brief essay of A. Momigliano, "Sul pensiero di Antifonte il sofista," *Rivista di Filologia e di Istruzione Classica,* 58 (1930): 129 ff., also in *id., Quarto contributo alla storia degli studi classici e del mondo antico* (Rome: Edizioni di Storia e Letteratura, 1969), 135 ff. Also worthy of attention is J. De Romilly, *La Loi dans la pensée grecque: Des origines à Aristote* (Paris: Les Belles Lettres, 2nd ed., 2001), 74 ff., esp. 76 ff. (also for the possible links between the thought of Antiphon and that of Hippias and Thrasymachus, known to us—partially—through Plato). I have already examined this text in "L'eguaglianza degli antichi fra politica e diritto," in A. Heller, C. Müller, and A. Suspène, eds., *Philorhômaios kai philhellèn: Hommage à Jean-Louis Ferrary* (Geneva: Droz, 2019), 27 ff., esp. 28 ff.

4. "Pasin anthropois."

5. References can be found in A. Schiavone, *La storia spezzata: Roma antica e Occidente moderno* [1996] (Rome: Laterza, 2002), 260, in English as *The End of the Past: Ancient Rome and the Modern West,* trans. M. J. Schneider (Cambridge, MA: Harvard University Press, 2000; reprint 2002), 266, note 14.

6. Herod., 3, 80–83.

7. E. Hartog, *Le Miroir d'Hérodote: Essai sur la représentation de l'autre* (Paris: Gallimard, 1980), esp. 330 ff.; R. Thomas, *Herodotus in Context: Ethnography, Science and the Art of Persuasion* (Cambridge: Cambridge University Press, 2000), esp. 115 ff.; G. Carillo, *Katechein: Uno studio sulla democrazia antica* (Naples: Editoriale Scientifica, 2003), 13 ff.

8. Herod., 3, 80, 6.

9. Arist., *Pol.* 3, 6–9, 1279a–1281a; Plat., *Pol.* 31–40, 291d–303b; "government of one, of a few, of many": Arist., *Pol.* 3, 7, 1279a.

10. Arist., *Pol.* 3, 7, 1279a.; thus, for example, in the whole text of *Pol.* 3, 6–9. On these passages there is an excellent commentary by P. Accattino and M. Curnis in *Aristotle, La politica,* eds. L. Bertelli and M. Moggi, vol. 3 (Rome: L'Erma di Bretschneider, 2013), 176 ff. (the most important and up-to-date critical edition of Aristotle's *Politics*).

11. Arist., *Pol.* 7, 1, 1328a.

12. Arist., *Pol.* 3, 6, 1279a.

13. S. Mazzarino, *Fra Oriente e Occidente: Ricerche di storia greca arcaica* [1947] (Milan: Rizzoli, 1989), 193.

14. A point of reference is C. Meier, *Die Entstehung des Politischen bei den Griechen* (Frankfurt am Main: Suhrkamp, 1980),in English as *The Greek Discovery of Politics*, trans. D. McLintock (Cambridge, MA: Harvard University Press, 1990), 29 ff., esp. 50 ff.

15. M. Ostwald, *Nomos and the Beginnings of the Athenian Democracy* (Oxford: Clarendon Press, 1969), esp. 96 ff., remains an important work. By the same author bear in mind also *From Popular Sovereignty to the Sovereignty of Law: Law, Society and Politics in Fifth-Century Athens* (Berkeley: University of California Press, 1986). See also S. Todd and P. Millett, "Law, Society and Athens," in P. Cartledge, P. Millett, and S. Todd, eds., *Nomos: Essays in Athenian Law, Politics and Society* [1990] (Cambridge: Cambridge University Press, 1993), 7 ff.; De Romilly, *La Loi* 9 ff.; Stolfi, *Introduzione*, esp. 23 ff. and *id., Quando la legge non è solo la legge* (Naples: Jovene, 2012), esp. 17 ff., 49 ff. Some points had already been touched on in A. Schiavone, *Ius: L'invenzione del diritto in Occidente* [2005] (Turin: Einaudi, 2nd ed., 2017), in English as *The Invention of Law in the West*, trans. J. Carden (Cambridge, MA: Harvard University Press, 2012), 85 ff.

16. The fragment from Heraclitus is in H. Diels and W. Kranz, *Die Fragmente der Vorsokratiker* (Berlin: Weidmann, 12th ed., 1966), 22 B, F. 101 (from Plut., *mor. adv. Col.* 20).

17. See, for example, Thuc., 2, 40, 1: *philokaloumen te gar met'euteleias kai philosophoumen aneu malakias*: "For we are lovers of beauty yet with no extravagance and lovers of wisdom yet without weakness": it is Pericles speaking here, as recounted by Thucydides, but more about this shortly.

18. Thuc., 2, 37, 1; Musti, *Demokratía*, 10 ff.; Carillo, *Katechein*, 49 ff. Though rich in interesting ideas, as always, I am unable to share the analysis of Isaiah Berlin, "The Birth of Greek Individualism," in *id., Liberty*, ed. H. Hardy (Oxford: Oxford University Press, 2002), 287 ff., who overstretches the significance of the concept.

19. Meier, *The Greek Discovery of Politics*, 183.

20. Pind., fr. 169a (Snell–Maehler); Herod., 3, 38, 4 and 7, 104, 4; Plat., *Gorg.* 484b; Arist., *Pol.* 4, 4 1292a; Chrys., *Stoicorum Veterum Fragmenta* (= SVF), vol. 3, 314 (= Marcian. 1 *inst.* in D. 1. 3. 2): a book still worthy of attention is M. Gigante, *Nomos basileus* [1956] (Naples: Bibliopolis, 1993, new edition with appendix). Other references can be found in Schiavone, *The Invention of Law in the West*, 287 and 513.

21. A fundamental and in many ways unparalleled work is F. M. Cornford, *Principium sapientiae: The Origins of Greek Philosophical Thought* (Cambridge: Cambridge University Press, 1952), esp. 159 ff.

22. I have already touched on this aspect in *The End of the Past*, 204 ff.

23. I refer again to *The End of the Past*, 3 ff., 175 ff. The words form the title of a celebrated book by S. Mazzarino, *La fine del mondo antico* [1959] (Milan: Rizzoli, 1988).

24. *Areop.*, 144, 23–24.

25. I am thinking of M. Riedel, *Metaphysik und Metapolitik: Studien zu Aristoteles und zur politischen Sprache der neuzeitlichen Philosophie* (Frankfurt am Main: Suhrkamp, 1975), in Italian as *Metafisica e metapolitica: Studi su Aristotele e sul linguaggio politico della filosofia moderna* (Bologna: il Mulino, 1990), esp. 91 ff.: an important work that I have borne greatly in mind, and which in turn presupposes J. Ritter, *Metaphysik und Politik. Studien zu Aristoteles und Hegel* (Frankfurt am Main: Suhrkamp, 1969), in Italian as *Metafisica e politica: Studi su Aristotele e Hegel* (Casale Monferrato: Marietti, 1983), esp. 3 ff. The common point of departure is W. Dilthey, *Einleitung in die Geisteswissenschaften: Versuch einer Grundlegung für das Studium der Gesellschaft und der Geschichte* [1883], in *id., Gesammelte Schriften* [Leipzig 1914–], vol. 1 (Stuttgart: Teubner, 6th ed., 1966), in Italian as *Introduzione alle scienze dello spirito: Ricerca di una fondazione per lo studio della società e della storia* (Florence: La Nuova Italia, 1974), esp. 282 ff., which speaks, perhaps more correctly, of "social metaphysics" (Italian trans. 295). "Social ontology" was already in E. Husserl, *Soziale Ontologie und deskriptive Soziologie* [1910], in *Zur Phänomenologie der Intersubjektivität: Texte aus dem Nachlass ff. Erster Teil: 1905–1920*, ed. I. Kern (The Hague: Nijhoff, 1973); and see also the essays translated and collected in *Ontologia sociale, potere deontico e regole costitutive*, P. De Lucia, ed. (Macerata: Quodlibet, 2003), esp. 9 (De Lucia) and 27 ff. (J. R. Searle). See also P. Aubenaque and A. Tordesillas, eds., *Aristote politique: Études sur la "Politique" d'Aristote* (Paris: Presses Universitaires de France, 1993), especially the contributions in sections 1, 3 ff. and 2, 133 ff. I touch on these themes briefly in *The Invention of the Law in the West*, 505, note 13. There are penetrating observations on Riedel's work in R. Esposito, *Politica e negazione: Per una filosofia affermativa* (Turin: Einaudi, 2018), in English as *Politics and Negation: Towards an Affirmative Philosophy*, trans. Z. Hanafi (Cambridge: Polity Press, 2019), 77 ff.

26. An excellent work is L. E. Tise, *Proslavery: A History of Defense of Slavery in America 1701–1840* (Athens: University of Georgia Press, 1987), esp. 183 ff., 323 ff.

27. Arist., *Pol.* 1, 1, 1252a; *Pol.* 1, 1, 1252a.

28. *Pol.* 1, 2, 1252a. *Archè* is a category of Aristotelean metaphysics as well, later also analyzed by Heidegger, *Die Grundbegriffe der antiken Philosophie*, ed. F.-K. Blust (Frankfurt am Main: Klostermann, 1993), in English as *Basic Concepts of Ancient Philosophy*, trans. R. Rojceziez (Bloomington: Indiana University Press, 2008), 26 ff.

29. Arist., *Pol.* 1, 2, 1253a: "In truth, by nature [*physei*], the city comes before the household and each of us. For the whole must necessarily come before the part."

30. Arist., *Pol.* 1, 2, 1253a.

31. Arist., *Pol.* 1, 2, 1253a.

32. Arist., *Pol.* 1, 2, 1252b.

33. Arist., *Pol.* 1, 5, 1254b.

34. Arist., *Pol.* 1, 4, 1254a.

35. Arist., *Pol.* 1, 1, 1252a, and also 6, 1, 1317b.

36. In the section of the *Politics* that we are principally referring to, "nature" is mentioned 21 times: G. Besso, in *Aristotele, La politica*, vol. 1, ed. M. Curnis (Rome: L'Erma di Bretschneider, 2011), 205. Also important with regard to this part of Aristotle's text are the observations of E. Schütrumpf, in *Aristoteles, Politik Buch I* (Berlin: Akademie, 1991), esp. 238 ff., and T. J. Saunders, in *Aristotle, Politics. Books I and II* (Oxford: Clarendon Press, 1995), esp. 73 ff.

37. "Any human being that by nature belongs not to himself but to another is by nature a slave": Arist., *Pol.*, 1, 4, 1254a.

38. Arist., *Pol.* 1, 5, 1254b.

39. Arist., *Pol.* 1, 3, 1253b.

40. Arist., *Pol.* 1, 5, 1254a.

41. The identification, though highly probable on the historical plane, is only conjectural in textual terms: G. Cambiano, "Aristotle and the Anonymous Opponents of Slavery," in M. I. Finley, ed., *Classical Slavery* (London: Frank Cass, 1987), 21 ff., esp. 30 ff.

42. "instrumentum vocale," according to Varro's definition in *de re rustica*, 1, 17, 1—perfectly in line with Aristotle on this.

43. Anaximander sources are in Diels and Kranz, *Die Fragmente der Vorsokratiker*, vol. 1, 12th ed., 1966, 81 ff.

44. Aristophanes, *The Clouds*, through the caricature of Socrates: vv. 200 ff.

45. Arist., *Pol.* 1, 2, 1252b.

46. Francis Bacon, *Novum Organum*, in *The Works of Francis Bacon*, J. Spedding, R. L. Hellis, and D. D. Heath, eds., vol. 1 (London: Longman, 1879), 185 ff. (lxxvii–lxxix). See also P. Rossi, *Francesco Bacone: Dalla magia alla scienza* (Turin: Einaudi, 2nd ed., 1974), 92 ff.

47. I have already developed some points of this argument in *The End of the Past*, esp. 148–49. In it, I also spoke of an "individualistic mentality which, as we have already mentioned, was emerging in the aristocracies and later in the city-states of Greece, the Tyrrhenian region, and Italy" (139): but I was wrong to use the concept of individualism to describe the phenomenon to which I was referring—though I was in good company. The end result was to confuse matters rather than clarify them. Individualism, strictly speaking, is a purely modern form, not found outside of that age—as I will try to make clear in the course of this book. In the ancient contexts that I referred to there were strong aristocratic subjectivities, in which the individual isolation of responsibility and destiny counted for nothing, but an essential role was played instead by membership of the community—city, social order, kinship group—and the recognition that stemmed from the strength of these bonds. In short, it was a totally different world.

48. See *The End of the Past*, esp. 204 ff.

49. Ter. *Heautontim.*, v. 77: intelligent observations, albeit in a framework that is in part questionable, in M. Bettini, *Homo sum: Essere "umani" nel mondo antico* (Turin: Einaudi, 2019), esp. 26 ff., 88 ff.

50. *SVF*, vol. 3, no. 352. "No man is slave by nature" cannot be related directly to Chrysippus, as far as we know, but it certainly dates back to ancient Stoicism.

The philosopher did, however, share the doctrine assimilating the slave solely to a *perpetuus mercenarius*—to a permanent wageworker: no. 351 (from Sen., *de benef.* 3, 22). For Cicero, see Chapter 2.

2. The Roman Imprint

1. Thuc., 2, 37, 1.

2. Cic., *de orat.* 1, 42, 188.

3. There would appear already to be a hazy perception in Homer: M. Riedel, *Metaphysik und Metapolitik: Studien zu Aristoteles und zur politischen Sprache der neuzeitlichen Philosophie* (Frankfurt am Main: Suhrkamp, 1975), in Italian as *Metafisica e metapolitica: Studi su Aristotele e sul linguaggio politico della filosofia moderna* (Bologna: il Mulino, 1990), 61 ff.; E. Stolfi, *Introduzione allo studio dei diritti greci* (Turin: Giappichelli, 2006), 97 ff. See also C. Meier, *Die Entstehung des Politischen bei den Griechen* (Frankfurt am Main: Suhrkamp, 1980), in English as *The Greek Discovery of Politics*, trans. D. McLintock (Cambridge, MA: Harvard University Press, 1990), 140 ff.

4. Arist., *Pol.* 1, 2, 1253a: "anthropos physei politikon zoon."

5. Everything that follows in this chapter presupposes A. Schiavone, *Ius. L'invenzione del diritto in Occidente* [2005] (Turin: Einaudi, 2nd ed., 2017), in English as *The Invention of Law in the West*, trans. J. Carden (Cambridge, MA: Harvard University Press, 2012), 86 ff. See also M. Humbert, *La Loi des XII Tables: Édition et commentaire* (Rome: École Francaise de Rome, 2018), esp. 1 ff., 22 ff.

6. Cic., *de orat.* 1, 42, 188.

7. Gell., *noct. Att.* 10, 20, 4: "veteres 'priva' dixerunt, quod nos 'singula' dicimus."

8. D. Musti, "I Greci e l'Italia," in *Storia di Roma*, vol. 1, ed. A. Momigliano and A. Schiavone (Turin: Einaudi, 1988), 39–51; L. Canfora, "Roma 'Città greca,'" *Quaderni di storia* 39 (1994): 5 ff.; T. J. Cornell, *The Beginnings of Rome: Italy and Rome from the Bronze Age to the Punic Wars (c. 1000–264BC)* (London: Routledge, 1995), 86 ff.

9. Gai., *inst.* 1, 55 (then partially reproduced in D. 1, 6, 3, and in 1, 1, 9pr): "fere enim nulli alii sunt homines, qui talem in filios suos habent potestatem qualem nos habemus. Idque divus Hadrianus edicto . . . significavit": F. Casavola, "Potere imperiale e stato delle persone tra Adriano e Antonino Pio," in *id.*, *Giuristi adrianei* (Naples: Jovene, 1980), 199 ff.

10. I am referring here to historians from Ennius to Livy (by way of Polybius) and legal thinkers of the Augustan age. The reciprocal extraneity between the two spheres—that of the people and the private one—far removed, with its force, from any Greek experience but constitutive of the Roman idea of citizenship, is at the root of that acute self-perception of ethnic and cultural particularism that traversed the whole history of the Roman mind, reflected in the many historiographic and literary elaborations of the Trojan myth as the foundation of an original alterity with respect to the other Italic peoples, including those most closely

linked to Greece—"distanced" Rome: important observations can be found in A. Giardina, *L'Italia romana: Storie di un'identità incompiuta* (Rome: Laterza, 1997), esp. 64 ff., 74 ff. As regards law, the first and most significant aggregating nucleus of *ius,* from the age of the Twelve Tables onward, consisted of the law of succession: and hence the private stability of the family structure, a point more critical than any other in the relationship between order and time, the abiding preoccupation of the whole of Roman legal thought.

11. R. Syme, "Lawyers in Government. The Case of Ulpian," *Proceedings of the American Philosophical Society* 116 (1972), 5: 406 (= *id., Roman Papers,* vol. 3, ed. A. R. Birley [Oxford: Oxford University Press, 1984], 863).

12. Cic., *pro Caec.* 25, 70.

13. Cicero writes here: "quid suum, quid alienum sit"—what belongs to him and what to others; but in *de inv.* 2, 53, 160, defining justice, he had said: "iustitia est habitus animi communi utilitate conservata suum cuique tribuens dignitatem," probably reprising the formulation of *rhet. ad Her.* 3, 2, 3, again relating to justice: "Iustitia est aequitas ius uni cuique rei tribuens." Both definitions certainly form the basis for Ulpian's most celebrated formulation in the first of his books *regularum,* in D. 1, 1, 10pr: "Iustitia est constans et perpetua voluntas ius suum cuique tribuendi" (= I. 1, 1, 1pr, with a small variant): T. Honoré, *Ulpian: Pioneer of Human Rights* (Oxford: Oxford University Press, 2002, 2nd ed.), 215–216; G. Falcone, "Ius suum cuique tribuere," *Annali del Seminario Giuridico (AUPA)* 52 (2007): 135–176. See also J.-L. Ferrary, V. Marotta, and A. Schiavone, *Cn. Domitius Ulpianus: Institutiones, De censibus* (Rome: L'Erma di Bretschneider, 2021).

14. Cic., *pro Caec.* 26, 74: "Quod enim est ius civile? Quod neque inflecti gratia, neque perfringi potentia neque adulterari pecunia possit."

15. The expression is again Cicero's, in a letter: *ad fam.* 4, 1, 1.

16. *pro Caecina*: 25, 71: "in iure nihil est eius modi, recuperatores, non tabulae falsae, non testis improbus, denique nimia ista quae dominatur in civitate potential in hoc solo genere quiescit; quid agat, quo modo adgrediatur iudicem, qua denique digitum proferat, non habet."

17. Here, once again, see *The Invention of Law,* esp. 190 ff. I returned to this theme more recently in "Astrarre, distinguere, regolare. Forme giuridiche e ordine teologico," in J.-L. Ferrary, A. Schiavone, and E. Stolfi, *Quintus Mucius Scaevola: Opera* (Rome: L'Erma di Bretschneider, 2018), 29 ff.

18. Gai. *inst.,* 2, 12–13: "Quaedam praeterea res corporales sunt, quaedam incorporales. <Corporales> hae <sunt>, quae tangi possunt, veluti fundus homo vestis argentum et denique aliae res innumerabiles. Incorporales sunt quae tangi non possunt, qualia sunt ea quae iure consistunt, sicut hereditas ususfructus obligations quoquo modo contractae": I have followed the edition of M. David and H. L. W. Nelson (Leiden: Brill, 1954), except at one point: for the explanation of this departure, see *The Invention of Law,* 483, note 18.

19. F. Savigny, *Vom Beruf unserer Zeit für Gesetzgebung und Rechtswissenschaft* [Heidelberg 1814; 3rd ed., 1840] (Hildesheim: Olms, 1967), 28–29. The *Beruf*

can also be read in H. Hattenhauer, ed., *Thibaut und Savigny: Ihre programmatischen Schriften* (Munich: Vahlen, 1973), 95 ff., or in J. Stern, ed., *Thibaut und Savigny: Ein programmatischer Rechtsstreit auf Grund ihrer Schriften* [Berlin: 1914] (Darmstadt: Wissenschaftliche Buchgesellschaft, 1959), 69 ff. (our citation is on p. 114 of the Hattenhauer edition). The *Beruf* is in English as *Of the Vocation of Our Age for Legislation and Jurisprudence* [1831], trans. A Hayward (New York: Arno Press [reprint edition], 1975), esp. 17 ff. and 43 ff; the quotation (slightly modified) is on 45.

20. Besides Schiavone, *The Invention of the Law,* see also J.-L. Ferrary, "Una vita nel cuore della repubblica. Saggio di biografia politica," in *id.,* Schiavone, and Stolfi, *Quintus Mucius Scaevola,* 3 ff.

21. Ulp., 1 *inst.,* in D. 1, 1, 1, 2: "publicum ius est quod ad statum rei romanae spectat, privatum quod ad singulorum utilitatem."

22. Cic., *de fin.* 3, 67, 3.

23. The subtitle of the second edition of Tony Honoré's previously cited *Ulpian: Pioneer of Human Rights* is, in my opinion, something of an accident, a pointless modernizing concession. The book certainly had no need of such expedients— fortunately extraneous (barring a few unfortunate pages, 76–94) to the substance of the study—to be acknowledged as a fine and important work, entirely befitting the deserved prestige of the author. To start with, the expression "human rights"— untranslatable in Latin, and not just in the Latin of the jurists—is not part of that whole world; to say nothing of the fact that Ulpian never assumes the perspective of the concept indicated by it as a point of view even remotely related to his own positions.

24. Once again a foreshadowing of Kant: R. Esposito, *Communitas: Origine e destino della comunità* (Turin: Einaudi, 1998), in English as *Communitas: The Origin and Destiny of Community,* trans. T. Campbell (Stanford, CA: Stanford University Press, 2009), 75.

25. Ulp., 11 AD *ed.,* in D. 4, 2, 9, 1: "et ideo sive singularis sit persona, quae metum intulit, vel populus, vel curia vel collegium vel corpus, huic edicto loco erit"—where the distinction is presented between the figure of singularity and that of some unified wholes, without any mention of a theory of legal subjects: as usual, this is clearly seen by R. Orestano, *Il "problema delle persone giuridiche" in diritto romano,* vol. 1 (Turin: Giappichelli, 1968), 9 and 94.

26. I have already used the expression "bourgeois-Roman law" elsewhere: see A. Schiavone, *Alle origini del diritto borghese: Hegel contro Savigny* (Rome: Laterza, 1984), esp. 61 ff.

27. Gai., *inst.,* 1, 8: "Omne autem ius, quo utimur, vel ad personas pertinet vel ad res vel ad actiones": E. Stolfi, "La nozione di 'persona' nell'esperienza giuridica romana," in *Filosofia politica* 3 (2007): 379 ff. and *id.,* "Riflessioni attorno al problema dei 'diritti soggettivi' fra esperienza antica ed elaborazione moderna," in *Studi senesi* 118 (2006): 120 ff. The Roman jurist I am referring to is Hermogenian, who reproposed it perhaps only partially but in any case altered its meaning

substantially. Justinian's compilers placed it at the foundation of the entire exposition in the manual of imperial institutes: see I. 1, 2, 12.

28. Cic., *de orat.* 3, 14, 53: "qui idem ita moderantur, ut rerum, ut personarum dignitates ferunt."

29. Examples from Cicero are *de leg.* 2, 19, 48–49; *de orat.* 2, 47, 194; *Lael.* 1, 4; *ad fam.* 6, 6, 10; *ad Att.* 8, 11; *pro Cluent.* 29, 78. In Seneca, see, for example, among many uses, *de ben.* 1, 12, 3; 2, 13, 2; 2, 15, 3; 2, 16, 2. According to V. Scarano–Ussani, "La 'scoperta' della persona," in *id., Disciplina iuris e altri saperi* (Naples: M. D'Auria, 2012), 7 ff., esp. 11 ff., Cicero's *de leg.*, 2, 19, 48–49, just cited, contains an underlying basis of Scaevola's writing, to which the use of the word *persona* relates; however, this seems to me to be a very flimsy conjecture, though it cannot entirely be ruled out: E. Stolfi, in Ferrary, Schiavone, and Stolfi, *Quintus Mucius Scaevola,* 396 and notes 1084 and 1085.

30. H. Kelsen, *Reine Rechtslehre* (Vienna: Deuticke, 1960), in English as *Pure Theory of Law,* trans. M. Knight (Berkeley, CA: University of California Press, 1978), 173.

31. Gai., *inst.* 1, 9: "Et quidem summa divisio de iure personarum haec est, quod omnes homines aut liberi sunt aut servi."

32. Gai., *inst.* 1, 52.

33. "Persona servi" recurs literally, in fact, both in Paul, the other great jurist of the Severan age, in the *liber singularis ad legem Fufiam Caninam,* in D. 50, 16, 215, together with "persona magistratuum" and "persona liberorum"; and in Ulpian, in the fifty-seventh book *ad edictum,* in D. 47, 10, 15, 44; while in the twenty-eighth book *ad Sabinum* (in D. 50, 17, 22pr), Ulpian uses the expression "persona servilis."

34. Gai., *inst.* 2, 13.

35. The theme is developed, with very perceptive considerations, by R. Esposito, *Le persone e le cose* (Turin: Einaudi, 2014), in English as *Persons and Things: From the Body's Point of View,* trans. Z. Hanafi (London: Polity Press, 2015), 24ff., 57ff.

36. Everything I sustain in the text presupposes *The Invention of Law,* 354 ff., 399 ff., 431 ff. and A. Schiavone, "Per una storia del giusnaturalismo romano," in D. Mantovani and A. Schiavone, eds., *Testi e problemi del giusnaturalismo romano* (Pavia: Iuss Press, 2007), 3 ff.

37. The absence is evident in modern historiographic readings, even if the issue is never thematized directly: see, for example, B. Straumann, *Crisis and Constitutionalism: Roman Political Thought from the Fall of the Republic to the Age of Revolution* (New York: Oxford University Press, 2016), esp. 239 ff., and, more generally, C. Rowe and M. Schofeld, eds., *The Cambridge History of Greek and Roman Political Thought* (Cambridge: Cambridge University Press, 2000), esp. 401 ff. (though the essay on the Roman jurists, 616 ff., is poor and ill informed). A book worth reading is V. Marotta, *Ulpiano e l'impero* (Naples: Loffredo, 2000), vol. 1, esp. 9 ff., 111 ff. and vol. 2, 2004, esp. 19 ff.

38. Ulpian refers to the "true philosophy" at the beginning of his books *institutionum,* in D. 1, 1, 1, 1: "veram nisi fallor philosophiam."

39. I have already explored this theme, albeit briefly, in "Astrarre, distinguere, regolare," 57 ff.

40. "Iuri operam daturum prius nosse oportet, unde nomen iuris descendat. Est autem a iustitia appellatum," we read in the text just cited: a false etymology that serves to establish a conceptual genealogy that Roman legal thinking had always ignored.

41. "Iuris prudentia est divinarum atque humanarum rerum notitia, iusti atque iniusti scientia": Ulp., 1 reg., in D. 1, 1, 10.

42. In D. 1, 1, 1pr.

43. *Aequitas naturalis* is a key category in Ulpian's thought; for him it was a universal principle of distributive and proprietary equilibrium, to which *ius* could and had to adhere, constructed by re-elaborating Cicero, Labeo, and (probably) Gaius: A. Schiavone, *The Invention of Law*, 403 ff.

44. 1 *inst.*, in D. 1, 1, 4.

45. Ulp., 43 AD *Sab.*, in D. 50, 17, 32.

46. Flor., 9 *inst.*, in D. 1, 5, 4, 1; Tryph., 7 *disp.*, in D. 12, 6, 64.

47. *de rep.*, 3, 25, 37: "Sed et imperandi et serviendi sunt dissimilitudines cognoscaendae. Nam ut animus corpori dicitur imperare, dicitur etiam libidini, sed corpori ut rex civibus aut parens liberis, libidini autem ut servis dominus, quod eam coercet et frangit, sic regum, sic imperatorum, sic magistratuum, sic patrum, sic populorum imperia civibus sociisque praesunt ut corporibus animus, domini autem servos ita fatigant ut optima pars animi, id est sapientia, eiusdem animi vitiosas imbecillasque partes, ut libidines, ut iracundias ut perturbationes ceteras." I have already interpreted this text in A. Schiavone: "Legge di natura o convenzione sociale? Aristotele, Cicerone, Ulpiano sulla schiavitù-merce," in M. Moggi and G. Cordiano, eds., *Schiavi e dipendenti nell'ambito dell'"oikos" e della "familia"* (Pisa: Ets, 1997), 173 ff., esp. 175 ff.

48. I can refer here to A. Schiavone, *Spartaco. Le armi e l'uomo* (Turin: Einaudi, 2011), in English as *Spartacus,* trans. J. Carden (Cambridge, MA: Harvard University Press, 2013), 147 ff. A still important work, from which there is much to learn, is K. Hopkins, *Conquerors and Slaves: Sociological Studies in Roman History*, vol. 1 (Cambridge: Cambridge University Press, 1978), esp. 115 ff.

49. See *de leg.*, 1, 10, 29: "Nihil est enim unum uni tam simile, tam par, quam omnes inter nosmet ipsos sumus" ("For no single thing is so like another, so exactly its counterpart, as all of us are to one another"): it is the evident reproduction of a Stoic motif, a doctrine repeated in a rather scholastic fashion, without any implications on the political or social plane.

50. In Y. Thomas, "L'institution juridique de la nature," in *id., Les Opérations du droit*, M. A. Hermitte and P. Napoli, eds. (Paris: Ehess, 2011), 21 ff.

51. "Astrarre, distinguere, regolare," to which I have already referred, and also A. Schiavone, "Dai giuristi ai codici. Letteratura giuridica e legislazione nel mondo tardoantico," in *Storia di Roma*, vol. 3.2, 1993, 963 ff. (= *id., Linee di storia del pensiero giuridico romano* [Turin: Giappichelli, 1994], 249 ff.).

52. What has survived of his writing is gathered together in O. Lenel, *Palingenesia Iuris Civilis* [Leipzig 1889] (Rome: Led, 2002), vol. 1, coll. 341–344.

53. Jn 13, 34; also: 15, 12 and 17: see A. Schiavone, *Ponzio Pilato: Un enigma tra storia e memoria* (Turin: Einaudi, 2016), in English as *Pontius Pilate: Deciphering a Memory,* trans. J. Carden (New York: Liveright Publishing Corporation, 2017), 96 ff; Gen. 1, 26–27: see A. Schiavone, *Storia e destino* (Turin: Einaudi, 2007), 93 ff; Gal 3, 28–29.

54. *de trin.* 15, 51.

55. *adv. Praxean,* 25, 1: "So the close series of the Father in the Son and the Son in the Paraclete makes who cohere, the one attached to the others. And these three are one <thing>, in the sense in which it was said, *I and the Father are one,* in respect of unity of substance, not of singularity of number": *Tertullian's Treatise Against Praxeas,* ed., with an introduction, translations, and commentary by E. Evans (London: SPCK, 1948), 169: (Ita connexus Patris in Filio et Filii in Paracleto tres efficit cohaerentes alterum ex altero [in 24, 8 he had just said: igitur et manifestam fecit duarum personarum coniunctionem]. Qui tres unum sunt, non unus, quomodo dictum est, "Ego et Pater unum sumus, ad substantiae unitatem non ad numeri singularitatem"). On Tertullian's language and style, a key work is E. Löfstedt, *Zur Sprache Tertullians* (Lund: Gleerup, 1920). The theologian was an extraordinary inventor of words: 509 nouns, 284 adjectives, 28 adverbs, 161 verbs, according to the research of H. Hoppe, *Beiträge zur Sprache und Kritik Tertullians* (Lund: Gleerup, 1932), 132 ff.

56. *adv. Praxean,* 29, 2; 30, 2.

57. Jn 18, 36 ("this world": "tou kosmou toutou"); Mk 12, 13–17; Mt 22, 15–22; Lk 20, 20–26.

58. I refer again to *Pontius Pilate,* 74 ff., esp. 84 ff.

59. On these themes the magnificent research of P. Brown has opened up new horizons in recent decades, in particular, *Power and Persuasion in Late Antiquity: Towards a Christian Empire* (Madison: University of Wisconsin Press, 1992), esp. 3 ff., 35 ff.; but already before that, *Religion and Society in the Age of Saint Augustine* (London: Faber and Faber, 1972), esp. 74 ff., 161 ff., 279 ff.; and then *The Rise of Western Christendom* (Oxford: Blackwell, 1996), esp. 18 ff., 112 ff., and *The Ransom of the Soul. Afterlife and Wealth in Early Western Christianity* (Cambridge, MA: Harvard University Press, 2015), esp. 31 ff.

60. *de trin.* 7, 6, 11: "Nam si esse ad se dicitur, persona vero relative, sic dicamus tres personas patrem et filium et spiritum sanctum quemadmodum dicuntur aliqui tres amici aut tres propinqui aut tres vicini quod sint ad invicem, non quod unusquisque eorum sit ad se ipsum. Quapropter quilibet ex eis amicus est duorum ceterorum, aut propinquus aut vicinus quia haec nomina relativam significationem habent. Quid ergo? Num placet dicamus patrem personam esse filii et spiritus sancti, aut filium personam esse patris et spiritus sancti, aut spiritum sanctum personam esse patris et filii? Sed neque persona ita dici alicubi solet, neque in hac trinitate cum dicimus personam patris aliud dicimus quam substantiam patris. Quocirca ut substantia patris ipse pater est, non quo pater est sed

quo est; ita et persona patris non aliud quam ipse pater est. Ad se quippe dicitur persona, non ad filium vel spiritum sanctum; sicut ad se dicitur deus. . . . Et quemadmodum hoc illi est esse quod deum esse, . . . ita hoc illi est esse quod personam esse."

61. *de trin.* 15, 7, 11: "Quapropter singulus quisque homo qui non secundum omnia quae ad naturam pertinent eius sed secundum solam mentem imago dei dicitur una persona et imago est trinitatis in mente. Trinitas vero illa cuius imago est nihil aliud est tota quam deus, nihil est tota quam trinitas."

62. In truth it must be said that, after Tertullian, but before Augustine, it had again been legal thinking, from which, as we have seen, the first conceptualization of the notion of *persona* for descriptive–systematic purposes had come, that returned to the original theological elaboration of the word and used it in a way which, while it seemed to draw on Gaius, did so in reality already with a Christian interpretation. I am thinking of the books *iuris epitomarum* of Hermogenian (the remnants of which are in Lenel, *Palingenesia*, vol. 1, coll. 265–278), where, at the beginning of the first book (modifying Lenel's order), we can read: "Cum igitur hominum causa omne ius constitutum sit, primo de personarum statu ac post de ceteris, ordinem edicti perpetui secuti et his proximos atque coniunctos applicantes titulos, ut res patitur, dicemus" (in D. 1, 5, 2 = Lenel, Pal. 1, col. 265)—the person referred to here is no longer Gaius's, but, as if were, Tertullian's, and it is connected in fact to an idea of man ("hominum causa") which, if it appears to draw on a Ciceronian motif (about which we have already spoken), is in fact already completely infused with the new theology.

63. Cic., *de fin.* 1, 6, 17; *Tusc.* 1, 18, 42.

64. P. Hadot, *Marius Victorinus: Recherches sur sa vie et ses oeuvres* (Paris: Études augustiniennes, 1971), 385; also, Vict., *de def.* 25, 19 (Stangl) and Porf., *Isag.* 2, 17, 20; 7, 20–27.

65. *de trin.* 7, 6, 11: "Cum enim definiero quid sit homo, quod est nomen speciale, singuli quique homines quae sunt individua eadem definitione continentur, nec aliquid ad eadem pertinent quod homo non sit."

66. *de trin.* 7, 6, 1: "Quod si dicunt substantiae vel personae nomine non speciem significari sed aliquid singulare atque individuum."

3. The Equality of the Moderns

1. Sticking to the twentieth century—that is, setting aside for a moment the great modern tradition on the subject, from Locke to Marx, of which we shall speak later—I consider the most intelligent and perceptive book on this theme to be Hannah Arendt, *The Human Condition* (Chicago: University of Chicago Press, 1958), despite differing from it on many points, which also concern a general idea of history and historicity, as will become increasingly clear in the pages that follow. From a different perspective, an overall view is offered by L. Dumont, *Homo aequalis, I: Genèse et épanouissement de l'idéologie économique* (Paris: Gallimard,

1977, 1985), in English as *From Mandeville to Marx: The Genesis and Triumph of Economic Ideology* (Chicago: University of Chicago Press, 1977), esp. 33 ff., 111 ff. (the second volume, *Homo aequalis, II: L'idéologie allemande. France–Allemagne et retour* [Paris: Gallimard, 1991], is less interesting).

2. I have intentionally used the expression that forms the title of the celebrated book by P. Sraffa, *Production of Commodities by Means of Commodities: Prelude to a Critique of Economic Theory* (Cambridge: Cambridge University Press, 1960).

3. It will suffice to refer here to the classic studies of E. Garin. Besides the works cited below, see the essays in *id., L'età nuova: Ricerche di storia della cultura dal XII al XVI secolo* (Naples: Morano, 1969).

4. Q. Skinner, *Visions of Politics*, vol. 2: *Renaissance Virtues* (Cambridge: Cambridge University Press, 2002), esp. 10 ff., 13. A book that should be read, though not all its views can be shared, is J. M. Headley, *The Europeanization of the World: On the Origins of Human Rights and Democracy* (Princeton, NJ: Princeton University Press, 2008), esp. 9 ff.

5. I presuppose my reconstruction in A. Schiavone, *La storia spezzata: Roma antica e Occidente moderno* [1996] (Rome: Laterza, 2002), in English as *The End of the Past: Ancient Rome and the Modern West*, trans. M. J. Schneider (Cambridge, MA: Harvard University Press, 2000; reprint 2002), 108 ff., 165 ff.

6. Arist., *Pol.* 1, 4, 1253b; see Schiavone, *The End of the Past*, 133 f.

7. Arist., *Pol.* 1, 4, 1253b; *Eth. nic.*, 8, 11, 1161b; *Pol.* 1, 4, 1253b (*ktema*, "a piece of property").

8. I am referring to the contractual scheme of *locatio operarum*: F. Schulz, *Classical Roman Law* (London: Oxford University Press, 1951), 542 ff.; V. Marotta, in A. Schiavone, ed., *Diritto privato romano: Un profilo storico* (Turin: Einaudi, 2nd ed., 2010), 405 ff.

9. J. Locke, *Some Considerations of the Consequences of Lowering of the Interest and Raising the Value of Money: In a Letter to a Member of Parliament* [1691] (London: Awnsham and John Churchill, 1692), 91.

10. J. S. Mill, *On Liberty*, ed. G. Himmelfarb (Harmondsworth, UK: Penguin, 1974), 69.

11. J. Locke, *Two Treatises of Government* (Cambridge: Cambridge University Press, 1967), 287–288 (second treatise, para. 27).

12. A. Smith, *An Inquiry into the Nature and Causes of the Wealth of Nations* [1776], ed. E. Cannan (New York: The Modern Library, 1937, 1965), 33–34; D. Ricardo, *The Works and Correspondence of David Ricardo*, eds. P. Sraffa and M. H. Dobb, vol. 1, *On the Principles of Political Economy and Taxation* [3rd ed., 1821] (Cambridge: Cambridge University Press, 1951, 1990), 15–16.

13. This is the analysis that opens *Capital*—pages which changed the history of the world: K. Marx, *Das Kapital: Kritik der politischen Ökonomie. Erster Band* [1867] (Berlin: Dietz, 3rd ed., 1979) (= MEW, vol. 23), 49 ff., in English as *Capital: A Critique of Political Economy*, 3 vols., vol. 1, trans. B. Fowkes (Harmondsworth, UK: Penguin Books, 1976), 142 ff.

14. Ricardo, *On the Principles,* 22 ff.

15. I presuppose Schiavone, *The End of the Past,* esp. 87 ff., 108 ff.

16. A picture of the discussion, in relation to themes not far removed from the ones in this book, can be found in the vast and important fresco of P. Costa, *Civitas: Storia della cittadinanza europea,* vol. 1, *Dalla civiltà comunale al Settecento* (Rome: Laterza, 1999), 50 ff. A classic continuant position—with all the limitations of method inevitable in such approaches, is that of P. O. Kristeller, *Studies in Renaissance Thought and Letters* (Rome: Edizioni di Storia e Letteratura, 1956), esp. 38 ff., 359. An important book is J. Goody, *Capitalism and Modernity: The Great Debate* (Cambridge: Polity Press, 2004), esp. 19 ff., 50 ff.

17. I share Skinner's position in *Renaissance Virtues,* 1 ff.

18. M. Heidegger, *Sein und Zeit* [1927] (Tübingen, Germany: Niemeyer, 18th ed., 2001), in English as *Being and Time,* trans. J. Macquarrie and E. Robinson (Oxford: Basil Blackwell, 1962), 123 ff.

19. G. Galilei, *Dialogo sopra i due massimi sistemi del mondo* [1632], ed. L. Sosio (Turin: Einaudi, 1970), 140 (= Ed. Naz. Firenze 1890–1909, reprint 1964–1966, vol. 7, 139), in English as *Dialogue Concerning the Two Chief World Systems,* 2nd revised ed., trans. S. Drake (Berkeley: University of California Press, 1967), 113.

20. M. Stewart, *The Courtier and the Heretic: Leibniz, Spinoza and the Fate of God in the Modern World* (New Haven, CT: Yale University Press, 2005), 164.

21. G. Manetti, *De dignitate et excellentia hominis* [1451–1452], ed. E. R. Leonard (Padua: Antenore, 1975), esp. l. IV, 100 ff.

22. F. Bacon, *De principiis atque originibus secundum fabulas Cupidinis et Coeli: Sive Parmenidis, et Telesii et praecipue Democriti philosophia, tractata in fabula de Cupidine* [1623–1624], in *The Works of Francis Bacon,* eds. J. Spedding, R. L. Hellis, and D. D. Heath, vol. 3 (London: Cambridge University Press, 1876), 92 ff. See T. C. Allbutt, "Palissy, Bacon and the Revival of Natural Science," in *Proceedings of the British Academy,* 6 (1913–1914), 223 ff. (which in part reiterated A. B. Hanschmann, *B. Palissy und F. Bacon* [Leipzig: Dieterich, 1903], followed by P. Rossi, *Francesco Bacone: Dalla magia alla scienza* [Turin: Einaudi, 2nd ed., 1974], 13–14).

23. F. Rabelais, *La vie très horrifique du grand Gargantua père de Pantagruel* [1542], ed. J. Boulanger (Paris, 1955), 76–77 (chap. 24), in English as *Gargantua and Pantagruel,* trans. M. A. Screech (London: Penguin, 2006), 286.

24. F. Guicciardini, *Considerazioni sui Discorsi del Machiavelli* [1528], in *id., Scritti politici e ricordi* (Bari: Laterza, 1933), 8, in English in *id. Selected Writings,* ed. C. Grayson, trans. M. Grayson (London: Oxford University Press, 1965), 66. Guicciardini was discussing forms of government, on the basis of chapter 2 of the first book of the *Discorsi.* Worth bearing in mind is F. Gilbert, *Machiavelli and Guicciardini: Politics and History in Sixteenth Century Florence* (Princeton, NJ: Princeton University Press, 1965), esp. 153 ff., 236 ff. The quote from Machiavelli is in N. Machiavelli, *Discorsi sopra la prima deca di Tito Livio,* in *id., Opere,* ed. C. Vivanti, vol. 1 (Turin: Einaudi Pléiade, 1997), 245 (book I, chap. 17), in English as

The Discourses, ed. B. Crick, trans. L. Walker (London: Penguin, 1970): Q. Skinner, *The Foundations of Modern Political Thought*, vol. 1, *The Renaissance* (Cambridge: Cambridge University Press, 1978), 152 ff., esp. 166 ff. Research into Machiavelli has been a tradition in Italian studies at least since Francesco De Sanctis: for the twentieth century, just think of Gramsci's comments in Notebooks 13 and 18 (*Quaderni del carcere*, ed. V. Gerratana, vol. 3 [Turin: Einaudi, 1975], 1553 ff., 1951 ff.), partially in English in *Selections from the Prison Notebooks of Antonio Gramsci*, ed. and trans. Q. Hoare and G. Nowell-Smith (London: Lawrence and Wishart, 1971), and the essays of F. Chabod, *Scritti su Machiavelli* (Turin: Einaudi, 1964), in English as *Machiavelli and the Renaissance*, trans. D. Moore (London: Bowes & Bowes, 1958) esp. 30 ff., 126 ff., a tradition that is still alive today, seeking out new paths with varying degrees of success: I have in mind the pages of R. Esposito, *Pensiero vivente: Origine e attualità della filosofia italiana* (Turin: Einaudi, 2010), in English as *Living Thought: The Origins and Actuality of Italian Philosophy*, trans. Z. Hanafi (Stanford, CA: Stanford University Press, 2010), 45 ff., of C. Ginzburg, *Nondimanco: Machiavelli, Pascal* (Milan: Adelphi, 2018), 19 ff., in English as *Nevertheless: Machiavelli, Pascal* (London: Verso, 2022), and of A. Asor Rosa, *Machiavelli e l'Italia: Resoconto di una disfatta* (Turin: Einaudi, 2019), esp. 65 ff.

25. F. Patrizi, *De institutione reipublicae libri IX,* editio postuma Montisbeligardi 1594, l. I, tit. vi, *de aequalitate civium,* 33 ff.

26. L. Bruni, *Oratio in funere Nannis Strozae,* in *Stephani Baluzii Tutelensis Miscellanea: Novo ordine digesta,* ed. G. D. Mansi, vol. 4 (Lucca 1764), 3–4.

27. See Skinner, *The Foundations,* 212 ("the northern humanists"). Also useful are the essays in D. Crouzet, É. Crouzet-Pavan, P. Desan, and C. Revest, eds., *L'Humanisme à l'épreuve de l'Europe: XVᵉ–XVIᵉ siècles. Histoire d'une transmutation Culturelle* (Ceyzérieu, France: Champ Vallon, 2019), esp. 41 ff. (C. Kiluchi), 59 ff. (P.-A. Salvadori), 80 ff. (J. Miernowski), 285 ff. (G. Chaix).

28. E. Panofsky, *Renaissance and Renascences in Western Art* (Stockholm: Almqvist & Wiksell, 1965), 113.

29. G. Pico della Mirandola, *De hominis dignitate,* ed. B. Cicognani (Florence: Le Monnier, 1941), 3, 5: observations on Pico that have stood the test of time can be found in E. Garin, *L'umanesimo italiano: Filosofia e vita civile nel Rinascimento* (Bari: Laterza, 1964), in English as *Italian Humanism: Philosophy and Civic Life in the Renaissance,* trans. P. Munz (Oxford: Blackwell, 1965), 105 ff.

30. In truth, Garin himself is not extraneous to that tradition: besides *L'umanesimo italiano,* see also E. Garin, *La cultura del Rinascimento* (Bari: Laterza, 1967). Also worth bearing in mind is M. Cacciari, *La mente inquieta: Saggio sull'umanesimo* (Turin: Einaudi, 2019), esp. 29 ff., 52 ff.

31. Garin, *Italian Humanism,* 49–50; L. Valla, *De voluptate* [1431], in *id., Scritti filosofici e religiosi,* ed. G. Redetti (Florence: Sansoni, 1953), 246, 73, on which Garin, *Italian Humanism,* 52.

32. On the criticism of Boethius—L. Valla, *Elegantiarum linguae latinae libri sex,* in *Prosatori latini del Quattrocento,* ed. E. Garin (Milan: Ricciardi, 1952; re-

printed Turin: Einaudi, 1977), book 6, chap. 33—see M. Ciliberto, *Giordano Bruno: Il teatro della vita* (Milan: Mondadori, 2007), 33 ff.; Esposito, *Living Thought*, 58 ff.

33. M. de Montaigne, *Les Essais*, ed. J. Balsamo, M. Magnien, and C. Magnien-Simonin (Paris: Gallimard–Pléiade, 2007), on the first page, "au lecteur": "car c'est moy que je peins," 27, in English as *The Complete Essays*, trans. M. A. Screech (London: Penguin Books, 2003), lxiii.

34. Montaigne, *Les Essais*, 490–491 (book 2, chapter 12). The translation is from *The Complete Essays of Montaigne*, trans. D. Frame (Stanford CA: Stanford University Press, 1958), 343.

35. The debate and its context are quickly and effectively reconstructed by P. Costa, *Civitas*, vol. 1, 121 ff., with an extensive bibliography. A wonderful book is the brief work by A. Dupront, *Espace et Humanisme* [1946], reprinted in *id.*, *Genèses des temps modernes* (Paris: Gallimard–Seuil, 2001), 47–112, in Italian as *Spazio e umanesimo: L'invenzione del Nuovo Mondo* (Venice: Marsilio, 1993), with an introduction by R. Romano, 9 ff., who in turn gathered together all of Montaigne's "American" pages in *De America* (Paris: Utz, 1991). Two important works are T. Todorov, *La Conquête de l'Amérique: La question de l'autre* (Paris: Seuil, 1982), in English as *The Conquest of America: The Question of the Other* (New York: Harper & Row, 1987), and A. Pagden, "Dispossessing the Barbarian: The Language of Spanish Thomism and the Debate over the Property Rights of the American Indians," in A. Pagden, ed., *The Languages of Political Theory in Early Modern Europe* (Cambridge: Cambridge University Press, 1987), 79 ff.; see also A. Prosperi and W. Reinhard, eds., *Il Nuovo Mondo nella coscienza italiana e tedesca del Cinquecento* (Bologna: il Mulino, 1997), esp. 287 ff. (G. Imbruglia), and 401 ff. (A. Prosperi). Going back in time, we must not forget two memorable works by L. Hanke, *Aristotle and the American Indians: A Study in Race Prejudice in the Modern World* (Chicago: Henry Regnery Company, 1959), esp. 44 ff., and *id.*, *The Spanish Struggle for Justice in the Conquest of America* (Philadelphia: University of Pennsylvania Press, 1949), esp. 132 ff., and R. E. Quirk, "Some Notes on a Controversial Controversy: Juan Ginés de Sepúlveda and Natural Servitude," *Hispanic American Historical Review* 34 (1954), 3: 121 ff. See also Headley, *The Europeanization of the World*, 103–104.

36. See M. Traversino, "Bruno e il 'Nuovo mondo': La condizione degli indigeni e il dibattito con Gentili," *Il Pensiero Politico* 44 (2011), 2: 241 ff. An overall view in M. Ciliberto, *Il nuovo umanesimo* (Rome: Laterza, 2017), 181 ff. (and see also *id.*, *Giordano Bruno*, 274 ff.). Bruno's words cited in the text are from *De immenso*, in *Opere latine*, ed. C. Monti (Turin: Utet, 1980), 784–785. T. Campanella, *Del senso delle cose e della magia*, ed. G. Ernst (Rome: Laterza, 2007), 224 (the text is also in Ciliberto, *Il nuovo umanesimo*, 189): "Those of the new world came to ours, and Plato writes of a very ancient story in the Atlantic, that there was the Atlantic island which joined one hemisphere with the other, and then it was flooded and submerged, such that all memory of it was lost in very ancient times, just as among us many origins are unknown. . . . But all men are similar, and can invent similar things."

37. G. Bruno, *De gl'heroici furori*, 2, 2 (Paris, 1585), anastatic reprint in *id.*, *Opere italiane*, ed. E. Canone (Florence: Olschki, 1999), vol. 4, 1454, in English as *The Heroic Enthusiast*, trans. L. Williams (London: Bernard Quaritch, 1889): I share the position of G. de Ruggiero, *Storia della filosofia*, vol. 3, *Rinascimento, Riforma e Controriforma* (Bari: Laterza, 1961), 454–455.

38. N. Machiavelli, *Il Principe*, in *id.*, *Opere*, vol. 1, 119; in English as *The Prince*, eds. Q. Skinner and R. Price (Cambridge: Cambridge University Press, 1988), 5.

39. C. S. Maier, *Once within Borders: Territories of Power, Wealth, and Belonging since 1500* (Cambridge, MA: Harvard University Press, 2016) esp. 50 ff., is a work from which there is much to learn. By the same author, see also *id.*, *Among Empires: American Ascendancy and its Predecessors* (Cambridge, MA: Harvard University Press, 2006), 78 ff. Also worthy of consideration is A. Pagden, *Lords of All the World: Ideologies of Empire in Spain, Britain and France, c. 1500–c. 1800* (New Haven, CT: Yale University Press, 1998).

40. G. W. F. Hegel, *Vorlesungen über die Philosophie der Weltgeschichte*, ed. G. Lasson (Leipzig: Meiner, 1919–1920), vol. 1, 196, in English as *Lectures on the Philosophy of World History*, trans. H. Nisbet (Cambridge: Cambridge University Press, 1975), 167.

41. I. Kant, *Beantwortung der Frage: Was ist Aufklärung?* [1784], in *id.*, *Werke*, ed. W. Weischedel, vol. 11 (Frankfurt am Main: Suhrkamp, 1968), 51 ff., in English as "Answering the Question: What is Enlightenment?" in *Practical Philosophy*, trans. and ed. M. Gregor (Cambridge: Cambridge University Press, 1996), 18. The philosopher attributes the sentence to Frederick II, his prince: "raisonniert" had a semantic coloring that also nudged the word in the direction of "contradict," "contest," "dissent."

42. F. Guicciardini, *Ricordi* [1530], ed. R. Spongano (Florence: Sansoni, 1951), 33 (para. 28) and 76 (para. 66) (*Selected Writings*, 12, 20–21).

43. M. Weber, *Die protestantische Ethik und der Geist des Kapitalismus*, in *id.*, *Gesammelte Aufsätze zur Religionssoziologie* (Tübingen, Germany: Mohr, 1920), vol. 1, 1–206, in English as *The Protestant Ethic and the Spirit of Capitalism* [1930], trans. T. Parsons (London: Routledge, 2001), 177, note 16, which cites, in praise, the book by E. Dowden, *Puritan and Anglican* (London: Kegan Paul, 1900), 234: "the deepest community is found not in institutions or corporations or churches, but in the secrets of a solitary heart."

44. T. Hobbes, *Elementa Philosophica de Cive* (Amsterdam, 3rd ed., 1647, though it appeared early in the following year); English trans. from the Latin: *On the Citizen*, ed. and trans. R. Tuck and M. Silverthorne (Cambridge: Cambridge University Press, 1998), 25–26.

45. T. Hobbes, *The Elements of Law, Natural and Politic*, ed. F. Tönnies (London: Frank Cass & Co, 1969), 70.

46. T. Hobbes, *Leviathan* [1651], ed. C. B. Macpherson (Harmondsworth, UK: Penguin, 1968), 183–185.

47. Hobbes, *On the Citizen*, 3, through Vell. Pat., *Hist. Rom.*, 2, 27, 1.

48. Here Hobbes reveals the distance from the whole ancient tradition, Aristotle included: I share the position of R. Esposito, *Politica e negazione: Per una filosofia affermativa* (Turin: Einaudi, 2018), in English as *Politics and Negation: Towards an Affirmative Philosophy*, trans. Z. Hanafi (Cambridge: Polity Press, 2019), 79 ff. See also M. Riedel, *Metaphysik und Metapolitik: Studien zu Aristoteles und zur politischen Sprache der neuzeitlichen Philosophie* (Frankfurt am Main: Suhrkamp, 1975), in Italian as *Metafisica e metapolitica: Studi su Aristotele e sul linguaggio politico della filosofia moderna* (Bologna: il Mulino, 1990), 169. Also H. Worrender, *The Political Philosophy of Hobbes* (Oxford: Clarendon Press, 1957), Worth bearing in mind, more generally, is the magnificent book by P. Hazard, *La crise de la conscience européene. 1680–1715* [1935] (Paris: Le livre de Poche, 1994), in English as *The European Mind 1680–1715*, trans. J. May (Harmondsworth, UK: Penguin, 1964), 73 ff. It is in fact from the condition of original equality that there derives "warre, as is of every man, against every man," and its disastrous results: Hobbes, *Leviathan*, 183 ff.

49. For example, by Carl Schmitt, *Der Nomos der Erde im Völkerrecht des Jus Publicum Europaeum* [1950] (Berlin: Duncker & Humblot, 1974), in English as *The Nomos of the Earth in the International Law of the Jus Publicum Europaeum*, trans. G. Ulmen (New York: Telos Press, 2003), 95 ff.: and in actual fact there is an explicit reference to America in the *Leviathan*, 121.

50. P. Costa, *Civitas*, vol. 1, 164–165. For more about the social orders of seventeenth-century England and the ideas that traversed them, a fundamental work is C. Hill, *The World Turned Upside Down: Radical Ideas during the English Revolution* (London: Pelican Books, 1972), esp. 39 ff., 107 ff., 339 ff.

51. Schmitt, *The Nomos of the Earth*, 95.

52. Hobbes, *On the Citizen*, 22.

53. Hobbes, *Leviathan*, 185.

54. Hobbes, *On the Citizen*, 22.

55. Hobbes, *Leviathan*, 186, 188.

56. Hobbes, *On the Citizen*, 22; *Leviathan*, 186.

57. Hobbes, *Elements*, 75.

58. R. Esposito, *Due: La macchina della teologia politica e il posto del pensiero* (Turin: Einaudi, 2013), in English as *Two: The Machine of Political Theology and the Place of Thought*, trans. Z. Hanafi (New York: Fordham University Press, 2015), 106 ff. His reading should be accompanied as a minimum by the now classic interpretations of Hobbes's thought, those of N. Bobbio, *Thomas Hobbes* (Turin: Einaudi, 1989), esp. 3 ff., 73 ff., and of Q. Skinner, *Reason and Rhetoric in the Philosophy of Hobbes* (Cambridge: Cambridge University Press, 1996); see also Q. Skinner, *Liberty before Liberalism* (Cambridge: Cambridge University Press, 1998), 101 ff.

59. In chapter 16 of the first part of the *Leviathan*, 217 ff.: Q. Skinner, "Hobbes and the Purely Artificial Person of the State," *Journal of Political Philosophy* 7 (1999), 1: 1 ff.

60. J. Locke, *Two Treatises of Government*, ed. P. Laslett (Cambridge: Cambridge University Press, 1988), 269. An excellent overall view is provided by *John Locke's Two Treatises of Government: New Interpretations*, ed. E. J. Harpham (Lawrence: University Press of Kansas, 1992). Also important is C. A. Viano, *Il pensiero politico di Locke* (Rome: Laterza, 1997).

61. Together with Engels, in *Die Deutsche Ideologie. Kritik der neuesten deutschen Philosophie in ihren Repräsentanten Feuerbach, B. Bauer und Stirner, und das deutschen Sozialismus in seinen verschiedenen Propheten* [1846], but published in 1932, in MEW, vol. 3, 1978, in English as *The German Ideology* (London: Lawrence & Wishart, 1974), 111.

62. Locke, *Two Treatises of Government*, 304.

63. J. Locke, *Of the Conduct of the Understanding* (New York: Teachers College, Columbia University, 1966), 33-34.

64. Locke, *Two Treatises of Government*, 304.

65. F. De Sanctis, "Lavoro, proprietà, industria. Il capitolo V del Secondo Trattato di Locke," *Materiali per una storia della cultura giuridica* 18 (1988): 311 ff.

66. Locke, *Two Treatises of Government*, 289: S. Buckle, *Natural Law and the Theory of Property: Grotius to Hume* (Oxford: Clarendon Press, 1991). Also K. Olivecrona, "Appropriation in the State of Nature: Locke on the Origin of Property," *Journal of the History of Ideas* 35 (1974), 2: 211 ff., now in R. Ashcraft, ed., *John Locke: Critical Assessments* (London: Routledge, 1991), vol. 3, 309 ff. Also worth reading: Esposito, *Politics and Negation*, 103 ff.

67. Locke, *Two Treatises of Government*, 291.

68. Locke, *Two Treatises of Government*, 127.

69. The expression comes from C. B. Macpherson, *The Political Theory of Possessive Individualism: Hobbes to Locke* (Oxford: Clarendon Press, 1962), esp. 1 ff., 263 ff.: the judgment of Skinner, *The Foundations*, vol. 2, 347, note 1, is largely correct. See also Costa, *Civitas*, vol. 1, 285-286 and M. Gauchet, *L'avènement de la démocratie*, vol. 1, *La révolution moderne* (Paris: Gallimard, 2007), 77 ff., who speaks of an "invention de l'individu."

70. C. Thomasius, *Institutiones Jurisprudentiae Divinae* [Halle 1720] (Aalen: Scientia 1963), 2, 3, 1, 22-24, 116-17; G. Tarello, *Storia della cultura giuridica moderna*, vol. I, *Assolutismo e codificazione del diritto* (Bologna: il Mulino, 1976), 113 ff.; Costa, *Civitas*, vol. 1, 255 ff. See also Hazard, *The European Mind*, 204 ff.

71. P. Stein, *Roman Law in European History* (Cambridge: Cambridge University Press, 1999), 61, 64 ff.

72. A. Duck, *De usu et auctoritate Iuris civilis Romanorum in Dominiis Principum Christianorum libri duo* (Leipzig, 1668; there is a reprint of the 1654 edition: Pranava Books 2018). The English translation appeared, together with the translation of another work on the same theme by C. J. de Ferrière, under the title of *The History of the Roman or Civil Law* (London, 1724; reprints: Clark, NJ: The Lawbook Exchange, 2005, 2010).

73. R. Orestano, *Introduzione allo studio del diritto romano* (Bologna: il Mulino, 1987), 166—a book of great importance and one of the high points in twentieth-century studies of Roman law.

74. J. Domat, *Les lois civiles dans leur ordre naturel* [1689–1694], in *Oeuvres complètes de J. Domat*, ed. J. Rémy, vol. 1 (Paris: Alex–Gobelet, 1835), 1, in English as *The Civil Law in Its Natural Order*, 2 vols., vol. 1, trans. W. Strahan (Boston: C. C. Little and J. Brown, 1850), 107; Tarello, *Storia*, 177. Important observations can be found in M. Brutti, *Interpretare i contratti: La tradizione, le regole* (Turin: Giappichelli, 2017), 106 ff.

75. M. Brutti, *Interpretare i contratti*, 107, note 8; also Tarello, *Storia*, 157 ff. (who emphasizes Domat's links with Pascal).

76. Domat, *Les lois civiles*, 15 (*The Civil Law*, 132–133).

77. Brutti, *Interpretare i contratti*, 118 ff.; O. Diliberto, "L'eredità fraintesa. Il diritto di proprietà dall'esperienza romana al Code Napoléon (e viceversa)," in P. Bonin, N. Hakim, F. Nasti, and A. Schiavone, eds., *Pensiero giuridico romano e giuristi moderni: Eredità e genealogie* (Turin: Giappichelli, 2019), 89 ff., esp. 99 ff.

78. The phrase is from the celebrated opening sentence of Marx's *Capital: Das Kapital: Erster Band*, 49 (*Capital*, vol. 1, 125). Marx was citing himself: *Zur Kritik der Politischen Ökonomie* [1859], in MEW, vol. XIII, 1974, 21, in English as *A Contribution to the Critique of Political Economy*, trans. S. W. Ryazanskaya (London: Lawrence & Wishart, 1971), 27.

79. The expression is found in Caecilius Statius, *com.*, 264 Ribbeck, 3rd ed.: "homo homini deus est, si suum officium sciat"—which in some ways anticipates the "humanism" of Terentian, and consciously overturns the original formulation by Plautus, "lupus est homo homini" (*Asin.*, 495), picked up by Hobbes. The contrast then returns, articulated differently, in Erasmus ("Homo homini aut deus aut lupus," *Adagia* [1500], in Italian as *Adagi*, ed. E. Lelli [Milan: Bompiani, 2013], no. 70), in Francisco Vitoria ("Contra ius naturale est, ut homo hominem sine aliqua causa aversetur, non enim homo homini lupus est, ut ait Ovidius, sed homo," *Relección primera, de los Indios*, 3 [Madrid: Editorial Católica, 1960], 709), in Bacon ("Iustitia debetur, quod homo homini sit Deus, non lupus," *De dignitate et augmentis scientiarum* (Turnhout, Belgium: Brepols, 2010), 6, c. 3), and in John Owen ("Homo homini lupus, homo homini deus," *Epigrammata* [Amberg: Libreria Uhlmanniana, 1811], 3, 23).

80. See Schiavone, *The End of the Past*, 113 ff., esp. 119. An evocative book is T. Hansen, *Slavernes skibe, Nordisk Forlag* (Copenhagen, 1968), in English as *Ships of Slaves* (Legon-Accra: Sub-Saharan Publishers, 2007), esp. chapters 1 and 2. A classic now is H. Thomas, *The Slave Trade: The Story of the Atlantic Slave Trade 1440–1870* (New York: Touchstone, 1999), esp. 291 ff.

81. According to the census of 1790, 3,929,326 residents lived in the United States, 697,681 of whom were slaves: First Census of the United States, at www2

.census.gov, 6: W. Dollarhide, *The Census Book: A Genealogist Guide to Federal Census Facts, Schedules and Indexes* (North Salt Lake: Heritage Quest, 2001), 7. Still useful is R. Hofstadter, *America at 1750: A Social Portrait* (New York: Vintage, 1973), 66 ff. See also the essays of W. D. Jordan and Ira Berlin in G. Heuman and J. Walvin, eds., *The Slavery Reader* (London: Routledge, 2003), 112 ff. and 122 ff. Also by Berlin is *Many Thousands Gone: The First Two Centuries of Slavery in North America* (Cambridge, MA: The Belknap Press of Harvard University Press, 1998), esp. 29 ff., 93 ff. Bear in mind also J. Black, *A Brief History of Slavery* (London: Running Press, 2011), esp. 69 ff. and O. Pétré-Grenouilleau, *Les Traites négrières: Essai d'histoire globale* (Paris: Gallimard, 2004), esp. 34 ff., 119 ff. A memorable picture is painted by S. Schama, *Rough Crossing: Britain, the Slaves and the American Revolution* (London: BBC Books, 2005), esp. 26 ff., 252 ff. At the height of slavery in classical times, the percentage of slaves in Athens and Rome exceeded 30 percent of the overall population: see Schiavone, *The End of the Past*, 112.

82. D. Defoe, *A Plan of the English Commerce* (Oxford: Blackwell, 1927), 76–77: D. Hackett Fischer, *The Great Wave: Price Revolutions and the Rhythm of History* (New York: Oxford University Press, 1996), 102 ff. For many of the themes touched on in this section, we must now bear in mind E. Traverso, *Revolution: An Intellectual History* (London: Verso Books, 2021), which, as it appeared two years after the Italian edition of my book and a year after the French one, I was unable to use.

83. The definitive text is the result of a stratification of writing between 1705 and 1729: B. Mandeville, *The Fable of Bees: Or, Private Vices, Public Benefits: With an Essay on Charity and Charity-School: And Search into the Nature of Society* (Oxford: Oxford University Press, 3rd ed., 1966), 2 vols: an important work is J. Robertson, *The Case for the Enlightenment: Scotland and Naples 1680-1760* [2005] (Cambridge: Cambridge University Press, 2006), 261 ff.

84. In the diary of a traveler, *Voyage en Angleterre,* held in the Victoria and Albert Museum (86 NN 2, f.14), cited by F. Braudel, *Civilisation matérielle, economie et capitalisme (XVe-XVIIIe siècle): Les jeux de l'échange* (Paris: Armand Colin, 1979), in English as *Civilization and Capitalism, 15th-18th Century,* vol. 2, *The Wheels of Commerce,* trans. S. Reynolds (Berkeley: University of California Press, 1992), 41–42.

85. D. Landes, *The Unbound Prometheus: Technological Change and Industrial Development in Western Europe from 1750 to the Present* (Cambridge: Cambridge University Press, 1969), esp. 5 ff., 41 ff.—an essential and unsurpassed work. For the purposes of the argument we are pursuing, see D. Landes, ed., *A che servono i padroni? Le alternative storiche all'industrializzazione* (Turin: Bollati Boringhieri), 1987, esp. 80 ff. Also important are N. F. R. Crafts, *British Economic Growth during the Industrial Revolution* (Oxford: Oxford University Press, 1985), *id.,* "The Industrial Revolution. Economic Growth in Britain, 1700-1860," in A. Digby and C. Feinstein, eds., *New Directions in Economic and Social History* (Chicago: Macmillan, 1989), 64 ff., and Hackett Fischer, *The Great Wave,* 117 ff., 142 ff.

86. Smith, *The Wealth of Nations*, 3: "Of the causes of Improvement in the productive Powers of Labour, and of the Order according to which its Produce is naturally distributed among the different Ranks of the People."

87. As J. Starobinski comments in the introduction to his edition of the *Discours sur l'origine et les fondements de l'inégalité*, in J.-J. Rousseau, *Oeuvres complètes*, vol. 3 (Paris: Gallimard, 1964), 51.

88. F. Furet, *Penser la Révolution francaise* (Paris: Gallimard, 1978; reprint 1985), 65–66, in English as *Interpreting the French Revolution*, trans. E. Forster (Cambridge: Cambridge University Press, 1981), 36–37—a book that is now a classic, and a masterly example of how, with the force of the historic intelligence alone, it is possible to radically transform, in the course of a few hundred pages, the study of a great theme about which we believed everything was known. See also the fine book by A. Lilti, *Le Monde des salons: Sociabilité et mondanité à Paris au XVIIIe siècle* (Paris: Fayard, 2005).

89. Voltaire, *Dictionnaire philosophique* [1764; definitive edition, 1769], ed. A. Pons (Paris: Gallimard Paris, 1994), in English as *Philosophical Dictionary*, trans. T. Besterman (Harmondsworth, UK: Penguin Books, 1971). The quotations are respectively in the entries on "Property" (my translation) and "Equality." Still important is G. Della Volpe, *Rousseau e Marx e altri saggi di critica materialistica* (Rome: Editori Riuniti, 1971), 115–116.

90. Rousseau, *Discours*, 123. In English as *Discourse on the Origin and Foundations of Inequality Among Mankind*, in *The Social Contract and The First and Second Discourses*, ed. S. Dunn (New Haven, CT: Yale University Press, 2002), 82.

91. Rousseau, *Discours*, 132–133 (*Discourse*, 88).

92. Rousseau, *Discours*, 178 (*Discourse*, 125).

93. Rousseau, *Discours*, 164 (*Discourse*, 113).

94. Fifty years on, Colletti's essays on the relationship between Rousseau and Marx are still exemplary: "Rousseau critico della 'società civile'" and "Mandeville, Rousseau e Smith," both in L. Colletti, *Ideologia e società* (Bari: Laterza, 1969), 195 ff. and 263 ff. (and, also by Colletti, bear in mind his pages on the theme in *Il marxismo e Hegel* [Bari: Laterza, 1969], 410 ff., and in his posthumous *Lezioni di filosofia politica*, ed. L. Albanese [Soveria Mannelli: Rubbettino, 2017], 29 ff.).

95. Rousseau, *Discours*, 193–194 (*Discourse*, 138).

96. Rousseau, *Du Contract social: Ou, principes du droit politique*, in *id., Oeuvres completes*, vol. 3, 429 (*Social Contract*, 221).

97. Rousseau, *Discours*, 131 (*Discourse*, 87).

98. The expression "état social" was already in the first draft of the *Social Contract*, the so-called Geneva Manuscript, in *id., Oeuvres*, vol. 3, 292.

99. Rousseau, *Contract*, 429–430 (*Social Contract*, 221).

100. Rousseau, *Contract*, 169 ff., esp. 171–172 (*Social Contract*, 171 ff.): some good observations in Esposito, *Politics and Negation*, 94 ff., who draws in part on H. Arendt, *On Revolution* (New York: Viking, 1963), 65 ff.

101. Rousseau, *Contract*, 429–430 (*Social Contract*, 221).

102. Rousseau anticipated the significance of that century's history with amazing foresight—which says a lot about the climate of France in those decades, when the unthinkable was being prepared: in the third book of *Émile* [1762], speaking of his own present, he wrote: "We are approaching a state of crisis and the age of revolutions": in *Oeuvres*, vol. 4 (Paris: Gallimard,1969), in English as *Emile*, trans. A. Bloom (New York: Basic Books, 1979), 194. It was exactly what would happen.

103. Montesquieu, *De l'esprit des lois*, in *id., Oeuvres complètes*, vol. 2 (Paris: Gallimard,2008), 274, in English as *The Spirit of the Laws*, ed. and trans. A. Cohler, B. Miller, and H. Stone (Cambridge: Cambridge University Press, 1989), 43.

104. Montesquieu, *De l'esprit des lois*, 274, 278–279 (*Spirit of the Laws*, 43, 46–47).

105. Montesquieu, *De l'esprit des lois*, 279 (*Spirit of the Laws*, 47).

106. Costa, *Civitas*, vol. 1, 377 ff.

107. R. R. Palmer, *The Age of the Democratic Revolution: A Political History of Europe and America, 1760–1800*, 2 vols. (Princeton, NJ: Princeton University Press, 1959, 1964); H. F. May, *The Enlightenment in America* (Oxford: Oxford University Press, 1978); J. T. Kloppenberg, *Toward Democracy: The Struggle for Self-Rule in European and American Thought* (Oxford: Oxford University Press, 2016); J. Israel, *Revolutionary Ideas: An Intellectual History of the French Revolution from "The Rights of Men" to Robespierre* (Princeton, NJ: Princeton University Press, 2014) and, above all, *id., The Expanding Blaze: How the American Revolution Ignited the World, 1775–1848* (Princeton, NJ: Princeton University Press, 2017)—a pair of works without equal not just in contemporary historiography (preceded, moreover, by *id., A Revolution of the Mind. Radical Enlightenment and the Intellectual Origins of Modern Democracy* (Princeton, NJ: Princeton University Press, 2010). Also worthy of attention: C. A. Bayly, *The Birth of the Modern World: Global Connections and Comparisons, 1780–1914* (Oxford: Blackwell, 2004).

108. F. von Gentz, *Der Ursprung und die Grundsätze der Amerikanischer Revolution, vergleichen mit dem Ursprunge und den Grundsätzen der Französischen* [1800], *Historishes Journal* 2 (1800): 3 ff., 97 ff., in English as *The Origin and Principles of the American Revolution, Compared with the Origin and Principles of the French Revolution* (Philadelphia: Asbury Dickins, 1800); new edition ed. R. A. Kirk (Chicago: Gataway, 1955); D. Armitage, *The Declaration of Independence: A Global History* (Cambridge, MA: Harvard University Press, 2007), 68, and Israel, *The Expanding Blaze*, 355–356.

109. Palmer, *The Age of the Democratic Revolution* (on p. 6 the author also speaks of an "Atlantic Civilization"); Israel, *The Expanding Blaze*, esp. 600.

110. Arendt, *On Revolution*, esp. 13 ff., 45 ff., 85 ff. 109 ff., 171 ff.

111. Israel, *The Expanding Blaze*, 606.

112. As is well known, this is the title of the great work by F. Venturi, *Settecento riformatore*, 5 vols., (Turin: Einaudi, 1969–1990): and it is a real pity that this work

does not feature in the bibliographies—rich and carefully compiled—of Israel's two books. Another unsurpassable, though rather dated work, is G. De Ruggiero, *Storia del liberalismo europeo* [1925] (Bari: Laterza, 1958) (I am referring here above all to 1–94).

113. Israel, *The Expanding Blaze*, 7 ff.

114. Arendt, *On Revolution*, 85.

115. Foreign gazes of extraordinary acuteness, directed at America more than a century apart by two figures who, out of vocation or necessity, had made travel a state of mind.

116. P. Finkelman, *Slavery and the Founders: Race and Liberty in the Age of Jefferson* (New York: M. E. Sharpe, 1996), esp. 105 ff., 138 ff.

117. Israel, *The Expanding Blaze*, 613–614, who in turn takes it from W. Hutcheson, "The Louisville Riots of August 1855," *Register of the Kentucky Historical Society*, 1971, 150 ff.

118. Armitage, *The Declaration of Independence*, 165.

119. J. Bentham, *An Answer to the Declaration of the American Congress* [London 1776]; the text is in Armitage, *The Declaration of Independence*, 173 ff.; H. L. A. Hart, "Bentham and the United States of America," *The Journal of Law & Economics* 19 (1976), 3: 547 ff.; Israel, *The Expanding Blaze*, 9, 30.

120. Bentham, *An Answer*, in Armitage, *The Declaration of Independence*, 173. See also Headley, *The Europeanization*, 188 ff.

121. M. White, *Philosophy, The Federalist, and the Constitution* (New York: Oxford University Press, 1987), esp. 3 ff., 193 ff.

122. In a letter dated May 30, 1790, in *Papers of Thomas Jefferson*, vol. 16 (Princeton, NJ.: Princeton University Press, 1961), 449.

123. The image used by Landes in the title of his well-known book.

124. N. Copernicus, *De revolutionibus orbium coelestium* [1543], in *id., Opere* (Turin: Utet, 1979), 168 ff., in English as *On the Revolutions*, trans. E. Rosen (Baltimore: Johns Hopkins University Press, 1992), but in eighteenth-century France the word had already acquired a fully historic-political meaning: just consider the *Histoire des Révolutions arrivées dans le gouvernement de la République romaine* by Abbot Vertot, 2 vols. (Paris: P. and F. Didot, 1719, 1816). A useful work is A. Rey, *"Révolution": Histoire d'un mot* (Paris: Gallimard, 1989), esp. 21 ff., 109 ff. Some fundamental observations in Arendt, *On Revolution*, 32 ff.

125. A useful collection of essays is J. P. Euben, J. R. Wallach, and J. Ober, eds., *Athenian Political Thought and the Reconstruction of American Democracy* (Ithaca, NY: Cornell University Press, 1994), esp. 29 ff. (S. Wolin), 59 ff. (E. M. Wood), 319 ff. (J. R. Wallach).

126. In England too, in fact, republican Rome was greatly in vogue. Essays like the *Reflections on the Rise and Fall of the Ancient Republics* by Edward Worteley Montagu [1760], ed. D. Womersely (Indianapolis: Liberty Fund, 2015), the *Antiquities of Rome* by Basil Kennet [1696] (London: Longman, 1793), or the *History of the Progress and Termination of the Roman Republic* by Adam Ferguson, 3 vols.

(London: Strahan, 1783), were known to all highly educated people, while George III himself read Livy together with Benjamin West, and suggested to him the subject for a *Departure of Regulus* [1769] that then remained among his favorite pictures: just a few years earlier Winkelmann had published the *Geschichte der Kunst des Alterthums* (Dresden: Walther, 1764), which in many respects can be regarded as the consecration of the myth of the "classical." An important collection of essays is M. Pacini, ed., *La virtú e la libertà: Ideali e civiltà italiana nella formazione degli Stati Uniti* (Turin: Fondazione Giovanni Agnelli, 1995), in particular the contributions of G. S. Wood, "L'eredità di Roma nella rivoluzione americana," 21 ff., R. A. Ferguson, "La scoperta di Roma: il modo di vedere e di rappresentare nella repubblica americana," 47 ff., and M. Reinhold, "L'interpretazione dell'età di Roma," 87 ff.

127. I share the judgment of Israel, *The Expanding Blaze*, 14–15, regarding the indeterminateness, in this context, of the category of "liberalism." The clear-cut opposition between "moderates" and "radicals" should also be used with care: see the important studies of G. Nash, *The Unknown American Revolution* (London: Penguin, 2006), S. Cotlar, "Languages of Democracy in America from the Revolution to the Election of 1800," in J. Innes and M. Philp, eds., *Re-imagining Democracy in the Age of Revolutions: America, France, Britain, Ireland 1750–1850* (New York: Oxford University Press, 2013); S. Wilentz, *The Politicians and the Egalitarians* (New York: W. W. Norton & Company, 2016); and naturally the observations of Israel, *The Expanding Blaze*, 14 ff. Another book to bear in mind is G. S. Wood, *The Radicalism of the American Revolution* (New York: Vintage, 1993).

128. Hegel, *Vorlesungen*, 925 (my translation).

129. Furet, *Interpreting the French Revolution*, 61 ff., 69 ff.

130. Israel, *Revolutionary Ideas*, esp. 450 ff., 503 ff.

131. "Men are born and remain free and equal in rights. Social distinctions may be based only on considerations of the common good."

132. In the preamble: "the happiness of all."

133. "The aim of every political association is the preservation of the natural and imprescriptible rights of Man. These rights are Liberty, Property, Safety and Resistance to Oppression."

134. Israel, *Revolutionary Ideas*, 83, and S. Rials, *La Déclaration des droits de l'homme et du citoyen* (Paris: Hachette, 1988), 220 ff., 236 ff.

135. "Since the right to Property is inviolable and sacred, no one may be deprived thereof, unless public necessity, legally ascertained, obviously requires it, and just and prior indemnity has been paid."

136. E. Sieyès, *Essai sur les privileges* (Paris: Alexandre Correard, 1788), 5, now also in *Écrits politiques*, ed. R. Zapperi (Paris: Éditions des Archives Contemporaines, 1985), 95.

137. This model was discussed at length between July and October 1789—Israel, *Revolutionary Ideas*, 106–107—and was then incorporated into the constitution of 1793.

138. Furet, *Interpreting the French Revolution*, 27.

139. In a letter to his brother, in 1789, cited by Arendt, *On Revolution*, 40.

140. Arendt, *On Revolution*, 38–39.

141. This is the title of chapter 13 of Israel, *Revolutionary Ideas*, 345.

142. Furet, *Interpreting the French Revolution*, 46ff. Israel speaks of "an authoritarian populism prefiguring modern fascism" (*Revolutionary Ideas*, 695). I well understand, and can share, the reference to authoritarian populism, but fascism is much else besides, and matchings like these do not assist historic understanding.

143. Furet, *Interpreting the French Revolution*, 38.

144. Cited by Israel, *Revolutionary Ideas*, 507.

145. Cited by A. Mathiez, *La Révolution francaise*, 3 vols. (Paris: Armand Colin, 1927). In his view, liberty and the political equality of the majority of citizens tended to vanish with the growth of social inequalities—a real problem, as we shall see: G. Lefebvre, *La Révolution francaise* (Paris: Presses Universitaires, 1951), 396.

146. Furet, *Interpreting the French Revolution*, 26.

147. Cited by Arendt, *On Revolution*, 50.

148. Robespierre, *Oeuvres*, vol. 9 (Paris: Presses Universitaires de France, 1958; reprint Paris: Phénix, 2000), 124—we are in the December of 1792: the occasion was the debate about the request to sentence Louis XVI to death without a proper trial.

149. On the constitutional outcome of the Revolution, see M. Troper, *Terminer la Révolution: La Constitution de 1795* (Paris: Fayard, 2006), esp. 91 ff., 109 ff.

150. It "horrifies a soul," Kant writes in *Metaphysische Anfangsgründe der Rechtslehre* [1797], in English as *The Philosophy of Law*, trans. W. Hastie (Edinburgh: T. & T. Clark, 1887), 178.

151. I. Kant, *Rezension vom Moscati Schrift: Von dem körperlichen wesentlichen Unterschiede zwischen der Structur der Thiere und Menschen*, 1771, in English as "Review of Moscati's Work *Of the Corporeal Essential Differences between the Structure of Animals and Humans*," trans. G. Zöller, in I. Kant, *Anthropology, History, and Education*, eds. G. Zöller and R. Louden (Cambridge: Cambridge University Press, 2007), 80.

152. Cited by A. Illuminati, *Kant politico* (Florence: La Nuova Italia, 1971), 138.

153. Kant, *Beantwortung der Frage: Was ist Aufklärung?* ("What Is Enlightenment?" 18).

154. See A. Schiavone, *Alle origini del diritto borghese: Hegel contro Savigny* (Rome: Laterza, 1984), esp. 61 ff.

155. I. Kant, *Von der verschiedenen Racen der Mensche*, in English as "Of the Different Races of Human Beings," trans. H. Wilson and G. Zöller, in *Anthropology, History, and Education*, 84–85.

156. I. Kant, *Zur ewigen Frieden: Ein philosophischer Entwurf von Immanuel Kant* [1795], in English as "Toward Perpetual Peace: A Philosophical Project," in *Practical Philosophy*, trans. M. Gregor (Cambridge: Cambridge University Press, 1996), 323.

157. Kant, *Über den Gemeinspruch: Das mag in der Theorie richtig sein, taugt aber nicht für die Praxis* [1793], in English as "On the common saying: That may be correct in theory, but it is of no use in practice," in *Practical Philosophy*, 292 [trans. modified].

158. Kant, "On the common saying," 291 (in section 2, "On the relation of theory to practice in the right of a state").

159. Kant, "On the common saying," 290.

160. Hegel, *Differenz des Fichteschen und Schellingschen Systems der Philosophie* [1801], in *id.*, *Werke* (Berlin, 1832–1844), vol. 2, *Jenaer Schriften 1801–1807* (Frankfurt am Main: Felix Meiner, 1986), 9–138, in English as *The Difference between Fichte's and Schelling's System of Philosophy*, trans. H. S. Harris and W. Cerf (Albany, NY: State University of New York Press, 1977).

161. Kant, "On the common saying," 290.

162. Hegel, *Vorlesungen*, 920 (my translation).

163. Israel, *Revolutionary Ideas*, 708. The page in question was clearly familiar to J. Hyppolite, *Genèse et structure de la Phénoménologie de l'esprit de Hegel* [1946] (Paris: Aubier, 1978), 439–440, in English as *Genesis and Structure of Hegel's Phenomenology of Spirit*, trans. S. Cherniak and J. Heckman (Evanston, IL: Northwestern University Press, 1974), 454. Israel knows the work of Spinoza well though, and carefully appraises its importance.

164. B. de Giovanni literally says "extraordinary weight," and he is quite right, in his research on Hegel and Spinoza, to which we will return shortly: *Hegel e Spinoza: Dialogo sul moderno* (Naples: Guida, 2011), 248–249 (and also 73)—one of the greatest works of European philosophy in recent decades.

165. E. Weil, *Hegel et l'état: Cinq Conférences* [1950] (Paris: Vrin, 5th ed., 1980); J. Ritter, *Hegel und die französische Revolution* (Frankfurt am Main: Suhrkamp, 1965); M. Riedel, *Studien zu Hegels Rechtsphilosophie* (Frankfurt am Main, Suhrkamp, 1969); B. de Giovanni, *Hegel e il tempo storico della società borghese* (Bari: De Donato, 1970); K.-H. Ilting, *Hegel diverso* (Rome: Laterza, 1977) (which brings together essays that appeared in Germany between 1971 and 1976, with a final and previously unpublished work); R. Bodei, *Sistema ed epoca in Hegel* (Bologna: il Mulino, 1975), 2nd ed., revised and expanded, with the title *La civetta e la talpa: Sistema ed epoca in Hegel* (Bologna: il Mulino, 2014); and again with regard to Bodei, see also *Scomposizioni: Forme dell'individuo moderno* (Turin: Einaudi, 1987), esp. 6 ff.

166. I am referring to B. de Giovanni, *Hegel e Spinoza*.

167. See G. W. F. Hegel, *Enzyklopädie der philosophischen Wissenschaften*, in *id.*, *Werke* [Berlin 1832–44] (Frankfurt am Main: Suhrkamp, 1969), vol. 8, 132, para. 50, in English (part 1) as *Hegel's Logic*, trans. W. Wallace (Oxford: Clarendon Press, 1975), 80 ff.; Hegel, *Die Vernunft in der Geschichte* [posthumous, 1837], in *Vorlesungen*, 166 (*Lectures*), which should be compared with a manuscript note by Hegel.

168. K. Löwith, *Von Hegel zu Nietzsche: Die revolutionäre Bruch im Denken des 19: Jahrhunderts* (Zurich: Europa, 1949²), in English as *From Hegel to Nietzsche:*

The Revolution in Nineteenth-century Thought, trans. D. Green (London: Constable, 1965), 208 ff.

169. K. Marx, *Kritik des hegelschen Staatsrecht* [posthumous, 1927], in MEW, vol. 1, 17th ed., 2017, 201–333, in English as *Critique of Hegel's 'Philosophy of Right,'* trans. J. O'Malley (Cambridge: Cambridge University Press, 1970), 12.

170. "The objective logic thus takes the place rather of the former *metaphysics* which was supposed to be the scientific edifice of the world as constructed by *thoughts* alone.—If we look at the final shape in the elaboration of this science, then it is *ontology* which objective logic most directly replaces in the first instance": Hegel, *Wissenschaft der Logik,* vol. 1, in *id., Werke,* vol. 5, 1983, 61, in English as *The Science of Logic,* trans. and ed. George Di Giovanni (Cambridge: Cambridge University Press, 2010), 42.

171. Hegel, *Vorlesungen,* 137 (*Lectures,* 131).

172. Hegel, *Enziclopädie,* 295, added to paragraph 151, (*Hegel's Logic,* 214); de Giovanni, *Hegel e Spinoza,* 37.

173. "This private [Roman] law is thus equally a non-existence of the person, a non-recognition, and this state of law is a complete lack of law. The subject, according to the principle of his personality, is authorized only to possess, and the person of persons to possess everyone, as the single law is at the same time abolished and deprived of legal force. This contradiction is the misery of the Roman world": *Vorlesungen,* 716; and see also 715–716: "And in the immense [Roman] empire was one who included all with himself. Before this one were individuals, as private persons, an infinite mass of atoms. They were absolutely equal (slavery was nothing but a slender difference) [this is a colossal mistake on an almost incalculable scale, which sensationally contradicts Hegel's own thought] and without any political rights . . . But despite this equality among citizens, tyranny continued to exist; indeed, it was precisely despotism that introduced equality. This also acquired the characteristic of freedom, but only of the abstract kind, that of private law. Private law developed and completed this equality. The principle of abstract interiority . . . was now realized in the concept of the person within private law."

174. De Giovanni, *Hegel e Spinoza,* 37, also 193–194. Hegel's view is expressed in a brief gloss that Ilting, in his edition of the *Vorlesungen über Rechtsphilosophie 1818–1831: Edition und Kommentar in sechs Bänden* (Stuttgart: Frommann Holzboog, 1973–1974), vol. 2, 95 attributes to the course of 1824–1825: "Vernunft ist gegenwärtig"—"reason is present."

175. Hegel, in *Berliner Schriften,* ed. J. Hoffmeister (Hamburg: Meiner, 1956), in English as "On the English Reform Bill," in Hegel, *Political Writings,* ed. L. Dickey and H. B. Nisbet, trans. H. B. Nisbet (Cambridge: Cambridge University Press, 1999), 239. N. Bobbio, *Studi hegeliani: Diritto, società civile, stato* (Turin: Einaudi, 1981), 109.

176. Hegel, *Vorlesungen,* 198 (*Lectures,* 169).

177. *Hegels Schriften zur Politik und Rechtsphilosophie,* ed. G. Lasson (Leipzig: Meiner, 2nd ed., 1925).

178. G. W. F. Hegel, *Grundlinien der Philosophie des Rechts*, ed. J. Hoffmeister (Hamburg: Meiner, 4th ed., 1955), 214–215, in English as *Elements of the Philosophy of Right*, trans. H. Nisbet (Cambridge: Cambridge University Press, 1991), 282.

179. Hegel, *Grundlinien*, 207–208 (*Elements*, 275).

180. Hegel, *Enzyklopädie*, vol. 3, para. 486, in English (part 3) as *Hegel's Philosophy of Mind*, trans. W. Wallace (Oxford: Clarendon Press, 1971), 242. But "das beschränke juristische Recht" should be understood as "of the jurists," in the sense of jurisprudential rather than "juridical" law, which would not have sense, as is translated by B. Croce in his version of the *Encylopedia* [1907] (Bari: Laterza, 1967), vol. 2, 446. The error did not escape N. Bobbio, *Studi hegeliani: Diritto, società civile, Stato* (Turin: Einaudi, 1982), 36.

181. Hegel, *Grundlinien*, 214 ("das innere Staatsrecht") (*Elements*, 281).

182. The expression forms the title of Savigny's most important work, *System des heutigen römischen Rechts*, vol. 1 [Berlin 1840] (Aalen: Scientia, 1981) in English as *System of the Modern Roman Law*, vol. 1, trans. W. Holloway (Madras: Higginbotham, 1867).

183. See Schiavone, *Alle origini del diritto borghese: Hegel contro Savigny*, esp. 10 ff. and note 11.

184. Hegel, *Grundlinien*, para. 357, 295–296 (*Elements*, 379).

185. Hegel, *Grundlinien*, para. 3, 23 (*Elements*, 34; translation modified).

186. G. W. F. Hegel, *Die Phänomenologie des Geistes* [1807], in *id., Werke*, vol. 3, 1986, 355, in English as *The Phenomenology of Spirit*, ed. and trans. T. Pinkard (Cambridge: Cambridge University Press, 2018), 277.

187. *Phänomenologie*, 355 (*Phenomenology*, 277).

188. Marx, *Critique of Hegel's "Philosophy of Right,"* the quote is on p. 79.

189. *Phänomenologie*, 150–154 (*Phenomenology*, 113–115). I have already addressed this text in *The End of the Past*, 166 ff.

190. A. Kojève, *Introduction à la lecture de Hegel* [1947] (Paris, 1976), 27, in English as *Introduction to the Reading of Hegel: Lectures on the Phenomenology of Spirit*, ed. A. Bloom, trans. J. Nicholls (New York: Basic Books, 1969), 22.

191. Kojève, *Introduction à la lecture*, 25 (*Introduction*, 19).

192. Hegel, *Grundlinien*, para. 198, 173–74 (*Elements*, 232–233).

193. Hegel, *Grundlinien*, para. 207, 179 (*Elements*, 238).

194. H. Melville, *Moby Dick or the Whale*, ed. Hayford-Parker (New York, 1967), 104–105 (chap. 26).

195. F. Ames, in L. P. Simpson, ed., *The Federalist Literary Mind: Selections from the Monthly Anthology and Boston Review, 1803–1811* (Baton Rouge: Louisiana State University Press, 1962), 54.

196. E. Smith, in *The Loving Kindness of God Displayed in the Triumph of Republicanism in America* [1809], cited by Wood, *Radicalism*, 231–232.

197. Wood, *Radicalism*, 233.

198. A. Jardin, *Alexis de Tocqueville 1805–1859* (Paris: Hachette, 1984), in English as *Tocqueville: A Biography*, trans. L. Davis with R. Hemenway (London: P. Halban, 1988), esp. 88 ff., the best biography of Tocqueville.

199. A. de Tocqueville, *De la démocratie en Amérique I* [1835], in *id., Oeuvres,* ed. A. Jardin, vol. 2 (Paris: Gallimard–Pléiade, 1992), 3, in English as *Democracy in America* [1966], ed. J. P. Mayer, trans. G. Lawrence (New York: HarperPerennial, 1969), 9.

200. I am thinking, for example, of chapter 8 of the first part of volume 2, *De la democratie,* 542 ff. (*Democracy,* 452 ff.), which seems to closely evoke the Hegelian idea of the infinite potential of the finite.

201. Tocqueville, *De la democratie,* 50 (*Democracy,* 50).

202. J. T. Schleifer, *The Making of Tocqueville's Democracy in America* (Chapel Hill: University of North Carolina Press, 1980), 263 ff.—an important book. The word "irridescence" is used by R. Nisbet, "Many Tocquevilles," *The American Scholar,* 1976–1977: 62.

203. L. Cafagna, "Tocqueville dalla democrazia in America all'aristocrazia in Francia," which serves as the introduction to the Italian translation of Tocqueville's other great work, *L'ancien Régime et la Révolution* [1856]: *L'Antico Regime e la Rivoluzione,* ed. C. Vivanti (Turin: Einaudi, 1989), vii–xlii (the sentence I am referring to is on p. xxv). In the vast bibliography on Tocqueville—largely French and American—two fine Italian books worthy of attention are F. De Sanctis, *Tempo di democrazia: Alexis de Tocqueville* (Naples: Editoriale Scientifica, 2005), esp. 81 ff., 121 ff., and *id., Tocqueville: Sulla condizione moderna* (Naples: Editoriale Scientifica, 2005), 25 ff. (both reprints of earlier editions: Naples 1986 for the first, Milan 1993 for the second). I would also just add F. Furet, "Naissance d'un paradigme: Tocqueville et le voyage en Amerique," *Annales* 39 (1984), 2: 225 ff.

204. Montesquieu's influence on Tocqueville is clearly highlighted by J.-C. Lamberti, *Tocqueville et les deux démocraties* (Paris: Presses Universitaires de France, 1983), esp. 27 ff., 93 ff., 123 ff., 217 ff.—another very important piece of research.

205. Tocqueville, *De la démocratie,* 60 (*Democracy,* 58–59).

206. Tocqueville, *De la démocratie,* 62 (*Democracy,* 60).

207. Tocqueville, *De la démocratie,* 193–194 (*Democracy,* 173).

208. Tocqueville, *De la démocratie,* 194 (*Democracy,* 173): "quoique."

209. Tocqueville, *De la démocratie,* 223 (*Democracy,* 198).

210. Tocqueville, *De la démocratie,* 542–544 (*Democracy,* 452–454).

211. Tocqueville, *De la démocratie,* 394 (*Democracy,* 340).

212. Tocqueville, *De la démocratie,* 398 (*Democracy,* 343).

213. A. de Tocqueville, *Voyage en Amérique* (posthumous, ed. G. de Beaumont, 1865–1866), in *id., Oeuvres,* vol. 1, 1991, 26 ff., esp. 360 ff., in English as *Journey to America,* trans. G. Lawrence, ed. J. P. Mayer (New Haven, CT: Yale University Press, 1960), esp. 360 ff.

214. *Voyage en Angleterre de 1833,* in *Oeuvres,* vol. 1, 450, in English as *Journeys to England and Ireland,* ed. J. Mayer, trans. G. Lawrence and K. Mayer (New York: Anchor Books, 1968), 52: L. Cafagna, "Tocqueville dalla democrazia in America" xxvii.

215. Tocqueville, *De la démocratie,* 615 (*Democracy,* 509).

216. Tocqueville, *De la démocratie*, 607–608 (*Democracy*, 503–504).

217. Tocqueville, *L'ancien Régime* , in English as *The Old Regime and the Revolution*, vol. 1: *The Complete Text*, ed. F. Furet and F. Mélonio, trans. A. Kahan (Chicago: Chicago University Press, 1998), 181.; Cafagna, "Tocqueville dalla democrazia in America," xix, xxxi.

218. Tocqueville, *De la démocratie*, 610 (*Democracy*, 505).

219. Tocqueville, *De la démocratie*, 609 (*Democracy*, 504); Montesquieu, *De l'esprit des lois*, vol. 1, 352: "De l'esprit d'egalité extrême," book 8, chap. 3 (*The Spirit of the Laws*, 114).

220. Tocqueville, *De la démocratie*, 612 (and note on 1113) (*Democracy*, 506 [and note on 735]). The same holds true for English: see I. Watt, *Myths of Modern Individualism: Faust, Don Quixote, Don Juan, Robinson Crusoe* (Cambridge: Cambridge University Press, 1997), 120 and note 1.

221. Tocqueville, *De la démocratie*, 607–620 (*Democracy*, 503–513).

222. W. Channing, "Remarks on Associations," in *The Works of William Channing* (Boston: American Unitarian Association, 1877), 139–140: but it should be observed that the debate about "American" character, often with references to Tocqueville, was very extensive between the nineteenth and twentieth century: I will refer just to H. S. Commager, *The American Mind: An Interpretation of American Thought and Character since the 1880s* [1950] (New Haven, CT: Yale University Press, 1959).

223. Tocqueville, *De la démocratie*, 612 (*Democracy*, 507).

224. Tocqueville, *De la démocratie*, 614 (*Democracy*, 508).

225. Cited by Wood, *Radicalism*, 243.

226. Tocqueville, *De la démocratie*, 614 (*Democracy*, 508).

227. Tocqueville, *De la démocratie*, 618, 621–622 (*Democracy*, 511, 513–514).

228. Tocqueville, *De la démocratie*, 613 (*Democracy*, 507).

229. I have already discussed this in *Spartaco. Le armi e l'uomo* (Turin: Einaudi, 2011), in English as *Spartacus*, trans. J. Carden (Cambridge, MA: Harvard University Press, 2013), 98 ff., 101 ff. More generally, see also *The End of the Past*, chapters 8–10.

230. K. Polanyi, *The Great Transformation* (New York: Farrar & Rinehart, 1944), 130 ff., offers an unrivaled overall picture.

231. The analysis in these pages returns to and develops what I sustain in *I conti del comunismo* (Turin: Einaudi, 1999), esp. 18–76.

232. K. Marx, *Der achtzehnte Brumaire des Louis Bonaparte* [1852], in MEW, vol. 8, 1972, 115 ff., in English as *The Eighteenth Brumaire of Louis Bonaparte*, in K. Marx, *Later Political Writings*, ed. and trans. T. Carver (Cambridge: Cambridge University Press, 1996), 31 ff.

233. K. Marx, *Thesen über Feuerbach* [1845, but published in 1888], in MEW, vol. 3, 1969, 5 ff., in English as "On Feuerbach," in K. Marx, *Early Political Writings*, trans. J. O'Malley with R. Davis (Cambridge: Cambridge University Press, 1994), 118. The *but* was added by Engels in his edition of 1888.

234. Marx, *Critique of Hegel's 'Philosophy of Right*,' 32.

235. Marx, *Zur Kritik der politischen Ökonomie*, 15 (*Contribution to the Critique*, 21).

236. K. Marx, *Theorien über den Mehrwert 3*, in MEW, vol. 26.3, 1968, 468, in English as *Theories of Surplus Value*, trans. G. Bonner and E. Burns (London: Lawrence & Wishart, 1951). The original phrase is: "Wie alles in dieser Produktionsweise sich verkehrt darstellt." L. Colletti, *Il marxismo e Hegel*, esp. 357 ff., 403 ff., remains one of the most significant achievements of Italian and European Marxism in the 1960s and 1970s.

237. Marx, *Zur Kritik der politischen Ökonomie*, 15–16 (*Contribution to the Critique*, 21).

238. According to the analytic framework and lexical choices of Marx ever since the *Oekonomisch-philosophische Manuskripte aus dem Jahre 1844*, in MEW, vol. 1, 1968, 465–588, in English as *Economic and Philosophic Manuscripts of 1844* (Moscow: Progress Publishers, 1977). See p. 68: "Under these economic conditions this realization of [the worker's] labour appears as *loss of realisation* [*Entwirklichung*] for the workers; objectivization as *loss of the object and bondage to it*; appropriation as *estrangement* [*Entäusserung*], *as alienation* [*Entfremdung*: the same word used, in another context, by Freud]."

239. Marx, *Das Kapital: Erster Band*, 562 (*Capital*, 680). I discuss this text in *The End of the Past*, 169 ff.

240. A debate that is now covered in dust: P. Sraffa, *Production of Commodities*, 34 ff.; P. Garegnani, *Marx e gli economisti classici: Valore e distribuzione nelle teorie del sovrappiú* (Turin: Einaudi, 1981), esp. 5 ff., 55 ff.; C. Napoleoni, *Discorso sull'economia politica* (Turin: Boringhieri, 1985), esp. 7 ff., 77 ff. Here too I can refer to one of my earlier books: *La sinistra del terzo capitalismo* (Rome: Laterza, 1989), esp. 55 ff.

241. K. Marx, *Kritik des Gothaer Programms* [1875, but published in 1891], in MEW, vol. 19, 4th ed., 1973, 13–32, in English as *Critique of the Gotha Programme*, in *Later Political Writings*, 222: "Between capitalist and communist society there is a period of revolutionary transformation of one into the other. There is also correspondingly a period of political transition, in which the state can be nothing else but *the revolutionary dictatorship of the proletariat*" [Marx's italics].

242. Marx, *Critique of the Gotha Programme*, 215; K. Marx, *Das Kapital: Kritik der politischen Ökonomie, Dritter Band*, in MEW, vol. 25, 1975, 859: the term for "accounts" is "Buchführung" (*Capital*, vol 3, trans. D. Fernbach [Harmondsworth, UK: Penguin, 1981], 991.

243. N. Badaloni, *Per il comunismo: Questioni di teoria* (Turin: Einaudi, 1972), 24 ff.

244. T. W. Adorno, *Negative Dialektik* (Frankfurt am Main, Suhrkamp, 1966), in English as *Negative Dialectics*, trans. E. Ashton (London: Routledge, 1990), xix.

245. Marx, *Zur Kritik der politischen Ökonomie*, 252 (*A Contribution to the Critique*, 210).

246. Marx, *Critique of the Gotha Programme,* 223: "Even the most vulgar democrats, who see the millennium in the democratic republic and have no inkling that it is in this last form of the state for bourgeois society that the class struggle will definitively be decided with weapons" ["mit Waffen"]; translation slightly modified.

247. B. de Giovanni, *Marx filosofo* (Naples: Editoriale Scientifica, 2018), esp. 30 ff.; Hegel, *Wissenschaft der Logik,* vol. 1, 61 "Die objektive Logik" (*The Science of Logic,* 47).

248. Marx, *Das Kapital: Erster Band,* 12 (*Capital,* 90).

249. Marx, *Zur Kritik der politischen Ökonomie,* 230 (*A Contribution to the Critique,* 191).

250. Marx, *Das Kapital: Erster Band,* 184 (*Capital,* 274).

251. K. Marx, *Grundrisse der Kritik der politischen Ökonomie* [1857–1858, but published in 1939–1941] (Berlin: Dietz, 2nd ed., 1974), 592, in English as *Grundrisse: Introduction to the Critique of Political Economy,* trans. N. Nicolaus (Harmondsworth, UK: Penguin, 1973), 704–705. I have already discussed this text, in A. Schiavone, *La sinistra del terzo capitalismo,* 69 ff., and *I conti del comunismo,* 39 ff.

252. "We know only a single science, the science of history": K. Marx, *Die deutsche Ideologie,* in MEW, vol. 3, 18 (a variant of the text) (*The German Ideology,* 28); A. Schmidt, *Geschichte und Struktur: Fragen einer marxistischen Historik* (Munich: Hanser, 1971), in English as *History and Structure: An Essay on Hegelian-Marxist and Structuralist Theories of History,* trans. J. Herf (Cambridge, MA: MIT Press, 1981), 29 ff. Around this point—the Marxist theory of history—Althusser and then his school developed their work from the 1960s on. In particular, bear in mind L. Althusser, É. Balibar, J. Rancière, R. Establet, and P. Macheray, *Lire le Capital,* 4 vols. (Paris: Maspero, 2nd ed., 1971–1973), esp. vol. 1, 150 ff., in English as *Reading Capital,* trans. B. Brewster (London: NLB, 2nd ed., 1977), esp. 119 ff.

253. According to de Giovanni, *Marx filosofo,* 86, Marx "does not know the negation of negation": "for Hegel the negative is the continual spirit of the original mediation that includes the negation of negation, or double negation; for Marx the scenario is the struggle against achieved Mediation that has become real Abstraction," with the result that "Marx rigidifies Hegel's *Philosophy of History* into *Science of History* capable of morphological prediction." If I understand correctly, de Giovanni also in any case ends up supposing the existence of a block, of a kind of insuperable freeze frame of historicity, in Marx's historical and morphological analysis. That this, with all the consequences it brings, can be traced back merely to a logical (or ontological) error seems to me to be an explanation of overly theoretical acuteness, of the kind that attracted the not unjustified irony of Luciano Cafagna, when he also wrote about the "negation of negation" in Marx ("Tocqueville dalla democrazia in America"), xxxvii—we are in 1989 here). Without a doubt, theory explains many things—and we should never forget it. But always protruding beyond it there is what we might call the density of the historic-natural structure of the real, with its own reasons that theory never knows in advance; what

now, I believe—and again, if I have understood correctly—de Giovanni tends to call "Life": Roberto Esposito does so too, in truth (see, for example, Esposito, *Living Thought*, esp. 105 ff.), and it is a significant convergence—as if one of the very best traditions of Italian philosophy (the Neapolitan one) has returned to where it broke off, that is, to the late Croce!—but this is another story.

254. Marx, *Zur Kritik der politischen Ökonomie*, 227–228 (*A Contribution to the Critique*, 188–189).

255. Marx, *Theorien über den Mehrwert*, 127 (*Theories of Surplus Value*).

256. Colletti, *Il marxismo e Hegel*, 388 ff.; Marx, *Economic and Philosophic Manuscripts*, 146: "But man is not just a natural being: he is a *human* natural being. That is to say, he is a being for himself. Therefore he is a *species-being*, and has to confirm and manifest himself as such both in his being and in his knowing."

257. See Sraffa, *Production of Commodities*, 34 ff.; Garegnani, *Marx e gli economisti classici* 5 ff., 55 ff.; Napoleoni, *Discorso sull'economia politica* 7 ff., 77 ff.; Schiavone, *La sinistra del terzo capitalismo*, 55 ff.; C. Napoleoni, introduction to L. Colletti and C. Napoleoni, eds., *Il futuro del capitalismo crollo o sviluppo?* (Bari: Laterza, 1970), viii ff., and *id.*, *Lezioni sul Capitolo sesto inedito di Marx* (Turin: Boringhieri, 1974), esp. 174 ff.

258. S. Weil, *Journal d'usine* [1934–1935], in *id.*, *La condition ouvrière* [1934–1942] (Paris: Gallimard, 1951), in English as "Factory Work," in *The Simone Weil Reader*, ed. G. Panichas (New York: David McKay Company, 1977), 53–72.

259. I am referring to G. Lukács, *Geschichte und Klassenbewusstein* [1923] (Bielefeld, Germany: Aisthesis, 2013), in English as *History and Class Consciousness: Studies in Marxist Dialectics*, trans. R. Livingstone (London: Merlin Press, 1971).

260. V. I. Lenin, *The Proletarian Revolution and the Renegade Kautsky* (1918, first German edition 1919). See also *id.*, *Marxism and Revisionism* [1908].

261. The next few pages presuppose H. Arendt, *The Origins of Totalitarianism* (London: George Allen & Unwin, 3rd ed., 1967), esp. 305 ff.

262. For instance, the classic research of F. Chabod, which saw the light in dramatic years in the form of *L'idea di nazione* [1943–1944, with variants in 1946–1947] (Bari: Laterza, 1967), esp. 17 ff. His work should be read together with Hazard, *The European Mind*.

263. "If Germany had been guided only by the hand of time along the thread of its own culture, undoubtedly our manner of thinking would be poor, narrow, but true to our land, archetype to itself, not so disfigured and divided": this is Herder, the inventor of the word "nationalism," writing in 1774, cited by Chabod, *L'idea*, 50, and the critique—anticipating strictly Romantic motifs—of the universalistic intellect of Enlightenment thinkers appears already fully deployed: we can sense in it a foreshadowing of Nazism—speaking of archetypes and roots. For more on Herder's positions, see the analysis by Z. Sternhell, *Les anti-Lumières: Du XVIIIe siècle à la guerre froide* (Paris: Fayard, 2006), in English as *The Anti-Enlightenment Tradition*, trans. D. Maisel (New Haven, CT: Yale University Press, 2009), 274 ff.

264. An important book is J. Keegan, *The First World War* [1998] (New York: Vintage and Random House, 2000). Also worth reading is J. Glover, *Humanity: A Moral History of the Twentieth Century* (New Haven, CT: Yale University Press, 1999), 155 ff.

265. In truth it seems that the word was first used by Giovanni Amendola, in an article written in 1923 ("totalitarian system"), in reference to the recently victorious Fascism: see S. Forti, *Il totalitarismo* (Rome: Laterza, 2001), 3 ff.; but its theoretical consecration, as it were, came from Giovanni Gentile, who writes: "for the Fascist everything is in the State and nothing human and spiritual exists and, far less, has value outside of the State. In that sense Fascism is totalitarian . . ," in *Enciclopedia Italiana*, vol. 14 (Rome, 1932), s.v. "Fascismo (dottrina del)," 835 ff.

266. See F. Furet, *Le passé d'une illusion: Essai sur l'idée communiste au XXe siècle* (Paris: Robert Laffont–Calmann–Lévy, 1995), in English as *The Passing of an Illusion: The Idea of Communism in the Twentieth Century*, trans. D. Furet (Chicago: University of Chicago Press, 2000)—a "one-sided" work, but of extraordinary intelligence; the pages on Arendt are magnificent: 431 ff.

267. V. I. Lenin, *Philosophical Notebooks* [1895–1915, but published in 1929–1930], in *Collected Works* (London: Lawrence and Wishart, 1960–1970). Perceptive observations in L. Althusser, *Lenin et la philosophie* (Paris: François Maspero, 1972), in English as *Lenin and Philosophy, and Other Essays*, trans. B. Brewster (London: New Left Books, 1971), esp. 103 ff.

268. It will suffice to look at Lenin's *State and Revolution* [1917], trans. R. Service (London: Penguin, 1992), to realize this—notes written in the heat of battle.

269. The text was circulated in the West on June 4, 1956, by the U.S. Department of State, and published the following day by the *New York Times*.

270. Marxism as a theoretical body is in reality the great absent figure in Arendt's book: a kind of spectral phenomenology of totalitarian power without background—or, if we wish, without flesh and blood: see in particular *The Origins of Totalitarianism*, 389 ff.

271. The expression is Gramsci's, used in an article that appeared in *Avanti* on November 24, 1917, and was reprinted in *Grido del Popolo* in January 1918: now in *Opere di Antonio Gramsci: Scritti giovanili 1914–1918* (Turin: Einaudi, 1958), 149 ff.

272. See E. H. Carr, *A History of Soviet Russia: The Bolshevik Revolution 1917–1923*, 3 vols. (London: Macmillan, 3rd ed., 1953), vol. 3, esp. 170 ff., and *id., The Interregnum 1923–1924* (London: Macmillan, 1954), esp. 201 ff. Also bear in mind, by the same author, *1917: Before and After* (London: Macmillan, 1969), esp. 58 ff.

273. Lenin, *State and Revolution*, esp. 75 ff.

274. It forms the title of a manifesto by Ilya Makarychev from 1925, "Every cook should learn to govern the State." Though the sentence is attributed to Lenin, it was not in fact written by him in these terms.

275. I am referring to the so-called democracy of the workers' councils that fascinated the early Gramsci: "The essential fact of the Russian Revolution is the establishment of a new type of State: the State of Workers' Councils. . . . Every-

thing else is contingency," he wrote in *Ordine Nuovo* on May 15, 1919, now in *Opere di Antonio Gramsci: L'Ordine Nuovo 1919–1920* (Turin: Einaudi, 1955), 374. See the extensive research of M. Salvadori, *Gramsci e il problema storico della democrazia* (Turin: Einaudi, 1970), esp. 5 ff., and C. Buci-Glucksmann, *Gramsci et l'État* (Paris: Fayard, 1975), in English as *Gramsci and the State*, trans. D. Fernbach (London: Lawrence and Wishart, 1980), esp. 47 ff. Also A. Tosel, "Gramsci face à la révolution francaise: la question du jacobinisme," in *Philosophie de la Révolution francaise: Représentations et interprétations,* proceedings of the conference at the Centre de recherches d'Histoire des idées de l'Université de Nice, January 21–22, 1983 (Paris: Vrin, 1984), 285 ff.

276. Interesting observations in A. Bullock, *Hitler and Stalin: Parallel Lives* (New York: Knopf, 3rd ed., 1993) (modeled on Plutarch's *Parallel Lives*), esp. 18 ff. Some considerations that are worth bearing in mind, albeit conceived from a particular point of view, are in A. Roccucci, *Stalin e il patriarca: La Chiesa ortodossa e il potere sovietico* (Turin: Einaudi, 2011), esp. 173 ff.

277. Some interesting ideas in Esposito, *Living Thought*, 185 ff.—and it is a real pity that the author does not explore this theme further, even though it is not the center of his focus. Also important: M. Gauchet, *L'avenement*, vol. 4, *Le nouveau monde* (Paris: Gallimard, 2017), esp. 145 ff., 203 ff.

4. Never So Equal, Never So Different

1. At the beginning of the twentieth century, just eight of the forty-eight independent nations in the world possessed the fundamental institutions of representative democracy. At the beginning of the following century, out of 190 independent nations, around eighty-five had sufficiently developed democratic structures and were inhabited by about 60 percent of the world's population: A. Karatnycky, "The 1999 Freedom House Survey: A Century of Progress," *Journal of Democracy* 11 (2000), 1: 187 ff. F. Fukuyama now counts more than 110, in *Identity: The Demand for Dignity and the Politics of Resentment* (New York: Farrar, Straus and Giroux, 2018), 3.

2. The word "race" was also part of the democratic lexicon: it can still be found, for example—albeit to deny its political and legal effects—in the Italian Constitution of 1948 (Article 3, paragraph 1).

3. J. Schumpeter, *Capitalism, Socialism, and Democracy* [1942] (London: George Allen & Unwin, 1976), esp. 61 ff.

4. P. Samuelson, *Economics* (New York: McGraw-Hill, eighth ed., 1970), 831.

5. F. Nietzsche, *Sämtliche Werke,* vol. 8, *Nachgelassene Fragmente 1887–1889* [ed. Colli–Montinari] (Berlin: De Gruyter, 1980), even though his thought certainly cannot be reduced to this: see R. Esposito, *Bios: Biopolitica e filosofia* (Turin: Einaudi, 2004), in English as *Bíos: Biopolitics and Philosophy,* trans. T. Campbell (Minneapolis: University of Minnesota Press, 2008), esp. 80 ff., 93 ff., 105 ff.

6. E. Hobsbawm, *The Age of Extremes: The Short Twentieth Century 1914–1991* (London: Michael Joseph, 1994), esp. 2 ff.

7. M. Sandel, *Democracy's Discontent: America in Search of a Public Philosophy* (Cambridge, MA: Harvard University Press, 1996), 250 ff. See also *id., Justice: What's the Right Thing to Do?* (New York: Farrar, Straus and Giroux, 2010), esp. 212 ff., and, with many observations that can be shared, *id., The Tyranny of Merit: What's Become of the Common Good?* (New York: Farrar, Straus and Giroux, 2020).

8. A book to unquestionably bear in mind is A. Supiot, *La Gouvernance par les nombres: Cours au Collège de France (2012–2014)* (Paris: Fayard, 2015), esp. 53 ff., 103 ff., 119 ff., 157 ff. An Italian classic is E. Ruffini, *Il principio maggioritario: Profilo storico* [1927] (Milan: Adelphi, 1976; 3rd ed., 2002). Some very acute observations can also be found in an invaluable old book: G. Rensi, *La democrazia diretta* [1902] (Milan: Adelphi, 1995), esp. 50 ff., 135 ff., 183 ff.

9. A. Gramsci, *Quaderni del carcere*, ed. V. Gerratana, vol. 3 (Turin: Einaudi, 1975), 1624 ff. (Quaderno 13, 30), partially in English in *Selections from the Prison Notebooks of Antonio Gramsci*, ed. and trans. Q. Hoare and G. Nowell-Smith (London: Lawrence and Wishart, 1971), esp. 192–194. Important considerations in Z. Sternhell, *Les anti-lumières. Du XVIIIᵉ siècle à la guerre froide* (Paris: Fayard, 2006), 418 ff., in English as *The Anti-Enlightenment Tradition*, trans. D. Maisel (New Haven, CT: Yale University Press, 2009), 315 ff.

10. E. Gabba and A. Schiavone, eds., *Polis e piccolo stato tra riflessione antica e pensiero moderno* (Como: New Press, 1999).

11. I have touched on this point elsewhere: *Non ti delego: Perché abbiamo smesso di credere nella loro politica* (Milan: Rizzoli, 2013), esp. 38 ff.

12. As is rightly observed by R. Dahl, *On Political Equality* (New Haven, CT: Yale University Press, 2006), 21.

13. See H. Arendt, *The Human Condition* (Chicago: University of Chicago Press, 1958), esp. 38 ff.

14. J. M. Keynes, "National Self-Sufficiency," *Yale Review* 22 (1933), 4: 755 ff.

15. M. Walzer, *Spheres of Justice: A Defense of Pluralism and Equality* (Oxford: Blackwell, 1983), 316.

16. An overall picture, perceptive and informed as usual, is in P. Costa, *Civitas: Storia della cittadinanza europea*, vol. 4, *L'età dei totalitarismi e della democrazia* (Rome: Laterza, 2001), esp. 3 ff., 151 ff.

17. United Nations General Assembly, *Universal Declaration of Human Rights* [1948], in G. Brown, ed., *The Universal Declaration of Human Rights in the 21st Century: A Living Document in a Changing World* (Cambridge: OpenBook, 2016), "Appendix A," Art. 1: "All human beings are born free and equal in dignity and rights. They are endowed with reason and conscience and should act towards one another in a spirit of brotherhood."

18. *Costituzione italiana: Testo vigente*, edition of the Senate of the Italian Republic 2017, 8–9.

19. V. De Grazia, *Irresistible Empire: America's Advance through Twentieth-century Europe* (Cambridge, MA: Belknap Press of Harvard University Press, 2005)—a fine work. Ford's five-dollar daily wage is discussed on page 95. See also C. S. Maier, *Among Empires: American Ascendancy and its Predecessors* (Cambridge, MA: Harvard University Press, 2006), 191 ff., 238 ff.

20. T. Piketty, *Le Capital au XXIᵉ siècle* (Paris: Seuil, 2013), 33, in English as *Capital in the Twenty-first Century,* trans. A. Goldhammer (Cambridge, MA: Belknap Press of Harvard University Press, 2014), 16, which draws on and uses Kuznets's pioneering research on American inequality.

21. An overall picture of those years can be found in J. T. Patterson, *Grand Expectations: The United States, 1945–1974* (New York: Oxford University Press, 1996), esp. 39 ff., 311 ff., 442 ff.

22. Some perceptive observations, though I cannot say whether they move in the direction I am trying to indicate, in R. Esposito, *Communitas: Origine e destino della comunità* (Turin: Einaudi, 1998), in English as *Communitas: The Origin and Destiny of Community,* trans. T. Campbell (Stanford, CA: Stanford University Press, 2009), 101 ff.

23. Some good but all too brief observations (and it is a real pity) on Gramsci are in R. Esposito, *Pensiero vivente: Origine e attualità della filosofia italiana* (Turin: Einaudi, 2010), in English as *Living Thought: The Origin and Actuality of Italian Philosophy,* trans. Z. Hanafi (Stanford, CA: Stanford University Press, 2012), 159, in a fleeting comparison with Croce and Gentile: this is perhaps the most significant lacuna of this book, the arguments of which can in many respects be shared. The interest that Gramsci's thought still attracts outside Italy is not, it seems to me, being matched by a new season of studies in Italy, after that of the communist orthodoxy, based entirely on the continuity between Gramsci and Togliatti.

24. J. Rawls, *A Theory of Justice* [1971] (Cambridge, MA: Harvard University Press, 1999; 6th ed., 2003). The most important of his other studies are "Justice as Fairness," *Philosophical Review* 67 (1958), 2: 164 ff., to which he returned in *Justice as Fairness: A Restatement* (Cambridge, MA: Harvard University Press, 2nd ed., 2001); "The Sense of Justice," *Philosophical Review* 72 (1963), 3: 281 ff.; "Distributive Justice," in P. Laslett and W. G. Runciman, eds., *Philosophy, Politics, and Society* (London: Macmillan, 1967), 58 ff., and "Distributive Justice. Some Addenda," *The American Journal of Jurisprudence* 13 (1968), 1: 51 ff.

25. J. O'Connor, *The Fiscal Crisis of the State* (New York: St Martin's Press, 1973; London: Routledge, 2001).

26. A. Sen, "Equality of What?" in S. McMurrin, ed., *The Tanner Lectures on Human Values,* vol. 1 (Salt Lake City: University of Utah Press, 1980), 196 ff.

27. Dahl, *On Political Equality,* 30 ff., 50 ff., 98 ff. S. Verba and N. H. Nie, *Participation in America: Political Democracy and Social Equality* (New York: Harper and Row, 1972) is still a useful work; and see also S. Verba, N. H. Nie, and Jae-on Kim, *Participation and Political Equality: A Seven-Nation Comparison* (Cambridge: Cambridge University Press, 1978), esp. 1 ff., 286 ff.

28. Rawls, *A Theory*, 53.

29. Rawls, *A Theory*, 72.

30. Rawls, *A Theory*, 266.

31. J. Rawls, *Political Liberalism* (New York: Columbia University Press, 1993, expanded edition 2005). See also J. Rawls, *The Law of Peoples* (Cambridge, MA: Harvard University Press, 1999), esp. 59 ff.

32. F. Hirsch, *Social Limits to Growth* (London: Routledge and Kegan Paul, 1977), 124 ff.; S. Veca, *Questioni di giustizia: Corso di filosofia politica* (Turin: Einaudi, 1991), 117 ff., esp. 125–126. Interesting, in relation to Rawls's thought, is C. Audard, *John Rawls* (Stocksfeld: Acumen, 2007), esp. 25 ff., 275 ff. Also worthy of note is S. Freeman, *Rawls* (London: Routledge, 2007).

33. Rawls, *A Theory*, 242–243.

34. I am thinking of positions like those of R. Dworkin, *Taking Rights Seriously* (London: Duckworth, 1977), or of R. Nozick, *Anarchy, State and Utopia* (Oxford: Basil Blackwell, 1974).

35. Walzer, *Spheres of Justice*, 318.

36. Walzer, *Spheres of Justice*, 14.

37. Walzer, *Spheres of Justice*, 19. Also worth considering is M. Walzer, *The Exclusions of Liberal Theory* (Frankfurt am Main: Fischer, 1999).

38. J. Meade, *Agathotopia: The Economics of Partnership* (Aberdeen: Aberdeen University Press, 1989).

39. Besides *Taking Rights Seriously*, see also by R. Dworkin, *Sovereign Virtue: The Theory and Practice of Equality* (Cambridge, MA: Harvard University Press, 2000): some well-grounded observations on his thinking are offered by A. Sen, *The Idea of Justice* (Cambridge, MA: Belknap Press of Harvard University Press, 2009), 264 ff. Worth considering is T. Nagel, *Equality and Partiality* (New York: Oxford University Press, 1991), and, above all, "The Problem of Global Justice," *Philosophy and Public Affairs* 33 (2005), 2: 113 ff. Finally, see T. M. Scanlon, "The Diversity of Objections to Inequality," in M. Clayton and A. Williams, eds., *The Ideal of Equality* (London: Macmillan, 2000, 2002), 41 ff. and *Why Does Inequality Matter?* (New York: Oxford University Press, 2018). Also worth reading is G. A. Cohen, *Rescuing Justice and Equality* (Cambridge, MA: Harvard University Press, 2008).

40. A. Sen, *The Idea of Justice*. By Sen see also *Inequality Reexamined* (New York: Russell Sage Foundation, 1992).

41. The expression "biological roots"—*racines biologiques*—is from F. Varela, "L'individualité: l'autonomie du vivant," in P. Veyne et al., *Sur l'individu* (Paris: Seuil, 1987), 88.

42. Rawls, *A Theory*, 10–11.

43. Rawls, *A Theory*, 11.

44. Rawls, *A Theory*, 222.

45. Rawls, *A Theory*, 11.

46. Sen, *The Idea of Justice*, esp. 52 ff., 291 ff.

47. Walzer, *Spheres of Justice*, 320.

48. Walzer, *Spheres of Justice*, 319–320.

49. As R. Dahl correctly says in *On Political Equality*, 45–46.

50. In the sense clarified by Arendt, *The Human Condition*, esp. 7 ff.

51. Perceptive observations in C. S. Maier, *Once within Borders: Territories of Power, Wealth, and Belonging since 1500* (Cambridge, MA: Harvard University Press, 2016), 260 ff., 278 ff. See also Z. Bauman, *Retrotopia* (Cambridge, UK: Polity Press, 2017), 1 ff.—also on the basis of M. Mutscher, "On the Road to Liquid Warfare?" Bonn International Centre for Conversion Working Paper 3 (2016).

52. Marx, *Das Kapital: Erster Band*, 640 (*Capital*, vol. 1, 762): "die organische Zusammensetzung des Kapitals"; Piketty, *Le Capital*, 82 (*Capital in the Twenty-first Century*, 61).

53. I touched on this point in A. Schiavone, "Le travail des anciens et des modernes," *Quaderni di storia* 86 (2017): 21 ff., and earlier in *id.*, *La storia spezzata: Roma antica e Occidente moderno* [1996] (Rome: Laterza, 2002), in English as *The End of the Past: Ancient Rome and the Modern West*, trans. M. J. Schneider (Cambridge, MA: Harvard University Press, 2000; reprint 2002), 108 ff., 165 ff.

54. As analyzed in the works of Alain Touraine, above all *La Fin des sociétés* (Paris: Seuil, 2013), esp. 11 ff., 35 ff., 187 ff., 413 ff., but also in *Un nouveau paradigme: Pour comprandre le monde aujourd'hui* (Paris: Fayard, 2005), esp. 28 ff., 39 ff., 85 ff., 187 ff., in English as *New Paradigm for Understanding Today's World*, trans. G. Elliott (Cambridge: Polity Press, 2007), esp. 9ff., 19ff., 44ff., 101ff.; and, again, *Pourrion-nous vivre ensemble? Égaux et différents* (Paris: Fayard, 1997), esp. 33 ff., 73 ff., in English as *Can We Live Together? Equality and Difference* (Stanford, CA: Stanford University Press, 2000), esp. 19 ff., 52 ff. More recently: *Nous, sujets humains* (Paris: Seuil, 2015). It would be very interesting to be able to discuss more closely the results of this extraordinary laboratory of ideas and interpretations—Touraine is, together with Bauman, the thinker who has strived the most to understand the revolution we are living through—many of which are highly intriguing even though I do not share them, but unfortunately this would go far beyond the aims of this book.

55. A Marxian concept, still very useful for the purposes of historic reconstruction: *Das Kapital: Erster Band*, 741 ff., "die sogenannte ursprüngliche Akkumulation" (*Capital*, 871 ff.).

5. The New Equality

1. B. Snell, *Die Entdeckung des Geistes: Studien zur Entstehung des europäischen Denkens bei den Griechen* [1946] (Hamburg: Claassen, 1955), in English as *The Discovery of the Mind: The Greek Origins of European Thought*, trans. T. G. Rosenmeyer

(Oxford: Basil Blackwell, 1953), esp. v ff.; J.-P. Vernant, *Mythe et pensée chez les Grecs* [1965] (Paris: Maspero, 3rd ed., 1990), 373, in English as *Myth and Thought among the Greeks,* trans. J. Lloyd with J. Fort (New York: Zone, 2006), 371 ff. See also A. Schiavone, *La storia spezzata: Roma antica e Occidente moderno* [1996] (Rome: Laterza, 2002), in English as *The End of the Past: Ancient Rome and the Modern West,* trans. M. J. Schneider (Cambridge, MA: Harvard University Press, 2000; reprint 2002), 159.

2. The concept of the "axial age" ("Achsenzeit") is from K. Jaspers, *Vom Ursprung und Ziel der Geschichte* (Zurich: Piper, 1949), in English as *The Origin and Goal of History,* trans. M. Bullock (London: Routledge & Kegan Paul, 1953), 1 ff.

3. I have already touched on this point in A. Schiavone, *Storia e destino* (Turin: Einaudi, 2007), esp. 22 ff., 39 ff., in French as *Histoire et destin,* trans. G. Bouffartigue (Paris: Belin, 2009), 27 ff., 45 ff.

4. T. L. Friedman, *The World Is Flat: A Brief History of the Twenty-First Century* (New York: Farrar, Straus and Giroux, 2nd ed., 2006).

5. J. Stiglitz, *The Great Divide: Unequal Societies and What We Can Do About Them* (New York: W. W. Norton & Company, 2015). See also *id.,* "Inequality and Economic Growth," *The Political Quarterly* 86 (2015): 134 ff., and A. Renaut, É. Brown, M.-P. Chartron, and G. Lauvau, *Inégalités entre globalisation et particularisation* (Paris: Presses Universitaires de France, 2016), esp. 33 ff., 161 ff., 361 ff.

6. The "liquid" concept is Bauman's: see in particular, Z. Bauman, *Liquid Life* (Cambridge: Polity Press, 2005) and *id., Liquid Modernity* (Cambridge: Polity Press, 2000); but also *id., Retrotopia* (Cambridge: Polity Press, 2017).

7. Stiglitz, *The Great Divide,* esp. 88 ff., 185 ff.; T. Piketty, *Le Capital au XXIᵉ siècle* (Paris: Seuil, 2013), esp. 373ff., in English as *Capital in the Twenty-first Century,* trans. A. Goldhammer (Cambridge, MA: Belknap Press of Harvard University Press, 2014), 297 ff. See also by Stiglitz, *The Price of Inequality: How Today's Divided Society Endangers Our Future* (New York: Norton & Company, 2012), esp. 1 ff., 52 ff., 187 ff. 265 ff., and *Globalization and Its Discontents* (New York: Norton & Company, 2002; 2nd ed., 2017), esp. 23 ff., 180 ff., 214 ff.

8. Stiglitz, *The Great Divide,* ix, which is at the basis of what Tim Wallace, writing in the *New York Times* on November 16, 2016, calls "the two Americas"; a theme well analyzed by M. Revelli, *Populismo 2.0* (Turin: Einaudi, 2017), 44 ff.

9. For this reason, I regard as misleading all those analyses that speak, in relation to the present age, of "post-capitalism." Among the many: P. F. Drucker, *Post-Capitalist Society* (New York: HarperBusiness, 1993), or P. Manson, *Postcapitalism: A Guide to Our Future* (London: Penguin, 2015)—forgetting that the existence of capital, both economic (in the form of incredible concentrations of productive investment capacity) and social (in the form of a radical divide between people who receive their income from labor and those who derive it from capital), continues—albeit in a new way—to be the dominant feature of our times. More interesting ideas with regard to my perspective can be found in J. Lukacs, *At the End of an Age* (New Haven, CT: Yale University Press, 2002), esp. 45 ff., 85 ff., and

in Y. Moulier Boutang, *Le capitalisme cognitif: La nouvelle grande transformation* (Paris: Amsterdam, 2nd ed., 2007), esp. 31 ff., 81 ff.

10. Gramsci claimed to have taken, and reworked, the notion of the "historic bloc" from Sorel (though the expression cannot literally be found in the latter's writings, there is a passage that speaks of "elements . . . that . . . must be taken as a whole, as historic forces") (G. Sorel, *Réflexions sur la violence* [Paris: Librairie de "Pages libres," 1908], in English as *Reflections on Violence* [Mineola, NY: Dover Publications, 2004], 42): *Quaderni del carcere,* ed. V. Gerratana, vol. 2 [Turin: Einaudi, 1975], 1300 (Quaderno 10, 33; and see also vol. 1, 437 (Quaderno 4, 13), partially in English in *Selections from the Prison Notebooks of Antonio Gramsci,* ed. and trans. Q. Hoare and G. Nowell-Smith (London: Lawrence and Wishart, 1971); notebook 4 is in vol. 2 of the multivolume *Prison Notebooks,* ed. and trans. J. Buttigieg (New York: Columbia University Press, 2011).

11. Piketty, *Le Capital,* 835 ff. [*Capital,* 663 ff.]. By Piketty see also *L'économie des inégalités* (Paris: La Découverte, 2nd ed., 2014), in English as *The Economics of Inequality,* trans. A. Goldhammer (Cambridge, MA: Harvard University Press, 2015), 26 ff., and *id., Une brève histoire de l'égalité* (Paris: Seuil, 2021).

12. M. Benasayag, in an interview with *la Repubblica,* June 23, 2020: 30–31. See also, by the same author, *Organismes et artefacts: Vers la virtualisation du vivant?* (Paris: La Découverte, 2010), esp. 7 ff., 13 ff., 85 ff.

13. This is a line of thought that he has been developing, not without some oscillations, in all of his research since the end of the 1990s: I have cited some of his books in the course of this work, but will mention them once again: R. Esposito, *Communitas: Origine e destino della comunità* (Turin: Einaudi, 1998), in English as *Communitas: The Origin and Destiny of Community,* trans. T. Campbell (Stanford, CA: Stanford University Press, 2009), esp. 28 ff., 43 ff., 54 ff., 86 ff., 94 ff., 118 ff.; *Immunitas: Protezione e negazione della vita* (Turin: Einaudi, 2000), in English as *Immunitas: The Protection and Negation of Life,* trans. Z. Hanafi (Cambridge: Polity, 2011), esp. 23 ff., 116 ff.; *Bios: Biopolitica e filosofia* (Turin: Einaudi, 2004), in English as *Bios: Biopolitics and Philosophy,* trans. T. Campbell (Minneapolis: University of Minnesota Press, 2008), esp. 34 ff.; *Terza persona: Politica della vita e filosofia dell'impersonale* (Turin: Einaudi, 2007), in English as *Third Person: Politics of Life and Philosophy of the Impersonal* (Cambridge: Polity, 2012), esp. 64 ff., 104 ff.; *Pensiero vivente: Origine e attualità della filosofia italiana* (Turin: Einaudi, 2010), in English as *Living Thought: The Origin and Actuality of Italian Philosophy,* trans. Z. Hanafi (Stanford, CA: Stanford University Press, 2012), esp. 58 ff.; *Due: La macchina della teologia politica e il posto del pensiero* (Turin: Einaudi, 2013), in English as *Two: The Machine of Political Theology and the Place of Thought,* trans. Z. Hanafi (New York: Fordham University Press, 2015), esp. 5ff., 83ff., 102ff., 151ff., 159ff., 176ff.; *Le persone e le cose* (Turin: Einaudi, 2014), in English as *Persons and Things: From the Body's Point of View,* trans. Z. Hanafi (Cambridge: Polity Press, 2015), esp. 16ff., 99ff.; *Da fuori: Una filosofia per l'Europa* (Turin: Einaudi, 2016), in English as *A Philosophy for Europe: From Outside,* trans. Z. Hanafi (Cambridge: Polity Press, 2018), esp. 131 ff.

14. S. Weil, "La Personne et le sacré" [1942–1943, published in 1950] (Paris: Payot & Rivages, 2017), 37, in English as "Human Personality," in *The Simone Weil Reader*, ed. G. A. Panichas (New York: David McKay Company, 1977), 318.

15. See, in particular, Esposito, *Third Person*, 64 ff., 104 ff., and *Two*, 83 ff.

16. The *Commentary* can be read in *Averrois Cordubensis, Commentarius magnum in Aristotelis De anima libros*, S. Crawford, ed. (Cambridge, MA: Mediaeval Academy of America, 1953). A fine book is E. Coccia, *La trasparenza delle immagini: Averroé e l'averroismo* (Milan: Mondadori, 2005), esp. 57 ff., 181 ff.

17. The trail has been carefully reconstructed by Roberto Esposito, especially in Esposito, *Two*, 143 ff.

18. See in particular M. Foucault, *Le sujet et le pouvoir* [1982], in *id., Dits et écrits*, vol. 2, 1976–1988 (Paris: Gallimard, 2001), 1041 ff., esp. 1046 ff. I note in passing that in a text from 1981 that closely resembles the one I have just cited, "Les mailles du pouvoir," 1001 ff., Foucault proposes, on 1005–1006, that the second book of Marx's *Capital* should be read as an analysis of bourgeois power—an extraordinary intuition that has yet to be developed.

19. G. Leibniz, *Considérations sur la doctrine d'un Esprit universel unique* [1702], in *id., Système nouveau de la nature et de la communication des substances et autres textes 1690–1703*, C. Frémont, ed. (Paris: Flammarion, 1994), 219 ff.; the reference to "boundaries of reason" is on 221. The strand of Italian humanism runs from Petrarch to Lorenzo Valla: Esposito, *Two*, 144.

20. I am again referring to Esposito, *Two*, 143 ff.

21. B. de Giovanni, *Hegel e Spinoza: Dialogo sul moderno* (Naples: Guida, 2011), which we have already encountered in this work. It is a pity that there has not yet been an explicit convergence between de Giovanni and Esposito on the theme of the impersonal. Both have reflected on it, opening new horizons, and seem to brush against each other without ever really coming together.

22. In a letter to his friend Henry Oldenburg, a man of letters and the ambassador of the parliament of Bremen to Cromwell: in B. Spinoza, *Opera* (Heidelberg: Winters, undated but 1924), vol. 4, in English in *Spinoza: The Letters*, trans. S. Shirley (Indianapolis: Hackett Publishing Company, 1995), 194–195 [trans. modified]. I know of it from B. de Giovanni, *Hegel e Spinoza*, 65 ff.

23. G. Hegel, *Wissenschaft der Logik*, vol. 1, 59–60, in English as *The Science of Logic*, ed. and trans. George Di Giovanni (Cambridge: Cambridge University Press, 2010), vol. 1, 41.

24. Hegel, *Wissenschaf*, vol. 2, 253 [*Science of Logic*, vol. 2, 514].

25. Hegel, *Wissenschaf*, vol. 1, 61 [*Science of Logic*, vol. 1, 47].

26. S. Schama, *The Embarrassment of Riches: An Interpretation of Dutch Culture in the Golden Age* (New York: Vintage, 1987), in which, however, Spinoza's name never appears.

27. De Giovanni, *Hegel e Spinoza*, 165.

28. De Giovanni, *Hegel e Spinoza*, 91 ff.; Esposito, *Two*, 160–161.

29. De Giovanni, *Hegel e Spinoza*, 49; Spinoza, *Ethica Ordine Geometrico demonstrata* [1675, but which appeared posthumously in 1677], in *Opera*, vol. 2, 45–308, in English as *Ethics* (New York: Hafner Publishing Company, 1974).

30. *Opera*, vol. 4 (*Letters*, 333): de Giovanni, *Hegel e Spinoza*, 51.

31. Spinoza, *Opera*, vol. 4 (*Letters*, 270; trans. modified).

32. See also Esposito, *Two*, 159 ff. Another book to bear in mind is É. Balibar, *Spinoza politique: Le transindividuel* (Paris: Presses Universitaires de France, 2nd ed., 2018), esp. 199 ff., in English as *Spinoza: The Transindividual*, trans. M. Kelly (Edinburgh: Edinburgh University Press, 2020).

33. S. J. Gould and N. Eldridge, "Punctuated Equilibria. The Tempo and Mode of Evolution Reconsidered," *Paleobiology* 3 (1977), 2, 115 ff. See also: S. J. Gould, *The Structure of Evolutionary Theory* (Cambridge, MA: Harvard University Press, 2002). By Gould—an extraordinary historiographic talent with great literary powers at the service of paleontology—see also his final volume of collected essays, *I Have Landed: The End of a Beginning in Natural History* (New York: W. W. Norton & Company, 2002).

34. A crucial point, which touches on a theme that has been taking root with difficulty in contemporary and especially European debate, the diffusion of which is still tinged with certain excessive (and sometimes misleading) antiproprietary and anticapitalistic ideological overtones that some observers are unable to shake off. For a preliminary approach, see U. Mattei, *Beni comuni: Un manifesto* (Rome: Laterza, 2011), and *id., Il benicomunismo e i suoi nemici* (Turin: Einaudi, 2015), esp. 17 ff., 66 ff.; P. Linebaugh, *The Magna Charta Manifesto: Liberties and Commons for All* (Oakland, CA: University of California Press, 2009); A. Ciervo, *I beni comuni* (Rome: Ediesse, 2012); P. Dardot and C. Laval, *Commun: Essai sur la revolution au XXIᵉ siècle* (Paris: La Découverte, 2014), in English as *Common: On Revolution in the 21st Century*, trans. M. MacLellan (London: Bloomsbury Academic, 2018), esp. 59 ff., 157 ff., 365 ff. See also M. Fioravanti, E. I. Mineo, and L. Nivarra, "Dai beni comuni al commune: Diritto, Stato e storia," *Storia del pensiero politico* 1 (2016): 89 ff., and E. I. Mineo, "Oggettivazione e storicità dei beni comuni," *Economia della cultura* 27 (2017), 1: 27 ff. There also some interesting ideas in M. Ainis, *La piccola eguaglianza* (Turin: Einaudi, 2015), esp. 28 ff., 43 ff., and in L. Ferrajoli, *Manifesto per l'eguaglianza* (Rome: Laterza, 2018), esp. 78 ff., 137 ff.

35. The pages I am referring to are in "Human Personality," 323 ff, on which see Esposito, *Third Person*, 100 ff. Weil's anticipation of Arendt is noted by G. Agamben, in the introduction to S. Weil, "La Personne et le sacré," 11. Arendt's observations are in *The Origins of Totalitarianism* (London: George Allen & Unwin, 3rd ed., 1967), 267 ff. (though she could not have read Weil's text, published only in 1950).

36. They are authors touched on at various times in Esposito's reflections, especially in *Third Person*, 104 ff., in *Two*, 176 ff., and in *A Philosophy for Europe*, 120 ff.

To them I feel we should also add P. Ricoeur, *Soi-même comme un autre* (Paris: Seuil, 1990), esp. 21 ff., 39 ff., 237 ff.

37. G. Deleuze, *Logique du sens* (Paris: Éditions de Minuit, 1969), 129, in English as *The Logic of Sense*, trans. M. Lester with C. Stivale (New York: Columbia University Press, 1993), 106, but I am referring to the whole chapter, 100 ff.

38. M. Foucault, *La vie des hommes infâmes* [1977], in *Dits et écrits*, vol. 2, 237 ff.

39. Weil, "Human Personality," 335.

40. I have already touched on this crucial point elsewhere, in Schiavone, *Storia e destino*, esp. 56 ff (*Histoire et destin*, 66).

41. The expression, as is known, was first used by Marshall McLuhan in *Understanding Media: The Extensions of Man* (London: Routledge, 1964, 2001). See also M. McLuhan and B. R. Powers, *The Global Village: Transformations in World Life and Media in the 21st Century* [1989] (Oxford: Oxford University Press, 1992).

42. Some fundamental observations and ideas can be found in T. C. Heller, M. Sosna, and D. E. Wellebery, *Reconstructing Individualism: Autonomy, Individuality, and the Self in Western Thought* (Stanford, CA: Stanford University Press, 1986), especially the essays in the second part of the book, 106 ff. Another significant book is L. Jaume, *L'Individu effacé ou le paradoxe du libéralisme francais* (Paris: Fayard, 1997), esp. 447 ff. Also worth reading is M.-C. Blais, *La solidarité: Histoire d'une idée* (Paris: Gallimard, 2007), esp. 235 ff.

43. Often debatable, but with reflections that should be taken into consideration, is J. Rifkin, *The Third Industrial Revolution: How Lateral Power is Transforming Energy, the Economy, and the World* (New York: Palgrave Macmillan, 2011), and, before that, *id., The End of Work: The Decline of the Global Labor Force and the Dawn of the Post-Market Era* (New York: Putnam, 1995).

44. A book that remains of current interest is P. Rosanvallon, *La contre-démocratie: La politique à l'age d'or de la defiance* (Paris: Points 2006), in English as *Counter-Democracy: Politics in an Age of Distrust*, trans. A. Goldhammer (Cambridge: Cambridge University Press, 2008), esp. 249 ff. See also N. Urbinati, *Representative Democracy: Principles and Genealogy* (Chicago: University of Chicago Press, 2006), and the discussion on "The Prospects and Limits of Deliberative Democracy," *Daedalus: Journal of the American Academy of Arts and Sciences* 146 [2017], 3: 6 ff. Among the most recent Italian reflections, I should mention S. Cassese, *La democrazia e i suoi limiti* (Milan: Mondadori, 2017), esp. 27 ff., 47 ff., and G. Zagrebelsky, *Diritto allo specchio* (Turin: Einaudi, 2018), esp. 113 ff., 159 ff.

45. I speak more about this in A. Schiavone, *Non ti delego: Perché abbiamo smesso di credere nella loro politica* (Milan: Rizzoli, 2013), esp. 63 ff., 87 ff. An interesting book is J.-F. Bayart, *Le Gouvernement du monde: Une critique politique de la globalisation* (Paris: Fayard, 2004), esp. 133 ff., 251 ff., in English as *Global Subjects: A Political Critique of Globalization*, trans. A. Brown (Cambridge: Polity, 2007), esp. 83 ff., 163 ff.

46. B. de Giovanni, *Hegel e Spinoza*, esp. 155 ff., 227 ff.

47. Weil, *La Personne*, 86–87 ("Human Personality," 338); G. Agamben, introduction to Weil, *La Personne*, 16–17.

INDEX OF NAMES